ONCE A CATHOLIC

ONCE A CATHOLIC ?~

Prominent Catholics and Ex-Catholics
Discuss the Influence of the Church
on Their Lives and Work

Peter Occhiogrosso

HOUGHTON MIFFLIN COMPANY · BOSTON · 1987

Library of Congress Cataloging-in-Publication Data

Occhiogrosso, Peter.
  Once a Catholic.

  Bibliography: p.
  1. Catholics — United States — Psychology.
2. Ex-church members — Catholic Church — Psychology.
3. Catholic Church — United States — History — 20th
century.   4. United States — Church history — 20th
century.   I. Title.
BX1406.2.O24   1987   282'.092'2   87-2772
ISBN 0-395-42111-X

Printed in the United States of America

P 10 9 8 7 6 5 4 3 2 1

Permission is gratefully acknowledged to use lines from the following songs on page 332: "St. Alfonzo's Pancake Breakfast" from *Apostrophe (')*. Lyrics by Frank Zappa © 1974 Munchkin Music ASCAP. "Heavenly Bank Account" from *You Are What You Is*. Lyrics by Frank Zappa © 1980 Munchkin Music ASCAP. Reprinted by permission. All rights reserved.

To Margery

By temperament and intellect, religion as such strikes me as a desperate attempt on the part of mankind to bore itself to death in expiation of some forgotten excitement. But what we had was never quite religion. It was a whole life and a merry one, and it never occurred to me not to live it. It was simply the thing we did.

— Wilfrid Sheed
  Frank and Maisie

I'm always looking for a spiritual discipline I can live with. When I stopped being religious, being a Catholic, it was — as I did not realize at the time, but have come to since — devastating to me. It was a spiritual and moral devastation — shattering. And yet there was no trauma at the time; it seemed painless, it felt like ordinary maturation. But it left a great hunger.

— Robert Stone
  The Paris Review, Winter 1985

Nobody leaves the Catholic Church.
— Jimmy Breslin

ACKNOWLEDGMENTS

❧ I CANNOT RECALL all the people who suggested which Catholics I might interview and how to get in touch with them. But several friends and acquaintances were extraordinarily helpful in coming up with ideas, names, addresses, and telephone numbers. Only a small percentage of these suggestions led to published interviews, but for that very reason I am especially grateful to those who continued to generate new ideas and helpful clues. Karen Schwarz, Thomas Boland, S.J., and William McBrien were three of the most prolific and resourceful, followed closely by Paul Slansky, Earl Blackwell, Jr., Gerard Van der Leun, Jeff Sweet, Ed Rubin, Gideon Phillips, Jane Friedman, Jim Faller, Meme Black, Jonathan Black, Gary Ahlskog, Eric Ashworth, Eileen Tracy, Beverly Brumm, Kate Nolan, and Christopher Guest. In addition, a number of people whose interviews appear in this book were gracious in directing me to still other Catholics: Michael Novak, Martin Scorsese, Christopher Buckley, Robert Hoyt, Daniel Callahan, and Mary Gordon.

These distinctions may seem frivolous, however, since suggestions and contacts tended to lead from one party to another until the actual chain of discovery had long since disappeared beneath the surface. At last, the whole expedition assumed an appropriately Catholic sense of community, reinforcing in me the notion that both those Catholics who emphatically defend Church orthodoxy and those most evidently at odds with the Church, including ex-Catholics, do form a communion, I would even presume to say a mystical body, of Catholics aware of one another and of their divergent and consonant viewpoints. The vitality of that community, which has remained largely submerged from popular awareness, is what I set out in the first place to explore and to expose in my book. To those Catholics I owe whatever sense of excitement and dialogue may have emerged in these pages, for in a very real way I couldn't have done it without them.

Nor could I have done without the services of the people who helped me with research, transcriptions, telephone calls, typing, and all the other components of the book: Margery Dignan, Jane Freeman, Joslyn Williams, Melissa Powell, Heidi Elshtain, and Ben Jennings. My thanks also to Sean Kelly for his inspiration in the earliest stages of conceiving the book; to my agent, Stuart Krichevsky, and my editor, Larry Kessenich, not only for their many suggestions and fruitful efforts to arrange specific interviews but also for having faith in my book in the first place. Finally, I'd like to applaud my manuscript editor, Barbara Flanagan, for her perceptive help with a difficult manuscript and for the opportunity she provided me to engage in some enjoyable dialogue about it. Perhaps as much as anyone I worked with, she proved the value of a good Catholic school education accompanied by the intuitive wit to transcend it.

CONTENTS

INTROIT

I think it has always been the case that everybody defined Catholicism for himself or herself, and there are millions and billions of Catholicisms running around embodied that don't fit the standard operating definition.
—Robert Hoyt
 Founding editor, *National Catholic Reporter*

IT HAS ALWAYS seemed to me that Catholics carry their religion around with them in ways that others simply do not. Garry Wills once wrote that he could tell Senator Eugene McCarthy was Catholic just by talking to him for a few minutes, even without discussing theology. Frank Zappa claims that as a child he could spot other Catholics from the characteristic creases incised in their shoe tops by hours of kneeling. And Timothy Leary, that most lapsed of Catholics, is said to have once accurately singled out the other Catholics among a whole roomful of academics — although it's not clear if he did this by observing their language or their shoes. But an indelible mark does appear to have been imprinted on most Catholics — whether or not they continue to practice the faith — as a result of Catholic school education, religious instruction, home training, and communal piety; like a tenacious dinner guest, it comes early and stays late. That so many people from such ethnically and socially divergent backgrounds have experienced a remarkably similar imprinting and have responded to it with the galactic multiplicity suggested by Robert Hoyt makes its exploration all the more compelling.

By assembling the interviews in this book I hoped to recall for my subjects and my readers, as well as for myself, the provenance and effects of that imprint, which were to be the book's principal theme. The stamp of Catholicism shows up so prominently in the work of certain artists and performers—not only in specifically Catholic characters but in imagery and the kinds of questions their work addresses—that I had only to begin with a few favorites. The Martin Scorsese of *Mean Streets*, Mary Gordon of *Final Payments*, Robert Stone of *A Flag for Sunrise*, Wilfrid Sheed of *Transatlantic Blues*, George Carlin of *Class Clown*, and Christopher Durang of *Sister Mary Ignatius* were obvious choices, as were the artist Thomas Lanigan-Schmidt and novelist and newspaper columnist Jimmy Breslin.

The connection between Catholic roots and public image was not so apparent in other figures—such as New York State Supreme Court Justice Bruce Wright, *Penthouse* publisher Bob Guccione, and rock musician and composer Frank Zappa—but I had my suspicions. Certain Catholic theoreticians, clerics, and activists whose lives and identities have been inextricably intertwined with the Church were more self-evident: Michael Novak, Daniel and Sidney Callahan, Elizabeth McAlister, Robert Hoyt, Father Terrance Sweeney, and Sister Joan Chittister fell into that group.

Yet few of these people were as predictable or monomaniacal as I might have preferred, and most could not be prevented from taking unexpected turns or answering questions they hadn't been asked. In this fashion, other motifs drifted into our conversations as the project went along, expanding it beyond its original boundaries. Explanations for the increasing popularity of fundamentalist and Evangelical sects, for the crisis of authority in the Church, and for the pervasive influence of Jansenism (a dualistic and Puritanical heresy which lingered in France long after being condemned in the eighteenth century) became major subplots in more than one interview. Not least among these new motifs was the search for transcendence, whether within Catholicism itself or in the apparent vacuum left by the so-called loss of faith.

Considering that nearly half the people with whom I spoke are lapsed Catholics—or, as we sometimes like to call ourselves, "cultural Catholics"—and that a number of the rest are outspoken critics of the Vatican, I was rather surprised that the overall tone of the interviews was so optimistic. The men and women who have remained in the Church either embrace it wholeheartedly or are working to reshape its commitment to social justice. And most of those who have left the Church acknowledge at least a few residual benefits from their Catholic background, some even retaining a longing for what the Church had once given them. Inevitably, a few profess no fondness for the Church at all. Yet in their harshest outcries one can sometimes sense an undertone of disappointment: waylaid by parents and clerics intent on promoting discipline over love, they may have been prevented from experiencing the fullness of the Church's prom-

Yet after that bit of quotidian surrealism, no narrative of corporal in-justice has ever seemed especially surprising to me. The good news, I suppose, is that many of the people I interviewed told stories to the contrary, most of which I've retained. They speak of the less highly touted side of Catholic school education that included the occasional enlightened fostering of creativity and intellectual excellence. A few even commend the unacknowledged strengths of a school system administered and staffed almost entirely by the women of various religious orders, creating in the psyches of some girls a positive image and role model of women as competent achievers and leaders.

As with most of what appears in these pages, I leave it to the reader to determine the relative significance both of the actual events recounted and of the impression those events left embedded in the hearts and minds of the tellers. I have exercised the greatest selectivity in favor of reducing the obvious and predictable; the bias I have shown has been largely toward those narratives that may confound the reader's expectations, as they confounded mine.

ONCE A CATHOLIC

JOAN CHITTISTER, O.S.B.

"Sister Says"

God is not "nice."
God is not an uncle.
God is an earthquake.
—Joan Chittister, O.S.B.
  "The Thirteenth Disciple" in *Winds of Change*

The changes in the Church since the Second Vatican Council may have no better emblem than the sight of a nun in mufti. (As Catholic kids growing up we found that, if we waited long enough, we could eventually catch Father Hagen dressed in his civvies for the paper drive or lounging around the pool in his trunks. But in the seemingly interminable years of parochial grammar school, we came to believe that Sister must *sleep* in her habit.) And worse for some Catholics than the change in appearances has been the transformation in the substance of what those women, once referred to as the Good Sisters, are now engaged in.

Following Vatican II renewal, "women religious began to move from classrooms to soup kitchens, to neighborhood action centers, to public welfare programs, to legal aid offices, to diocesan peace and justice offices, to safe-houses for battered women. At the same time . . . they stayed in education but changed textbooks and curricula to deal with the problems of the time. . . . Whole communities adopted corporate commitments to specific social questions—housing, nuclear disarmament, poverty, justice—and pledged themselves to promote these questions wherever each of them might be: in education, in health care institutions, in office work, in either the private or parochial sector." So writes one civilian-frocked nun who may be the most articulate and riveting representative of that change. Sister Joan Chittister has appeared sans habit in the pages of the

New York Times and *People* magazine and has written and lectured at
length on the growing interaction of religious life and secular involvement.
She is well equipped: as prioress of Mount St. Benedict priory in Erie,
Pennsylvania, Chittister helped lead her Benedictine order through the
rigors of religious renewal during perilous times.

Through books about renewal in religious life, from *Climb Along the
Cutting Edge* to *Winds of Change*, Chittister has established herself as the
foremost authority on the subject. More than that, she is, according to
Tom Fox, editor of the *National Catholic Reporter*, where Chittister's
column has appeared for the past three years, "one of three or four women
in the U.S. Church today who have a very strong national following."
Fox's evaluation is that Chittister's unique alloy of articulate intelligence
and "enormous spiritual depth" makes her a charismatic figure in the lay
Church as well as in the ranks of American women religious.

Chittister may also personify the overlooked fact that the women of
religious orders are among the most highly educated women in the country.
Apart from her series of books on renewal, Chittister has also published
two volumes of meditations on the Psalms. And in addition to her *NCR*
column, her writing appears frequently in *America*, *Commonweal*, the
Way, and *Sojourners*, a largely Protestant journal. At her best, her articles
resonate with a tension that comes of rooting one part of the work in the
spiritual and the other part in a reflection on society or Church affairs,
moving from the gospel values or the teachings of the Church fathers to
the social, economic, or political realm.

The particular value of Chittister's perspective reveals itself in this
interview as she draws on her comprehensive knowledge of the history
of the Church to discover precedents for changes that may seem on the
surface to fly in the face of tradition. Catholics who feel unsettled by the
notion of married priests or women in the ministry may find some comfort
in Chittister's ability to identify in those propositions a return to an earlier
sensibility within the Catholic Church. (Failing that, they may turn to
Michael Novak's impassioned and equally informed defense of orthodoxy
later in the book.)

The Catholic school system and the women who administer it with
largely unacknowledged aplomb have been critiqued as zealously as has
the Inquisition (nor will they escape entirely in these pages). But Joan
Chittister lets us know both through her stories and by the evidence of
her considerable intellect that the sisters were often more subversive and
inspirational than many of us are willing to admit.

۶ AS FAR AS I KNOW, my mother is French-Irish Roman Catholic. My father was Irish Roman Catholic, probably second generation. But my biological father died when I was about three years old, and my mother married again, a Presbyterian—I always say, in an era in which ecumenism was neither a word nor a virtue. From him I learned truth; truth-telling was his major virtue. My father *genuinely* believed that as long as you *never* told a lie you were *always* on God's side. My mother honestly believed and formed in me a notion that you were to be everything that God had made you to be, and that was the basis for salvation: Did you return to God what God had given to you to steward? Kind of that gospel on coming at the twelfth hour. I didn't know it then, but I know very clearly now what she was talking about.

My father was a welder. He worked for the American Bridge Company during my formative years in Ambridge, Pennsylvania, during World War II. He welded LSTs apparently, and it was the reason he was given a deferment during the war. Ambridge was named for the company, which has long since disappeared. The fact of the matter is that the town itself is still physically there, it's on the map, but with what purpose other than nostalgia, I don't know. American Bridge has died and the town with it. That's the whole point, there's *nothing* left there at all. It was once a nice, kind of thriving little—before we had the word *suburb*—suburb of Pittsburgh.

To be frank, my parents were probably a microcosm of the Hundred Years War. The Protestant family didn't like the fact that he was marrying an Irish Roman Catholic, and the Roman Catholic part of the family certainly were very concerned about the fact that she was marrying a Protestant. Neither one of them was devout, although she was a closet Catholic. She was busy trying to hold the marriage together when absolutely nothing else was going right. Protestants were never known for devotion, just for ideology, and so neither one of them *practiced* in the strictest sense of that word—but *both* of them provided me with the fruits of the practice. She said that since her going to Mass caused a rupture in the family, it was better for her not to go to Mass; every time she went to church it seemed to anger my Protestant father and result in some kind of tension in the home. She decided that the home was more important and that was her obligation of conscience. And my father never gave me an explanation for why he didn't go to church except that he didn't believe that churches were much. So there was absolutely *no* connection between the liturgical life of the Church, the teaching cycle of the Church, or the organization of the Church that influenced my life. That's a joke; I didn't know the difference.

The funny thing is that out of all that negative, or at least passive, response came this ardent churchgoer. I don't have any explanation for that, outside of the fact that both of them saw church as valuable. She had given it up for the sake of the family, and he didn't believe that organized church was any necessary reflection of virtue or Christianity. I guess I went to see what they both valued but neither one worked at.

I think my mother took me to church in the beginning — I have recollections of that — but my real churchgoing began with school: Saint Veronica's in Ambridge, taught by the Sisters of Saint Joseph. He didn't like the idea of my going to a Catholic school, but she insisted. And I loved it. I was crazy about the sisters. They were kind, they were omniscient, they were present, they were beautiful people, and I loved it. I loved school; I could have been a professional student if given half the chance. I got a lot of sense of achievement and reward there. I can remember very, *very* distinctly people coming to the house to talk to my mother about — apparently they had done some kind of tests on me — moving me into school before I should have been there and then, later, moving me through school at a greater rate. And my mother said, "No, absolutely not. There has to be another way to do this. I want her to progress as quickly as she can, intellectually, but I think there is a difference, and I don't want her moved ahead of her age."

Now, my mother was not an educated woman, but she was a brilliant woman. There is a difference, and I always knew all my life that my mother was brilliant. It never occurred to me to doubt what she had figured out or what she had said. So I can remember that the sisters, the Baden Josephs, sat me deliberately, every year, by the encyclopedias. And then they told me in my ear, privately, that when I was finished with the work they gave me in various classes, I was to read, and I was permitted to read anything I wanted to on those shelves.

I've looked back after all this time, and, frankly, I think they did the right thing. If you want the absolute truth, I had no idea how they assessed me at that age, but apparently they were struggling with the kinds of things that people are struggling with now in special education for children. But all those wise women got together. My father said to me, "I don't care what grades you get in anything else. You can come home with F's in everything except two subjects: I want you to have an A in reading and I want you to have an A in arithmetic. And after that I don't care what you do. But if you get an A in reading and an A in arithmetic, you can do anything you want to in life." All I can tell you is that I remember sitting in my second and third grade classrooms and reading everything that *Encyclopaedia Britannica*, and *Americana*, and Dickens had to offer. I'd completely finished them by the end of third grade. That's real education. Everything after that was kind of postlude.

Sister brought books in extra and, as she saw me finishing, just quietly fed the shelves. She must have brought them from the convent library; I don't know where she got the darned stuff. I would do my little exercises, and I was doing them in five minutes, and then I would reach over to my bookshelves and take off either the encyclopedia or the latest Dickens, and by the end of fourth grade I had read *A Tale of Two Cities* and there was no question in my mind what it was about. I loved it, and I took it for granted. It's only been in my adult years that I've looked back and said, "*What?* Are you sure?" But of course I'm sure. I went into college classes where they assigned things that I'd already read in the fourth grade. I was the only one I was aware of who was doing that, and somehow or other my little mind knew that something about it was mine, that I was supposed to do this.

I can remember, too, my mother taking me to the convent for music lessons and the sisters saying they *never* gave anybody music lessons at my age. And my mother said, "If I am willing to pay you, are you willing to take her?" And the sisters said they would give me a little test. That's how I began piano, the first month of my first grade year. The sisters didn't like to take anybody before the fourth grade, but my mother insisted. Then one day my father took me downtown in Ambridge, into a music store, and said, "Okay, kid, pick a piano." He didn't know anything about pianos. I was the expert; I was six. "I'll take this one. This is nice, Daddy." But I was aware of our finances. I was very aware of the fact that they should not be buying me a piano and I said to him, "Well, it's okay with me, Daddy, I don't really need a piano." And he said, "Yeah, fine, but we're going to buy a piano, so now you tell us which one to get." The man took me upstairs to the second floor, and I guess we finally bought a spinet of some kind that *I* liked because I thought it sounded good and that my mother said was a good piece of furniture.

I loved music and I never wanted to stop. It was never one of those cases where I had to be teased into practicing. Still, I remember quite distinctly my mother telling me that I could be a concert pianist and that even if I didn't want to be a concert pianist, if I practiced hard, it would be good for parties. You had to keep these things in balance. I always loved my music. Sometime during high school I took up the accordion instead of the piano because it was a better party instrument.

As I said, my biological father died when I was almost three, and I have a vivid memory of my mother taking me to the funeral home. I was an only child, and her family was unhappy, or at least concerned, about her taking "the baby" to a funeral parlor. But my mother was insistent that there was no choice, that if she didn't take me to the funeral parlor there would be no adequate explanation as to where my father had gone. When we came to the funeral parlor, at least the memory I have is of two sisters sitting at the end of the casket. When I asked my mother who those people were, her explanation was that they were friends of God, and they were also friends of Daddy's, and that when the angels came for Joan's daddy, the sisters would tell the angels that Joan's daddy had been a very good man and a good daddy and that God should take that soul. So my association was that sisters were people who gave the souls of children's daddies to God. And frankly, I thought that was a pretty good way to go through life. I began to follow them from one side of the street to the other side of the street, and I *waited* to go to school to be with people who gave little girls' daddies to God. I thought it was a pretty good trick. The respect started way before first grade. I know that it's just unlikely, and so I hesitate to tell the story, but the problem is, it's true and I have no other story to tell. I was really convinced that I would be a sister and give the souls of little girls' fathers to God. That's what I thought sisters did. I found the Baden Josephs—the Sisters of St. Joseph of Baden, Pennsylvania—and they were absolutely wonderful. They met all my expectations, and that was it.

Everything I do comes out of what I was trained to believe by the institutional, the organized Church. They won't be happy to hear that, but it's true. I must be one of their failures. The only thing I go on is the theology that my second grade teacher told me—they're not happy with it, but it sounded pretty good to me. It's about who God is, who the Church is, who Jesus was, and I believed it, I bought it all. For instance, when I was in second grade, I certainly don't know the day or the hour, but Sister taught us that only Catholics went to heaven. I know where I was sitting—by the bookcases—and I just felt that something terrible had happened. I sat there very quietly, very embarrassed, very ashamed— after all, my mother had married someone who wasn't going to go to heaven and I couldn't figure out how to get him there. I went home and my mother said, "What did you learn in school today?" So I went through most of the stuff, and then I said, "Momma, Sister said that Presbyterians don't go to heaven." And my mother said, "Uh-huh, and what did you say?" And I said, "I didn't say anything." My mother said, "What do you think about that?" And I can remember a great struggle, and I said, "I think Sister is wrong." And she said, "Why do you think Sister is wrong?'' And I said, ''Well, I've been wondering that.'' And she said, ''Well, did you decide?'' And I said, ''I figure, Sister just doesn't know my daddy.'' In other words, Sister is omniscient, there is no question that Sister is always right, but Sister lacks a piece of the data, and the piece of the data that would change her mind is to know my father.

So I was very young, but I decided that there were some things that I just had to figure out. One of them I had already figured out, but I just didn't bother to tell them: that they were wrong. Protestants *did* go to heaven, and I knew it because I lived with one who, by all their standards, was worthy of it. So when you're very little and you put a couple of those things together, after that it's open field.

We moved to Erie, Pennsylvania, when I was in fourth grade and I was *intent*, I just practically told them that I had no intention of going to school unless they found ''my sisters,'' who were the Sisters of St. Joseph of Baden. Erie just happened to be populated, controlled institutionally by the Sisters of St. Joseph of Erie, so there was very little problem in meeting my demands, except that they were a different order. When I got to high school age, though, through a series of circumstances, I found myself at the Sisters of St. Benedict, and in my opinion they seemed even more like the sisters that I had first known in terms of spirit and all the things that make up a charism, or a community personality. So ultimately they had an awful lot to do with the progression of my spiritual and personal life. You could see that they enjoyed one another and they respected one another. They were extremely good to us kids: they treated us like human beings. And they were beautiful people. I always say, it was a case of I came, I saw, they conquered.

You have to remember that I had been waiting to enter religious life from the time I was three. Since my father died, I had been waiting to be a sister. So I waited patiently, and then I made my freshman year retreat, and they told me religious life was a good thing to do, and then I made my sophomore year retreat and they were just as affirming. The retreat usually came around March, and my birthday is April 26. Our high school was in the motherhouse, same building, under one roof. So when all the sisters have disappeared, because I don't want the sisters to know, I go to what is commonly called the bell system, and I look up the prioress's number — which does not take an awful lot of intelligence. The prioress's number is always one, and it never occurs to me that nobody ever rings the prioress's bell. I ring one, and the door opens across the hall, and this little Mother Superior comes out, with a certain amount of chagrin, trying to find out who rang her bell. And I whisper, ''Mother, I rang your bell.'' She looks over her glasses and says, ''You, my dear? Well, what can I do for you, child?'' And I say, "Mother, I'd like to enter. I'd like to enter the convent." And she says, "Oh." And she looks at me long and hard, and she says, "How old are you, dear?" And I say, "I'm fifteen, Mother." And she says, "Well, that's very nice but nobody can enter the convent until they are sixteen, so dear, you just come back at that time," and disappears.

So I wait, one year goes by, it's April 26, 1952. I go to the bell, I ring one, she comes out of her office — same look — and starts down the hall. I say, "Mother, I rang your bell," and she says, with a slight frown over her glasses, "And what would you like, dear?" And I say, "Mother, I'm sixteen." She says, "Pardon me?" "I said, I'm sixteen." And she says, "Wonderful," and I say, "Mother, you told me to come back when I'm sixteen," and she says, "What for, dear?" and I say, "To enter." She says, "Oh yes, I remember you." So I say, "When can I come?" And she says, "I think we better go over here and talk." So she takes me in a little room and she talks to me a minute, and she says, "My dear, you are the only child your mother has and I really do not believe that we can take you. Your mother will need you someday." And I say, "But my mother is perfectly happy to let me go." And she says, "Well dear, you don't know that." And I say, "I'll bring my mother tomorrow." So the next day, I show up with my mother who tells her that she has never known me in all these years not to do *exactly* what I said I was going to do. So they might as well take me, or at least do us all the favor of saying they weren't going to take me, because otherwise they had trouble on their hands, forever.

So at the age of sixteen, I entered. And that was it, it was just that simple. On September 8 I showed up at the convent door and, I think with a certain amount of consternation, they took me. The normal minimum age would have been eighteen. We had just about no one else who came at sixteen. Someplace along the line I must have picked up the gem of canonical wisdom that when you're sixteen years old you can enter religious life. I was a sophomore in high school, and I thought I'd dated everybody in town. I entered the novitiate on September 8, and on October 16, I think it was, I got polio. And after that, it was kind of tough. The whole question was Would they keep me? I didn't walk for four years. I was in a wheelchair and a long leg brace and an iron lung, and when I think back, the Community must have had just a terrible time trying to determine whether or not in conscience they could keep this kid that they weren't sure could ever really live the life and who would always be, at best, an exception. And they kept me. And I'll tell you, people may look now and say, "What has happened to the Erie Benedictines, have they gone crazy?'' And I would say that if you had looked back at 1952 and seen how they dealt with the poor and disenfranchised then, in the person of Joan Chittister, you should have had fair warning about who this group was.

But what initially attracted me to them was that they were such loving people. And furthermore they were extremely prayerful people. When I went home at night, I used to walk out through the schoolyard and be able to hear the Divine Office being chanted and to this night — in fact, I'm missing prayer right now — the choral prayer of the Church has never ceased in this Community. There were two things in this Community that were never questioned during renewal, never came up in a *discussion*, although everything else was open for some kind of debate or a review. One was choral prayer and the other was the role of the prioress.

Before Vatican II, there is no doubt that the spirituality espoused was the spirituality of selflessness that led to self-obliteration. Spirituality after Vatican II was also a spirituality of selflessness, whether the current Church realizes it or not, but it is a selflessness that stems from self-development. The spirituality before Vatican II was a spirituality of interchangeable parts — the Singer Sewing Machine Company could have done as well. Everybody in the Community was a potential fourth grade teacher; everybody in the Community was a potential high school English teacher. What you did was send in warm bodies. After Vatican II, you began to ask, Who is this person, really? What gifts has she been given for the upbuilding of the Church? How can this Community affirm those gifts, and how can this person promote the charism of this Community? It's a different theological world view. Before Vatican II, the emphasis was on a kind of conflict between the spirit and the flesh: duels, struggles with the flesh, that there are two separate things, that one is capable of sanctity and the other one is not. After Vatican II you have a much more integrated world view, a much more incarnational world view. You're saying Jesus came enfleshed, and therefore all flesh is holy. Now all flesh has been redeemed and so *everything* speaks of the glory of God again, just as it did in the Garden, and *everything* must work for the coming of the reign of God, and everything does if you let it. Prior to Vatican II you had a religious life that was working *against* the flesh, to put it mildly, and after Vatican II you have a consciousness that the flesh is part of the Kingdom of God.

The Benedictine order is fifteen hundred years old. It began with St. Benedict in 529 A.D. Up until about the thirteenth century the parallel parts, male and female, are similar. In fact, we have periods of great abbesses and even great dual monasteries, where there are both men and women in a single monastery and the abbess is a female. Then in the thirteenth century we have the rising of the university system, and the university system closes all the schools to females. Only men may go to the universities. And about that time, in a parallel line, we have the imposition of clerical celibacy, and at a third parallel level, we have the imposition of cloister. The interesting thing is that cloister is imposed only on women. If you have any Catholicism in your background, you don't think of a cloistered Benedictine monk. You may think of a cloistered Cistercian monk, but you don't make cloister essential to Benedictinism. You make a cloister of the essence of Benedictine women, not Benedictine men.

In the nineteenth century, Boniface Wimmer, a Benedictine monk from Metten Abbey in Germany, in a kind of resurgence of the Benedictine missionary spirit that had missionized England, France, and Germany, decides it is time for Benedictines to go the United States, to the New World. He brings monks, and he goes to the cloistered women's monasteries in Europe and he asks for women. In the mid–eighteen hundreds, the Bavarians had passed a law. Just as today Germany is still the richest of the churches, in the mid–eighteen hundreds the Germans were already living on state pensions, and so the Germans say they will give pensions only to those religious who do something useful to the state. That is when you get the beginning of convent schools. And the Community in Eichstadt releases three to five women to go to the United States to aid with the education of the German immigrants in this country. That's Erie and St. Mary's, Pennsylvania, which is the first foundation here.

The point is we come from a cloistered Benedictine abbey: St. Walburga in Eichstadt, Bavaria. It was founded in the year 1035, and it is a thriving Benedictine monastery to this very night. They just elected a new abbess a couple of years ago. For a long time, that must have been the ideal for this Community: to get established and live as they lived in Eichstadt. But it never happened—you can't go home again. They became an educational Community for the German immigrants in Erie, Pennsylvania. Nevertheless, when I entered in 1952, one hundred years later, they were still identified as a "*semi*cloistered" Community—meaning that you could go into the Community, the sisters could and would talk to you and serve you, but the sisters themselves didn't go out. They didn't go to their own home, for instance. I entered in 1952 at the age of sixteen, and I never walked into my own home again until 1968. I used to say, as a matter of fact, we could use every Esso station in the country, but we couldn't go into our own home because it was some kind of an attack on our vocation.

We live today *exactly* like the Benedictine monks: we have schools and we're not cloistered. Have we loosened up? No, we've just become normative. If the norm in everything is the male standard, we've taken it, unlike communities of Benedictines who had papal cloister imposed on them.

I'm a perfect example of the unthinking conservative. I bought it all, meaning I never confronted it intellectually. I loved the Community, I loved its spirit, I loved its members. Even in 1952 I thought that a lot of the stuff we did was (a) groundless, (b) meaningless, (c) silly — all of the above, some of the above, none of the above. But I never questioned it. I just took it for granted that I'd be a second-class citizen in the Order, but it was okay with me because I really thought that the people I knew were worth it. Sometimes your most liberal people are your most conservative. I don't know if it makes them feel better to defend what they can't do or if the most that they can do is defend what they're incapable of. But the point is that no matter what the public image is, I did not lead renewal. I'd *love* to be able to say I did, but I really didn't. I feared it. I'm the intellectualist type, I want a footnote for everything, and when I would ask certain people, "But why would you give up the habit?" and they would say, "Because," that was not enough of an answer for me. I came to renewal slowly. The fact of the matter is that I am very considered, rational, thoughtful about everything I do, so I have come to my present posture through an *awful lot* of footnotes, the *most* conservative of footnotes, and I believe that where we are right now is *right*. And furthermore, I'm dumb enough to believe that this whole thing is *quite* traditional.

In 1971, when I was elected president of the Federation of Saint Scholastica, I was only by birth two months eligible. I certainly didn't want it — on the contrary, I avoided it like the plague. I was busy getting my doctorate at Penn State. I was thirty-five at the time. There are four Benedictine women's federations in the United States, and the Federation of Saint Scholastica is the largest of them.

I was elected for a three-year term and then, three years later, to a four-year term, and I had every reason to believe that I would probably have been elected to my third and last term as president in 1978. But my Community said at that point, in effect, You've been president long enough. We want you to come home and be prioress of Erie. So when I was forty-two years old, I became prioress of the local Community, and I've been prioress for eight years and am now in my last term. After this, I have no particular plans.

What was it like when the Order went through renewal? That's easy: it was a walk through the outskirts of hell. Absolutely everything that you had ever been taught, everything you ever saw, everything you ever believed, was now up for grabs. And the final principle—and I *don't* mean to be simplistic, but I'm just trying to tell you what happened in my life—the distinguishing principle became love. You just finally had to get to the point where you said, What really matters? Is it a veil that matters? Is it a skirt that matters? Is it a ministry that matters? What matters? And when I came right down to it, the only answer I could come up with was that Christ mattered, gospel mattered, and the people mattered, and that was it. So I just decided to go for those three.

I went so far as to go home to tell my parents in September that I was leaving in June 1970. I told them that I had not left religious life, that religious life had left me. The entire symbol system had gone—these are words I have now, they're not words I had then—and the entire purpose seemed to have gone. For instance, religious were beginning to talk about doing things other than simply teaching in the Catholic school system. Religious were beginning to talk about needing to be able to move in the public arena without habits and veils. Well, it's kind of embarrassing to hear myself say it tonight, but at the time that kind of looked like the essence—which of course it wasn't. It's silly, but so seduced had we been by the symbols that we couldn't imagine that you could have the faith without them.

People are in contemporary dress within the Order now, and the sign is See how they love one another and See what these people will do, at any cost, for the rest of humankind. They're not asking for privilege. It's a more incarnational thing. But it had become clear to me that as I seriously tried to listen to myself, I had been a very happy religious. I wasn't trying to leave religious life. I was really trying to stay, and the more I heard and really listened to the position papers, the principles of Vatican II, the more I realized that I was being called to the most authentic kind of religious life. That in turn put a great burden on me because all the symbols were gone, so the whole question was now whether I could really be what I talked about. And I found it was more than worth doing. I found that I was in the very same gospel position as the rich young man, and all the disciples, and Mary of Nazareth. It was so different. It was really being called to the center of everything you believed in and trying to make it real, rather than to everything that the *institution* was and trying to perpetuate it.

I don't have any statistics, but I think we were affected by as many as twenty or twenty-five percent of the religious in our Order leaving, which was the average figure for everybody else. It wasn't so much that professed sisters left but that younger people did not stay in the novitiate. It has very much leveled off. In fact, it's more than leveled off, it's been totally reversed. I genuinely believe that there are an awful lot of vocations out there. I always maintain that we must be intervening in life in a significant way, in significant times, and that if you are doing that, it's a basic gospel act and that there are phenomenal numbers of people who want to live the gospel by becoming a religious. Frankly, I don't have any questions about a vocation crisis. It's a crisis of significance and a crisis of spirituality. If we are doing significant gospel things, out of a significant spirituality of this time, the vocations are there.

What I'm trying to say is that I don't think religious life is dead. On the contrary, I think religious life is in a state of rebirth. But what was a significant reason to give your life one hundred years ago is no longer a significant reason. One hundred years ago, when my ancestors came to this country and they were torching convents in Philadelphia and Boston, they were torching them because nuns were a terrible threat to a white, Anglo-Saxon society. What nuns were doing at that time was making it possible for immigrant Catholics to preserve their faith and be inserted into a Protestant culture. They were making it possible by teaching immigrant children the faith and the language, and *nobody* really wanted that to happen, including Thomas Jefferson. Nuns came to this country as radicals — I have a friend who says performance punishes — and they were so successful they got co-opted into the establishment by moving up on the backs of the poor. Boston once had signs that said, "No Catholics need apply here." Let's not forget that. Nuns and the Church turned that city around — then all of a sudden they became the most establishment of the establishment. Now, since Vatican II, nuns have realized that the radical ministry of that century is over: Catholics *are* the establishment. They're the middle class; they're even the wealthy; they're certainly the educated. The whole question now is Who are the new poor? Who needs us now?

The very interesting thing is that the Catholics who came up on the backs of the nuns don't like it that the nuns are moving down instead of up — they don't like that *at all*. "Sister, you belong in the Catholic school system." Which at this stage of the game means "Sister, you belong with the wealthy, the established, the white, the Anglo, the system, and we don't want you mucking around with those kind." And I say that unless we are at those moments of life that are "breakdown" and "breakthrough" points, we don't deserve to be anyplace, and we ought to die out. We ought to be with the establishment in breakdown and with the poor for breakthrough. Breakdown points are pastoral points, retreat points, counseling points. Breakthrough points are soup kitchens, food banks, lower-class neighborhoods, advocacy positions, legislative research — wherever the voiceless need a voice.

I certainly would not want to sound as if I'm writing the parochial school system out of existence, if for no other reason than pure political theory. I think one of the very first things an authoritarian state does is get control of the school system, so I would always want an alternative school system, and I would die to defend that. I was misquoted on that some ten years ago, to my chagrin, and I was never sure if it was my bad rhetoric or their bad mind. I would never say that the parochial school system should go. As to whether or not nuns have to run it . . . if after one hundred and fifty years we have not developed a stratum of laity who are capable of that, frankly I wonder what we've all been about. If you could have lay Catholics at the highest level of government, including the presidency, surely they ought to be able to teach second grade. So if Catholics want a Catholic school system, I think we're more than capable of generating one. A synonym for a Catholic school system is not necessarily one run by an order of nuns. I don't think the Catholic school system is the only way in which the reign of God comes, and I'm really sorry that we gave anybody that impression.

I am definitely not being coy when I try to make the point that the women's question is a great deal broader than the ordination question or that, as a matter of fact, it is possible — and I think the situation does exist right now in other mainstream Christian churches — to ordain women and still be very sexist. I wouldn't want to leave the impression that ordination would do it, because my theory is that it wouldn't do it at all. The ordination question is crucial because it is highly symbolic, and it is ultimate. If we try to imagine the one thing that a black couldn't do in this country in 1955, that summed up with phenomenal power what it meant to be a black, I suppose that you would have something comparable — maybe the right to vote or the fact that they couldn't drink water out of a common drinking fountain.

The ordination issue is central because it has something to do with the quality of a woman's soul and the nature of women as God sees them, not the nature of women as men see them or as other people see them. It brings into question the credibility of all the best doctrines of the Church: baptism, grace, redemption, Incarnation, creation. Everything is wrapped up in that package called the female soul — and is it qualitatively different from the male soul? All of this talk about you can't ordain a woman because Jesus was male has got to be patent nonsense. Jesus did not come to be male, Jesus came to become flesh—"And the Word became flesh." You know, we have never said, in any of the Christian churches that I know of, "And the Word became male." They say you've got to have a male in order to be a sign of Jesus. *No* male can be a sign of Jesus, anymore than a woman can be. If you have to have a male who is like Jesus to be Jesus, then one of the criteria ought to be that the person has to be Jewish—that has a great deal more to do with being Jesus than being male does because the Redeemer was to have come from the line of David.

So there is a theological inconsistency that is more than inconsistency; it is absolutely the erosion of the value of the other doctrines of the Church. They will say, for instance, that a woman cannot be a priest because there were no women at the Last Supper. In the first place that is suspect, if it was a real Passover meal—but forget that. The fact is that if the Last Supper is the only and ultimate paradigm of the Eucharist, then who decided that women were allowed to receive the Eucharist? And why is it that when *they* depart from the model of the Last Supper it's called "ongoing revelation," and when *I* depart from the model of the Last Supper it's called "heresy"?

The ordination question is central to the nature of Jesus, to the nature of the Incarnation, of the human soul, and of discipleship and Christian commitment. It's an important one, obviously, and more than just socially. But now it has a particularly significant social power. Why now and not before? For some pretty obvious reasons, one of which is certainly the increased educational consciousness of women. It used to be that the *entire* institutional structure militated against being a full human being if you were a woman. But progress made in other arenas has got to affect this one.

So you have a new moment in history, with all new manner of information. It isn't that so many new things are happening necessarily, but you have to look at old things in a new way. You must begin to account for the fact that half of the institutional Church has been totally run by women. Who brought the hospital system to the United States, for instance? It was women. Who ran it and paid for it? Women. Dioceses didn't pay for those things; religious orders paid for them. Who built the Catholic school system in the United States of America? Women. You cannot look, even at Church history, and argue with the effectiveness, the quality, the ability of women. It's not going to go away. Every day more arenas open. The Church is going to have to re-examine its theology-biology of women. I have always argued that the problem with the role of women is that a very bad biology has been theologized. And because that biology is no longer tenable, everything else is going to change around it.

The diaconate is almost a better example of the corrosive theology of women than the priesthood is. At least with priesthood you've got a tradition. You must still look at the tradition and you must look at it seriously and respectfully. But when you get to the diaconate, the whole thing runs aground. That is where practice, possibility, and theology all go awry. Because, as a matter of fact, we did have women deacons. I think we had women deacons in the West for eleven centuries, and in the East for fourteen centuries, and later than that in some of the Eastern churches. When the Roman Catholic Church restored the permanent diaconate about fifteen years ago, they restored it for men only. Now that's blatant sexism. That's all there is to it. By virtue of their own criteria, that's sexism.

I should probably explain that the diaconate is one of the orders on the way to priesthood, the order given just prior to priesthood. It does not include, for instance, a faculty for consecration or for hearing confession, so it is not the fullness of the priesthood, but it is a clerical office. For a long time, the message was that a man could be ordained a married deacon, provided that if his wife died he would never marry again. That's a clear message: you got messed up once with a woman and we'll forgive you for that, but don't ever do it again, young man. Do not let yourself get involved with that lower creature again. Those are mighty negative messages. The notion that little girls cannot serve on the altar—all of that is sexism to the ultimate.

The best relationship of women's religious life to the celibacy question comes in the historical truth that cloister was not really imposed on women until about the thirteenth century, which is the very time in which celibacy was imposed on men. Up until the thirteenth century, you did not associate cloister necessarily with religious life. After the thirteenth century, cloister became the norm of *women's* religious life. The notion that women must be removed from the streets certainly was intended to protect them at a barbarous period in history, but most of all it was meant to control and restrict them. That derives from what Thomas Aquinas called their "carnal lust," so the whole notion became that a woman simply could not control herself carnally and that a woman's nature was such that she simply had to be engaged in very rigorous asceticism—not in education, for instance. Her purpose was for more menial kinds of service. What you are seeing at that point is the whole notion that the male vocation—which is apparently very fragile—and celibacy itself can be maintained only by making sure that there are no women present. As the centuries went by, that developed into the whole notion that religious life for men was open, but religious life for women was to be in a closed society. I always get a kick out of the fact that the Church theologians or teachers or administrators took the position that women were unreservedly carnal, whereas Freud took the position that they were unreservedly frigid—so if you're a woman, you can't win. You are either by nature absolutely without control or by nature so overcontrolled that you simply are incapable of response on a human level. Those are great messages to grow up with.

Likewise, if you look into the reasons for male celibacy, you come up with some interesting perspectives. Historians agree that estates were being divided through inheritance to the children of priests, resulting in a loss of Church property. So celibacy became as much an economic issue at one period in history as a theological or a clerical one.

At significant points in Church life, women have had input in significant ways. Yet at the present time, all jurisdiction is tied up in priesthood, so that's why all roads lead to Rome, that's why we keep coming back to the priesthood issue. But there are many other issues, so let me name a couple. One is the identification of women in the language of the Church—women are just invisible. You can have two hundred and fifty women and one man at the six o'clock Tuesday morning Mass, yet for centuries they will tell you that we are all meant to be sons of God, and nobody even has the grace to blush. Invisibility is no small psychological thing, and if you are allowed to erase people from the language, what isn't in the mind isn't going to be in the structures. But we have multiple approved versions of the Scriptures. Take any single passage and follow it through all the approved versions. Not only will the translations differ in word use, some of them even differ in content. But when somebody like me says, "We would like to see at least two pronouns, and we would like to see an expanded, less heretical version of God," they accuse us of tampering with the deposit of the faith. It doesn't make any sense.

So language is a big issue, a new theology of family is a big issue—the notion of parenting rather than mothering. The whole question of what marriage is about is a major issue for women, and women in decision-making positions in the Church is a major dimension of this. The Church is on record for legislation that makes possible the unmarried vocation for women. We say that there are three vocations: the married vocation, the religious vocation, and the single vocation. But it is almost impossible for a woman to follow the single vocation and lead a dignified life, until we are also on record supporting equal pay, housing subsidies, and contract and legal rights. All of those things are extremely important women's issues in the Church. That's the kind of stuff I'm talking about.

It is one of the reasons that women themselves have to take responsibility at the lowest possible levels for speaking up and making their presence known and their needs felt. Someplace along the line we have to rely on grace and conscience, and I have said repeatedly that we definitely need women of courage. We also need men of conscience—they have to begin to call their own system, and it is true that some are, and that is very heartening to someone like me. It's very painful, there is no question about that. But we have to realize that the Church didn't really inveigh against slavery either for years and then eventually came to a consciousness of the moral relationship—when you hear yourself say that, it's *breathtaking*; nevertheless they did, and there weren't any blacks in the Church then, so I just have to trust that the Holy Spirit does work and that men of good will do listen. I *have* to trust. Otherwise how would you stay, how could you take it? When I am out at public lectures, women invariably ask that question. They get conscious and they get desperate, and they don't know if they want their daughters subjected to this.

I do believe that when you move outside the system you can become its critic, but critics are a strange breed. If you stay inside the system, surely someone must see you as its lover. Prophets did not move outside the system; they stood right in the middle of their societies and tried to point out their consciousness of the will of God for that society. They didn't abandon it; they didn't run. But they also never acquiesced, and they never made the system feel good about itself by being quiet. I feel all the time that the model that we must take—certainly the model that I feel I must take—is, if not *for* us, then *because* of us. I owe the people of God this consciousness because it has something to do with the nature of God. Just moving out of that, just abandoning that to a narrowness of vision would be *my* sin.

I don't want to imply under any circumstances that women who do move out of the system are being unfaithful. On the contrary, I'm convinced that they are the signs to us of a new kind of grace working. Those women are very important to me in my own life because they are phenomenal signs of courage and strength. But at least at the present time, or God willing for all time, I feel called to stay at the center of this thing from which I get hope and strength and courage to see what the Church can be and to try to help it be that.

When I was a teacher, I always taught that wheat was the major export of the United States of America—now weapons are. We're not putting money into education, we're not putting money into child care, we're not putting money into housing subsidies, we will not put money into aid to dependent families, we don't want to put any more money into food stamps, and we decry these figures. I really see this as a demonic mask of some of the *real* issues of this society. I think we need a lot of study and a lot of concern for the whole nature-of-life question and not just at the level of conception, but at the other end of the spectrum. We are now becoming an older society, and people are beginning to make recommendations in the public arena that medical care of a life-sustaining nature or of a corrective nature should not be given after the age of eighty. These are going to become major questions as this century ends and the next century begins.

We simply cannot afford not to bring this discussion into a much broader context, and you'll find that this discussion is what will bring us to a critique of our society as well as a critique of our morality. It's not just the Church in Rome that's avoiding the issues—I think the government is, too, and they're of a piece.

We really are in a unique moment in Church history. For the very first time, questions control the arena before answers can possibly be worked out. You used to have ten, fifteen, thirty years before the word even got around that there was a question. Now you get the question on the evening news, and somebody demands an answer the next morning. We're talking about phenomenally complex issues, most of them based in science, all of them new, not just to our world but to any world. Someplace along the line, we are going to have to become more a Church of questions than of answers. We are going to have to admit that we are into some new arenas and this is the best evidence that we have at the present time. We have to have a Church that calls the local churches, the national churches to their questions. The Roman Church should be saying to the American Church, What is your position on consumerism, on affluence, on stewardship? Because your government, your national policies are affecting the lives of other people, and as a Church you must address this issue. So have you raised that question yet?

That and drawing people into the formation of conscience on those questions *is*, I think, an emerging role for a universal Church that has a transcendent perspective, that crosses national boundaries and sees the overlap in those boundaries. My fear is that if you keep a catechism Church in a complex society, where people know that old answers aren't working for new questions, you lose the credibility and power of the Church and the gospel.

You have to realize that the center of the world and the center of the Church is shifting. Walbert Buhlman in his book *The Coming of the Third Church*, using Vatican statistics, says that by the year 2000, sixty percent of the membership of the Church will live in the Third World, in Latin

America or in Africa. But by the year 2000, only sixteen percent of the world will be any kind of Christian at all. The point is that the center of gravity is shifting away from old institutions, away from old structures, away from old centers of control, and, therefore, into new centers of population and new agenda questions. It's a shift that brings the Church face to face with the whole question of an ecclesiastical imperialism and colonialism that is ceasing to work. You can't Romanize the entire Church around the world, and that's what we're going to have to face and work with. We need new ears because that Church is going to bring a whole new set of moral agendas and questions to the Church.

They've had our so-called system of free enterprise in the Third World countries like those in Latin America for over one hundred and fifty years now, and all they have to do is look around on the city square and they can tell you that it hasn't worked. It's no wonder they're suspicious of it. The whole notion that liberation theology flirts with Marxism is at least amusing, if not antihistorical. We have to realize that the theology of Thomas Aquinas was built on the philosophies of Aristotle and Plato, and nobody said, "They're pagan, and therefore we can't accept that." We said, "Isn't that a wonderful new cosmology, isn't that tremendous insight." In the words of Don Sergio Mendes Arceo from Cuernavaca, "The difference between Marxism and capitalism is that capitalism is immoral at its roots, but Marxism has to be corrupted to be immoral." I certainly believe that there is a way to have a free enterprise system that is Christian. Nevertheless, you've got to critique where their economic assumptions come from. What are they built on, and can you line it up next to the Scripture at all? I'm not an apologist for Marxism, but you cannot dismiss the needs of an entire people whom capitalism apparently has not served well — "We're sorry but we cannot allow you to eat today because that would be Marxist."

If there's a Communist revolution in Latin America, we have made them ripe for it — or at least have had plenty of complicity. When I say "we" I mean a so-called Christian capitalist society that should be coming out with a set of norms that would make liberation theology unnecessary and make Marxism antiquated. We have to look at what we're doing and what our assumptions are as Christian nations — and how we're implementing them — before we can so cavalierly dismiss those liberation theologies or seem to be mystified about why people would begin to move toward Marxism. We have managed to export our products and our factories, but we are not exporting our standard of living, fringe benefits, unions, or pension systems. That's pure exploitation — is that coming out of Christian capitalism?

You see the American bishops courageously and forthrightly calling us to these questions. I hope it's not too late. You don't have to be an economist to look at American society and see that we ourselves are facing a rising number of poor and that we are drawing back from the obligations of the state to care for those who cannot care for themselves. You don't have to have a Ph.D. in economics to be concerned about that. All you have to do is read the beatitudes and look at Jesus' compassion for the poor. The bishops are showing us the social sins that can happen when privatized Christianity sinks into itself and has a spree. They're telling us that the gospels have to be held up to society and to its structures and institutions.

The thing of value that I carry with me always from my training and that is at the basis of my love for the Church is the whole concept of sacramentality—of the sacred in life as human things, as channels of grace. My own feeling is not that I have departed from the Church's teaching. On the contrary, I believed it. It worked on me. I just keep looking for it. I believe very strongly in the interpenetration of the sacred and the secular and in the presence of God in the world. If I could have changed anything, it would be having been born at the tail end of a period that is quite Jansenistic and dualistic—having experienced the rigors of that and seeing the loss of a sense of the holy in some things. I do feel privileged to be alive at this time, but I wouldn't have told you that twenty years ago. I'm not one of those people who would stand on the edge of chaos and say, "Isn't it wonderful?" But having lived with a foot in both theologies, I have a great sense of the past and its traditions and as great a sense of the possibility and the presence of a real transformed Christ. And a marvelous sense of the Church as the people of God rather than the Church as only an institution. I feel richer to have had both. Would I want to go around again? No. A masochist I'm not. But I've gotten a lot of good things along the way. It's like the famous Chinese curse "May you live in interesting times." Do you know the other one that says, "Now people exploit people. But after the revolution, it will be just the opposite."

THOMAS LANIGAN-SCHMIDT

Incarnation and Art

The nuns always encouraged me to make art. They were really the ones
who gave me the idea of it as a mission in life and said it was a talent
that had to be developed for the glory of God and the good of the world.
They never talked about it as something that would become an occupation
or anything practical. They always spoke of it in grand, kind of cosmic
terms.

—Thomas Lanigan-Schmidt

Sometime after the Summer of Love but before the twilight of the sixties,
I found myself climbing the stairs to an East Village walkup out past
Avenue B. The apartment served as living quarters, studio, and informal
gallery for a young artist named Thomas Schmidt (out of feeling for his
mother, he later annexed her maiden name). I'd met Tom once or twice
through a mutual friend, but this day was to be my introduction to his
art. Not content simply to put his works on view, Schmidt had concocted
an elaborate premise for his private showings. Called "The Sacristy of
the Hamptons," the exhibit purported to house the gleanings of famed art
collector Ethel Dull, who had "realized that secular art was basically
religious in spirit, that the Bauhaus had failed, that form didn't follow
function." As an antidote, Dull had collected works of religious art and
was exhibiting them in her home: "*Bauhome* rather than Bauhaus." At
least, that's as much as I can recall of the setup, as impressive in its way
as the work itself, for which I wasn't really prepared.

For arrayed inside that dreary and crumbling Lower East Side ten-
ement was a sumptuous assortment of Catholic Church treasures: golden
chalices and ciboria, jeweled reliquaries, a gleaming monstrance, priest's
chasuble, bishop's miter, and more. Despite their having been created

from some of the cheapest materials available, including florist's foil, Saran Wrap, Baggies, and Elmer's glue (critics would later label these elements "kitsch"), the pieces bore a surprising resemblance to the actual objects. What intrigued me most about the artifacts, though, was not their verisimilitude but my sense that the copies were far livelier than the originals. Genuine Mass implements, which as an altar boy I had seen up close so many times, have a character and a solidity that derive not only from their sacred utility but also from the precious metals and materials of which they are constructed. Yet if the real things tended to wear their authenticity like a solemn Roman garment, Schmidt's ringers shimmered and danced in even the fading afternoon light of Avenue B. Somehow humor and deep reverence commingled in those art objects, a tribute to the painstaking craftsmanship and improvisational wit of an Old World sensibility.

What I saw that day and on subsequent visits was at once so fanciful and so thoroughly the product of a singular vision—an integral union of craft, play, and religious feeling—that I assumed it had little chance for survival in the commercial world of art. I surmised that Tom Schmidt would be forced to evolve in some other, more practicable direction in order to survive as an artist. I was excited to learn some years ago, then, that by dint of perseverance and realized gifts, Schmidt had indeed been flourishing. He had earned a long-standing relationship with the prestigious Holly Solomon Gallery, and his works had been featured in exhibitions in Bonn and Düsseldorf, Venice and Rimini; he had been exhibited at the Whitney and some of his work placed in the permanent collection of the Metropolitan Museum.

None of this, needless to say, convinced the man to move to the Hamptons or to silk-screen his designs on T-shirts for mass consumption. Genuine feelings of solidarity with the working class from which he sprang haven't encouraged him to dilute his art in order to popularize it. During a period when the art scene appeared to be beset by a peculiar mixture of insincerity and aggressive self-marketing (perhaps the legacy of the Warhol generation) Lanigan-Schmidt's work has continued to be affecting through its integrity and its absence of self-importance. It has maintained an inner quality that *New York Times* art critic John Russell described in 1977 as emanating from "an innocent nature . . . doing its best to convey an innocent vision to the rest of us."

Although Tom Schmidt was probably one of the first real East Village artists, he left the area long before it acquired its trendy cachet, relocating in the rigorously unfashionable Manhattan neighborhood known as Hell's Kitchen. One entire room of his walkup on West 47th Street is decorated

with a woodsy mural; from the ceiling depend cherubim fashioned from
toilet paper wrappers and tinfoil. When he turns on a small fan, the angels
(or ''Charmin babies,'' as he calls them) bob and cavort against their
pastoral backdrop. But the bulk of the apartment is crowded with industrial
shelving that holds the copper wire, many colors of foil, plastic soda
bottles, glitter, and other raw materials that are the stuff of his art. In a
kitchen hung with holy pictures, we sat down to talk—or, more precisely,
to continue a dialogue we had taken up some years before about art and
religion. Tom is one of the few lay people I know who is conversant with,
among other things, ecclesiastical history, liberation theology, and religious art. His self-proclaimed affection for his working-class roots is not
a pose but part of a deeply felt system of beliefs that find their ultimate
expression in his choice of materials. I mention this here simply to un-
derline the observation that for Lanigan-Schmidt, art, religion, and culture
are intertwined in a way that reaches back to the Renaissance and before.

꿍 MY PARENTS WERE BORN in Elizabeth, New Jersey. My mother is
Irish-German and my father is northern and southern German. His father
is Lutheran and his mother is Catholic, southern German. My mother's
mother is southern German and her father is half Alsatian and half Irish.
So I'm only a little bit Irish and mostly German. Both my parents went
to Catholic schools. My father went to an ethnic German Catholic school
which wasn't allowed to be too ethnic—it was right after the First World
War—but which kept up certain customs, like Corpus Christi processions,
that had a very German, rococo feeling. My mother went to mostly Irish
Catholic schools, which had a very different flavor—which is to say, not
much flavor at all compared to the southern Germans or Italians or Polish,
all of whom have more color in their churches.

Among the immigrants, the German and Irish Catholics were pretty
much in the same neighborhoods. My father was tutoring my mother's
brother in Latin because he was going to become a priest. My mother,
who had been working for some rich people down the shore, had hitchhiked
home one weekend. She was sick of working for these people because
they had tried to get fresh with her. So that was how she met my father.
They eloped after that because my grandmother didn't want them to get
married. She wanted my mother to become a nurse and marry a doctor,
and here my mother wanted to marry the guy from around the corner. So
she chased them out of the house with a knife and they eloped—and
when they came back she chased them out again with a knife. My aunt,

my mother's sister, who was there at the time, said to her mother, "You wouldn't let them get married, that's why they eloped." My grandmother said, "I would've let them get married." My aunt said, "Well, you won't let me become a nun, either." Then my grandmother said, "You can become a nun if you want. Now get out of here!" And my aunt became a nun because of that. So all these things happened at knifepoint.

When I was born they moved to Linden, New Jersey. The house had a lot of statues and holy pictures. It was very old-fashioned ethnic. It hadn't been Americanized to the point where ethnic culture wasn't considered part of life. The ethnic attitude is similar to the Old European one in which you have a lot of religious images and statues around just because it's part of the culture. And you talk to them and pray to them, but at the same time you do everything good and bad in front of them. They're just there.

In school during Lent we would get little boxes that we were supposed to put a dime in every day—mite boxes or self-denial banks they were called, because you were supposed to deny yourself everyday candy and put the money in there instead. But I never filled mine up because I thought a dime a day was a lot of money. Only once I did, because one of my aunts stuck a five-dollar bill in the box, and then I got the free mother-of-pearl crucifix with the gold plastic Jesus on it which still hangs in my parents' bathroom. It's a nice crucifix, it held up over time, and the gold plastic Jesus has a bit of a patina to it now. There were lots of saints' statues there, too: St. Anthony, St. Teresa, St. Joseph. They ranged from the dashboard-size plastic ones to the bigger plaster kind. And a few pictures have come down for generations, of the Blessed Virgin holding the Baby Jesus or the guardian angel with the two kids going across the bridge.

When I was a little boy, my father went to church but my mother didn't because she had had a fight with the priest. For health reasons, she was advised not to have any more children—she had four kids already—and she was using birth control. The priest told her that she should make herself ugly and sleep in a separate bed from my father rather than use birth control. So for many, many years she didn't go to church at all. Later on she got very religious, but for a while she wouldn't even talk about priests or nuns. She sent us to Catholic school all the same—it's just that every once in a while she'd say that the priests and nuns didn't know anything about life. A lot of times they don't, so maybe she had a point.

My first memory of church was of sitting on the kneeler and thinking that it was a little pew for children because it was just the right size. And

I remember hearing the choir sing and looking up and seeing a blue ceiling with stars on it. There was also a statue that one of my cousins had that lit up in the dark.

I started parochial school in kindergarten. Kindergarten was the only grade in which I thought I was approached in an intelligent and intuitive way. From then on I felt that there was too much emphasis on the intellectual side of things. Honestly speaking, ever since kindergarten, education has been a disappointment to me. But even that kindergarten had the usual layout of a Catholic schoolroom: a crucifix in the middle, above the blackboard, and a Virgin Mary statue — Our Lady of Grace with her hands spread out — off to the corner. Sometimes there would be an Infant of Prague statue, and there was one in kindergarten because we could relate to that as children.

I had Dominican nuns, Dominicans of Caldwell, New Jersey. They smelled nice. They were very clean and they had long white habits with stiff, cardboardlike squares around their heads with black veils. All that stuck out were their little hands, and I couldn't tell if they were men or women, but I didn't think about it. I never thought of them as having any gender until later on. That occurred one day when I was washing vigil lights in the convent kitchen — we were supposed to do things like that for the nuns, right? I was over the sink and I looked out in the backyard of the convent, where there were three clotheslines. Two had sheets on them, but one had bras on it. I knew that my mother wore one of those and my father didn't, so I figured they were more like my mother than my father, although I didn't understand those things yet.

The nuns always encouraged me to make art. They were really the ones who gave me the idea of it as a mission in life and said it was a talent that had to be developed for the glory of God and the good of the world. They never talked about it as something that would become an occupation or anything practical. They always spoke of it in grand, kind of cosmic terms. In a way, their whole manner of thinking came from a kind of medieval communal thinking that was pre-industrial. Northern European Christians, especially the Irish, never learned to deal very well with buying and selling. The Italians, because of Venice in particular, were always involved in trading, and so they had more of a sense of practical existence. But the Irish Church was made up of peasants who had no experience of buying and selling. Their world view was of the land, and they never thought of opening little stores. They opened bars where I lived, in Linden — bars, liquor stores, and funeral homes.

I designed the bulletin boards in school, especially the main bulletin board outside the principal's office, and they gave me more or less total freedom with this. If it was May, I knew enough to do something blue with the Blessed Mother on it. In June you did the Sacred Heart, and in October the rosary. But other than that, there was really a lot of artistic freedom. And since the sensibility that I liked in the Church was still accepted then — that kind of rococo feeling — they didn't give me a hard time. They didn't try to force me to do felt banners, which would come later, although by that time I was already out of Catholic school. I also used to design and draw the cover of the CYO newspapers, but I would do things that would annoy the priests. On the IHS, for instance, I would make the *S* look like a dollar sign: IH$. I think some people got it, other people didn't.

At the same time, I began to make churches out of cardboard on my own, which I would then show. The kind of altar I designed in grammar school was inside an open structure, as if you cut a church in half and just showed it from the middle up to the altar — like a doll house or a stage, so that you could play with it or look at it without any trouble. And I would put little holy pictures on the walls. Since the altar was only an inch or two long, a holy picture from a Christmas card would be the size of a mural in that scale. And I also made certain accessories that were actually used in our church. For instance, there's a little piece of square cardboard that goes on top of the chalice, called a pall. A pall was one of the things that could be decorated — it would have satin or different kinds of cloth stretched across it and then a little picture of the Sacred Heart or a dove painted on top of it. So I used to paint on those or put lace around the border and priests would use them on the altar. And I made a few stoles, the longer bands that priests wear around their necks to administer the sacraments.

But the nuns always liked those little toy churches. It was kind of nice the way they really coddled me and groomed me. I don't know if they do that to artists anymore. I mean, I would get days off from school just to draw pictures. I would be in school in a separate room drawing pictures to go on the bulletin board. This could mean three days of missing arithmetic and everything, so that was special treatment which I feel had a big influence on my developing some confidence as an artist. This had privilege attached to it. I was totally unaware of anything else that the outside world might think of art or artists because I was being raised in a way that had a sense of direct continuity through the Middle Ages and the Renaissance — the attitude that art was something very special.

The priests were different about it. We had a small wooden church at first that was very pretty. Then the parish population grew and they built this enormous airplane hangar–type fake Romanesque church. I remember telling the priest—I was only twelve at the time—that I thought the church would look better with more pictures in it. He stood me in the middle of the church and said, "See that altar? That's the focus of why we're in church, so there shouldn't be any pictures to distract." I thought this was a crazy attitude, kind of like the old movie star wanting to kill the young understudies and starlets so that her bad act would look good since there was nothing to compare it to. That attitude was slowly surfacing in the way the priests thought, and by the time Vatican II came along the "bare church" mentality had taken over, until now it's the dominant feeling—or lack of feeling.

Having society and religion and art connected isn't always so good because history tells us all the horrible things that can happen. But some elements that in retrospect are seen as cute exist side by side with so-called serious elements in art and culture. If you go to Italy, you'll see churches with cute little *putti* all over them carved in marble, and that's a very serious thing. *Putti* are those playful little child-angels, and in one church in Rome I remember seeing sarcophagi decorated around the sides with marble skulls. Sitting on the marble sarcophagi were little cherubs playing catch with the marble skulls, which got across its message: certainly, anyone who was a child when that tomb was made is a skull now, and so on. So it's a serious contrast between childhood and death. It's not like our society where everything has to be either Hallmark cards or nuclear disaster. What I'm trying to say is that there are positive aspects to those holistic ways of looking at life. The negative aspect is that sometimes it's difficult for people who don't think to incorporate something new into the pre-existing structure.

In my school, we were chosen to be altar boys in the fifth grade, but we didn't actually become altar boys until the sixth grade. The parish priests were Benedictines, and they liked everything to be recited clearly. They didn't like the Latin to be slurred, so we would spend a long time learning the prayers. It wasn't as if we were just put out there and learned on the job. We had a training program in which we studied with the older altar boys until eventually we got to serve Mass. But everything was carefully rehearsed. There were different outfits that you got to wear according to your rank. The new altar boys wore a red cassock and a white surplice with little red crosses on it, and the older ones got to wear lace surplices that were a lot like the priests', with crosses and flowers and all sorts of designs on them. A lot of the customs in our parish came from Bavaria, so there were little capes with gold trim that were worn on Corpus Christi, or white cassocks or purple or black cassocks, green capes and gold capes, too. I remember the beginning of minimalism, when the priest told us that we had to take the little red crosses off our surplices so they could all be plain white. I knew that he was the enemy of art then. I remember feeling bad—I saved the crosses and I still have them. But uglification was in the wind.

I was an altar boy from the sixth grade till the end of high school. I left right after they started changing things into English. I didn't mind it being in English, I just didn't like it being so stupid and ugly and without any sense of reverence. But that wasn't why I left the altar boys—that's another story altogether. The Catholic Youth Organization, or CYO, used to have dances. The parish was mostly white, but there were a few black kids—it didn't seem like there were many black Catholics because most of the black families around there were Southern Baptists, but there were a few. Now, if white kids brought friends who were Protestants, they could get into the dance. But when the black Catholics brought their black friends, they were told the friends couldn't get in because they were not members of the CYO. So I had a run-in with one of the CYO women, an older woman who was like a chaperone there. She was very prejudiced. She used to say there was a separate heaven for black people. I pointed out what was going on, and then a black family went to the priest and complained. The priest called me in and told me that I had made up the whole thing, that this wonderful white woman would never do anything like this. But in the middle of it, he admitted that he was afraid of getting called in by the chancery—although that probably wouldn't have happened because I have to assume that the chancery was just as prejudiced as everyone else. So I just handed in my cassock and left.

I went from St. Elizabeth of Hungary grammar school to St. Mary of the Assumption High School, run by Sisters of Charity, who seemed to be on a much lower intellectual level than the Dominicans. I don't know if it was because I liked the Dominicans' habits more and felt the Sisters of Charity had ugly habits or what it was, but they seemed sort of stupid to me. I left that school after one year—they asked me to leave because I was drawing what they called "dirty pictures." What really happened was this. There were a lot of tough kids at that school, and some of them liked me and some didn't. This was my first experience with secular art patronage—earlier, as I told you, I had experienced the patronage of the Church.

See, the historical development of art in Western civilization was happening within my consciousness, and I didn't even know it. The individual patron has a different kind of vanity from the Church patron, who concerns himself or herself with representations of salvation and saints. But these secular children were concerned with things like sex. They used to beat me up from time to time, and then finally they decided that I should draw pictures for them. So I would draw pictures of strippers for them that had nothing really showing — no tits or pussy — because the strippers would be holding fans in front of them. These would be lavish pictures — the formal continuity between them and the May shrines and rococo church ceilings was obvious to a discerning eye. And for their girlfriends I would draw hearts — "Tony & Angie," things like that. Because of this, I was able to avoid getting beaten up. The art patrons were pleased with the art I was creating for them, and so I was allowed to exist in relative peace. It was like the first basic level of civilization: people come out of the cave and then the tougher ones realize that maybe they need art and that someone can do it for them to enhance their personal image. They collected these things as status. I don't know if any of them later became art collectors; I haven't looked into it.

But eventually, the nuns found a whole bunch of these pictures, and some of these kids and I had to go to the office. It was a horrible scene where fathers had to come in and people were beaten up by their fathers and the nuns. They asked me to leave the school and I did, because I was highly insulted that they would even think that I was anything but a good Catholic. They even wanted to know why I drew the pictures in red ink — I think this had something to do with communism in their heads. They were funny about pens. You weren't even supposed to use a ballpoint pen back then — you had to use a fountain pen. They didn't like when I used peacock blue ink in my fountain pen, either, instead of that Waterman's dark blue. Peacock blue you had to buy in a little tiny bottle in the greeting card section of the five and ten — it was ultra-effeminate. They didn't like my using that because it was a very pretty blue that had a tinge of green in it. The nuns would always call me up to the desk and ask me why I was using such an affected type of ink.

After that, I had to go to public school, which was mostly filled with Catholic kids anyway. We were taught that Catholic kids who went to public school had no respect for anything, that they were almost Protestant except for the fact that they were baptized Catholics. They supposedly didn't go to church on Sunday and cursed all the time. When Catholic school kids did these things, it was because they were bad. When public school Catholic kids did them, it was because they went to public school. This was also the first time I met real Protestants and Jews, which was interesting since I couldn't believe that there were non-Catholics who weren't Communists. We were told that anyone who wasn't Catholic probably had something to do with communism, because Communists didn't like Catholics, and non-Catholics didn't like us either. The nuns made us believe that if we made friends with the Protestants, they would put a microscopic sliver of bacon in a cupcake and give it to us on Friday.

My first real doubts about Catholicism started when I left the altar boys, but there were different things that led up to it. When I was asked to leave Catholic school in ninth grade, I didn't doubt my faith so much as I began to doubt the people I was taught to respect as authority. I felt they weren't worthy of any respect. And I felt the same way when I left the altar boys, too. I realized I was dealing with people who weren't trying to get others even to pay lip service to Christian brotherhood, never mind actually practice it. Later on, when I went to Pratt Institute in Brooklyn, I was around people who didn't believe in anything for the most part, so I just stopped believing for a while. I went to church on Sunday and thought, What am I doing here?

But at the same time I was being made aware of what class I had come from because the only people from my background at Pratt were the women who worked in the kitchen. They were Irish and German and Italian Catholics. But very few people from ethnic working-class backgrounds actually *went* to Pratt. Most of the other students were from middle-class or upper-middle-class or upper-class backgrounds. So part of me was being pulled away from the Church by an environment that ignored its existence entirely, and another part of me was being drawn closer to it by the snobbishness of the school and by my awareness that I was part of a group of people who weren't as pervasive as I thought. When I was a kid I thought everyone was from my background. At Pratt, people would sing those songs about "My Plastic Jesus" and everything. Even though at that time I didn't believe in anything, I remember feeling culturally insulted because songs like that were being sung by people whose families had never had a plastic Jesus in their cars. I felt they were making fun of the people I came from more than simply ridiculing a religious practice. What they were doing was more or less a secularized version of good, old-fashioned American Protestant bigotry against things they didn't understand.

After that, I went to the School of Visual Arts in Manhattan, which seemed better than Pratt because it was less snobby and had more people from my background. That was where I learned that it is possible in this society to make art and have it be your work, your job. I realized then that I wanted to do what I had been doing since I was a little boy, but that I wanted to do it as my whole life and to express what I think is good about where I come from through my art. I think there are a lot of good values that come from the ethnic Catholic background that should be kept alive and made into a kind of synthesis with what is good in secular humanist society—because I don't necessarily think all of *that* is good. Somehow I feel I combine the two in the materials that I use and the traditions that I try to put into those materials.

For me to explain exactly which traditions I'm referring to, I'll have to make a little digression into art history. Shortly after the turn of the century and getting toward the nineteen twenties and thirties, there were movements like Constructivism and Neoplasticism, which were optimistic about the twentieth century and wanted life to be better than before. There were theories that art should be made out of the materials of the society, that "form follows function." Artists at the Bauhaus were going to build housing that would be functional for working-class people, which in turn would make society just the most ideal place ever. Everyone was somehow going to be as happy as bees in the hive making honey or as beavers working in the mud. But what happened was that, by the sixties, that theory had evolved to the point where, in reality, there were just a lot of ugly office buildings made of girders and glass, and it had become more dehumanizing than humanizing.

Back then, around 1967, I came to the conclusion that since a lot of the rhetoric and theory on which that stuff was founded was supposed to be about giving dignity to working-class people, perhaps we should be asking ourselves how working-class ethnic people defined their *own* dignity. The dignity that they were supposed to achieve through Bauhaus and Constructivist architecture was being defined for them by a different class from their own. Traditionally, the working class had always taken their dignity from their folk arts—which included holy pictures that were sometimes mass-produced—and the way they decorated their houses, which wasn't at *all* plain and functional. They were a little more complex than bees or beavers, in other words. So I decided to try to combine the basic theory of the new materials with the old esthetic of the small, intimate religious objects, fuse the two into something that was the esthetic of the peasant in the urban industrial environment.

That was when I started making religious art out of the materials that I use, which are always basically plastic and metal. This also represents the continuity of the peasant tradition of using what is around. I don't use I-beams and enormous pieces of Plexiglas. I use aluminum foil and Saran Wrap, which are the things that the "peasant" would use—and I say that in quotes because he's not a peasant anymore, but he still comes from those traditions. Even if he was on the farm, he might have used straw or corn kernels, whatever was around, but it would be very crazy and dishonest to use those things in the city—I mean, he could get them, but it just wouldn't be the same. Their art takes what is there and translates it into a form that gives humanity a sense of dignity and romance instead of just harsh practicality. So what I'm doing is trying to offset the harsh practicality by using the peasant feelings and intuitions to make art with these modern materials.

But I very consciously thought through Constructivism and all those idealistic movements that occurred in the first half of the twentieth century and were supposed to make a better world and didn't. I think they failed because they forgot that people need decoration, and that's a basic thing. Art is a basic thing that at the same time has intuitive depth, and the Constructivists were too worried about finding out how to do the steps of the dance instead of learning how to do the dance. Anyone who's ever danced knows that there are people who can learn all the steps but can never dance. Once you're doing it, it's a soul-felt thing, and peasant traditions always know that. The more middle-class traditions are always saying, Teach me the steps. They learn the steps and then they wonder why they look so stiff and stupid. It's the same with the art that comes out of that mentality; it's all about ideas and learning steps.

My art is never totally secular or unsecular. It stays within the culture I was raised in. I'm aware that within the culture I come from there is no possibility of making art because there is no support system for it. Unions don't own art galleries; parishes would never give an artist the support an artist needs. And because of that, they reduce art in their own perception to a hobby. By reducing it to a hobby and not supporting it, they discourage people from going into it. That way they have fewer artists, and they force the artists who do come out of the Church to be secular artists. By a secular artist, I mean an artist who shows in a gallery in New York City. It's very difficult for an artist to make art with any religious themes. I've been able to do it just because I've stuck with it and certain people have liked it. But I've gotten no encouragement through the Catholic Church or any organization connected with it. A few isolated, individual priests have given me a certain amount of encouragement, but they're not connected to any organizations that are going to offer to pay my rent or help me to continue.

The Church has a conscious hatred for art right now. It's being iconoclastic, to use one of the Church's old terms, in the worst sense of the word. There's a good sense of iconoclasm, when people want to destroy bad ideas or images. Then there's the traditional Christian definition of iconoclasm, which just means smashing art and images and hating them —and that's where the Church is at now. They're one-dimensional conceptualists. They can't imagine layers of ideas coexisting. The Church has never actually said anything *against* my art, and I'm glad they don't. I don't need any more trouble — it's hard *enough* being an artist. Of course, it might be good publicity if the cardinal decided to hate my art. Or if they publicly excommunicated me for saying bad things about them and espousing heresy in this book. I could get a lot of mileage out of that.

We were told that when you go to confession, the priest is the same as Christ at that moment, that Christ is forgiving you through the priest. The concept of Christ forgiving you through the priest I can accept, but I can't accept the ability of the priest to perceive and love another human being the way Christ would. If the priest is going to give you advice, it's not the same advice that Christ would give you. I think I can get better advice from my friends than I can from the priest, so I'll go to communion but I won't go to confession, and that's what I think every Catholic should do. Confession is just a vehicle of clerical control to keep the laity from becoming more a part of the priesthood of the Church, to give the priest the power to advise you, find out what you're doing and get into your personal life in a way that he has no right to — always peeking in people's bedrooms like that.

About ten years ago I went to a priest in a Russian Church and said that I wanted to become Russian Orthodox because I felt it was more Catholic than what the Roman Catholic Church had become. At its best, religion is very romantic, but sometimes in its ethical and practical applications it can be both arid and overbearing. When that happens you ignore that aspect, or take from it what you think is best, and approach religion as a source of romantic strength to get through the reality. That's why a beautiful Mass is very important, and the Russians and the Greeks have that. I'm not an intellectual — I can intellectualize, but I'm more intuitive and I like that whole multisensory approach where you can see and smell and feel instead of just having to think over and over again, This is holy, this is holy, this is holy.

I deeply resent Vatican II. Mother Church doesn't embrace you anymore. You go there and she says, "I love you — think about it." But she's not going to hold you and make you feel warm. She wants us to be tough — tough grown-ups who just think. Now it's all conceptual. It's as if at the Last Supper Jesus said, "Take and eat, this is My concept." That's what the Mass has become. So I think they're totally heretical in their approach — it's the Irish Catholic heresy of conceptualism replacing Incarnation. But man does not live by concepts alone.

Russian Orthodox Catholicism is a total experience that contains concepts within it. A Russian service hits every sense at once. There's a lot of singing, and there's the smell of the incense, and a lot of pictures. You're totally enveloped by a feeling of something going on everywhere. You're distracted, and because of the distraction you're attracted to the whole thing. You're constantly reminded that you're in some mystical setting, that what is happening is connecting the whole cosmos and going through time and space, that it's about the living and the dead and the future and the past and the present all at the same time — and about things that are outside of the past, present, and future. That's why these saints are all over the walls — these icons — to remind you that their presence is as much a part of things as yours.

The Russian Mass is basically the same as the Roman Catholic Mass of the Catechumens in its form, it's just embellished. It's in English sometimes, it's in Greek sometimes, it's in Slavonic sometimes, depending on where you go. It's just as good in English as it is in Greek or Slavonic because it still keeps a mystical feeling. The American Roman Catholic Mass could've been mystical and been in English, but for some reason they insisted on making it ugly. They wanted to make it conceptual instead of an experience. It's a theory Mass now, based on what they think is necessary to make it valid in legalistic terms. Maybe it's the product of celibate minds, whose experience of sex is just jerking off instead of an actual encounter with another human being — which becomes a process that can culminate in orgasm but that isn't just about the orgasm. They've made the Mass more or less like a sex act that's only about the orgasm with no emphasis on the love process. It's not about making love, it's about getting your rocks off.

The Catholic Church is probably guilty of the biggest sins of omission by no longer bothering to encourage art. Historically, it did for a long time; but recently, especially in the second half of the twentieth century, it just doesn't bother at all. It doesn't even enter their minds — they just think art is superfluous.

I have a feeling that because the Irish were on that little island and because they were conquered by England, while the rest of Europe was undergoing the Counter-Reformation they were stuck in the isolated past. The Counter-Reformation was very heavily involved in art because art was a primary tool of keeping people in the Church and winning them back into the Church in a charming way. Not only was it charming, but it also got people involved in the ritual of the Church through something that was very meaty and esthetically highly developed. The rococo and the baroque are ingeniously conceived theatrical settings for the drama of the liturgy. The Irish had no drama in their liturgy because they were busy having Mass in the caves in Ireland. Not only that, but their priests were being trained in France by the Jansenists, which is one of those heresies that was very puritanical. So the combination of having no stable edifice to decorate and make into a church and a kind of inbred inclination toward puritanism has had a devastating effect on them. They just do not see art as a necessary part of liturgy in the Church. They're not like Italy, which had art as a natural part of its life. Maybe something in them resents art, the way ugly people resent beautiful people.

They make themselves miserable and they make everyone else miserable. They want you to go to church because you're supposed to, and they tell you it's a mortal sin if you don't go. Now if the Mass is the most important event in the history of the world — if the Incarnation is made real in every Mass through the Body and Blood being present in the bread and wine — then to make it a totally inconsequential event is moronic to me. If the Mass is supposed to be the center of the totality of the universe and the transition between incompleteness and the renewed completeness of humanity, then to have it be so much less than incomplete is something I just don't understand.

Maybe it has to do with their not thinking that Christianity is about the Incarnation. Maybe they're more heretical than people realize because they're dematerializing the Mass to the point where it's become a concept. It's not about material things to them, it's about immaterial things — which I don't think are the same as spiritual things. Christ is spiritual and at the same time material in the Resurrection. He's not dematerialized. He walked through walls and St. Thomas stuck his hand into His side and felt a real human Being — different from us because He could walk through walls. But it's theologically significant because St. Thomas said, "My Lord and my God," which is kind of like saying that this Person is human and divine at the same time. I don't know if that's ever said at any other time in the New Testament.

It's significant that this happens just when Christ makes it clear that He is physical and that His spiritual substance is contained within His physical substance, inseparably. That's probably why bread and wine are used at Mass. Actual bread is the staff of life, and wine is something through which people get happy. So it's a symbol of life as something beautiful — not of just barely sustaining existence, as bread and water would signify, but something more. That implies that art, which is about a more completely embellished life, is totally appropriate. In addition, Christ's coming restores people to their original state of grace before the fall, so to speak, and that original state was in a garden — something that is an artistically prepared natural setting, not a forest and not a farm.

Adam and Eve existed in a place that was pleasing to the eye and in which the fruit was good to eat, according to Genesis, so in that sense it's a combination of an esthetic experience and an experience of nurturing. The split between art and life doesn't happen until after the fall, when God tells them they'll have to make their living by tilling the soil — that's when function is separated from esthetics. In the joining together and making complete of human beings, symbolized by the Mass, beauty and function are rejoined as they were in the Garden. Just the word *garden* is very significant here — it's not the farm and it's not the forest. God arranged the trees and the bushes and the waterfalls and the sun and the stars and everything in a way that looked right to Him. They weren't just there because they were functioning; they were there to be perceived as beautiful, and that's where the basic human perception of beauty comes from. St. Basil said that the memory of the Garden of Paradise is what makes people create art.

And looking forward to the Second Coming of Christ we also create art because that Second Coming is going to re-establish that order of beauty and everything else once again in a totality, not separate as they are now. But the Second Coming is there already in the bread and wine, and that's why it's totally appropriate to make the church and the Mass as beautiful as possible. In fact, it's heretical not to have art because then you don't acknowledge the Incarnation, and you don't acknowledge the connection of people to God as it existed in the Garden of Paradise and as it was re-established in Christ through the Incarnation.

ROBERT STONE

The Way the World Is

There is some sort of religious impulse in every novel I've written.
—Robert Stone
New York Times Book Review, October 1981

Gimme a rush, Jesus, if you truly want me for your personal sunbeam.
—Pablo in *A Flag for Sunrise*

"Whenever I'm starting a book, I read the Bible a lot, for obscure, deeply implanted reasons," Robert Stone told the *New York Times* some years ago. "This gets me into a bout of religious history." Undoubtedly, much of Stone's involvement—perhaps we should say obsession—with religion arises from sources that are deeply implanted, if not quite obscure. Replays of archetypical Christian scenarios flash through his novels with abundance: the martyrdom of Sister Justin in *A Flag for Sunrise*, Lu Anne's climbing a Mexican mountainside on bloodied knees, culminating in the stigmata, near the end of *Children of Light*, and so on. Like few other contemporary novelists—he himself cites only Mary Gordon in this regard—Stone consistently asks religious questions in his work. Though he is no longer a practicing Catholic or even an unequivocal believer, he treats the question of the existence of God as one of crucial importance, no matter how one answers it. (When the question is put literally to Holliwell, the lapsed Catholic in *A Flag for Sunrise*, he replies, "There's always a place for God, señora. There is some question as to whether He's in it.") It's not by accident that Stone and his characters are forever quoting Gerard Manley Hopkins, the Jesuit poet who experienced as dark a night as any soul.

Never having finished high school, let alone college, Stone made it a point "to be where things were happening." Following a three-year hitch in the navy, during which he witnessed the bombing of Suez, Stone spent time with Ken Kesey and his Merry Pranksters out in San Francisco amid the early days of psychedelia and later won an assignment as Vietnam correspondent for a short-lived British periodical so that he could witness the war. Those experiences furnished him with the raw material for his first two novels, *Hall of Mirrors* and *Dog Soldiers* (which were made into the films *WUSA* and *Who'll Stop the Rain*, respectively). Acknowledging that he travels "entirely too much," Stone nonetheless has used his extensive forays into Central America as the source for his latest two novels.

Robert Stone's books have been received generously by the critics — and have sold well. Yet apart from the acknowledged brilliance of his writing, one can't be sure if his popular appeal arises from the sense of spiritual questing that propels his characters or the staggering amounts of alcohol, drugs, and violence that follow them around (either of which may have moved one commentator to refer to him as "the last angry hippie"). A similar ambivalence divides Stone's statements to the press. "The myth of original sin is onto something," he once told the *Washington Post*, only to insist later, "I wouldn't want it to be thought that I represent a position of comfortable despair."

Sitting on the back deck of Robert Stone's home on the western Connecticut coastline, I found it hard to tie those loose and random ends of information about the man into a neat running bowline. As he began to answer questions, the cries of sea birds mingled with those of exuberant children playing in the "classic New England salt marsh" that is Stone's backyard. His voice, described by one journalist as "accentless," is not so much that as an amalgam of several dialects, none of them easily identifiable, each one teasing the ear with a bit of New England, a salty fragment of New York by way of London, but none of these precisely. In any case, the voice combines with his peppery beard and robustly haggard countenance to give the impression of an ever so slightly tormented but nonetheless genial sea captain.

I WAS BORN IN BROOKLYN on President Street, the border of Park Slope and South Brooklyn, in 1937. My mother was a schoolteacher in the New York public school system. My father worked for the old New Haven Railroad. My mother's family had been on the Brooklyn waterfront, working on the tugboats, for several generations. When I was still small, my parents separated. I moved with my mother to Manhattan and grew

up then in Yorkville and on the Upper West Side. My mother was schiz-
ophrenic, and when I was about five she was hospitalized for a while. I
went to St. Anne's at Lexington and Seventy-seventh Street, which later
became Archbishop Molloy High School. St. Anne's was somewhere
between a boarding school and an orphanage, run by the Marist Brothers.
I was at St. Anne's until I was nine and then I was out again.

I lived with my mother in SROs and rooming houses mostly on the
West Side. They weren't as bad in those days as they later became, so I
can't really say that I was in there with junkies. There was more variety
in the poverty of New York at that time — layers and layers. It was very
interesting to live on the West Side when it was only seedy, before it
became totally lethal. Now it's much more dangerous and less interesting,
which seems kind of unfair.

I stayed with the Marist Brothers, as if I couldn't get enough of them.
I stayed right through high school — almost through high school, actually,
because I never did quite finish high school. I never got a diploma from
them, and yet they have this capacity to find me — and I'm not very easy
to find. But they always find me, I don't know how. They send me pitches
for donations, and they send me the class list, which I am not on. They
never seem to put it together; they're always trying to awaken my nostalgia
by sending me these class lists on which my name does not appear. Every
once in a while I get their alumni notes, and they always get the names
of my books wrong. Such prizes as I've won, they get the names of those
wrong. It's completely scrambled. I just really don't want these people
finding me. I go through a week-long depression when I see something
from them in the mail. I really try to put all that *far* behind me, and it's
a tremendous bringdown to see their little coat of arms with its beehive
and its corny Latin motto. It awakens a kind of panic, as if there's nothing
I can do to get that out of my life.

The Marists were savage, but in those days I don't know where they
stood in terms of relative savagery — you were always hearing about some
order of Irish troglodytes down the road, you know, who were actually
permitted to use flails. They certainly slapped people around right and
left; it was very dreary, very tiresome. But, of course, you assumed this
was the way the world was supposed to be. Where else would anybody
tell you to offer your humiliation to the Holy Ghost? That always stayed
with me. One of my earliest anxieties was whether I was going to be lined
up outside the prefect's room at night to get my hands slapped with a
razor strop. There *was* a strop and he actually did sharpen his straight
razor on it, and he had these little kids of five and six lined up outside
his room to hit them on the hands.

It's very hard to escape that take on the world. And when you come right down to it, the world *is* like that, after all. I mean, first you think the world isn't like that, and you feel very liberated to find that it isn't. But after a while you work your way to the point where you discover that actually *is* the way the world is. So the preparation probably had some usefulness after all, some grim utility. There are good things that you get from Catholic upbringing, although it's the hard way to get them. Then again, life is not supposed to be easy. Anything you get you get the hard way. In some ways, Catholicism is very good training for making the best of a hard world, which is what you have to do. That is what they're telling you, on a certain level.

My mother was Scottish and Irish, so her family was religiously mixed; I think my father's was, too. But she really foisted Catholicism on me. Her father was a Presbyterian, her mother was Irish Catholic. She liked the idea of Catholicism. She thought it gave kids something to adhere to — she was quite right — so she sort of elected me to be the house Catholic. As soon as I stopped going to church, when I was about fifteen or sixteen, she immediately stopped. My high school years were a complete disaster. I don't know whether as a result of my experiences as a kid or just because of my temperament generally, I was never able to come to terms with formal education. My punishment was to become a professor in later life. I went on to teach writing and literature at Stanford, UC/Irvine, Harvard, Princeton, Amherst, and the University of Hawaii. Irvine was the most fun because the students were already writers, some of whom had published in small magazines and were willing to work day jobs as waiters and mechanics and cabbies just to support themselves in writing fiction. I had a lot of fun with them and actually took them to the racetrack — to Hollywood Park — to cruise for dialogue. I was always a Writer in Residence — my only real degree was a high school equivalency diploma I got while I was in the navy.

I joined the navy when I was seventeen, in 1955. I was a radio operator, first attached to a tactical air control squadron in the Norfolk Naval Air Station in Virginia, and then I went to sea. I was in the amphibious force and was finally rated as a journalist. I was transferred to a ship called the U.S.S. *Arneb*, an attack transport that was part of the 1958 Antarctic expedition. That trip to Antarctica took most of my last year in the navy and passed the time very interestingly. Now that I'm able to think about it with some detachment, I really had quite a good time in the navy. It just never occurred to me at the time. In 1956 in the Mediterranean, we saw the air attack on Port Said by the French during the bombing of Suez.

We got caught in the harbor and were sitting right in the middle of that. We were not a target, but the Egyptians in the harbor around us, and everything that could float, came as close to us as they possibly could. We had this enormous American flag which we were flying and which we illuminated at night. The harbor was being shot up indiscriminately; there was no attempt that I could determine to find military targets. The firing was coming from flights of Mystère jets.

I got out after three years and started at NYU, Washington Square College. My wife worked in the Figaro, back when it was really the Figaro, when Gregory Corso used to read there. Before she worked at the Figaro, she was a guidette at the RCA building, and she had another job at the Seven Arts coffeehouse, which was between Forty-second and Forty-third streets on Ninth Avenue. That was a great spot, where all sorts of celebrated events took place. Kerouac was very often there, Ginsberg read there, Corso read there, and LeRoi Jones, as he was known then. It was a great scene. I think I always had had literary aspirations of one kind or another, even when I was in high school. I had read *On the Road* when I was in the navy. If I'm not mistaken, I think my mother had turned me on to it. I think I'm probably the only person who ever read *On the Road* at his mother's suggestion.

Also, my mother was really kind of anticlerical. I was the solid citizen of that duo, and I took Catholicism much more seriously than she did. It was just not in her temperament to be religious. She went to church only when she went with me. I think she went only to please me, whereas I thought I was going to please her. So finally we were both going to accommodate each other, and we both quit when I did. But I took it seriously enough to imprint quite deeply a lot of aspects and attitudes that I think are religious and Catholic. Also, I left it — at least I abandoned any attempt to practice it — when it was still unreconstructed, unenlightened, post-Tridentine, nineteen fifties Catholicism, so the Church that I left really no longer exists. But I think that I certainly had made an association between ethical systems and religion — an association that I think a great many Catholics make — to the degree that I still tend to associate ethical coherence and religion. It's very hard for me to disassociate the two, and I think that's a very important philosophical attitude. I have trouble with nonreligious humanism as an ethical system. It's not that I don't understand it; it simply doesn't have any meaning that I can respond to. I mean the kind of secular humanism that merely tells you to do good, as opposed to its being tied to ultimates.

That kind of secular humanism tends to make you not a bad citizen if you're brought up that way, of course. Because if, on the other hand, you lose your religious anchor, then you tend to go into utter nihilism—it certainly is an option—and you tend to go on asking the kinds of broad and total questions that you got in trouble for asking in catechism class. And you don't get any better answers from a humanistic society than you did from a dogmatic religion—which I think is good, actually. Because there is a certain aspect of Catholicism that, to me, is its most appealing and attractive tradition, and that is the tradition of Catholic skepticism which I associate with people like Montaigne and Erasmus and Pascal. I think that's a very intellectually wholesome tradition, and I can still identify with that to some degree.

Perhaps because I left Catholicism at a relatively early time, I never really tried to make it relevant, and in a way this kept up its appeal for me. I never tried to live as a Catholic adult, which means that it can be there as a kind of illicit love for me, as a forbidden pleasure, because I never tried to live it out in a responsible, day-by-day way. So there's a kind of real-life Catholicism, as opposed to my nostalgia trip of long-vanished Catholic comics, like *Treasure Chest* and Chuck White and all that stuff—the only secret plans and worlds that we all are party to. This new Catholicism is vaguely left wing and feminist: folk Masses. All the scorn of the ex-Catholics that I know is focused on the folk Mass as an exercise in utter fatuousness. It seemed like just common sense at the time, but it turns out to have been really a mistake.

In 1962 I got a Stegner Fellowship to the writing program at Stanford. So I happened to be in Palo Alto at the right time when this strange scene was going on with Ken Kesey and the rest, and one aspect of it, of course, was psychedelics—taking acid. I think this kind of impelled me to re-examine my attitudes toward religion because my experiences with acid were very much charged with religion. I guess it would have been strange if they weren't. I was taking acid, and I was taking it seriously. I felt very much that I was consciously developing a view of the world, and when I had these religious experiences as a result of taking acid, I really felt that they demanded to be reconciled with my intellectual attitudes generally. So it made me less able to develop a totally secular intellectual system of my own. I again had to make allowance for the numinous—if not the supernatural, at least the nonrational, the extrarational. I think this probably served as a process through which my adolescent religious attitudes were transformed but somehow reinforced. My adult secular life was subverted again by something very intrusive and very strong. I began to have to afford to the extrarational a certain importance in terms of how I saw things, and as a result these religious areas of experience came to be reflected in my writing. The drug experience forced me not to dismiss those things as simply part of my childhood gear but to realize that I had to continue to think about and deal with them.

A couple of the acid trips that I had that were most memorable brought me into confrontations with aspects of things like God — or the absence of or presence of. I felt, as the result of one time that I took acid in Wales sometime in the middle sixties, that I really was experiencing God, and I don't know where that came from. It wasn't particularly Catholic, this experience; it was as close to that celebrated oceanic experience as I've ever personally been. So I realized that I was not going to build a personal system or live in a personal system that was free of those concepts, and so I don't.

There was a night in 1963 in San Francisco when a bunch of us had bought a lot of peyote and refined it, went to a pharmacist and bought a lot of plastic capsules, and put this refined peyote in the capsules — and I swallowed twelve of them. We piled into a Volkswagen bus and headed into the city. We saw John Coltrane at the Jazz Gallery and later went out onto Broadway, and that was where I totally lost it. The rest of the people I was with went from seeing Coltrane to catching Lenny Bruce at the hungry i and then Jonathan Winters. So they saw the sixties in one great night. But unfortunately, I was not with the main band of people because I had just completely come apart watching John Coltrane, and I left because I was seeing the music, which was kind of disconcerting. I just couldn't stop seeing it, and that began to get to me. So I went out, and what was outside, of course, just around the corner on Broadway, was Chinatown. I had a tough time with that — I mean, I knew it was Chinatown, but I just found it altogether too visual, that being the nature of mescaline.

You do get to a point where you expect, as one of your satisfactions, an experience of the transcendent — at least you acquire a need to connect yourself with something transcendent. The result is, of course, that things never are quite enough after that, so you have to go higher. It's not for nothing that Marx calls religion the opiate of the people. How does that whole quote go? "Religion is the opium of the masses, the heart of a heartless world." I can't remember it precisely.* It's funny how the diagram becomes basically one of salvation: you have to achieve salvific

* The quotation from the introduction to *The Critique of the Hegelian Philosophy of Right* (1844) by Karl Marx reads in full: "Religion is the sigh of the oppressed creature, the feelings of a heartless world, just as it is the spirit of unspiritual conditions. It is the opium of the people."

experience. Suddenly the only thing you'll settle for as the end of your evening is a kind of ultimate contact with God. That becomes what you're going for all the time, what you expect from music, say—and in a way it's not a bad thing to expect from the arts. It's what you get a sense of in Beckett. You kind of find it in all the best things, somehow, that sense of being in touch with the numinous, with something transcendent. In a way it's vain and foolish and sort of spoils everything for you because you're expecting too much—that kind of spiritual orgasm is what you're always going for. But on the other hand when you do get it, it wakens that sense.

I think that finally my attraction for Catholicism remains sentimental. I'm never really able to approach the idea of a serious intellectual commitment to Catholicism or Christianity, although I think it's intriguing how belief has been redefined. Catholicism of the fifties was an inheritor of that rather meretricious, pseudorealist, pseudomaterialist Catholicism of the nineteenth century where they really became absurdly literal with things like the Immaculate Conception. They reified these religious notions and made them mechanistic, real things in a totally fractured way that simply was not going to bear examination. One of the interesting things in Catholicism now, as I perceive it, is the success with which they have come down from that stance and have been able to say, Look, these are entities of which we cannot speak very precisely because we don't understand them, they belong to another dimension. That's a sophisticated attitude toward those things, which has its appeal.

Those of us who left the Church in its unreconstructed phase probably ask ourselves every once in a while, Well, on the new terms, as they've been redefined, can we perhaps accept this now so we can do something sort of neat, like go to church on Sunday and see what that would be like? Or go to church on Christmas, or whatever? But I have never really come to the point of seriously contemplating that.

I certainly find myself being scornful of such former Catholics as I see going up and getting born again for some Southern person in a polyester suit, but apparently there are numbers of former Catholics who have been born again—which, of course, is a very un-Catholic thing. You only do it once in Catholicism. Then there is also charismatic Catholicism, which I have no experience in. When I was living in Honolulu in 1979 and 1980, one of the Catholic churches there used to have joint services with a Pentecostalist church—I mean, this was sort of Holy Rolling. Nuns and seminarians really got off on this. It was a chance to carry on and speak in tongues and the whole number, which certainly seems to me on the face of it to be the very opposite of everything that Catholicism is all about. I guess it was forbidden fruit for Catholics. They got to sing "There's an Old Rugged Cross" and they got to talk in tongues and things like that.

Given its way of conducting early childhood education, you might be excused for thinking that Catholicism is a particularly violent religion. Certainly there is an intimate connection between violence and Catholicism, because Catholicism partakes of all the melodrama of history. If you look at the iconography of Catholicism—just think of the history of European painting from Giotto on—the violence in Catholic iconography is limitless. Just think of all those people carrying around the evidence of their violent deaths, carrying around their various crosses, their grills, their gibbets, the guy walking around with the knife through his head, Peter Martyr. There it is. Obviously, if you think about the iconography and the principal mysteries of the rosary, you have an awful lot of blood, an awful lot of violence. On the other hand, that's the way the world is, too. So it's appropriate, in a way, that Catholicism and its iconography reflect all this, because the world, after all, *is* like that. It *is* full of violence, and religion would have to incorporate that. It tells you that you have to accept this, it tells you that the world is this way. Catholic pacifism is a fairly new development in modern Catholicism. It was a small minority in the time of Dorothy Day [cofounder of the Catholic Worker movement in the thirties]; it's a larger minority now, apparently.

But you certainly were conditioned to accept all the violence, to accept war as a given, and, of course, to look on death as something vaguely . . . death was certainly better than sex. Death was something that could be more comfortably incorporated into Catholicism. There was a way in which I think fifties Catholicism definitely could be said to be pro-death. If it came down to life or death, death was undoubtedly the more virtuous aspect. Dying was an approved Catholic thing to do. You could exist totally within the Catholic culture as a dead person. It was a kind of total resolution of Catholicism. Death was better than fucking, certainly, because it was eminently Catholic. You could be done up with rosaries and tombstones and crosses and holy water. All the accouterments of death were absolutely orthodox. But sex, on the other hand, was unacceptable, and the Church was not with you. Whereas it was totally with you in death, and you were with it. As a corpse, you could be an ideal Catholic.

War was generally approved of by the Church, partly because it contributed to people dying, which was always a good thing. I don't think that's unfair. I think there's a level on which dying was really approved of, practically as a virtuous act in and of itself. It was good for religion because it turned people's minds to the ultimate reckoning. But I don't know if that's more true in Catholicism than in another religion. Certainly it's more true in Catholicism than it is in Unitarianism, but that doesn't make me feel any more warmly toward Unitarianism, which to me is the worship of a potted palm.

The way I see it consciously, speaking of my own work, I address the things that frighten me. Writing is what I do to deal with the world and things generally; that's my response to the implied question of living. So I would say that violence is in my writing because it's in the world. Whether being a Catholic conditions my interior world, and consequently my perceptions, so that I'm more attuned to violence, I don't know. It's certainly possible.

In Mexico and Central America, you have this bizarre coupling of the machismo sense with the religious impulse and with the desire for "physical humiliations," as they're called. This *penitente* syndrome is prevalent among certain Hispanic Catholics, particularly the so-called Spanish Americans of New Mexico, and consists of torturing themselves — literally carrying crosses, being scourged — something the official Church has been trying to suppress all over Mexico, Central America, and the American Southwest. Those people seem to have worked toward some kind of synthesis of the sun dance and the Stations of the Cross. It's what they used to call mortification or self-flagellation, and it particularly flourishes in New Mexico. It's as though they're inclined to compete with Christ to see who can take it more.

That is certainly what is going on in the mountaintop scene near the end of *Children of Light*. That's what Lu Anne is doing, she's trying to torture herself into some kind of sanity. She's trying to destroy her own madness by torturing herself, which is what people sometimes do. She also gives herself the stigmata; that's in her bag of tricks. That passage certainly refers directly to the Stations of the Cross, and I did call it "The Ascent of Mt. Carmel" [when it was excerpted in the *Paris Review*]. I wasn't doing it in a deliberate, ongoing way. But I invoke it, sure. I'm making a connection between her personal, self-destructive perversity, which is partly sexual, and the implied perversity of Catholicism generally, of the Catholic experience, which has within it a perverse, masochistic element, certainly for women.

One of the things that you see everywhere in Sicily — and this is not part of *Children of Light* because it's something that I've acquired since, but it makes the point — is Santa Lucia, the great saint in Sicily. Particularly, there's a shrine to her in the cathedral in Siracusa, and what represents her iconographically in Sicily is principally a goblet and a pair of eyes. She's supposed to have gouged her eyes out rather than get married. This isn't orthodox because I don't think it can be, but in the popular story she's supposed to have cut her eyes out and sent them in a goblet to the guy who was her suitor to discourage him, which presumably it did. That makes the point that within Catholic iconography — which, whether it's supposed to be or not, is a large part of the sense of Catholicism itself — there's so much violence, so much suffering and masochism and perversity. And certainly that is one element of Lu Anne's perversity at that point: she's going to transform herself into a martyr. There is in Catholicism this prospect of death as a kind of triumph — after all, martyrs are supposed to get the crown. That's a way of winning: by dying you triumph. In Catholicism, as I've already implied, the easiest and most successful thing you can do is die. We used to joke when I was in high school that the perfect Christian life was to graduate from that place and go to St. John's or Fordham and become an insurance actuary and be buried in Calvary Cemetery. That was the total Christian life.

Some of the same kinds of parallels, incidentally, turn up in *Dog Soldiers* and, of course, in *A Flag for Sunrise*, which has an awful lot of religion in it — just plain, flat-out religion and martyrdom and so forth. Not only is Sister Justin Catholic, but Holliwell is, and I guess Pablo is, too. Well, purely pro forma — he's a pagan, a pre-Columbian. But he always thinks everything that happens to him is there to enlighten him. He thinks he's on the receiving end of this ever-unfolding process of enlightenment — he's always trying to get off, and he thinks life is being conducted for his edification. If he could only find the right people who didn't keep turning him around. Poor Pablo, he's such bad news — that's the secret of life that he never discovers, that he's just terrible bad news.

Another aspect is the fact that my characters take all those drugs and drink all that alcohol. I really have to cut it out. They just go right ahead and do it. It approaches self-parody — I really have to watch it. They're certainly always trying to put something between them and the thorns of life itself, to live in a world other than the one they're presented with. In a way, they do a lot of my drug taking and drinking for me. They do a lot of things for me so that I don't have to do them, all that dying and rolling around. In a sense they're trying to find transcendence, and they have bad habits, and what's the difference?

What takes the place of those things now that I've cut down on my own indulgence? Supposedly, the mature satisfactions of life — and as soon as I find out what they are, then that's what I'll be into next, I'm sure. Any day now.

I think growing up Catholic, taking it seriously, compels you to live on a great many levels. It's not totally dead to believe in a whole lot of unlikely, preposterous things. It certainly enriches your sense of humor, if there are so many unlikely things that you are trying to juggle in your spiritual life at a tender age. At a certain point, there's something kind of touching and gallant and funny about the situation of being a kid and having to deal with eternity and all these absurd and monstrous concepts. I think there's an inherent comic aspect to all that which is inescapable. I think that probably is the cause of the specifically Catholic sense of humor. You could certainly find enough material within Catholicism to keep you performing for years and years and years.

When I once said, "In a sense I'm a theologian, and so far as I know, the only one," I meant that in terms of American writers. There is just more religion and more religious questioning in my work—it seems to me that I probably deal more with religion, that there is more overt Catholicism in the stuff that I write about—than in most writers that I am aware of, except Mary Gordon. I felt at various times that I was taking seriously questions that for most educated people were no longer serious questions, and I ascribed that to my Catholic background. I mean specifically the question of whether or not there is a God or whether or not you can talk about life and its most important elements in religious terms, the question of the absence of God—Heidegger's postulating God as an absence—all these things are, for the most part, not taken too seriously by educated people. I talk to my editor, for example, or most of the people that I know, and they aren't concerned with religious questions, not in quite the same way that I am. They might ask the same questions, but not in the same terms that I ask them. That's what led me to make that statement.

I'm really concerned with the idea of there not being a God as a kind of dynamic absence that is a constant challenge. Now if it never meant anything to you, then obviously it isn't a challenge, it's just the way it is. As a result of having been a Catholic, I'm acutely aware of the difference between a world in which there's a God and a world in which there isn't. For people who either have not taken religion seriously or have not been exposed to religion, the question of whether or not there's a God is an obviated question, a trivial or silly question. It's not a silly question for me. I don't see how anybody who took seriously their Catholic upbringing can be comfortable as an atheist—you'd have to doubt that, too.

The question of why there seem to be so few Catholic painters and visual artists may have a different answer. There really is a strong element of people with immigrant backgrounds, first- or second-generation working class, among Catholics, and working-class people as a rule are not oriented toward plastic or visual arts. Catholic education doesn't go out of its way to look for visual artists; you don't feel reinforced in your pursuit of the arts. Where I went to school, the whole of artistic endeavor in human history was something that you tried to cram into the college preparation course when you prepared for the Regents scholarship test. They just fed you all this information that you were supposed to memorize, without actually exposing you to the contaminating influences of the art itself. Basically they were saying, Here's a whole lot of stuff that the Gentiles believe and various shibboleths and names that you ought to know because they'll be on the test that the Jews will give us. It was all totally external from life, from the course of our being prepared for our careers with Hartford Accident and Indemnity and for Calvary Cemetery.

The intellectual world that underlies contemporary secular humanism, the intellectual substructure supporting our friends and contemporaries who don't worry about God and so forth, has really been exhausted. Logical positivism has really been exhausted. It's been taken as far as it can go — now in terms of philosophy and even science, we've come up against the exhaustion of that as a reference point. We have now got to deal with these questions again; they will reintroduce themselves. We're coming into another period of uncertainty. We're coming to the end of a world order, the middle-class world order of the nineteenth century. The empires and that optimistic, materialist, relatively comfortable world is breaking apart. Of course, all generations think they're living at the end of a cycle. But certainly it's happening that the empires are breaking down, that the European domination of the world is coming to an end.

As a result of all this, I do think that these questions are presenting themselves to be dealt with and they will do so increasingly in this country and other countries. We see the rise of the born-again evangelists — they're answering a need. They're taking advantage — some of them, I think, quite cynically — of a need in ordinary people who feel lost and disoriented. Secular positivism is not giving them anything, and they're lonely and lost and unhappy, and so they want to engage in that orgy of emotionalism and be born again. They're looking for the childhood that they lost and the certainties that they lost with that. It's probably happening less in Catholicism than in Protestantism, where the new evangelism is speaking to a need, and in Judaism, where there's a kind of neo-Hassidism and a kind of returning to orthodoxy that's visibly going on. Catholicism alone is still struggling toward a secular consciousness. It's still discovering the folk Mass — it's discovering the sixties. The Church can handle them twenty years later. It's kind of like my old school can handle me thirty years later. They just couldn't deal with me at the time.

WILFRID SHEED

"That's Entertainment"

Above all, you might as well enjoy yourself. If you yawned your way through Mass, for instance, you were only making things duller and worse. Contrariwise, if you prayed, pondered, paid attention in the right proportions, the time would fairly whiz by. Thus by simple habit and custom, my sister Rosemary and I and who knows how many thousands of others became what would now be considered freakishly devout Catholics. That it was not altogether dissimilar from being a Dodger fan does not trivialize it.
—Wilfrid Sheed
Frank and Maisie

On the ride out to Wilfrid Sheed's home in eastern Long Island, the bus — known as the Hampton Jitney — passes a soccer practice field studded with opposing goal posts, easily more than a dozen, arranged along both north-south and east-west axes in no particular sequence. At a quick glance, the field appears to be a croquet course for giants — the same ones, presumably, who walked away from a lighthearted game of dominoes some years back and left Stonehenge. Silly as it sounds, it is precisely the sort of nutty but *gemütlich* image that can come to mind after prolonged exposure to the writing of Wilfrid Sheed.

The fact is that, for all the steam-hiss-dripping, acid-on-iron acerbity of Sheed's critical prose, he remains eminently likable, and idiomatically Catholic. For example, in a piece on small-town baseball for the *New York Times Magazine* called "Diamonds Are Forever," Sheed asks rhetorically, "Where did the Death of Baseball theologians go bad?" And he closes the same essay by stating somewhat triumphally that "even the nonbeliever bends his knee to the World Series."

Nor does Sheed ever wander too far from his sense of humor. Asked by the *Times* to name the one literary composition he would most like to have written and why, he answered, " 'Ulysses,' I suppose, because it would save one the trouble of writing anything else." As a critic — and a genuinely catholic one who has taken on books, theater, film, and sports — Sheed can relate the humiliation of the central character in Mary Gordon's *Final Payments* to the sort encountered in *The Story of O*. As a novelist, he can cap a fumbled seduction scene (in *Transatlantic Blues*) by having the protagonist muse, "I was miserable and wet with rage. There is no sadness like unto a Catholic boy who has committed a sin with nothing to show for it."

Or take any of his concise ripostes at pop cultural wisdom, such as regarding the exercise boom: "The fitness business is about sex and immortality. By toning up the system, you can prolong youth, just about finesse middle age and then, when the time comes, go straight into senility." Or his one-line dismissal of assertiveness training: "As if the world needed more rudeness." But for sheer virtuoso lead-in writing, I'll take this opening of a 1980 meditation on, among other things, cyclical patterns in best-seller lists:

"Two things can confidently be said about history. One is that anyone who has ever heard Santayana's famous statement about the past is destined to repeat it; the second is that if you *do* remember the past, as George advises, you are, according to W. Churchill, in for an endless series of dismal shocks. Like Kim Novak, the intellectual starlet who read 'mostly prose and poetry,' history proceeds mostly in circles and straight lines."

And besides, he does the best John Simon impression you'd ever want to hear.

Perhaps because I spent most of what they call the formative years on Long Island and most of my adolescence trying to get off it, I find the place physically unappealing — little more than an overlong landing strip for desperate aircraft. Yet others appear to like it fine, especially its easternmost forked tongue, and are willing to pay extravagant sums to live in unpainted shelters built among its fading sand dunes. Wilfrid Sheed lives in a rather more congenial section of the island known as Sag Harbor. Out there, although the trees still don't amount to much more than overfed shrubbery, there are some lovely old houses, and the quality of sunlight is not strained as it illuminates their freshly painted clapboards.

I meet Sheed right off the Jitney on Main Street, and we proceed into a nondescript joint with the pretentious title of J. W. Ryerson's Eating & Drinking Est'b. The interview session itself launches inauspiciously as Sheed announces, half shell in hand, "I hope you're going to take notes and not use one of those tape recorders." Taking a sip of seafood bisque,

I assure him that, out of respect, my Sony won't see the dim light of J. W. Ryerson's. (But wasn't it a Sony tape recorder that was prominently featured in *Transatlantic Blues*, Sheed's somewhat autobiographical tale of a talk-show host who spends the entire novel confessing into one somewhere over the Atlantic Ocean?) "As a Luddite," Sheed is saying, "I don't like the electronic buzz. I don't like the sound all those electronic things make." Fine, notes it is.

We begin; my pen, working furiously below table line and, I imagine, out of sight, is trying to take down Sheed's salty remarks about Michael Novak when he interrupts himself to say, "*That* better not be going in!" Of course not. We move on to Robert Stone, whom he likes a great deal. "Stone told me," Sheed confides, "that he'd let the Church go rather too completely and was sort of sorry he did." He adds that they've spent years trying to find "ferries in common" between their Connecticut and Long Island shores, but to no avail — when suddenly he's on me once more. "That pen has got to go," he says.

Forty minutes later, tape recorder humming contentedly, I'm informed that I'll have to drive his car back to the Sheed compound after he picks up a second car at the repair shop. This, as I soon discover, is somewhat more than it appears. For Sheed's car is one of those wonderful old boats that nobody drives anymore except in Bruce Springsteen videos. Flick the steering wheel a couple of degrees to the right and you're suddenly chewing up road shoulder; hit the brakes and nothing much happens at all. When a squirrel later darts suicidally across the road ahead, I don't even flinch — it's him or me, and I don't plan to check the tires for fur when we get back, *if* we get back.

But somehow we do, and under a cumulonimbus of cigar smoke, we spend the better part of the next two hours discussing everything but the obvious. (For readers who are not familiar with Wilfrid Sheed's illustrious parents, I can't do better than direct you to his convivial memoir, *Frank and Maisie*, wherein he recounts, amid the occasional divagation, the story of Sheed and Ward, the single most influential Catholic publishing house in American history. To quote his own succinct evaluation, "If one had to boil the Sheed/Ward American mission down to one sentence, it would be that Frank and Maisie finally gave Catholics permission to think without benefit of clergy.") Among other things, Sheed has made a career of crisscrossing the Atlantic since leaving his English homeland fifty-three years ago. I can't think of a writer better equipped than he is to detail the nuances of Anglo-Irish-American Catholicism and the whole import-export business that has made the Church in America what it is today. Or one who could make the explaining such fun.

I INHERITED a somewhat cranky point of view on education from my father. He was really against primary education altogether because he thought kids should learn directly from life as long as they could. That was partly because his father had the same theory and didn't send *my* father to school until he was ten years old or so. Until that point my father had enjoyed a full kind of Huckleberry Finn life in Sydney, and because he had the necessary gifts he proceeded to sweep through school like a juggernaut. I don't think the theory works for everybody, but at any rate I in my turn inherited the old family position, to which I added my own observation that more kids come to hate the Church through its schools than through anything else that happens to them. I don't think that the Church should ever be in that authority position because kids can never remember whether something or other was fair or not, they can only remember injustices. And they're not going to pick up any religious instruction that's worth much at that age anyway — although I believe that religion is taught much more brightly these days, as the tide of half-baked vocations recedes.

Cardinal Cushing had the same theory — to close up the parochial grammar schools. I never knew quite what went on in Cushing's head — it's hard to imagine — but he tended to come out with fairly smart conclusions, one of which must have been that the parochial school system at the lower level creates more trouble than it's worth. All the nasty stories told by ex-Catholic authors about being forced to clean up whatever mess they made on the floor and atrocities of that sort — all those brutish nuns in Brooklyn, where they seemed to grow like weeds, cuffing little kids over the ear — could easily be avoided. (The nuns could be sent to mental homes, say.)

But again, as I said in *Frank and Maisie*, it's best if the practice comes before the theory anyway. First you simply come to enjoy what you're doing: the ritual and the liturgical seasons and so on. It is your year. You begin marking off the seasons by saints and feast days, all somehow leading up to the Big Bang after Lent — and, of course, the special American dispensation to let go on St. Patrick's Day. We used to have a *ball* on St. Patrick's Day, but that's a subject for a less ethereal conversation than this one.

It's not literally true, as I seemed to imply in *Frank and Maisie*, that if I hadn't been born into that family I might not have been a Catholic at all. That's a little too precious, and it wasn't quite intended that way. It wasn't "we happy few" at all. It could have happened for me in any number of families, and it might even have happened in a few schools, but as far as I was concerned it had to be a living situation. And I had that feeling about the Church that it tended to exist in living situations more than other churches. The idea of simply churchgoing just seemed like staying in after school to me. The people who did it were religious types, and Catholics really prided themselves on not being religious types — they were Everyman. I think our mix of sacraments and ritual did make it much more like theater. As kids, the operatic aspects of the Church — indeed, the music and the smell — were among the hooks that drew us in. But our theater wasn't all opera by any means. A low Mass at dawn in a side chapel was another kind of theater, close to a Graham Greene sort of theater. Crawling to confession on a rainy night in South Kensington was another kind of theater, and so on: Mass on a battlefield, Mass in Bavaria where they use a brass band in place of bells, a missionary Mass on a packing box — "that's entertainment," as the song says of more secular diversions.

The pleasures we got from these things were frequently secular, and I think the mix did wonders for our sanity. I was delighted to find, when I was training to be an altar boy shortly after coming over here, that I could memorize the Mass card and that I could say it as quickly as the fastest priest could demand. There was one such at our school who absolutely craved a cigarette, which he couldn't have until after Mass. And so he always called for me because I was the original eleven-minute kid. We *moved*. Father Felix was a French Canadian from Maine, and he was also the baseball coach, and I trust that it is not sacrilegious to say that he said Mass a little bit like an infielder turning a double play. My tendency to move the book to the wrong side, of course, maddened the guy, because his fingers were practically shaking by then for that first butt. But we understood that that was part of the fun of the Church — a kind of grave comedy, in which we abided scrupulously by the rules and then went like the wind.

Thus — theater of all kinds. I think Genet said that the most dramatic moment in the world is when the priest raises his hands in consecration. Without believing a word of it, Genet imagined the concentration of all the world's forces in that one moment. I think there's probably a new kind of drama today. For instance, the host turning up in some Third World village can still be as exciting as it was in Elizabethan England or Graham Greene's Mexico. I don't think the drama depended on the particular props I grew up with — the central proposition is exciting enough.

Did I think sex was such a big deal as some Catholics — mostly ex — have made it? Mercifully not. When I was about sixteen or seventeen and

absolutely on fire with those things St. Paul warns us about, I decided
that I would never quit the Church over sex. I thought there was bigger
game afoot. I also thought that sex was a totally inscrutable subject and
I didn't find anybody else's solution to it any better than ours. I'm glad
I made that decision then, because at that point I hadn't thought realistically
about things like marriage and birth control, and I might have been a good
deal more shaken when those matters came along; but I already knew
there was more to it than that.

However, despite my brave resolutions, I had as much trouble as the
next Catholic framing even a coherent language for sexual experience. In
Walker Percy's novel about filmmaking, *Lancelot*, he stages an orgy
because it's absolutely necessary, but he has it done on defective film
that's sort of shimmering, so you can't tell exactly what's happening. I
gather that was the only way Walker felt he could do explicit sex with a
straight face. By now, if my own sensibility is anything to go by, I don't
think an American Catholic novelist would have quite so many moral
qualms as we did about erotic writing, but he might share Percy's difficulties with the straight face. One's view of sex and human dignity is too
complicated to go into, but at its simplest it instinctively draws curtains
over the sacred and over profanations of the sacred.

There were two things that particularly bothered me about the Church
as I grew up because they both seemed to be keeping me childish. One
was the habitual prayer of supplication, asking for favors. After I got
polio at fourteen, I used to volley these out every night, and at a certain
point I thought this was a pretty childish thing to be doing, that it really
was like writing to Santa Claus. And, of course, nothing came of it
anyway. I remember some elderly nun type saying, ''You don't get exactly
what you prayed for, you get what God thinks is best for you,'' and I
thought, Well, I'll just sit back and wait for that anyway. I won't bother
to mention anything in particular.

The other thing I had serious trouble with is the one that I make fun
of in *Transatlantic Blues*, which is confession. It wasn't funny to me
at the time to find myself, as a grown-up, still assuming a kind of
supplicant position and blurting my sins like a child. I never had the
kind of airy-fairy temperament necessary to believe, other than ''no-
tionally,'' that I was talking directly to God. What I was actually talking
to was this heavy-breathing, gray-faced creature over whom I seemed
to be fawning and begging forgiveness. I realized that this nightmare
version was basically false and untheological, but I never learned an
adult way to do it, and I'm afraid that if I did so now, the old reflexes
would still betray me.

I did have my day in the confessional, though, a day when I didn't feel the least wormlike. I had been reading the Acts of the Apostles and thought, This is *really* mumbo jumbo. I'd swallowed all the rest with relative ease, but the wonder stories in Acts seemed like *Alice in Wonderland.* So I said words to that effect to a man who I'd been told was the brightest priest in, as I recall, Clifton, New Jersey. And he pulled the hoariest old routine on me. He said, "Have you ever seen Australia?" To this you are supposed to say, "No, I haven't," after which *he* says, "But there are those who have, and so it is with the mystery of faith, etc." Well, by chance, I had recently been to Australia, so I said, "Yes, I have," and left the box in triumph.

Anyway, I have always been very much in favor of general absolution to prevent all these forms of embarrassment. I know there are some people whose temperaments are much suited to private confession, and I think the idea of having to confess to humanity rather than simply in your head is an important part of the Church, so I am not a strict abolitionist. But if it stays, I don't think people should have to go to it too early in life or at too sensitive an age. I think they should know what they're doing, and I think they should meet the priest as a human equal so that then the sin itself could be the problem and not you against him. Ideally the subject should be the sinfulness of mankind as represented by yourself that particular day and by him, perhaps, the next. You are telling the Christian community — as opposed to just talking to yourself — that you did it and that you're sorry you did it.

There was a point at which I had gotten bored with going to church, and I must add that I was also theoretically excommunicated because of my divorce — although at that time this was a pretty much fingers-crossed situation. I already found a lot of younger people not taking excommunication terribly seriously by the late sixties — if they wanted to go to the sacraments they went to the sacraments. But during that brief period of being cut off, when I had the sense of being an outcast, going to church became an immense effort. The English Mass turned out to be an unqualified bore as far as I was concerned. The worst of it was that I had been in favor of it once upon a time, but I was expecting better English than this. I thought we'd get something like the Book of Common Prayer; I didn't know that we were going to get this flavorless mush. I have trouble with repetition anyway, so Mass in English every week is pretty much like reading the same editorial every Sunday. On the other hand, I have the usual Catholic predisposition not to want to be anything else. A universal Christian Church remains not merely an ideal but, once tasted, the only possible ideal, and I'm not about to drop it because of some quibble over prose.

.   .   .

I was a great friend of Joe Flaherty's, and talk about your battle-scarred, or at least eraser-scarred, ex-Catholics. . . . He had an enormous head and he claimed it was from the nuns belting him so often. But, naturally, he also got a funny story out of it. His father had been head of some grain haulers' group which defied the Mafia, as a result of which his father was East Rivered. So every Friday when school was let out to go to the movies, the nun would announce very loudly, "Everybody has to pay a quarter, except for Joe Flaherty, whose father was murthered."

No matter how lapsed Joe was rendered by all this, he remained very much a Catholic writer. And I was thinking as we were driving through Sag Harbor just now about some of the things that phrase might mean. And I saw three hopelessly fat, plain girls, who by the sound of it were also stupid, and I thought that a certain pagan friend of mine might quite reasonably say, "Why do these fat, ugly people marry and procreate and produce such hideous children?" And I thought, No Catholic could ever say that. Nobody is altogether worthless to us, and that shows up in one's work. But with it goes a sense that nobody's that great either, that human greatness is probably a deception, and if you think you've got it you're better off without the information. (And, of course, all our real saints are dead.) Gene McCarthy was a practitioner of the attitude: Don't take yourself too seriously, jump on anyone who does, and be absolutely merciless to anyone's pretentions. To pluck another instance out of the air: when Nathaniel Crosby—from the last litter of Crosby kids—won the U.S. Amateur, he was asked, "What would your old man have said?" And he answered, without missing a breath, "He would've said, 'Don't let it go to your head.' " That was the Catholic upbringing. You could be very vain indeed, as Senator McCarthy also demonstrated, but you couldn't quite make egomaniac.

This didn't *have* to lead to an exaltation of bums, in the Peter Maurin manner, because bums were not intrinsically better than bank managers: by their fruits, however bizarre, you must know both of them—but not easily. Because *everybody* was precious in the eyes of God and therefore worth a look. And we were taught that Christ is there among the least likely of them, that He is in this one or that one—He hops about a lot. I have a particularly cranky theory of my own that has nothing to do with the Church, which is that God the Father is no liberal—in His job, He couldn't be—but that His Son the human had to be a liberal, being One of us. These are shifting fantasies in one's mind. The Holy Ghost may simply be history, who moves the whole thing along—or call Him Harpo if you like. Obviously Yahweh was very far from a liberal—there was never such an authoritarian figure.

But then we have a God that was human, and He can express what humans should feel for each other — not necessarily what God would feel for us but what a God who is human would feel for us. That's why ''No one goeth to the Father except through Me'' was always a very important saying for me — that you have to go through the human, that trying to go directly to God is a presumption very close to insanity. I guess this was where we really locked horns with the Puritans, in that they wanted nothing to come between them and God, and we thought, Hey man, you going to get burned if you get that close.

And so we go instead through this rich intermediate world with patron saints and strange architectures and different kinds of religious experience, and along the way we get sidelong glimpses of God as through a train window.

But to get back to that notion of nobody — you or anybody else — being so hot: this is something that the Irish may have laid on us double thick because of their history of disappointments. Irish history, perhaps like Jewish history, wasn't always as bad as the parts they choose (perhaps wisely) to remember. I think that a great deal of eighteenth-century Ireland would have been a wonderful country to live in. That's when all the great Irish music was collated for the first time, all the great piping and jigging, and Brian Merriman was writing wonderful poetry. The Rising of '98 was simply an annihilating heartbreak: the French fleet, you'll recall, got all the way to Bantry Bay and then the ''Protestant winds'' came up and the fleet never landed — and the Irish rose anyway and were wiped out. First of all, there had been a rising in the east which would have been successful if it could have been coordinated with the west. But the Irish in the east barely spoke the same language as the west. In fact, when the eastern rebels went to the west, they were considered fops by the farmers out there — them and their fancy songs and English and all.

By now, of course, most Irish Americans have forgotten even the bad parts of their history, retaining only, in some cases, a vague sense of grievance. My father once tried to publish some little-known Irish classics. And he thought that since Irish Americans carry on so much about their heritage, he'd found a heaven-sent new market. But as it turned out, they not only didn't buy the books, but when he despairingly put a quiz into Sheed and Ward's own *Trumpet* asking them to name five things that happened between the Battle of the Boyne and the '98, they seemed barely aware of the two events, let alone five things in between. At which point he simply gave up on the American Irish as readers, feeling that they'd rather boast about their heritage than *learn* about it. For all that, and for all my native Englishness, the American Irish became my game when we moved over here during the war, and I identified most closely with their form of Catholicness then and what's left of it now.

It's my experience of the English and American Catholic Churches—with just enough European mixed in to throw sand in my eyes—that each of the regional churches has certain crippling defects but doesn't have the ones that the others have. Thus, if you found Catholics almost neurotically prudish in Ireland, you might find them much less so in France, say. The usual explanation for the famous Irish puritanism is that it was a Jansenist import, like Japanese flu or something. But it's been my experience that the Protestant churches of Scotland and Wales are equally harsh, and I believe it's for the same reason: poverty. I think it's very much based on the idea that the parish will eventually have to take care of the pregnant girl and her child, and this gets built into a tradition until you don't know where the tradition came from—as with kosher food.

When the Irish came over here, this harshness was still necessary for the people who came crawling off those verminous ships and tried to set up in this country. They needed the same rules—everybody but Joe Kennedy, the million-dollar exception. There may have been a tacit understanding among some of the more genial Irish that you could get away with one weakness, but not two. If you really were abstemious, as Joe was, and didn't drink at all, that bought you a certain license in the *other* sin.

Unfortunately, those once practical historical sexual restrictions also made for a great division between the sexes. The coldness of husbands and wives in Ireland is one of the wonders of the world. I remember asking once, after we'd been a couple of months in Dublin, why it was that, although everybody was very generous to us in pubs, we were never invited to people's homes. And the journalist I was with said, "Because our wives would hit us with a frying pan if we came home at all. If we came home with a strange friend, the fat would really be on the fire."

The English, for their part, used to be absolutely fierce about not going to any kind of Protestant service. For historical reasons, there was a lot of bad blood involved, of course. But beyond that, it was so easy for a Catholic to advance in English life by becoming an Anglican that—as that famous parking sign in Charleston says, "Don't even THINK of parking here." What fatal seductions lay in wait in Anglican churches I never found out because of those parking regulations. The sin involved was known as "indifferentism" and the English, perhaps by temperament, seemed to be sinfully tempted by it.

The English Church was also very strict about discipline in general, so in a sense it didn't come out so different from the Irish Church, but I think they got there by different routes. The English felt that they had to hang on to their tiny garrison of Catholics, and this meant hard training. For instance, the English could be quite urbane about some matters, and certainly it was a lot easier to confess a minor sexual sin in England than it was here. But in matters of Church practice, they could be needle-eyed. Take, for instance, the business of weighing one's food during Lent so that you couldn't have more than eight ounces or whatever for lunch. I couldn't imagine a Spaniard, say, going through this rigamarole. But in English houses I actually used to find these scales, doing a brisk business.

Garry Wills and Walter Kerr may be exemplars, at opposite ends of the spectrum, of a kind of Catholic critical sensibility that's a mixture of bluntness, of hardheadedness, combined with personal forbearance. Something you got from scholastic philosophy is the notion that the object of intellect is truth, not cleverness, so truth must be rooted out, however painful. But the pain should not be made worse than it has to be by tap-dancing on the author's, or performer's, grave. I myself pretty much gave up reviewing because I found I was hurting people without even knowing it, and I didn't think my little epiphanies were worth it. Maybe confession, again, had something to do with all this, because we had to strip ourselves bare and we realized how it feels to have your skin peeled off. There's a certain kind of arrogance that's out of bounds for Catholics. Confession gives you the habit of thinking that you're possibly as much at fault as anyone else in a given situation. Examination of conscience is a very strange habit, but I think it can lead to a certain fair-mindedness — in the right hands. In all these instances, I am referring, to use Cardinal Newman's image, to those who take their religious medicine, and not those who "pour it down the sink."

I think that if you're a serious Catholic, it's very hard to fall for religious fads. As a Dominican friend of mine once said, "Having embraced the one great superstition, I don't feel a need for any other." I never even saw how one could become a Communist, although I sensed the natural affinity. A book that influenced me very much — and don't bother looking for it, because I don't think it exists anymore — was *The Catholic Center* by E. I. Watkin. The thesis was that if you're going to have a universal Church, it's got to say something to every variety of religious experience. And so Watkin considers the Church in terms of Buddhism and Shinto and so on and finds the elements in it that could live with each of those faiths with some parallel tradition of its own. But communism just seemed incredibly cramped to me. Also, Communists seemed to think that humor was a bourgeois trick. I never met one that you could have a jolly evening with, unless he was out of, or on his way out of, the party. Of course, humor *is* a way of changing the subject—it's the great evasion, indeed, and that's why we like it. There's a saying of G. K. Chesterton's that I've always liked. Talking about Bernard Shaw as a puritan, he said, "A puritan is someone whose *mind* never takes a holiday." He can't play, and when he plays there's got to be some point to it.

When the Church decided that everybody should go vernacular, I think they were imagining some terrific flowering of some specifically local cultures that would feed into the Church. But what we got here were bad guitar Masses or desperately uninspired hymns belonging to no time or place because we don't at the moment have a culture that's suitable. To take away one you've already got—and, which, however foreign to begin with, is already part of the American Catholic soul—and say, "Well, now you can do one of your own . . ." well, it can't be produced on demand. The Episcopal culture is vernacular, but it goes back to the seventeenth century, when the English language was just right and English music was just right, so they could produce something that stands. But we don't have either a suitable culture or a tradition to supplant what we lost. And I hope they don't have to invoke a whole other council to restore things. I don't think that we're groping toward anything better than a total restoration right now.

I'm delighted that the American bishops are not just the sort of colonial civil servants they used to be. The change in the bishops has been extraordinary, to find them saying anything of use at all. I think it's also interesting that they are so accustomed to marching in lockstep that right-wing bishops like Kroll will not break with the other bishops even when it hurts: if the rest of the bishops have moved leftward then they will not find significant open opposition from the right-wing bishops. I'm sure you would find in different dioceses enormously different emphases, but if it comes to a joint statement, they understand that such a statement with a quarter of the spokesmen abstaining would be useless—just as the Supreme Court *had* to be nine to nothing on the segregation issue. (It was probably closer to five to four, but if they were going to make a statement at all it had to be nine–nothing or forget it.)

I've always thought of the Church as being somewhat like the Democratic party: totally disputatious and infinitely varied and colorful, but traditionally capable of pulling itself together to act as one. That, after all, is our proposition: but it wouldn't add up to much if we didn't fight each other every step of the way.

When an argument comes up—and it could be on any one of a number of subjects—Catholics and ex-Catholics are likely to be on the same side. There really is a similar way of looking at life, don't ask me to explain it. If I'd never been told what the Catholic position on abortion was, I would have known. And if I hear someone across the room defending a vilified public figure, that may well be a Catholic, ex or otherwise, speaking. It also seems that what some people left the Church over very often turns out to be marginal to the whole thing. That's why I had the feeling that I wasn't going to leave about sex. Michael Harrington, for instance, was outraged into leaving by the doctrine of hell: he believed that this dogma simply had caused so much misery in people's lives, so much fear, that any church that taught it was inhuman. Yet he couldn't get many Catholics—even the great Dorothy Day—to accept that he was leaving just over that: there was so much *more*.

I can't tell if I was experiencing God or experiencing my own excitement, but at my first communion I was absolutely beside myself. I thought, This is it. But then again, music has always moved me in the same way. They say that Winston Churchill always cried when he heard the old Harrow boating song. Well, now that my mother is gone, I cannot listen to Gilbert and Sullivan, particularly *The Gondoliers,* dry eyed or throated. Music gets me directly in that way, and if someone were to offer a proof for the existence of God through Mozart—well, I've heard worse ones.

Naturally, I was a big Benediction man. There was plenty of music and all the incense your tiny lungs could handle. English anti-Catholics have, by the way, a particular thing against incense, which may have fueled my own taste for it. They used to call us "bloody incense burners," not realizing that when they purged their own services of the exotic and the strange, of "otherness," nobody went anymore. And if I ever happen to smell that nouveau, non-Catholic incense coming from Hare Krishnas or worse, I just bless myself and hurry down the road. That's *our* smell, boy.

As to mystical experience, or intuition of Being, whenever I have come remotely close to it, it has not been in a specifically religious context, which I think is as it should be—and in my youth more or less had to be. Metaphysically the Church was never just about the Church, but about God and His whole creation; practically and diurnally, I found it to be mostly about things like being a good Catholic (who sounded like, and usually was, a dull good fellow not much given to spiritual adventure). Mysticism was simply not on the menu of the quotidian Church; in fact it was generally distrusted, so you had to send out for it—probably at your own peril. A good many free spirits, of course, never came back.

All the old Church really did for most of us was to keep us alert and on our toes for the unpredictable pinprick visitations of grace, which was not nothing. Beyond that, its trappings were bathetically richer than the daily life it proposed for us — us lay people at least. Now of course they've flattened out the trappings as well, but I think Catholics are marginally freer than we ever were — if they have the wit — to live interesting lives that are still authentically Catholic.

MARY GORDON

The Irish Catholic Church

The Catholic Church in America is an immigrants' church, but unlike the
institutions founded by the immigrant Jews and Protestants, Catholics view
education as a threat. They're afraid you'll leave the Church if you're
educated. Their attitude is that by thinking, you're going to get yourself in
a lot of trouble. As long as Catholics maintain a separate educational system
they'll remain outside the highest intellectual circles. Fordham is not Harvard, not Columbia. Catholic schools are separate, not equal.
—Mary Gordon
Women's Wear Daily, February 13, 1981

As a child, I was obsessive about religion. I wanted to get leprosy and be
miraculously cured. I used to sleep with a little plastic cross. One morning
I woke up with an imprint on my chest and I knew I had the stigmata. I
ran to my mother and said, ''Mom, I've got it—the stigmata!'' She said,
''You goddamn fool—you've slept on your crucifix.''
—Mary Gordon

Mary Gordon lives with her husband, Arthur Cash, and their two children,
Anna and David, in a large old house with a wraparound stone porch on
a shady side street in New Paltz, New York, three blocks from her mother's
house. Cash, who is the biographer of Laurence Sterne, teaches English
literature at the State University in New Paltz. Gordon taught English at
Dutchess Community College and Amherst College but gave it up when
her children were born because she felt that teaching was ''too much like
being a mother. College kids need so much nurturing, and when you're
being nurturing and patient and attentive to books that you're trying to
write and to little children, it gets to be entirely too much nurturing.''
    The furniture in her living room is warm and comfortably unpretentious,

much like the writer herself, who loves the paintings of Vuillard and has named her daughter and son after her mother and her father. In fact, as we sit down to talk, Mary Gordon appears particularly maternal. Anna has a cold and twists in her lap while, under the guise of submitting to Mom's tender ministrations, she is carefully taking in every word of the interview. When the subject of sex comes up, Gordon simply explains that she'd like Anna to go upstairs because she is going to say some things that she doesn't want her daughter to hear. Anna isn't delighted with this arrangement but is told in the most straightforward manner that her mother doesn't think it's appropriate.

Gordon has compared her father, a Jewish convert to Catholicism who died when she was quite young, alternately to Danny Kaye and Ezra Pound. She counts her literary influences as Virginia Woolf, Elizabeth Bowen, and Margaret Drabble. Probably more than any other novelist today, Gordon has explored the ramifications of a Catholic upbringing. Her ethnic background is a mixture of Irish, Italian, and Jewish, making her perhaps the ultimate New York immigrant scion. She grew up in Queens, but by the time she'd started high school she was regularly seeking cultural refuge in the Manhattan her parents had been happy to leave.

Mary Gordon's first novel, *Final Payments*, was that rarity of modern publishing, a best-seller that was critically lauded. It was singled out by the *New York Times Book Review* from those "herds of novels bristling with bright anarchy and loopy apocalypse, and a more recent rut of feminist self-advertisement" and was praised for being simply "an old-fashioned realistic novel." Its themes certainly have an element of the old-fashioned about them — sacrifice and moral development, for openers. Isabel Moore, the book's protagonist, is given to observations such as this: "Goodness ought to make people happy as it did in other ages. But now goodness was a private, esoteric hobby, like painting miniatures, or putting ships in bottles."

In some ways, Gordon narrates the classic tale of the Catholic intellectual who grows up in a world in which she is ridiculed for being out of place yet suspects that she is better than the rest of the kids because she's smarter than they are. It's a syndrome that Mary McCarthy commented on in *Memories of a Catholic Girlhood* and that is familiar to those of us who underwent a more or less cloistered parochial school education. To discover by comparison later that in certain ways Catholic schools had relatively low standards could be quite devastating, as McCarthy realized.

"I stood at the head of my class," McCarthy wrote, "and I was also the best runner and the best performer on the turning poles in the schoolyard; I was the best actress and elocutionist and the second most devout. . . . No doubt, the standards of the school were not very high, and they gave me a false idea of myself; I have never excelled in athletics elsewhere. Nor have I ever been devout again. When I left the competitive atmosphere of the parochial school, my religion withered on the stalk.'' Gordon sounds a less discouraging variation on this theme, as she also brings typically unconventional insights into archetypical conventions such as the all-girls school and the relationship of the priest to Catholic girls growing up.

Mary Gordon is at work on a novel chronicling an Irish family that migrates to America, and judging from her remarks in this interview about the Irish influence on American Catholicism, her book may raise hackles from here to Ballycastle. The Irish have clearly manifest a controlling interest in the Roman Catholic Church of America almost from the beginning, and it's no coincidence that their name arises so frequently and in such variegated hues of anger, delight, and perplexity in these pages — or that so many of the Catholics one finds prominently ensconced in the American landscape are of Irish parentage. Their impact was felt everywhere in the Church most of us grew up with, right down to the songs the Sisters had us sing in ''music class.'' (To this day, I know the lyrics to ''MacNamara's Band'' and ''You're as Welcome as the Flowers in May to Dear Old Donegal'' a lot better than I care to recall.)

Finally, Gordon makes a strong case for the Biblical premise that Terrance Sweeney has identified as ''the spirit of God written in the hearts of all.'' If, as she suspects, there is no place for Catholics like her in the Church, then the Church may be in more precarious shape than even its severest critics suggest.

I THINK THE FIRST THING that you really need to know about me is that my father was a Jew who converted to Catholicism and became an absolute zealot. During the entirety of my parents' marriage, they had absolutely nothing in common except a zealous Catholicism. My mother was Irish and Italian. My father went to Harvard, dropped out and went to Europe, lived in Paris in the twenties, and Oxford in the late twenties, and then converted to Catholicism in the thirties because he was a Francoist. So the whole bond between my parents was a very zealous, right-wing, devotional Catholicism. They even met through a priest — my mother used to go on retreats, and she was introduced to my father by the retreat priest. You may never find anybody more Catholic than my family.

My father was an unsuccessful journalist who was always trying to start
magazines — which would last about two issues and then fold. They were
all very right-wing, Catholic, crazy stuff. Meanwhile my mother supported
us by working as a secretary. My father was a great failure in every sense,
really, except that he was a wonderful, wonderful father. But because he
was in debt all the time and because nothing he started succeeded, he
thought of himself as a failure. He was obsessed with the decline of the
modern world, and he particularly hated Protestantism. As he saw it, the
American Church was getting more secular, more Protestant, and more
Rotarian, blurring distinctions between the sacred and the secular. And
this was before Vatican II, since he died in 1957.

My father had a real romance about Irish working-class Catholicism,
which is why he married my mother; but on the other hand he was not
at all working class. One of his failed businesses was an attempt to market
liturgical greeting cards with holy pictures. In trying to get people away
from the Ivory Soap madonnas usually found on such cards, he would
instead put in a Grünewald madonna or the Goya St. Jerome. And, of
course, the line bombed. But we did end up with a lot of high-class
religious pictures and objects around the house.

I went to a Catholic grammar school called Holy Name of Mary in
Valley Stream on Long Island and then to Mary Louis Academy in Jamaica. We had Josephite nuns, who were very strict but also very dumb.
They managed to combine being very ill educated with being very strict
about all the wrong things. Everything seemed to center on neatness and
appearance, and content was really pretty irrelevant. People always talk
about how they learned grammar and Latin in Catholic schools, but that
was not my experience at all. I had teachers with terrible Brooklyn accents
who were illiterate and spoke ungrammatically and a lot of very old nuns
who had no business being in classrooms. It got better in high school,
but here again I think it came down to a matter of class. Theirs was a
very working-class order, with primarily a working-class constituency.
On College Day, instead of having people from colleges come and talk
to us, they had people from secretarial schools and nursing schools come
in. There'd be a couple of colleges — like D'Youville College in Buffalo,
a little Catholic college run by some nuns, that has about fourteen
students — but there'd be a whole procession of people from business
schools.

But the real tragedy of my high school was that there were some very
smart girls in there — it was fairly hard to get in and you had to take a
competitive examination — and nobody to teach them. As a matter of fact,
I used to have to hide books under my desk, like Nancy Drew or *The
Secret Garden*, just because the idea of reading a book was suspect or

threatening. Some of the nuns were good at teaching grammar—I mean, I can diagram a sentence better than anybody in the world. But on the other hand, they didn't use the language well.

That was the terrible aspect of my whole intellectual life, because by the time I was ten years old I was smarter than my teachers. It was very bad for my intellectual discipline, since I wasn't old enough to create my own structure for intellectual discipline, and theirs was absurd. I had no model, and so it was totally easy for me to do that silly busywork. It wasn't until I got to college—and then I got the shock of my life going to Barnard—that I really had to learn some sort of intellectual discipline, which I had lost at age ten. What you can't get people to understand is that learning, to the Church, was not something to be treasured but something to be feared. Again, I'm obsessed by the notion of class. Maybe there were some wealthy parishes somewhere who had some awareness of Sheed and Ward or some alternate track where you would be learning something of value under Catholic domination. But in a working-class environment, it was just sheer, unadulterated hostility to learning and to any inquiry. It's not even that they were *only* against inquiry—you could understand that in a way—but they were against any intellectual achievement at all. And I think that was partly class and partly the authoritarian structure of the Church.

It was all about standing up to the enemy. They did see themselves as being in a very beleaguered position, from which vantage the enemy appeared to be protean in its manifestations. It could be Communists, Jews, Protestants, or atheists, but it was also pornographers, intellectuals, and sociologists, almost without distinction. What you were made to understand was that all those things were nonsense and that you were holding on to pure bedrock—and that was your goal, to withstand all those corruptions that were everywhere about you. Nothing else mattered, including learning, or even real achievement.

But taken in the context of the schools I went to, there was the added complication that we were girls who were going to grow into women. I think the relationship of nuns and girls is very odd and complicated. What they are theoretically training girls for is the life that they have turned their backs on. There was lip service paid to the fact that you were all going to get married, but what it was really about was keeping men at bay—that was what they were really interested in. So you now had an extra area in which you had to consider yourself beleaguered. Not only were you beleaguered as a Catholic, but you were beleaguered by males, who were out of control. And the message was always "We know that you're not interested in these things, but you know how boys are."

When I was going to grammar school, the nuns were very glamorous to me, but as I became an adolescent and saw them up close, that changed. There were a couple in my high school who were awfully smart, but they were really crazy, too. I don't know why nuns seemed to feel they had some sort of license to go into crazy rages. They would just go into rages and hit and throw things and scream. There was no notion that you had any recourse against it or that it was particularly unusual. It was just, "Oh, that was Sister Imelda—Oh my God, I got her for fifth grade." There was never any notion that your parents would step in between you and the nuns or the priest to protect you. And do you remember that whole penny candy business? That was capitalism at its absolutely most unleashed.

I don't want to paint an unmitigatedly negative picture. I think that in some ways, because we were all girls taught by all women, the one thing that was good was that you never had to refrain from saying something in class for fear of seeming smart and therefore losing the love of boys. My two best friends are still people I went to high school with—one's a doctor and one teaches at Notre Dame. Oddly enough, what was extremely valuable to me in that educational system was that because we were all girls, and we were the smart girls in an environment that we knew was not equal to us, we were very dependent on each other for sustenance. We gave each other that sustenance, and extremely intense bonds between us grew up as a result. I feel that the smartest person that I have ever met I met when I was thirteen years old, and she has continued to enrich and challenge my intellectual life for twenty-five years.

There was a way in which we were all discovering the wheel secretly. We would say, "Oh, I think Camus is somebody you should read, I don't know." I remember hearing that D. H. Lawrence was somebody you should read, but I didn't know *what* you should read—I knew you probably shouldn't read *Lady Chatterley's Lover*, but I didn't know what the good ones were. I went to the Donnell Library and I found a book called *Kangaroo*, which I read thinking that was representative Lawrence. You had no clues and no help, yet you were secretly, with each other, groping for a hidden intellectual world that you sensed was out there but for which you had no map. This created a tremendous intimacy and sense of intellectual purpose and adventure. I think if there had been boys around and the social or sexual ante were upped, we wouldn't have had that sense of adventure and thrill and camaraderie.

So, on the one hand, I have an odd feeling that it was better in some ways to grow up a Catholic woman than in certain other kinds of organizations because there existed a separate but equal world for women. The very sexual segregation spared you from a lower place in the hierarchy run by males. Eventually of course, in liturgical terms, you would always be totally out of it. But because of the existence of that separate but equal world, you didn't deal with men for a large part of your day. There was a way in which the experience of femaleness was given a kind of validity—it wasn't as if you were always looking over your shoulder for the approval of some male because the males weren't around. I think paradoxically that this gave young women a kind of strength and a notion that other women were important—and that, I think, is the most valuable thing that the women's movement says, that the lives of women are important. Since you were in a sexually segregated structure, the lives that you took seriously were female lives.

Then, on the other hand, you have the business of the priests, who operate out of a different, male context. The priest is the untouchable male, which renders him very potent but also keeps him from getting too close. In some ways you never assume that you're known well by a priest. But then there's the moment when they fix you with that Bishop Sheen look—which can pierce lead—when only they see through to your soul. It functions on a lot of different levels. Because the priest is distant and honored, he is both the person who doesn't know you very well *and* the only person who really knows you. You don't see him a lot but, because he is distant and hyperpotent, his opinion is the one that really matters. So that when the priest who rarely turns his attention to you, as a woman, *does* turn his attention, then you feel absolutely anointed.

All women have a complicated relationship to male authority, but Catholic women must deal with a heightened dimension wherein the priest is the sacred personage. Only a male can be this sacred personage; therefore his attention and his judgment become tremendously important and yet remain distant. Since you never know him as he knows you, as a Catholic woman you develop a very odd notion of what the male is. It's a whole new frame of reference that I think other women don't have. It's very much like the relationship of fathers to daughters in traditional nuclear families. Priests, because they don't have to get their hands dirty, as it were, with the daily lives of people, can offer a sort of kindness and sweetness. Whereas mothers are bad cops, fathers are good cops, and priests can be good cops in the same way because they don't get close. And some of them were actually smarter than either the nuns or your parents. There was a way in which, if they marked you and touched you, they gave you confidence to go out into the larger world.

I actually had extremely kind treatment from many priests. The kindest treatment I got was from a priest who later left and got married. What one finds about most women who are accomplished is that they got a lot of encouragement from their fathers. I think that when Catholic women are accomplished, they've often gotten a lot of encouragement from priests. Maybe it was because, if you were a smart girl, they saw you as desexed somehow and therefore not dangerous. Maybe some of them liked the smart girls because they didn't have to deal with them as grossly physical characters. In my life, I received quite a bit of encouragement and praise and support from some priests. By the time I was sexual, I was out of the Church, so the things they could say that were destructive to women had nothing to do with me. In that regard, I think it's a very ambivalent relationship. Because sex is taboo, priests and women can communicate on some ground other than the sexual. But because the priests have all the power, all the standard power games between men and women become exacerbated. And priests can be quite punitive to women as well. In my particular experience, though, I had much better relations with priests than with nuns, because I was untidy and mouthy, and I was not demure. There was a way in which certain kinds of priests would like you for that, but nuns never would.

In terms of what the Church thinks about female sexuality — well, who thinks anything good about female sexuality? Where would you have gone for a better message? In some ways, because the Church hated sex so much across the board, at least it was fairer. To get a message that sex is all right for men but it's not all right for women is more difficult than to get the message that it's not all right for anybody. At least that's more democratic.

In the eighth grade, I remember, there was a funny kind of sexual charge in the air all the time. There were graduation parties where there was more sex than I'd ever seen before. It was just necking — but you would go into these basements and you would neck with ten different boys with the lights out. And I've never been in a situation like that that was so kinky, before or since. But then it all stopped when you got to high school.

As a child, I was very devotional and very religious, and all our family life was shaped around Church events. I remember processions, which I loved, and Benediction, which was very important to me — the elevation of the monstrance, the gold vestments. It was also a way of being close to my parents. I've never had an event in which the real so closely approximated the ideal as my first communion. I prepared for it well and thoroughly and I felt absolutely pure. I remember that feeling of purity — it was an occasion and an event that was exactly what I had dreamed of. I was all white and everybody was all white and people were singing "Little White Guest," and it really was to me in all my life the hallmark and paradigm of purity. And confession, too. After you had made a good and, sometimes, a difficult confession, walking out of that church and feeling a lightness and singleness was beautiful and very valuable, and I don't think the secular world has any replacements for it, including the esthetic experience, which is the thing that comes closest to it. I don't think that sense of utter purity and lightness and singleness can be duplicated outside of the Church context.

The trouble with the Church now is that anybody who wants to retain the old ritual also seems to want to invade El Salvador. You have to be really suspicious of people who want to return incense and Latin, because they often have a political and a sexual agenda that's really scary. On the other hand, the people on the Left who are doing all sorts of good works want to play Peter, Paul, and Mary for you and have Sister Corita posters hanging on the walls. They kind of got stuck in 1965. I don't know what there is to move forward to — you can't replace Peter, Paul, and Mary with Prince. But when you get stuck in a not particularly distinguished historical moment, that's a real tragedy. Better to get stuck in the thirteenth century than in 1965; better to get stuck in ''Pange Lingua'' than ''Blowin' in the Wind.'' And that seems to be what's happened to the Church esthetically. When you have created an environment that doesn't value the esthetic and that essentially pushes artists out, then you can't expect to have a liturgy with any esthetic content. And so it seems to me they're reaping what they've sown. Also, if you have a situation which only allows male celibates into positions of central power, you're stuck, because the chance of a male celibate being really accomplished is probably not very high.

The Church has been criticized for having celibate males instruct the faithful on their marriages, but what's worse now in the modern Church is when the married couples advise you. When you hear Kevin and Jean telling you about bringing Jesus into your bedroom — I'll take Father O'Malley any day. A friend of mine overheard one of these Catholic couples at a meeting actually say, ''We've come to look on oral sex as a quasi sacrament.''

They're still supposed to tell you not to practice birth control — now you're supposed to test your cervical mucus instead. I have gone, just for a goof, into some of these Catholic stores and they have little cutouts that you paste on the calendar to indicate when you can have sex because your cervical mucus is okay, and so on. Meanwhile women are shoving things up inside themselves every fifteen minutes, which I guess is marginally more effective than rhythm, but not too much so. It's the same ethic slightly tarted up by pseudotechnology. They're holding hands and taking communion together, and that's supposed to be modern and hip. But you still can't get divorced, you still can't practice birth control, you can't have sex outside marriage or before marriage, and God forbid you should have any homosexual experiences. The agenda is the same, but it's all tarted up with this fake openness which is no more open than Father O'Malley. At least his language fit his message, and at least the form and the content had a kind of conjunction.

I feel an absolute sense of anomaly in trying to hold on to faith in some way. I have very marginal communities. I'm involved in the fight for Catholic abortion rights, for example, and I have a kind of community there and among some Catholic feminists. And then I have isolated friends who have religious lives, too. But when I go into a regular church, I feel like a total freak. And so I'm constantly thinking that there's no place for me in the Church—it's just that there's no place else for me to go if I want to have some sort of religious life. I'm still practicing Catholicism, but I'm not sure that the Pope thinks I am. At a certain point during my adolescence, the whole thing began to seem so ridiculous that it had no pull for me. It wasn't any big trauma wherein I wrestled with demons in the dark and either won or lost. It just began to seem of no interest to me. I guess as I began writing more and more and I began confronting in my writing a lot of the issues which really stemmed from my child-hood, I began to see that I had a kind of religious hunger and that I had shaped many experiences in religious terms. But there still is no place for me to go in the Church. It's only because it is a potential source for me —and has been in the past in isolated moments—of such beauty, of a kind of beauty that cannot be replicated in the secular context, that I sort of stay in.

At its best, the Church is also a source of tremendous idealism and charity. It's a combination of the esthetic ideal and the ethical ideal, both of which, to me, have a kind of purity that you don't find elsewhere. The best of what I consider Catholicism that I can feel touched by and touch combines that esthetic and moral intensity, and an image of love and responsibility and beauty that feeds you and enables you to go on with it. But the reality of life in the Church now has nothing to do with that. So I don't know, I'm probably after some fantasy. There are places like St. Joseph's in the Village that are very politically active—and they have a really extraordinary music program. It's a beautiful building, and it doesn't have Sister Corita all over the walls. They're also always in trouble with the archdiocese.

The American Church is an immigrant Church, and immigrants—except for Jews, who are anomalous in valuing learning and culture—don't value

the arts. What's important to them is feeling financially secure. Many of
them came from absolutely terrible conditions, so you can't blame them.
But the American Church is not only an immigrant Church but an *Irish*
immigrant Church. If you go to Ireland, you won't find any architecture
to speak of. You have a whole country with about three decent buildings
in it. It's just extraordinary. There's also no painting, there's no cuisine,
and there's no fashion. Anything having to do with the corporeal is of no
interest to the Irish. All their genius goes into language, it seems to me,
because language is incorporeal and therefore not so corrupted, or at least
somewhat free of the taint of the body.

In Ireland, you also have a whole culture in which sexual repression
was successfully institutionalized and carried out. It has been traditionally
a culture with the latest marriage age and the smallest illegitimacy rate at
the same time. The result was a whole bunch of people who, during their
most productive sexual years, were not engaging in sex. They were waiting
till their thirties to get married—it was like China.

I think that the American Church follows in being Irish, immigrant,
and working class. Why would you expect anything else of it? To expect
that you're going to have the Medicis because the Medicis happen to be
Catholic, too, is really illusory. A friend of mine said, "The proof that
it's really Jews who keep culture alive in America is that the only block-
buster show at the Met that has bombed was the Vatican show." The
Catholics couldn't get people out for that. And so it seems to me that we
are all Irish Catholics in America, whatever our ethnicity. The Church is
shaped by the Irish, certainly the hierarchy is, particularly in the East—
people tell me the Midwest is more German. But the whole tone is Irish,
so to be Catholic in America is to be Irish Catholic.

Historically, Ireland didn't have the Renaissance, and it didn't have the
Enlightenment. It was really a Third World country. The great age of
Irish culture and artistic achievement was over by the end of the Middle
Ages, so they didn't have the great public buildings, the squares, the
fountains, the roads, the avenues, the courthouses, all those things which
are Renaissance and then eighteenth- and nineteenth-century phenomena.
Ireland didn't have that; they were too poor. They were a very poor colony
of England, and that accounts for an awful lot. Esthetically, Ireland went
from the Middle Ages to the twentieth century—and the twentieth century
is not such a great century for public art. Whereas the Italians had a rich
visual tradition which had a continuity from the Middle Ages through to
the modern, the Irish didn't. There's no Irish street life—it's too cold,
it rains too much, and people are much more inward. When the Irish
Church started to get a lot more puritanical and repressive in the nineteenth

century, communal dancing, for instance, was very much frowned upon
as sexually dangerous and improper.

One of the reasons for this sexual repression was the famine which
occurred in the 1840s — although you have to understand that that was
only the most well known in a series of famines. One of the prevailing
popular interpretations of the famine was that it happened because people
had too many children too quickly and then they subdivided the land and
the land in turn became untenable. So it was very much encouraged, from
the mid-nineteenth century on, that it was only the bog Irish who got
married and had sex and propagated all the children. And then death
followed. I think there's a very strong race memory in the Irish that sex
is linked with death in a literal way. What they were told was that to keep
the land viable you couldn't be getting married and having all those
children. It was only after the famine that primogeniture became the
rule — and that created its own kinds of heartaches, too, because there
was then nothing for the younger sons. The notion of the succeeding sons
entering the priesthood and the military and so forth didn't apply because
again you're talking about a poor country: Ireland didn't have an army,
and to go into the Church you had to have an education. These poor people
didn't have access to that either. So what they did was emigrate to America.

The Church has an easier time with homosexuality than with abortion.
Abortion is what really frees women. If you can't put them under the
interdiction of pregnancy, then they have a lot more power, and power
is something the Church really doesn't want to give up. You cannot get
excommunicated for being homosexual or advocating homosexuality, but
you can be excommunicated just for being the taxi driver who drives a
woman to get an abortion. There are only six grounds for excommunication
in canon law now, and four of them are connected with abortion.

There were some good things about growing up in the Church. But I
think all the good things got lost, and what got retained was the authoritarian structure and the prejudices against women and sexuality, and that's
never been touched. But the part of the Church which said, "We are
distinct from the world and from the corruption of the world" — which
had a certain value — *that* got lost. Now they want to be just as yuppie
as everybody else.

One of the great sadnesses is that most of the people I know who left
the Church left it because of sex. That's not all that the Church is about,
but it has become *the* thing, that if you can't knuckle under sexually then
you have to leave. Well, I'm not going to give in to them on that because
there are other issues and sex is not one of the most important ones in a

religious life. There are things that a religious life can give you that no other kind of phenomenon can, and to lose it all because you disagree with somebody about masturbation is unfair. "They" set it up that way. If people who really long to be back in the Church don't come back because they disagree with the Church on sex, then "they" have won. Then "they" have the whole Church to themselves on a minor issue. And by "they" here I guess I mainly mean the forces of reaction — some of them are lay, some are clergy, some are hierarchy. But they are the prevailing power structure at every level of the Church, from the parish council to the Vatican.

I think you just have to address this issue by witness. If you say, "I am not going to let you reserve the riches of the Church only for people who agree with you on these things," then you're at least a witness. You're saying, "You do *not* reflect the hearts and minds of all Catholics, because there is another way of being Catholic. Eventually you are going to come around, because the future is on our side, not yours." I mean, I hate to see the Church being taken over by inferior people because they're the only ones who don't have problems with the Church's sexual message. That's the real tragedy.

I guess what I see as valuable in the Church is a very high ethic of love which exists in the context of the whole of European civilization and a very rich history — as opposed to Protestantism, which always seems very limited in either a historical or a geographical context. And there's a great esthetic experience which I guess isn't around anymore but used to be and which could potentially be recovered in some way. The fact is that I do like, on the whole, Catholic cultures better than Protestant cultures. I like France and Italy and Mediterranean cultures, and I like Ireland, whereas I have *no* attraction to Scandinavia or Germany. If I die without ever seeing Sweden, that's just fine by me. If I die never having spoken the word *fjord*, that's okay. There is something about the impress of Catholic culture that I seem to be esthetically attracted to beyond the confines of religion. Although I'm not particularly proud of the fact, I'm not at all drawn to Eastern cultures, either. Buddhism is too radically dualistic, and Hinduism is just too busy for me — there's too much going on.

In addition, some of the nuns and priests are really in the streets, doing things that you and I wouldn't have the stomach for, and they do it every day. They *are* with the homeless and the poor and the imprisoned, they are performing the corporal works of mercy in a very pure way that I find impressive. I think that kind of idealism still goes on in the Church. You certainly don't find that in the Christian Right, with the fundamentalists. One of the things that I do value in the Church is a reverence for the poor—as opposed to the notion that our mission is to make them stop being poor and that if they would stop being poor, then we would have fulfilled our mission. The subtext to a lot of Protestant fundamentalists is that if you get your act together with Jesus you'll also raise your yearly income, and I don't think that's part of the Catholic Church. There has never been a real notion that being a good Catholic will help you get ahead in the world—as a matter of fact, there was a kind of reverse pride, to the effect that if you have gotten ahead in the world maybe you'd better question whether you're a good Catholic or not.

I think the whole question of humility is an interesting one. It seems to me that probably the only place in the twentieth century where the word *humility* was regularly used was in a Catholic church or school. But it does have an importance as a virtue. It was so misused by the Church that it turned into self-hatred or fear or sycophancy, but that's the perversion of it. There is a kind of genuine humility which tells you that you are *not* the center of the universe, and I think a lot of people could use a nice dose of that.

JOSÉ TORRES

The Religion of Machismo

> We are cultural Catholics. . . . Catholicism is to us now not so much a
> system of beliefs or a set of laws but a shared history. It is not so much
> our faith as our past.
> —Anna Quindlen
> *New York Times*, June 18, 1986

When José Torres was coming up in the boxing world, collecting six of
his first eight straight wins by knockouts, writers such as Gay Talese
rhapsodized that he was bringing the blood back to a sport etiolated by
television. "Fight managers have complained for years," Talese wrote
in 1958, "that today's boxers, handicapped by literacy and slum clearance,
lack the killer instinct of the ring's former maulers and Piltdown types."
As sometimes happens in the clairvoyant world of sports writing, it worked
out both ways. Fighters like Torres and Cassius Clay did revivify a fight
business that was on the ropes. But they also showed a different era of
boxing, peopled with a different kind of boxer, to its seat. Even more
than Muhammad Ali, Torres was surrounded from the beginning by writers
and intellectuals who were attracted to him as much for his spirited punch-
ing ability as for his desire to be more than a mere athlete.

Norman Mailer, Pete Hamill, Jimmy Breslin, Victor Navasky, and Budd
Schulberg all seemed fascinated by his combination of brawn and literacy.
Perhaps predictably, their relationships brought down the confused ire of
both athletic and intellectual circles. "For some reason," Torres once
complained to Hamill, "all the sports writers think there's something
wrong with me because I hang around with people like Norman. I don't
understand the logic. Would I be a better fighter if I hung around with
drug addicts or bank robbers or vacuum cleaner salesmen? When I say

I'm working on a novel, everybody says, What's a fighter doing writing a novel? I say, What's a fighter doing *not* working on a novel?'' On the other hand, there were skeptics like Tom Wolfe, who once referred to the New York socialites' ''courting of pet primitives such as the Rolling Stones and José Torres.''

Torres emerged not only as the first Puerto Rican ever to become light heavyweight champion of the world but also as the author of *Sting like a Bee*, the best-selling book on Muhammad Ali, and as columnist and feature writer for *El Diario*, the *New York Post* and the *Village Voice, Ring* magazine, and the *Atlantic Monthly*. His writing debunked boxing myths while giving a voice to the expanding Puerto Rican population of New York. In 1982, Torres was named a commissioner of the New York State Athletic Commission and since 1984 has served as chairman. Although his number one ambition is still ''to write a great novel,'' his goal as commission chairman has been to educate fighters, ''at least so they can read their contracts.'' The job has attracted no less attention than his early literary forays: Torres's rigorous maneuvers to clean up the boxing business in New York State have been pounded by both the fight promoters and the media. As for those who feel that boxing should be abolished altogether, Torres aligns himself with the conservative black academic Thomas Sowell, who holds that people who want to put an end to boxing are invariably white liberal elitists—who he feels have lost sight of the fact that few other vehicles out of the social cellar exist for America's perennial underclass.

Torres maintains that he himself was never really poor, that his father—an independent businessman in Puerto Rico, where José was born—was actually a Republican. He knows that he lives better than most immigrants in a country that has largely done its best to ignore its Hispanic population. Torres thinks that the Church has had much the same attitude, a situation which would appear to be foolhardy when one considers that the fastest rising subgroup of American Catholics is Latins. In the past, the Vatican has shown more concern for Latin Catholics in countries like Brazil and Argentina than for their North American counterparts. One could even speculate that the pontiff's tour of the American Southwest may have been aimed specifically at changing that perception.

Clearly, José Torres thinks of himself as a cultural Catholic, and pretty much has from childhood. On the summer day he came to my apartment to talk, he was dressed in a pale blue *guayabera* shirt, white slacks, and black Beatle boots—and a small gold crucifix dangled prominently from a chain around his neck. He's the first to admit that he never had much affection for the Church and never felt much in return. But I wouldn't want to be the one to tell him to take off the crucifix.

IN PONCE, Puerto Rico, and so was my mother. My
k-skinned, black. His name is Andrés Torres, and his
Francisco. I can remember when my grandfather died,
/ anything about death then, so it wasn't a sad moment
eird, though, because I saw my father going berserk and
dfather must have been a slave when he was young, I'm
was a carpenter who used to build wooden houses and
fore that, he told me, he used to work at the Puerto Rico
a guy who eventually became the governor of Puerto Rico,
campaign for him also. Later he became the first president
union on the docks, then he became president of the local

I used to go to private school — I assume that the payment
en a dollar a month or something. And my grandfather used
the penny every day for school — this was in 1939 or 1940,
ed when I was five or six and he was around ninety. He was
k man. When he was dying in bed he called my father and
bring me a woman, and bring me food, and I will not die.''
ty-three children by seven or eight women, but he married my
father's mother. My father was proud that he married *his* mother. I met
only about twelve of those thirty-three kids.

My mother is very light-skinned. She was an illegitimate child. Her
mother, my grandmother, whom I met — she's still alive — is a mixture
of Spanish white and Caribbean Indian. She used to work for a landowner
who fucked around with all the women who worked for him, and that's
how she got pregnant. My mother was illegitimate for a while. When I
was coming up in boxing, the guy called my mother and gave her his
legal name. He died about fifteen years ago. Once in a while I'll go to
some big activity in Puerto Rico, and I'll find relatives on his side that I
never met — they come out of the woods because I'm now a celebrity.
Professional guys, too. ''Hello, I'm Dr. Rivera,'' a guy will say to me.
''I'm your mother's first cousin.''

My father is now about seventy-one, my mother is sixty-nine. They
had seven children. My father was very close to his father, very conservative and Republican, but over time he came to be more pragmatic. In
Puerto Rico, for instance, he once voted for a Democrat because I was
campaigning for the Democrat, and in New York he voted for Mario
Cuomo because I worked for Cuomo. And he would vote for Badillo
because blood is thicker than water. But before that he was a very staunch
Republican in Puerto Rico. The experience I had when I was a kid, which

I only became aware of much later, was that people used to praise my father by saying, "You know, your father is a *white* black man." That was praise. In other words, he was black, which is no good, but he acted white. My father always had his own business, always had a job, and worked all his life for his seven children. He was considered middle class because we ate meat three or four times a week and because we would not line up with the rest of the people on the welfare line. I used to get beat up in my house if I went barefoot because it was considered an insult to the dignity of the family to have no shoes. Going barefoot was a symbol of poverty, just like standing on the welfare line. I came to that conclusion much later—when I was a kid, I figured it was just bad, period. Like smoking. Nobody can smoke around my father, even now. He would not let his wife or the kids smoke. My mother is sixty-nine and she still smokes in the bathroom.

The first time I got into trouble with the law, I was sixteen. Along with two other kids, I stole a car. My father was away in the United States and he had to cut the trip short to come back to Puerto Rico. When I found out that they had called him and he was coming back—I wasn't actually in the jail cell yet, I was in the prison office—I said, "Put me in the fucking cell." I beat the case, but my father had to spend a lot of money on lawyers. And the judge said to me, "Legally you are off the hook, but I know that you committed the crime." That was the *judge*. I am *sure* that my father used political clout to get me out—he was very close to the mayor.

At seventeen I went into the army and lied about my age—I forged my mother's signature to go and volunteer in the U.S. Army. They caught me nine months later, but at eighteen I joined the service anyway. When I went into the army, that's when I started boxing. I never boxed institutionally before. I used to box in the street, fistfight. I probably had three or four fistfights a week. Don't forget, during the war I was five, six, seven, and I saw many soldiers in Puerto Rico. I used to go on Sundays to see war pictures, and to me the tall, blond, English-speaking male was the superior being. That I remember. It came back to mind when I went into the service—my volunteering was a result of that childhood. I wanted to be an American. I wanted to have the uniform, which was also a symbol of superiority. When I began to box, I knew that I could not become champion of the world because I was not one of those people—I was not tall, blond, an authentic soldier. I was a phony soldier. Boxing taught me a lot of things. When I began to knock these guys out—Hey, shit, look at this white guy on the floor! But I didn't even look at them as white guys, particularly. He was an American to me—I'd hit an American and he went down. My head was full of that kind of bullshit.

Because I grew up in a subculture of poverty, even though I was middle class, boxing was considered a way out. It was a good thing to do. Social conditions superseded religious considerations. My father did not oppose me. My mother did not accept it, but that wasn't because of religious reasons — she was more concerned for my health. She went to see one fight, the first one I ever had. She saw a minute or two, then she began to shake. She got diarrhea and had to go to the bathroom. She stayed in the bathroom praying until she found out I won. Never saw another fight.

We had an altar in the house with statues and pictures of saints, Jesus Christ, crosses, candles lighted all the time — and my family prayed to it. My wife is the same way. It was a Catholic culture. I used to go to church every Sunday, but there was no Catholic school there. I went to what we used to call "particular school," *escuela particular*, which means public school. Those were either Methodist or Baptist schools. (My youngest kids went to Catholic schools, and some of them went to private junior high and high school. One of them is now a colonel in the air force.) Eventually they got a Catholic school and my two brothers went there, but at the time there was no parochial school. The Baptist and Methodist churches had schools, so I went to those. But it was just part of the culture to go to church on Sunday — and movies. Church in the morning and movies in the afternoon.

Holy Week in Puerto Rico, which we called *Semana Santa*, was something very special. They had the procession and I used to go to sing in the procession. Most of the Catholic songs that I learned were learned in the procession. But I didn't like going to church, and I would not go to confession. Thinking back now, I realize that I really resisted Catholicism. I don't remember ever taking my first holy communion. They tried to make me go to Mass on Sunday and to receive communion, but I always looked for ways out of it. I think that my father was not very religious himself, in the sense of going to church, and that may be why they didn't put more pressure on me, since my father was the ruling force in my house.

I always considered myself a Catholic, even when I didn't go to church. When I got married, I told the priest, I said, I believe in God and I'm a Catholic. Unlike Pete Hamill, for example — he was an altar boy, and now he's an atheist. I'm not an atheist. I'm a believer in a very strange way. Some people consider me agnostic, but I think I'm a believer. But Pete, I think it was that background that forced him to be anti-everything. My kids are the same way. They're going to Catholic school, but they got so happy when the principal died. It was outrageous. Their Mother Superior was so tough that when she died nobody missed her. I felt so bad. But I sent my kids there for the discipline—because it was in New York City. If they were growing up in Ponce, there'd be no need to send them to a disciplinary school.

In my family, Catholicism was more culture and habit. We all went to church. My sisters all had communion, my brothers had communion. But I was excepted, I don't know why. I was a bad kid—a nice, bad kid. I used to fight a lot. I used to steal sugar cane and mangoes. I used to throw rocks at rooftops. My father felt that you didn't have to go to church to behave like a good human being. I assume that even though he was very Republican and conservative, he was also practical in that sense, and I'm the same way. We used to have a picture of Christ on the wall, and I remember one time my father's partner got mad because his son, who was working for him, misspelled *voucher* with a *b* instead of a *v*. He said, "How the hell could you write *voucher* with the *b* of *bicho* (which means 'prick') instead of *v* of *vaca* (which means 'cow')?" I was on the floor laughing. He said, "You know, I've got to curse somebody." He saw the crucifix hanging there and he said, "I don't want You to be the fucking witness to this shit." He slapped the crucifix and began to curse God for his son's misspelling of this word. He's dead now, this guy, but he used to be so funny. He used to drive drunk all the time—when it was okay to drive drunk!

We have a saying in Puerto Rico that is very insulting to God, which is: *Me cago en Dios*. That means "I shit on God." Whenever you get mad, "I shit on *God*!" I would never say that. I felt it was blasphemy. If anyone used that expression in front of me, I would cross my fingers. By the way, I still do it unconsciously. Just now when I was talking to you, I did it. Because that way I stop the curse from going to God.

I knew guys in Puerto Rico who used to go to church every Sunday—more than every Sunday, two or three times a week. They were married guys with girlfriends. They were very respectable, but they had girlfriends. Every week they would go to confession to get forgiveness from God for the girlfriend. I have the notion that in Puerto Rico every woman who is going to get married knows that the guy is going to have a girlfriend. You cannot confirm that—you cannot humiliate her with the girlfriend—but she knows that you're going to have a girlfriend. And they can get a gun and kill the girl if they know positively. Based on that notion, whenever a Puerto Rican man fools around or goes out with the girls and somebody tells his wife, he says it's not true. Even though she has evidence, he just acts like she's crazy. Because the doubt is very good—she's not absolutely sure, and that's the way you can control the situation. They expect you to have a girlfriend, but they don't want to be absolutely *sure* that you have a girlfriend.

And that has to be the result of Catholicism. For instance, I had an experience with a girl who would not accept oral sex. I know her mother, who is very Catholic and who controls her. I said to this girl, "How come you like to do it, and you don't like it to be done to you?" That's very strange because I've known a woman who would not do it to a man, but she would welcome it. So I know this has to be Catholicism. She's a good person, a professional, smart as hell. But she said it was because of hygiene, that it's not clean. At first I thought it was unusual. But if you go out with many Puerto Rican girls, you find out that it's not unusual. This girl doesn't go to church; she claims to be agnostic. Bullshit. In Puerto Rico, they think that the Puerto Rican girls in the United States are liberal, promiscuous, and that in Puerto Rico you have to marry the girl before she gives up her virginity. Over here, the Americans feel that the Puerto Rican woman, *in* Puerto Rico, is very promiscuous. But it's only a perception—I think that it's the same. The only difference is that here there's only one parent, usually.

Let me tell you one interesting story about Puerto Rican culture in terms of boys and girls. It is okay for a boy to be naked, but it's not okay for a girl to be naked. It is okay for a mother and father to play with a boy and to make comments about the boy's sexuality, but not about the girl. In other words, you can say to the boy, "What is this for? This is for the woman, right?" You cannot say the same thing with a girl. You cannot play with a girl's part the way you can with a little boy's. It is cute to see a boy naked, but not a girl. *Machismo* is part of the religion. *Machismo* is an extension of the idea that God is a man. If someone were coming to the house, even another woman, the mother would run to cover the girl if she was naked, but not the boy.

Also, even though racism is more subtle in Puerto Rico, it is still whispered about by upper-middle-class, middle-aged women—and they're all Catholic. These women will not allow their kids to marry somebody dark, boy or girl. They want the kids to marry somebody lighter "to improve the race." There is a stereotype of what a Puerto Rican should look like. My mother is absolutely white, almost blond, and my father is very black, as I said. Now, my grandmother's favorite of all us kids was the firstborn, Andrés. One time—I must have been ten or twelve—we did something bad. You have to understand that my father didn't pull any punches with us—he beat the shit out of us with his belt. So he started hitting my brother so hard that he drew blood. My grandmother pulled my brother away from my father, turned to my mother, and said, "I told you not to marry this fucking animal. These people are animals!" Meaning blacks. Meanwhile, she had this black kid in her hands and she was defending him.

The impression we always had of the Catholic Church when we were in Puerto Rico was that they are with the poor. But the Catholic Church in New York, for example, is an elite group. Not every Puerto Rican can talk to the cardinal. The cardinal shows up at places like the funeral of Javits, but if a poor Puerto Rican dies, forget it. And another thing. Three years ago, my mother and father wanted to celebrate their fiftieth anniversary. We decided to have it at St. Patrick's Cathedral. They said fine, do you want a big ceremony or a small one? I said I wanted a big thing because I wanted to invite a lot of people. Fine. We went to negotiate and they said they wanted a donation of two or three hundred, whatever it was. Okay. But we wanted to sing one particular religious song in Spanish. We had a nice celebration and took pictures and everything, but they would not sing the song we wanted to sing in Spanish. And if they think I'm going to give them a donation, they're crazy. I never paid them.

When I was boxing, I always prayed. I kept a picture of Christ. I had a crucifix, and I crossed myself before a fight. I prayed before the first round for the whole fight. Even now, I pray at night before I go to bed. I cross myself before I take a shower—that's a habit from my mother. My mother used to bathe me every day, but before she put the water on me she would make me cross myself, and I got the habit from her, even though I don't go to church anymore. When I fly on a plane, I cross myself because I'm afraid and I figure that God will help me. Cus D'Amato, my manager who died a few months ago, never flew. He was afraid of heights and afraid of planes. I said once, "Cus, when your number comes up, your number comes up." He said, "That's okay, but I don't want to be in the plane when the *pilot's* number comes up."

Sometimes I ask myself if I really believe in all this. I say I have to believe if I'm praying before I go to bed or on an airplane when I'm afraid. The thing is, I'm practical, and I have to have an explanation. And the explanation of the Catholic is—faith. You believe, period. You don't need any justification, any evidence of the existence of God. I had a couple of experiences when I was a kid, about fifteen. When we had heavy rainfall in Puerto Rico, the river used to do what we called "grow." And *el golpe*, the "punch," of the river was our word for a lot of water coming down the mountains bringing everything with it, outhouses and animals. And when that happened, we would jump into the river to get the pigs and chickens and goats that were going to drown. One time, one of us jumped in to grab a chicken and the current caught him. I jumped in to pull him back, but after I reached the kid I couldn't get back because the pressure from the current was so tremendous. So I closed my eyes and began to pray. Thirty or forty seconds later, I realized that I wasn't feeling any water pressure. I opened my eyes and saw that we were on the shore. No explanation. The only explanation was that something very mysterious happened, and I connected that with God. Also, I think about the way we're made — it's very mysterious. That has an explanation, of course, but how the fuck did it start? They say we're made of molecules, but where did the molecules come from? I hope there's something.

But it's hard for me to believe in any religion. No matter how good the intentions of the man who starts the religion, the politicians always take over.

MARTIN SCORSESE

In the Streets

You don't make up for your sins in church. You do it in the streets. You
do it at home. The rest is bullshit and you know it.
—Harvey Keitel in *Mean Streets*

Mean Streets is a religious statement. Can you really be a saint in this day?
—Martin Scorsese, *Time*, November 1973

Why does it seem as if the lapsed Catholic artists are the ones who can't
keep the religion out of their work? I don't know another major American
filmmaker whose movies are more thoroughly steeped in the ethos and
essence of Catholicism than Martin Scorsese. Although Scorsese probably
hasn't made a film so overtly obsessed with sin, penance, and redemption
and so loaded with literal Catholic images since his 1973 *Mean Streets*
—filled as it is with in jokes that only priests or former altar boys can
decipher—he still keeps his hand in. In his most recent work, *The Color
of Money*, which features its own versions of the fall and resurrection,
Fast Eddie Felson (Paul Newman) explains his motivation by saying, only
somewhat wryly, ''I get high on the Man upstairs.''
    Bits and pieces of Scorsese's message have shown up in each of his
feature films as recurring themes. But the movie that might come closest
to conveying what he has to say in its entirety is the one he hasn't yet
been able to make. Since 1973, Scorsese's attempts to realize a cinematic
adaptation of Nikos Kazantzakis's controversial novel *The Last Temptation
of Christ* have come up empty. By 1983, he had acquired a script by Paul
Schrader, scouted locations in Israel and Tunisia, and cast Aidan Quinn
as Christ and Harvey Keitel as Judas. Quinn was en route to the location
sometime around Thanksgiving that year when Paramount pulled the plug.
According to Scorsese, the film studio had received a series of letters

written by Christian fundamentalists warning Paramount not to get involved with the book's unorthodox depiction of Jesus Christ. Still, it's
unquestionably the film Scorsese wants most to make, the one he seems
almost fated to undertake.

Scorsese has said of *Mean Streets*—not his first feature film but the
first to get significant theatrical exposure in this country—"I wanted to
give all the hints about what I wanted to say, but not make the statement."
Presumably he's saving the statement for *Last Temptation*. But a revealing
precursor to *Mean Streets* is the treatment for a film Scorsese never shot,
which stands in relation to *Mean Streets* much the way *Stephen Hero* does
to *A Portrait of the Artist*—and it shows the influence of those books.
In his fifty-page outline for *Jerusalem, Jerusalem!* five Catholic school
boys suffer through a Jesuit retreat every bit as harrowing as the one
recounted by James Joyce half a century earlier—complete with Stations
of the Cross and a fire and brimstone sex sermon—and the protagonist
has a hallucination almost identical to the one Scorsese describes in this
interview. The epigraph for Scorsese's treatment is taken from the es-
teemed French director Robert Bresson's *Diary of a Country Priest:* "God
is not a torturer. . . . He only wants us to be merciful with ourselves."

Scorsese's interviews have been strewn with references to unconsum-
mated plans for films he wanted to make next—usually streetwise scenarios like the one set in the garment district (where both his parents have
worked) or the movie about a Mother Cabrini he envisions as an unsaintly
saint who "hustled in the streets and clawed her way through society."
Yet Scorsese's remarks merely serve to convince us that all of his films
are in some way about the neighborhood where he grew up and its claus-
trophobic sense of community. If the unifying theme of his movies is the
possibility of redemption, it's a redemption that has meaning only as it
is achieved in the context of those urban byways, from Little Italy to
Soho. The work of few directors can so clearly be tallied as a continuous
effort to transfigure their immediate surroundings, with no quarter asked
or given. And unquestionably, it seems, Catholicism is the determining
force in Scorsese's sense of that environment.

Although Scorsese is no longer a churchgoer, he does not so much
reject Catholicism in his films as try to find ways to bring Christ's principles
to bear on the narrow streets and close quarters of the city landscape. If
he ever does get to make *Last Temptation*, it will probably all be set in
back rooms, bars, and alleyways. No wonder the fundamentalists are
concerned.

Marty Scorsese talks fast, fitting, as the *Washington Post* once put it,
"four words in the space God made for one." In the format of this book,

it isn't possible to do justice to that kind of volubility without finally decaffeinating the speaker a bit. For a taste of the real thing, I suggest watching his all too brief appearance as a speed-rapping jazz club owner in Bertrand Tavernier's *Round Midnight*.

As it happened, our interview took place in the heart of the city at the Brill Building on Broadway, in a looping room — the studio where dialogue is sometimes dubbed onto films during postproduction. It was a cold, efficient kind of room, by contrast with his office, whose walls jump with Technicolor posters for *Two O'Clock Courage*, starring Tom Conway and Ann Rutherford, *Comanche Station* with Randolph Scott ("She wasn't the white woman he'd bought. . . . But she was the white woman he was going to keep!"), and Nick Ray's *Bitter Victory* ("The Desert Commando Raid They Wiped Off the Record Books!"). Yet even in the bareness of the looping room and dressed in a conservative suit, Scorsese appeared to be having a great time, laughing and talking to beat the band. More so than most lapsed Catholics, he appears to savor the Church he left and to hold no grudges.

ᕭ I WAS BORN and lived my first eight years in Corona, Queens. In 1950 we moved to 253 Elizabeth Street in Little Italy in Manhattan. My grandmother lived four doors down, at 241 Elizabeth Street. That's between Houston and Prince. The look of the four rooms we lived in is in my first theatrical feature film, *Who's That Knocking at My Door?* Literally. Part of that film was shot in my mother's bedroom, in that apartment. All the statuary in that bedroom is my mother's. That's real stuff that I grew up with in my house, especially the Madonna and Child. One scene, where she's combing her hair, starts in my little bedroom — the bedroom I lived in with my brother until he got married and moved out — goes to the living room, through the kitchen, and winds up in my mother's bedroom. That's exactly as I lived: in one shot you see everything. All the religious artifacts were as they were in the film; there was nothing extra-special put in. Especially the crucifixes over the beds — I think I had a little plastic one over mine.

My grandparents had very old, traditional, more European religious icons, like the large crucifix in *Raging Bull*. But my mother and father were never really very religious. They might go to Mass on Palm Sunday. That is, my mother might go, my father certainly wouldn't, but my grandparents would go. My parents never went around saying, "Oh, my children should become priests and nuns." But they would always say things like

"Go tell the priest that you said that, that's a disgrace." They used that as a weapon when they wanted to pull out all the stops. Here we get into the issue of my parents' becoming more Americanized, and not necessarily wanting to go to confession to discuss birth control with the "stranger," which is how they referred to the priest. Their attitude was that it's none of his business.

But what we had on Elizabeth Street was very interesting because around the corner on Mott Street was St. Patrick's Old Church, which was built around 1812 or 1821 when the Irish were there. There was also a parish school there, which at one time had been a Civil War hospital. The church and the school and convent are still there, in fact. They sent over Irish nuns to work in that parish — right from Ireland, with Irish brogues. But by the time I arrived, the neighborhood was all Italian, so you had a little enclave of Irish mafia religious thinking in the school which conflicted with the home lives of the Italian kids.

We had to move out of Corona for some personal reasons — I was never quite sure what those were — and we had to stay with my grandparents in their four rooms on Elizabeth Street for a while. I didn't know why I was there or what was happening. It was a very traumatic experience for me coming into a new neighborhood at that age, so I had to latch onto anything I could get my hands on for some sort of security. I had already had two or three years of public school in Corona, but I had no religious upbringing.

So I was thrown into school with these people wearing black, the nuns. I hadn't learned how to write in script yet, and my classmates already knew. The nun said, "You don't know how to do it? Just follow what I do on the board." So that's what I did. And the nuns liked me. I needed to be accepted somewhere. I couldn't do it in the streets — the kids were really rough. I had asthma, so I really couldn't play as strongly as the other kids, which meant making up games of knights in armor using garbage pails and stuff like that. They liked to play in the fire hydrants in the summer. But I wasn't allowed to do that because if I got wet, I'd get a cold and get sick.

I made some friends there, but it was a tough area, so I guess the acceptance I went for was in the Church. I started going to Mass, and those Masses were kind of theatrical. The church itself, St. Patrick's Old Church, was enormous to an eight-year-old — and it still is, it's quite a beautiful church. As a result of all that, I began to take it much more seriously than anybody in the family did.

I guess being that young and having experienced some traumatic things in that uprooting, maybe I was looking for some peace or an answer of some sort, an idea of how one achieves any kind of happiness. I wanted to be a painter, but I wasn't doing that. I began to see that the priests and the nuns were talking about God, and heaven, and hell, and religious vocations. And I started to say, Well, at least with a religious vocation a priest or a nun might have more of an inside line to heaven — into salvation, if you want to use that word. They might be a little closer to it than the guy on the street because, after all, how can you practice the Christian beliefs and attitudes that you are learning in the classroom in your house or in the street? Because my house is different, everything is different, the whole world is different.

So how do you practice these basic, daily Christian — not even specifically Catholic, but Christian — concepts of love and the major commandments? How do you do that in this world? I figured that maybe wearing the cloth you might be able to find a better way to do that. The final payoff will be salvation, therefore you'll be happy. That's when I started getting the idea of really wanting that vocation, selfishly, so that I'd be saved. Later on, obviously, it didn't work out, and I wound up finding a vocation in making movies with the same kind of passion.

The first, most important film to me was *Mean Streets*, which had the same theme: How do you lead a good life, a good, moral, ethical life, when everything around you works the absolutely opposite way? It's not necessarily criticizing all that to say that it just doesn't work that way. It's like being on another planet. That's the main theme of the picture, since I'd thought that would probably be my only film — I thought I'd be going off to direct other films, nonpersonal films, for other people, and that *Mean Streets* would never be released. That was the one I poured it all into in terms of this religious concept. That's why the opening line is "You don't make up for your sins in church. You do it in the streets." Meaning that you don't practice penance in the church, you don't hide out in the church, you don't hide out in a monastery like a monk. You gotta live amongst the people and change life that way or help people reach salvation *in the street*, through day-to-day contact, meeting by meeting. "In the street" could mean Hollywood, you know what I'm saying?

It's like a religious vocation. That's where I think a lot of my passion switched over from the priestly vocation, when I decided that wasn't the right way for me to act out these things. Mine was harder: I had to do it in the street, I had to do it in Hollywood — you gotta do it in Paris, you gotta do it in Rome, you gotta do it in New York. That's the sense of it all in terms of this Catholic thing we're talking about.

When I was thirteen years old, I went to a preparatory seminary on Eighty-sixth Street. By the time I was fourteen I got thrown out because

I wasn't paying attention anymore to my classes—I had fallen in love with some young lady, a young girl who was in another school. I just lost out on my grades. And so I went to another school called Cardinal Hayes High School; it took me four years to get my average back up to an acceptable level to get into college because I'd done so badly.

Cardinal Hayes High School was in the Bronx and was run by parish priests and brothers. The brothers were Marist Brothers—rough guys, rough guys, *really* tough. And one Franciscan priest who taught Italian was really murder—he was rougher than all of them. Then I tried to get into Fordham but I wasn't accepted because I was in the lower quarter of my class. So I decided that I wanted to go to NYU because I saw that film courses were being given. The first two years were just history and criticism in order to weed people out; hundreds of kids would sign up for it, and by the second semester they'd have five.

That was where I met Haig Manoogian [to whom *Raging Bull* is dedicated] in 1960 when he first came on the stage there and started giving his lecture about film history. He was the guy who inspired me to make movies, to put my feelings into action really. I asked my parents if I could start to take film as a major, but also English as a major somehow—because that way I would always have something to fall back on, be an English teacher, that sort of thing.

When Manoogian started talking about films that way, I became aware that the idea was to put all my feelings into films, that maybe acting out whatever good I would be doing with a vocation could be done through films. Of course, you're dealing then with the sin of pride, which is why someday I'd like to make a film about a priest who has to deal with the sin of pride—because they're human, too. But I thought that would be the thing, the same passion. Up until 1960, I had wanted to finish at Cardinal Hayes, maybe go to university for a few years, and then go into a seminary and become a priest. But once he started talking about film, I realized that I could put that passion into making movies, and then I realized that the Catholic vocation was, in a sense, through the screen for me.

When I was in grammar school with the nuns, they would tell stories and I would draw pictures of Christ on the cross. They loved it, and I would go show them to all the different nuns in all the different classes. They liked me a lot for some reason. First I said I wanted to be a missionary —they *loved* that. One nun, Sister Gertrude in my third grade, she was terrific. "A missionary!" She'd slap me in the face because she liked it so much. "Ah, this boy! I love 'im!" Either way, you got hit. "Ah, I love this boy!" Slap slap slap!

They were great, those nuns, the Sisters of Mercy. They'd tell those wonderful stories. But it's easy, in a book like this especially, to retell all of the silly stories that the nuns would say; it's like folklore. But I'll give you one, based on the notion that you should never chew the Eucharist when you get it into your mouth. You should swallow it, and you should never do any kind of desecration of the Eucharist. According to the nuns, there was a woman who wanted to take home the Eucharist. And she did. She got it in her mouth, she took it back to the pew, and she took it out and put it in her handkerchief, went home, and put it in a trunk. And that night while she was sleeping, the trunk started to glow. Then blood started coming out of the trunk, you know? And then she was terrified, and she had a priest come in, and the priest took the host and put it back where it should be. So we would never touch the Eucharist after that. Forget it! You want to bring it to your house, your father'll *kill* you if the trunk starts glowing in the middle of the night. What are you gonna do? That's rough stuff.

But I think, actually, Timothy Carey in his movie *The World's Greatest Sinner* did that. The film was never released, but it's one of John Cassavetes's favorite films, directed by and starring Timothy Carey. He takes the Eucharist from the tabernacle, and—I never saw the picture but they tell me that as he's running away, the Eucharist starts glowing and blood starts to follow him all through the streets, and over the hills as he's running blood is following him. It's a wonderful idea. He's a folksinger-preacher type, plays guitar and has a snake around his neck. I know the film exists. One day, ten years ago, when we were doing *New York, New York*, I went to screen my rushes and somebody was looking at it in the next room. I walked in and I saw this guy stealing something from a tabernacle and I said, ''That's Timothy Carey!'' Listen, nobody believed me. It was like, ''This film really exists, guys!'' and ''Oh, come on, Marty, let's go look at the rushes.''

We had a priest in high school who would always complain about the nuns. One day he was stopping over someplace and he had a gilded chalice with him. The nuns took it and as a favor they washed it, washing all the gold off it in the process. He wanted to kill them. I mean, what did they *use?*

In the seventh grade we had a nun who was a little older, who had an Irish brogue and the whole thing—she was a little dotty, actually, but she was very sweet. The younger ones, the sharper ones, the very stern ones were more difficult. But this older one had odd quirks, like if you were shaking your leg—you know that nervous habit—she'd yell, ''Stop that!'' You had to stop it because that was sexual, you were enjoying it sexually, according to her. In the seventh grade they were watching you because you were twelve years old and all the sex was coming out. You used to get in so much trouble for your leg doing that.

This nun also got upset if you'd write in red ink. "What are you, a Communist?" You had to use blue ink, not even black. You know, the funny thing is I don't write in anything else but blue today. Even the Sharpies have to be blue — I can't deal with the oranges and the greens, that's for scriptgirls, or, I should say, scriptpersons.

We can talk about nun stories and it's kind of cute stuff in a way. The implication is that these nuns are so dumb and so stupid — and I don't think that's the case. They have something else in mind and, out of love, they really want to help these kids. And sometimes out of love the most terrible things are done. But they really want to help you and get your soul saved; they're not there to play around. Even if it kills ya they're gonna save your soul, and that's it.

I mentioned pride before. I remember once, in the fourth grade, we were talking about what God could do. God could do anything — but the nuns opened it up and expanded the theory. God couldn't do a squared circle, for example. There's no such thing as a squared circle, so God couldn't do that; but he could do anything. One of the kids said, "What do you mean, you can't do a squared circle?" And I said, "Well, I can do a squared circle." Sister said, "You can?" I said, "Yes." She got very upset, which I couldn't understand. She said, "Why don't you bring it to me tomorrow?" So I went home and got a compass, and I drew a circle. Then I put a square on top of it, then I erased the lines where they connected, so it became like a piece of architecture. I brought it back the next day. She looked at it, looked at me, looked at the picture, and said, "That's not a squared circle."

It's a dilemma, though. I have two kids, and I don't have them in Catholic schools. But I would like them to have some aspect of religion, Christian thought. I always think it's much harder to deal with the idea of love without retribution, as opposed to Mosaic law. I think that's the thing everybody has to go for: forgiveness. What Gandhi did was extremely hard, obviously. Much easier for everybody to run around and start retaliating, like the Hindus and Moslems all killing each other. I saw a wonderful sign that epitomized the anti-Reagan feeling that followed the Libyan attack: "An Eye for an Eye Makes the Whole World Blind."

I think Mark Twain said, "Christianity is a great idea. Too bad nobody's ever practiced it." It would really be great for the kids to have a concept of that sort of thing while they were younger. You could do it yourself. You could read parts of the Bible, you could explain the stories, you could even show them movies about it. Unfortunately, I never lived with my two children.

Maybe Catholic schools today are a little bit different. But from a purely *Roman* Catholic point of view—not Russian Catholic or Greek Catholic—there's a lot of extraneous doctrine. For instance, it was a sin to eat meat on Friday, and then, suddenly, after a thousand years, it was no longer a sin. I've been divorced a few times—therefore, technically, I'm excommunicated. I haven't gotten any letter yet or anything, but. . . . I haven't made my Easter duty in years, which technically means I'm excommunicated also. That kind of stuff prejudices the mind. Where I think the Church has failed over the years is that they have never gotten across to people the actual concept that Jesus taught in day-by-day living.

And that's not just a Church problem, it's a family problem, too, because when the kids go out of the school, they go home. When I went to my home, they didn't say anything about God or religion—forget it. They had the same kind of fear, like, "Don't do that—God sees this." And "There's a film about God, let's watch it." That kind of stuff. But that was it.

The other thing the Church does is to promote intolerance toward other groups. Their attitude toward Protestants was one thing, but the worst was the racial intolerance and intolerance against Jews. I think this is something where the Catholic Church has a long, long way to go to make up for the past two thousand years. So that's something I wouldn't want my kids getting—they get enough of that in the street or at home. I don't mean that badly, but there's enough racial prejudice at home as it is.

The Italian-Irish thing is very interesting in the sense that where I came from was an Irish neighborhood, and Italians took over. And the way we felt about the Puerto Ricans, the Irish felt about us. We felt the same way about the Irish, of course. And yet, there was an incredible amount of respect on the part of the third generation of Italians for, let's say, the films of John Ford. Anything to do with the Irish—Irish poetry, *anything*. We felt a great deal of fascination, even obsession, with Irish history because of the Catholicism and because of the family structure. If you look at *How Green Was My Valley*—of course, that was about the Welsh and everything, but still it was Ford who directed it. You know, the way the mother is called "woman of the house" by Donald Crisp when she comes in. You saw that relationship in your grandparents, you saw it in your household, and the Irish were that way. It was done mainly through films, I thought. And my friends and I identified with it immediately. We never said, "Oh, look at these micks drinking!" We laughed when we saw the drinking stuff. *The Quiet Man* we *loved*. My family *adored The*

Quiet Man. I find Irish and Italians to be so similar that maybe that's why they can't get along. *So* similar.

Again, with organized crime, first you had the Irish gangs in New York, and then the Italians came over and showed them *really* how to do it. You want perfection, you bring Renaissance thinking into this and *realllly* make it pay, make it work. And they became the cops, the Irish. That was terrible because then they had a moral position over you. At least a bad guy's a bad guy—which is not to say that he's doing any better. But these guys, the Irish cops, are saying, "We are morally superior—but in the meantime, could you give us five bucks?"

I was just talking to a friend of mine, a guy who recently got into a car accident. He had two plates of lasagna in the car that he was bringing home for his family for Mother's Day. And when he went back for the car, the lasagna was gone. So everybody at the table said, "Ah, the cops got it." They didn't mean it badly. The cops probably said, "Why should it go to waste?"

Did I ever feel that I was communicating directly with God or having spiritual experiences? Constantly. I think that in a funny way that still goes on. A lot of it is still there. I hoped it was as simple as it was before, but it isn't anymore. It culminated in a retreat that I went to when I was in high school, in which I had a vision of some sort, which was really more a fright vision than anything else because I was feeling guilty about things. I wound up in a very bad state for which the priest's only advice to me was to see, when I got back, a very good Catholic psychiatrist.

These were new-type priests; when they spoke to you they had T-shirts on. They gave great sermons, but then eventually the old fire and brimstone sermon did it, you know? Exactly like *Portrait of the Artist.* Elements of it show up in *Mean Streets*, where Harvey Keitel is talking about the story of the girl and the guy who make love in the priest's car, and the car gets hit by a truck and blows up before they have a chance to make an act of contrition.

Now it's very important that we get this point across to anybody reading this: I happen to be extremely impressionable—very different from other people, I think. I may be overly sensitive to practically everything, which causes a lot of problems sometimes. This is a case where the Church got one kid like me, and I happened to take it a little too strongly. For example, my friends who were with me at the time on that retreat didn't react the way I did. And that's why in *Mean Streets* I have the guy saying, "And he *believes* the guy!" And Harvey Keitel—who is really playing my role—says, "Oh, they're not supposed to be just guys." What I meant by that is they're not supposed to be like you and me, they're supposed to be somebody to teach us, to show us. They're not supposed to lie to us.

When I explained that to my friend who was with me on the retreat, a very close friend of mine, he said, "Marty, a friend of mine a week later had the same story told at his retreat, and another guy, another guy, another guy. You understand, it's a business — they gotta get the end results. It doesn't matter how they get the result." And I said, "But I can't take it that way. There's a guy in front of a pulpit and he's *lying*. And he's taking us into his confidence. And I feel personally betrayed by it." Of course, this has more to do with me in a neurotic sense than it has to do with "Oh how horrible the Church is, look what they've done to these kids." It happened to affect me that way, so I want to be very fair about that. Although I can't have it both ways with the Church — I mean, everything they think I'll say, they'll be against, so what can I say?

I don't really think that they overemphasized sex, though, the way a lot of people say, although that business about not shaking your leg in the seventh grade was a little extreme maybe. I was more into looking at the little girls' uniforms and wondering what was underneath the uniforms. Those uniforms became very striking to me, so that later in *Who's That Knocking?* and in *Taxi Driver* I had them wear what look like parochial school uniforms. A blazer and a pleated, Scotch plaid type skirt — Cybill Shepherd wears that in *Taxi* as a kind of joke.

I had a young priest talk to us in high school and explain about the body temperature, the heat, the blood boiling in a sense — not in a literal sense, but becoming very hot, excited. And it's true, your temperature rises. They're talking about that and saying you have to be very careful, that these things happen and that they're a sign to turn away. He was trying to tell us the physical symptoms. And that was as close as they got to talking about sex in my time, which was in 1957.

At the retreat I was telling you about they did have a sex sermon — in fact they had sermons based on all the Ten Commandments. It was quite interesting and very entertaining in the way it was done. I wrote a script based on this whole retreat, called *Jerusalem, Jerusalem!*, which I never made into a film. It was the first part of a trilogy that finished with *Who's That Knocking?* and *Mean Streets*.

The fire and brimstone sermon was set off by a lecture on the Shroud of Turin and the punishment and the suffering of Jesus. Following that, one night I was in a little room in the retreat house. I was trying to read and I was kind of scared. There were no blinds on the window, at night in the country. I was also a city boy, so anything in the country, a noise, seemed scary. It became like an auditory hallucination where I heard crickets that got louder and louder and louder until they made me feel like I was going to burst. And then I saw the smudges on the window become like the face on the Shroud. That happened about three times during the night. I walked around the halls trying to get out of it.

And then I went to a special grotto to pray. If you stare at something long enough, you can make everything else fade away. It's an old trick for meditating—because meditation is the hardest thing. They always talk about meditating—"How are you going to meditate?" Any of the other thoughts that come to your mind you feel are sinful because they're distracting you. To this day I still don't quite understand what they mean by meditation.

The experience in the grotto was actually very pleasing; the one the night before was pretty bad. What I think I reached that time in the grotto was some sort of pure meditation wherein I accepted what was going to happen. It was really interesting, it was nice. I remember when I was doing *Taxi Driver*, saying to [scriptwriter] Paul Schrader, "You know what's going to happen, we're both going to wind up in a monastery somewhere, you and I." Luckily, we got over that. We were a good team because Schrader's a Calvinist.

I was an altar boy, but I was drummed out because I used to arrive late for seven o'clock Mass. My specialist altar boy training was for the Mass for the dead on Saturdays, the ten-thirty funerals. I was very good at that for some reason. They would always give me that, I don't know why—the priest wanted me to do it, so I did. I became very enamored of one particular young priest who was a breath of fresh air. I was eleven or twelve, and I really wanted to be like him, so I patterned my whole life after him.

Critically, he was also more interesting because he liked certain kinds of movies. He liked British films, especially Alec Guinness films. It kind of got into a snobby area, too, because *we* loved American movies. At any rate, I had become an altar boy before he was there and then went through four or five years with him. And then he threw me out because I would show up late—for the seven o'clock Mass, yet. I mean, gimme a break. The nuns were there to get communion and that was it, aside from maybe a few old ladies.

My disenchantment with the Church began the first time I got involved sexually with someone. I felt that it was coming out of a love state and not what they insisted was something evil. It couldn't have been evil. I remember facing that priest whom I liked a lot and going to confession and telling him all about it. He said, "Yes, but the idea is that it has to be sanctified by God. It's not evil what you did, but it has to be sanctified by God.'' It kind of made sense to me then, around sixty-four or sixty-five. I was still at NYU and making my first short films, so I was still very one-foot-here-and-one-foot-there. But I knew that sex wasn't intrinsically bad. And how offended could God get if it was something that was done out of a sense of celebration?

In 1965, I was still going to Mass. I was married then, and I had a child on the way. I went to a Mass in Union City, New Jersey, one Sunday. At that point I was a political virgin. I had no idea what was happening, but I did know that there was a lot of talk *against* the Vietnam situation. Yet a priest came out on a Sunday morning and preached from the pulpit in support of this holy war. Those poor parishioners were living in Union City, which is a depressed area. Their sons were probably going to go off and get killed. And here was this guy — an old man, too — who got up and told them it was right. I never went again. I had no political commitment, I just knew that there was something wrong.

If there's any religious theme or concept in my films, I guess the main one would be the concept in *Mean Streets* of how to live one's life. You take a microcosm like that neighborhood down there, and that becomes a macrocosm, becomes the whole world. It's a reflection of what's on the news and what's going on in the world. It's the same attitude, the same concept of greed, the same concept of pride, all that sort of thing — all played in that little play that happened in those few weeks down in Little Italy. The idea is How do you practice Christianity living this way and having to survive with these people? A lot of these growing-up pictures have the narrator or the protagonist a little more sensitive than the others: ''Oh, I'm the good, sensitive one, not like them.'' No, in *Mean Streets* we're all rotten, we're all no good in a sense, but we're still people, we're still human beings. And the lead character, being me, has to grapple with a sense of guilt because of this, because it isn't the way it is said in church. When you go two steps outside the door and you're in the street, it's totally different. And the only recognition that the Church gets is, let's say, if a priest walks by, the really strong wiseguys may tip their hat. That's a lot of respect. But that's all they ever saw.

Catholicism always comes out in the other films, too. *After Hours* has got tons of it — there it has a lot to do with the sexual aspects of it. *Raging Bull* has the idea of the suffering in it, I guess. I never really understood *Raging Bull* except after I had gone through a lot of problems myself in the mid-seventies during the making of *New York, New York* and after. There were three years between *New York, New York* and *Raging Bull*, and those were hard times. But I was able to put that suffering into the film. Later on, people told me that the suffering in that film had more to do with a Catholic sense of suffering, the daily struggle of just living.

I consciously put a few things in *Alice Doesn't Live Here Anymore*— like in the ladies' room where Diane Ladd shows Ellen Burstyn her crucifix made out of safety pins and says, "You know what this is? This is what holds me together." *Taxi Driver* is interesting because it's a clash between the Calvinist ethos and what someone called a decadent vision of Catholicism. Michael Chapman, the cinematographer, is a Protestant, and he would say, "This is so decadent!" Enjoying it, in the sense that it was so decadently Roman Catholic. He was teasing me about that one scene where the flowers were all returned and he was tracking along the flowers. He said, "Oh, that was the most decadent shot I've ever taken." We were laughing about it. I think there is also the sense of the camera sliding or crawling all through the streets, oozing with sin. You know how Travis wants to clean up the sin, and yet he's immersed in it himself. What he really wants to do is to clean *himself* up.

The Last Temptation of Christ, if and when I get to make it finally, represents my attempt to use the screen as a pulpit in a way, to get the message out about practicing the basic concepts of Christianity: to love God and to love your neighbor as yourself. Let's at least get that started, that's somewhere in the right direction—then the rest of the things we can talk about. It's almost like the mitzvahs for Jews. All these other things, the Mass and this and that for Catholics—we should reject that and start with the basics first. Let's get to understand the basics and how we can use them day by day. That was my idea—to open it up and put that on the screen. Maybe *The Last Temptation of Christ* could show that Jesus fought with the human side of His nature and let people say, "Hey, I identify with that." He had to go through the same stuff that we're going through, and yet He was able to push through because He was God also. That would've given some hope to people in the audience who had lost hope and had lost faith. And here they are complaining that the film was going to break people's faith, which is the last thing in the world I want to do, because faith is the most incredible thing you could have.

I hope *The Last Temptation* will get made because I think it's an important statement. I got a lot of resistance at first from the Moral Majority fundamentalist groups. They were the worst. The Catholic Church I think is not too happy about it, but. . . . We're not looking to shock anyone with the picture. We're not looking to do a *Hail Mary* like Jean-Luc Godard or any of that stuff. We're looking to make a film that will make people think, that will make people begin to see that maybe the best philosophy is the way Gandhi took it and to give people something to hope for.

PEGGY SCHERER

Living the Gospel

I started out committed to the "Church" and found myself committed only
to the Christ. Let those who think the two are the same, beware. The
problem is to determine where the two merge and where they do not. The
"safe" thing is to assume — as we've been taught — that there is no difference. The way of the Spirit is to struggle between the two.
—Joan Chittister, O.S.B.
    "Today I Saw the Gospel" in *Winds of Change*

It would have been hard to be a Catholic living on the Lower East Side
in the mid-sixties and not be aware of the Catholic Worker on Chrystie
Street. It was the sort of place where left-wing Catholic intellectuals liked
to go and hear Michael Harrington lecture on poverty and then break bread
with the homeless before heading off to see the latest Bergman film. I
don't mean that cynically; there was an idealism about the sixties that saw
no contradiction in such activities. The fact that there are now more
homeless than ever in New York City and that neither the Church nor the
government has taken adequate measures to house and feed them simply
underlines the relevance of the Worker's mission. The fact is that few
people have taken the gospel imperative to implement the corporal works
of mercy as seriously as have Peggy Scherer and the people with whom
she worked for many years at the Catholic Worker.

The Catholic Worker movement over the past five decades has, in
Harrington's words, "inspired Catholics to innovation in the trade unions,
the black freedom struggle, ecumenism and both the pacifist and peace
movements." That it could accomplish so much with so little institutional
support is mainly a tribute to its founders, Peter Maurin and Dorothy Day.

A convert from Episcopalianism, Dorothy Day came to live in Green-
wich Village and hang out with Eugene O'Neill and Hart Crane in the

twenties and early thirties. She had a Marxist lover and wrote for left-wing papers like the *Call* and the *Masses*, where she met John Reed. Her journalism was prescient: she wrote against German nationalism and anti-Semitism as early as 1933, attacked Mussolini's invasion of Ethiopia in 1935 and Franco's uprising in 1936. She also took on the bombing of Hiroshima and Nagasaki (*"Jubilate Deo,"* she wrote. "We have killed 318,000 Japanese") and warned against American intervention in Vietnam in 1954. On May Day 1933, with French itinerant laborer-philosopher Peter Maurin, she founded the *Catholic Worker*, a monthly newspaper that still sells for its original price of "a penny a copy." Envisioned as a direct competitor to the *Daily Worker* ("Is it not possible to be radical without being atheistic?" its first editorial asked), it was neither pro-Communist nor pro-capitalist. It was, instead, part pacifist, part agrarian idealist, always strongly pro-labor—siding, for instance, with striking New York gravediggers who left Cardinal Spellman holding the shovel in 1949. The paper reached a circulation peak of one hundred fifty thousand and no doubt helped advertise a Catholic alternative to Marxism at a time when that philosophy must have seemed attractive to a great many intellectuals and blue-collar workers.

But a better-known and possibly more significant outgrowth of the movement was the creation of a string of loosely linked Houses of Hospitality, which continue to serve the homeless in more than a hundred locations around the world. As with the *National Catholic Reporter*, Church spokesmen have sometimes tried to distance the official Church from the policies of the Catholic Worker movement, objecting to the word *Catholic* in its title. On the other hand, to admirers such as historian David J. O'Brien, Dorothy Day was "the most significant, interesting and influential person in the history of American Catholicism." Perhaps the outstanding theological contribution of Day and Maurin was their emphasis on the living out of specific teachings of Christ as revealed directly in the gospels—unfiltered by historical accommodation. The Worker's philosophy calls for literal adherence to biblical exhortations such as Christ's to the rich young man: "Go sell what thou hast and give to the poor and thou shalt have treasure in heaven. And come follow me." Such radical Christianity has found favor neither with the Church hierarchy (which has never encouraged real Bible studies anyway) nor with so-called Christian fundamentalists, who appear to cling strictly to selected lines of Scripture while mysteriously ignoring others altogether.

Peggy Scherer began writing for the *Catholic Worker* in 1975 and served as managing editor from 1979 to 1986. Although since the time this interview took place Scherer has left the Catholic Worker movement, she continues "to work for justice, to work with people who are poor and oppressed." That now includes fighting against what she feels are injustices toward the gay and lesbian community, particularly in light of the Church's recently proclaimed opposition to Dignity, a national organization of gay Catholics. Despite her differences of opinion with the Catholic Worker over this matter, she feels that the Worker taught her much about what the Church is and what participation in it means. "You can take me out of the Catholic Worker," she says, "but you can't take the Catholic Worker out of me. My pain at leaving is the greater because of how much I still love and respect and value the Worker. I don't know what the Worker as a group should be doing, but I do have a sense of what I should be doing."

What she is doing now is working with a literacy program in the Brooklyn library system, beginning paralegal study in immigration law, and continuing the work in Nicaragua which she describes in the interview. Her commitment both to the poor and to her faith remains unchanged.

I WAS BORN in Cincinnati, Ohio, as was my father before me, and grew up there. My mother was born in Kansas City, Missouri, and moved to Cincinnati at a young age. The presence of religion in my house was subtle but strong. My mother was ill when I was two or three and died of cancer when I was ten, and I remember some very kind and generous people during that time. I was aware from an early age that my father went to Mass every day. Very little was said about that, but I absorbed the fact that it was quite important to him. At the same time I could clearly see that my father was a very kind and generous person. Until I was five or six, he and a brother ran a grocery store, and then he began his own real estate business, which left him with some free time in his schedule. He was forever helping neighbors out or helping with class trips or chauffering people here and there. With almost nothing said about it that I remember, I got a sense that you kind of helped people out. And I knew that somehow that was connected to my father's faith.

I don't remember a great deal about the content of grade school, except for having to memorize the Baltimore Catechism. Lately I've even been thinking that it would be fun to go back and look at one. I remember the drawings of milk bottles that they used to illustrate varying states of sanctifying grace. At some point in my adult life it occurred to me to wonder if the fact that I liked chocolate milk had an impact on my life, because while I was being told that mortal sin — which in those drawings looked like chocolate milk to me — was bad, at the same time it tasted good. I don't want to analyze that too carefully, but. . . .

Later on I came to regret the fact that most of my understanding of my faith was by rote memorization. It all felt so Pavlovian that if somebody were to yell out "One twenty-three," I would probably respond with the appropriate answer. That's not entirely true, and I hope my life reflects that I absorbed something else along the line, much of it good. I have good memories of growing up and going to Catholic grade school at St. Cecilia's, where we had Sisters of Mercy. Various religious events go through my mind, like holy communion, but I think I have stronger memories of the party at my parents' house afterward.

Something I know has stuck with me is a sense of what truth is and that even if one fails to abide by that, the important thing is at least to recognize that you've done wrong. If you lied at home, that would be bad enough. But it would be worse to pretend you didn't lie than to admit it. My parents taught more by example than by screaming and yelling, and I'm grateful for that compared to other friends' experiences. We lived in a working-class neighborhood, and I remember a knock on the door and someone saying, "I'm hungry." I don't remember much conversation, but they would always be given food. That didn't happen often, but it did happen. So again I had the experience of what I viewed to be, then as now, a living out of the faith.

I think that in grade school, like many other people in first and second grade, I was preoccupied with the question Do nuns have knees? I don't think that lasted long. I don't remember having a hard time with any of my teachers. But I was not rebellious at that period of my life, so it was all kind of amicable. There was one other incident that in later years I realized might have had something to do with the way I view some things in the Church. In the seventh or eighth grade, our school got a new gym. And all of a sudden the girls were not allowed to go in the gym because they would mess up the floor, which was to remain nice for the boys to play basketball on. Now, I didn't like gym anyway, so in one sense I couldn't have cared less, but I did respond to what I thought was an unfair division.

I think that I grew up with less of a sense of sex roles than most of my friends. My father was a good cook and was quite capable around the house, although he wasn't mechanically inclined. With my mother ill and then eventually dying, he took over many of the household tasks. I wasn't conscious of it. All I knew was that I grew up seeing my mother working when she was well, making clothes and so on, and that my father was as likely to be in the kitchen as my mother. That just seemed right and how life should be, and I know it's had an impact on how I view things nowadays.

As I got older and entered a private girls' high school called St. Ursula's — I think the official name was St. Ursula's Convent and Academy Day School — I began to ask questions about what I was being taught in school. I began to wonder what the connection was between all these good things that I was hearing and a sense of living them out.

One of the few times I can remember ever arguing with a teacher was in my senior year when I stood up and said, "I cannot believe that everyone who is not a practicing Catholic is going to hell." And I was told that I was wrong. I didn't really know anybody who wasn't Catholic, but still it somehow didn't seem fair or correct.

About ten years after I graduated from high school and after I'd been at the Catholic Worker for two years, I was invited back to address the entire student body at St. Ursula's. Even though a number of my teachers had left, the ones still there were supportive of what I was doing. They weren't necessarily ready to engage in it, but they seemed quite intrigued that my faith had led me to refuse to pay federal taxes. The students were quite upset with what I had to say, however.

When I was fourteen and a sophomore in high school, I was invited by one of my teachers to go on a trip into the Appalachian Mountains. We went to a place called Berea, Kentucky, where a priest whose name escapes me now was doing mission work. Although in my grade school years, with the "Save a pagan baby" routine, the focus had been on foreign missions, it was suddenly time to begin to look a little closer to home. Foggy as my memories are, I recall spending most of that weekend sorting clothes that had been donated. But we also went into "hollers," and for the first time in my life I saw children who had swelled bellies and no shoes, people living in shacks with outhouses — people who clearly didn't have enough to live. On one level it was an outing, getting away from home, and I didn't think much about it. But I think it did have an impact on both my faith and my politics just to see hunger and poverty in this country.

In the meantime, I was fairly active in school, studied Latin, did all those kinds of things. But then I joined the Catholic Students Mission Crusade and became very active in that. By my senior year I was president of CSMC and went on several more trips into eastern Kentucky. Then, in October of 1966, I went with one of my teachers to what was called the Main Street Bible Center, which I later found out was sponsored by the Archdiocese of Cincinnati. It had been started by a person who at that time was a seminarian and fit into the pattern of mid-sixties social activism. It was a place where immediate emergency aid was given, and I probably had an overblown view of what my role was—I was going down there to help the poor. Well, we went into the place and a young girl who was probably ten at the time, named Belinda Waters, came up to me. She was a sullen, skinny little thing and, far from being grateful, one of the first things she did was to kick me in the shins. I don't know if I'm perverse or if other things I don't remember happened that night, but I was intrigued by the place, and within months I was spending all of my free time there.

We began to visit families. It was a black and Appalachian neighborhood, two cultures totally new to me. I graduated in May of 1967, and in June I started working there full time. By September I had moved into the neighborhood, and I have lived mostly in poor neighborhoods since then and done similar kinds of work.

Almost immediately after leaving high school, I entered a rebellious period, and as I became more socially conscious, I began to apply some of that to the Church. The fact that I turned the corner so quickly makes me wonder in retrospect if a lot of things weren't brooding and that once I was out of the house and had the freedom to explode, I exploded. Because I literally moved from my parents' house into a rectory. The rectory was run by German priests straight from Germany and two German housekeepers, and it was a huge fortress of a place built in the old German style. But they had an empty room which they offered to my friend Barbara, on the condition that she find a roommate. I jumped at the chance to move in with her. My father listened to my story and then went down and met the priests. He just assumed that if I lived in that fortress with all those Germans around—my father is of German descent—I would be safe and good. Well, some of the older Germans went to bed rather early and I had my own keys. I learned very quickly that because I cared about my father and cared about my own future, I just didn't let him know that I was running around at night.

The head priest, Father Porter, was a rather conservative, middle-aged fellow who, when I first met him, was driving a Cadillac. The center itself quickly became a stronghold of ex-religious who were angry with the Church. Father Porter soon sold his Cadillac and got a station wagon under pressure from his staff. These were people who felt very clearly that one should live out the gospel in a much more literal way than most of the Church did. All of a sudden I was thrown into a kind of training ground. Meanwhile at the rectory, the priests chose to relate almost not at all and very negatively to anyone who lived in the neighborhood. The poor were not really welcome to ring the doorbell. I began to realize that

I was living in a church and finding myself angrier against the Church than I ever was. Within months, I left the Church.

A year or so after that, I met a number of people including some Quakers who were involved in the antiwar movement, and it wasn't long before I was making the connection between poverty and injustice and war. That ended up being my college education. I had gone to the University of Cincinnati for one year and quit because it seemed so boring compared to all the other things I was doing. I had no desire to get training in any special area. And I must say that I have had an extremely rich education given all the things I've done. So the years went on and I lived in a couple of different community groups with people who were involved with the poor and with antiwar work. But toward the end of that seven-year period, I had a growing awareness that something was missing. I began to be conscious that I missed something about the Church, and I moved into a period where I was beginning to see the difference between institutions and the people in them and the difference between teachings — which could well be good — and the people who were practicing them.

I was still searching, not knowing what I was looking for or where I would find it. A pacifist group that I was involved with, called Peacemakers, was putting on two-week seminars every summer, and I offered to help. They wanted to see if the Catholic Worker farm at Tivoli in upstate New York would let us have a seminar there. I had heard of the Catholic Worker from two friends of mine, one who had had a bad experience there and spoke rather sarcastically about Dorothy Day and another who had had good experiences there. Eventually the Catholic Worker agreed to let us do the seminar, and so on June 2, 1974, I arrived in Tivoli after hitchhiking out with a friend. Walking onto the property I immediately felt at home. I think that what the Worker did for me was to bring together the core parts of the faith in which I had been raised with the political and social beliefs and practices I had come to embrace and feel I needed. They brought it into a whole which I had not previously found. I returned home long enough to finish up a commitment I had there and then packed up, returned to Tivoli, and moved in. That was twelve years ago.

I don't regret at all that I had a period outside the Church, that at some point in my life I stepped back and made a choice. As with anything you do, if you continue with it just because it's comfortable and familiar, it can become mechanical. That's not to say that everyone has to leave the Church in order to choose to be in it. But for me it turned out to be helpful to be able to stand back and look at what it was, with its imperfections.

It took me some time at Tivoli before I acknowledged to myself that I wanted to return to the Church, and at first I resisted going to vespers and compline. But one day, Dorothy Day called me over and said that there was a priest coming to visit and asked if I'd help him get ready for Mass. I didn't know beans about the chapel and was wondering what she had up her sleeve. I told the priest that I hadn't been to Mass in years and that I didn't know where anything was. We ended up talking and I began to feel at ease. That was the beginning of my re-entry, so to speak. After I eventually came back to the Church, I suspected that Dorothy indeed had something up her sleeve in asking me to do that. On the other hand, I'm told that she once expressed surprise that I had been brought up Catholic, saying, "But she works so hard, I thought she must be a Protestant." You have to bear in mind that Dorothy herself was brought up Protestant and converted, but I found it quite humorous.

I was able to re-enter the Church as an adult and within the setting of a community which I knew wasn't the whole Church but which was at least struggling to live out the gospel teachings which I had always found so good to begin with. On some levels it enhanced my anger and sadness that not everyone lived that way, but it showed me the possibilities and gave me a community of support. To understand this, you have to have a sense of what the Catholic Worker is. At any of our houses, large or small, there is likely to be a mixture of people — some who are troubled, who are very broken, and who come from all walks of life, economic strata, races, religions. Not everyone who lives in Catholic Worker houses is Catholic. But the volunteers who come on purpose are more likely to have a Catholic background or some religious background. And at almost any Mass or gathering there would literally be the lame, the halt, and the blind, helping each other. We live very simply on purpose, in accordance with our beliefs.

Many of the priests who come to the Catholic Worker to say Mass are themselves involved in social justice, and so reflections are somewhat down to earth and touch our lives. Our prayers have a lot to do with immediate, often life and death issues. My memory of the Church before that was that it had all been pretty distant. Now in our daily life and our dinnertime conversations and in our prayers at vespers and so on, we would raise a lot of questions about ecumenism, racial justice, war, or economic inequities. We would ask questions about what the responsibility of the Christian is. If you have more than you need and others are in need, what is your responsibility? The Worker is also an odd mix — for all its radical politics, we have people there who are probably more conversant with papal encyclicals than many seminarians or priests are. There are always people around who can repeat the lives of saints that no one ever knew existed. Even today, we're probably one of the few secular groups that can sing certain religious songs in Latin.

Yet all of that is not separate from but rather connected to the rest of what we do twenty-four hours a day, seven days a week. That has integrity — a word that means "wholeness" — a unity in our lives. Our work has always been a prayer as well, and often our prayer is work.

After I had been at the Worker for about four years, I went to Central America for seven months. By then I had already heard about some of the things happening in the Church in Latin America. One of the things I learned from going there is that there's a difference between faith and religion and that certain aspects of what I would see as religion are formed by the culture. If the Catholic Worker is different from the Church I experienced growing up in Cincinnati, I found yet a different Church in Guatemala and in Mexico and later in Nicaragua. Then again, one of the things that I hold precious about Catholicism is that there are things that are constant, or that should be, despite all.

It's unfortunate, but very often — particularly in more comfortable societies, and certainly in this country — what is preached and what is lived is a watered-down version of the gospel. I think that's sad, and I don't mean this in a self-righteous way at all, because I feel that people have missed out on the real meat and the real challenge and the real grace. Unfortunately, people can do things that are not in accordance with Christian belief and yet claim that their actions and political tendencies have never been condemned during their Catholic upbringing. In fact, these tendencies have also been shared by the Church — and I'm talking about degrees of wealth, giving in to political power either by joining in with it, blessing it, or not challenging it.

The last five years have been an exciting time, to see the bishops come to the point where the war and peace pastoral and the economic pastoral reveal that other people have begun to have questions and see the need to examine more closely how one lives out in every aspect of one's life the gospel teachings. The Church should be something more than the building you enter on Sundays, and the teachings should not be seen as some sweet stories or lessons that apply to everyone else but not to me. The Church must look at hard economic questions, and there is certainly among some religious orders and some areas of the U.S. Church an attempt to look at questions such as divestment. But I think that as an institution we are far too comfortable, and I think that comfort accomplishes exactly what we don't want it to accomplish. We have far too much time and leeway to think about what renovations we want to make on our church buildings rather than who is dying tonight on the streets of our own city.

Long ago it occurred to me that the richer people are, the more walls there are in their lives. If you have a larger bank account, you tend to have more homes with more rooms, more offices, and so on. The poorer you are, the fewer walls you have in a literal sense. Many poor people whom I know by name don't have *any* walls in their lives. In Central America, the walls may be cardboard or cornstalks with perhaps ten people in one room. The more walls we have, the less they offer us comfort and protection. They actually provide divisions and discomfort and separation from what is important. Again, I don't think that everyone should live in one-room houses. As a matter of fact, we should live in a world in which everyone can live with some variety. But I do feel it is wrong, and would even go so far as to say it is sinful, for people to have far more than they need when other people do not come near to having what is essential to life. I have seen people die of malnutrition that was preventable, and that has driven the point home to me. So while I would hesitate to say that any particular person with a large bank account is personally responsible, I think that those people who strive to take seriously the gospel need to examine that and are at some point responsible.

Neither should all the church buildings be torn down. Priests and sisters and certainly older religious need and deserve some degree of comfort. But there is something very wrong in a Church in this very city of New York where you might at times find one or two priests living in a building which has eight or ten bedrooms, when people are dying out in the cold.

Certainly the Catholic Worker is relatively more popular and more accepted at this point in history, for some good reasons and for some perhaps not good reasons. Many people tend to look at the good-works part and think it's wonderful that we feed the poor, and they either ignore or dismiss some of the other parts of what we do, even though we see it all as connected to the works of mercy and the gospel teaching. There are different views about where the line exists between religion and politics, for example. Much of what we do at the Worker would be interpreted as "political." The Worker has always been a pacifist group and has spoken out against every war since its beginning. It has often found itself opposed to deeds and, in fact, to the structure of the United States government in many ways — in how it treats the poor, its foreign policy, its militarism, the arms race, and so on. Some people within the Church obviously don't share the concerns or views that we have.

While not everyone could or should take all the same steps, the Catholic Worker publicly encourages people to consider such things as nonpayment of federal taxes, if they believe as we do that the gospel teaches that one should not take another's life. Since such a large part of that budget goes to deprive people of life — they call it war but we still see it as murder

—one should not willingly give funds to a body that would use them to that end. Most people in this country would think that was absolutely crazy, and some people are offended that we call ourselves Catholic. Other people may respect our views even if they disagree. Yet at this point in history we would agree with the statements of the Catholic bishops' conference more often than we would have five or ten years ago.

My experience of life is that no one of us can come up with the whole truth. The Quakers look at the task of trying to find the truth as a situation where you have a lantern in the center of a group of people. Each person can describe the angle of the lantern which he sees, but no person from the point at which he's sitting can see the entire lantern. Yet the beauty of it is that if everyone in the circle will offer their views, you will then come up with the whole lantern, the whole picture. That stresses the concept of interdependence and unity as opposed to what our culture pushes: independence and separateness at any cost. That's true within the Catholic Church as well, which does certainly have an authoritarian structure.

On the other hand, I've had experiences with individuals who have proved to be exceptions to that rule. Not long ago, we had [Paulo Evaristo] Cardinal Arns, the archbishop of São Paulo, Brazil, the largest archdiocese in the world, come and spend an entire day at our house. Dom Paulo, as he likes to be called, was going to take the bus down from midtown except that we happened to have a van that day and he was having some health problems, so we picked him up. But on the way down he insisted on stopping to talk with some workers on a picket line because he does so much work with the laborers in Brazil.

Then we got to the Worker house and it was time to introduce him to everyone. Most of my life I've seen cardinals and archbishops as distant people whom you're supposed to revere but with whom you often find yourself quite angry. It's as if they're on a pedestal or something. But this man is a very gentle, warm, loving person. There are several people who stay at the Worker who really don't like to be touched physically, probably because of experiences they've had. As the cardinal came in and was embracing everyone, a few of us noticed that he'd started to go for one woman who really didn't take kindly to such things. Yet somehow, when he went up and embraced her, she was beaming—she thought it was wonderful. Later we went to have dinner at our other house, St. Joseph House, and he jumped up and started serving people and helped clean up afterward. With him it was all so normal: the servant-leader was personified in this man. He is a very bright, strong-willed, powerful man in the Church—you don't get to be cardinal-archbishop without certain qualities. And yet he could be more effective in that office because he's the kind of person who does not hold himself apart physically or through his attitude.

I know it has helped me to have blessed encounters with people like that as well as with people whom I don't find to be such good ministers of Christ or the gospel.

I do believe that there is at times a difference between what I feel called in conscience to do and Roman teaching. I want to say immediately, though, that I think it's always important when we recognize that we're going off on a different road not to pretend that that isn't the case. Any decision that any of us makes needs to come from being well informed, prayerful, and reflective. There is within the Catholic Church the teaching of the primacy of conscience, and I value that. I've never studied theology and don't claim to be a theologian, but I certainly know there is a necessity to obey one's conscience. Again, a responsible person must do research if he or she is considering a position that takes a different route from Church teachings.

But one of the things I'm aware of in certain of these teachings, particularly anything to do with women, is that—even though the Holy Spirit can work within an imperfect situation—many of them clearly reflect the thinking of a small number of men. Very few of those men are working for their living—not to say that many of them might not have worked before they became priests. I think they have a somewhat limited view and experience of life—again, no single human being can grasp the whole lantern—and I think we see the results of it. I can respect their wisdom and sincerity and their authority, but at certain points it's possible that I or other people in good conscience, in an informed and prayerful way, can come to another view.

I know enough of Church history to know that we have seen some evolution in certain areas, as time has passed and science and culture and history and psychology have had an effect—even if it may take centuries sometimes. I don't see that as a solid justification—that someday, for instance, I'm sure the Church will believe that women should be ordained and therefore I can believe it now. And yet, on that issue in particular, I really believe there is no good reason women should not be priests if they are called to be and are seen by a community of people as such. Frankly, because there are other things that are more important to me, I've never spent much time or a huge amount of thought or energy on the issue of women's ordination. Part of that comes from the fact that I think the whole priesthood needs to be redesigned. I also do not see any good reason why priests should not be married.

But I wonder if, in some of these choices not to do certain things, we are avoiding some larger question. It looks like we don't want women ordained for such and such a reason — but is it really something deeper or more profound that we are trying to shy away from? Whether those making the decision are conscious of that deeper threat or challenge, I'm not sure. But I think it's quite possible that on various levels it's easier to talk about women priests than about whether the Church should divest of all its wealth. It's also likely that the Church will allow male priests to get married long before they would have women ordained.

Those things are important, but they don't happen to be that important to me personally. I've never had any desire to be a priest, and, besides, I think that the entire Church, priests and laity, should be looking at some other things as well — matters of life and death and the authenticity of our faith in our daily life. Some of these questions might become clearer if we dealt with some other things that Jesus called us to do.

In a similar regard, many people have come to decisions about birth control and abortion in a very prayerful, thoughtful, conscientious way. And I don't feel myself able to or entitled to judge their decisions. For me, though, there is a big difference between the seriousness of birth control and abortion. I do believe that abortion is murder, is the taking of a life. But at the same time, because of my own life experience, I think that it is sinful for people in the Church — and again they are mainly celibate male priests — to judge and in some way to condemn women who do that, when those same men have refused to look at their shared responsibility in that decision. I know women who have had abortions, poor women who live in difficult circumstances, who may be uneducated and who because of the social setup of our system may not have access to certain health care, and so on.

I know a few of those women who have made incredibly painful decisions. Certainly they were responsible, with the man involved, for becoming pregnant. Yet, once pregnant and faced with the reality, who would they turn to? This may all be changing, but we discovered through pregnant women calling up and coming to our door that there were many places in the archdiocese and around the country where you could get wonderful sermons about the rightness or wrongness of abortion, but no provision of a home. And in the few places where a pregnant woman could be taken in, perhaps even with some health care, once the baby was born they were off and out on the street. Perhaps an agency had come along and said they would help adopt out the baby, but that is a very limited and, I think, irresponsible support — which once more gets into the larger question of why so many people are poor and destitute to begin with.

If we are going to condemn people who have done something, we must look at our own role in that situation. And I don't think only priests and religious share that responsibility; the broader Christian community also does. Simplistic solutions are not applicable because the situations are far too complex, and a small group of people of only one sex cannot make the best decision. If it were a church in which women were listened to in an open and respectful and sincere way, perhaps I would think differently.

The first time I went to Central America, in 1978, I spent five months in Guatemala and two months in Mexico. One of the primary reasons for going was that I wanted to learn Spanish in order to continue to work with poor people in this country. I also knew that it would be good for me to learn what it was like to be a stranger in a strange land and to feel somewhat lost and alienated — to live in a culture somewhat different from my own and to see the Church in a different context. I also wanted to know what it was like to live in a country which my country had helped to destroy, and Guatemala certainly fit the bill. So embracing all those expectations and not knowing exactly how I was going to go about it — I would never do the same thing again — I went off with fairly little money and with plans for the language school but little idea of what I would do after that. I was pretty much alone, and I don't recommend that. They were among the five most depressing months of my life. But even in the midst of that I have since realized how rich an experience it was and how much I learned.

I then returned for a month in 1983 and subsequently spent seven months in Nicaragua in 1984. For one thing, it helped me to understand the distinctions among the Central American countries and the impact of history and the changes within the Church in each of those settings. The first thing I would say is that I learned there, in a way that I had not learned here, the value of life. I learned a lot from people who were so aware, because they were forced to be, of how precious life is and who knew how to live well in the best sense of that word. They had a better sense of love and friendship and of how they would spend the hours of the days. We're talking about situations of overt and covert oppression, destitution, and, in Nicaragua, war. In Honduras I spent two weeks visiting Salvadoran refugees — twenty-one thousand of them are living virtually in armed prison camps. I came face to face with people who had been tortured, who had seen their entire families machine gunned or beheaded before their eyes, or who lived in daily fear of that happening. It was particularly difficult for me, not only as a Christian but also as a citizen of the United States, to realize that all of the people whom I met in those circumstances were talking about deaths which occurred — in ninety-five percent of the cases — only because the U.S. had provided the funds and the guns.

Despite the grimness, people there had a vibrance, a life, a sense of humor and joy that was a gift to be associated with. Most of the people I met identified first and foremost with their faith as Christians and saw their Catholicism as the guiding force of their lives. There is great variety within the Church in Central America, and I don't think it's honest to give any simplistic definition of it. I certainly saw signs of what you might call a more conservative Church and also what one might call liberation theology, although I think very few people really understand what liberation theology is. But I felt at times that I could almost visibly see the Holy Spirit work among people, see incredible generosity and courage and self-sacrifice, and a sense of humility and joy despite extreme personal suffering. By contrast, life here and much of the Church here seem so dead and fake and mechanical. I'm very glad for the contacts I've had with the Central American Church.

In Nicaragua I was with Witness for Peace, which is a faith-based group. All of the people who work with it are committed to nonviolence in word and deed, though not all are pacifists. It's a small group started in 1983. There were six or seven of us then, and now there are about thirty. Partly we were there to keep a presence within the country and to say that because of our faith we are so opposed to U.S. policy that we are literally putting our bodies on the line to convey this message back to the powers in the U.S. as well as to friends and relatives and lawmakers. We also were there to observe what was happening and report that back. There is a short-term part of Witness for Peace during which a group of fifteen to twenty people — most of them church people from forty different denominations — spend a few weeks in the country observing. They must make a commitment upon returning to America to make some effort to change U.S. policy. While we were there, we made a conscious effort to make contact with people who were considered opposition, who held dissenting views from the Sandinistas. We were there with the permission of the Nicaraguan government, but definitely we were there at the invitation of church people, and our contacts within Nicaragua were church people. We wandered around and saw and listened and talked.

Judging by the newspapers and other standard media in this country, it's no wonder many people think the way they do. But when one has had access to different information from the source and has had the further opportunity to see and listen — there's a doubting Thomas within me, I admit — policies take on a different meaning, a more human meaning.

The Nicaragua that I saw has nothing to do with the one that the Reagan administration purveys. There's almost no resemblance. And the effects of U.S. policy, far from serving to protect democracy for us or anyone else, are serving to prevent democracy and to disrupt it for ourselves in this country as well as down there. If anything, the bungling, murderous way we're going about treating Nicaragua may well bring about a self-fulfilling prophecy, but we must take responsibility for that.

On the other hand, I feel that I saw and experienced in Nicaragua a degree of democratic participation in a society that I've never experienced here. I saw people making decisions about what happened to their lives. There were many complaints, and I certainly did listen more to people I got to know well and who, I felt, were very solid in their faith and were stable and balanced. But their experience of the kind of democracy that the U.S. helped to support during half a century of installing and supporting the Somoza family has been one of systematic repression, deprivation of the populace, increased poverty and destitution, and on and on. Whereas what is happening under the Sandinistas, despite great impediments including the U.S. economic boycott, is that everyone is getting food, which is a work of mercy. The hungry are being fed, the thirsty are being given to drink, the naked are being clothed, the homeless are being given shelter.

I don't care what you call the people who did one or the other of those actions, but the latter practices are Christian, and the former practices were un-Christian. Any of us can go around and claim any title or any ism, but I think the proof is in the pudding, and the way people live says everything about them. Teaching people to read is actually giving them a powerful political tool because once they can read they can make their own decisions. And the Sandinistas did that. The results of the funding of the contra were death and destruction. By that I mean that health workers, teachers, religious workers were all focused on by the contra and continue to be. And so the effect of the contra war was the destruction of schools, the destruction of clinics and food projects — and that to me does not further democracy or anything that is good.

I have friends who would describe two Churches in Nicaragua. My experience was that there are probably half a dozen, just as there are here. Certainly I encountered a few priests who were very politicized, to a point which I found offensive, who were implying that the Sandinistas were angels and the cardinal was a devil. Also, partly because he would not meet with our group, I never spoke with Cardinal Obando y Bravo. I did meet two of the people who were recently expelled. I had interviews with both Bishop Vega [Pablo Antonio Vega Mantilla of Juigalpa, vice president of the Nicaraguan bishops' conference] and Monsignor Bismark

Carballo [director of the Church-run radio station], who was the spokesman of the cardinal. It's a sad thing to say, but during those interviews I found both of them very evasive. At times I knew some of the things that Father Carballo said were lies, and I found that very disturbing. It was, at the least, an evasion of reality. At that point it was front-page news that the CIA was active in mining the ports and that millions of dollars had come from the U.S., and he refused to acknowledge that. His opinion about that was certainly his to have, but to refuse outright even to acknowledge a very important fact in the life of that country, I don't understand.

There are extremes there as in this country. But most of my experiences were of clergy and laity struggling together to reflect on and look at what the gospel said about their lives in terms of challenge. For the most part they live in a radical way that I found very much akin to my friends' lives at the Catholic Worker. That is not so surprising as interesting in terms of the two very different cultures. I have to laugh when I hear about the persecution of religion in Nicaragua. Our groups were full of pastors and priests and nuns, and by the time we left, some of them were so tired of religious meetings — they had never been to such a steady stream of intense religious gatherings.

Nicaragua is a very Christian country — you cannot forget Christ while you are in Nicaragua. I have never seen so many pictures of the Pope in my life. Often they were next to a picture of August Sandino, who was an early liberator of the country. Most people there, who might have had very limited education and yet were very wise and holy people, didn't quite understand why they should dislike the Pope because they also happened to like what the Sandinistas were doing — such as feeding their children. It seemed a false dichotomy, and I shared that perception.

Michael Novak

Orthodoxy vs. Progressive Bourgeois Christianity

Don't ever take a fence down until you know the reason why it was put up.
—Ascribed to G. K. Chesterton
    by John F. Kennedy

The theologians are becoming Communists and the Communists are becoming theologians!
—Fidel Castro
    Quoted in *Christians and Marxists* by José Bonino

Michael Novak, author of *The Open Church, Belief and Unbelief,* and *A Theology for Radical Politics,* was at one time a hero not only of young Catholic liberals but of radical students of all denominations. But somewhere between the postconciliar effulgence of the sixties, when he was writing those books, and the hierarchical backlash of today, Novak underwent a change of ideology, if not of heart, and has emerged as one of the country's leading Catholic apologists for the free enterprise system. This kind of reversal recalls Robert Frost's homey bromide to the effect that he was never a radical in his youth for fear that he would become a conservative in his old age.

Yet, in a curious way, Novak's championing of the morality of capitalism at a time when the American bishops have handed up a mordant indictment of democratic capitalism and inequalities in the distribution of wealth seems every bit as radical as his earlier stance—in the sense of opposing the mainstream while reasserting underlying causes and meanings. "The very root of capitalism, as the origin of the word suggests, is the human head," Novak said in a forum held at Cooper Union and reprinted in *Harper's* in 1986. ''The society which organizes its institutions to favor creativity, invention, and discovery will be the society best suited to liberate the poor and create an unprecedented economic dynamism.'' Novak's argument that capitalism exalts the individual and provides the freedom to innovate ''individual visions of the common good'' seems to be at odds with Catholicism's emphasis on community and tradition. But he insists that those visions, taken as a whole, ''produce a higher level of the common good than was previously possible.'' And he likes to substitute for the evil-sounding word ''profit'' the more palatable ''economic development.''

Much of the strength of Novak's case stands on his valuing the practical and the comparative. In criticizing the religious socialists in his book *The Spirit of Democratic Capitalism*, Novak noted, ''Seldom do they claim that the superiority of socialism lies in its works, its practicality, its proven fruits. Nearly always they justify it in terms of its vision.'' And in comparing capitalism to the other available economic political systems in the world, such as Marxist socialism, he finds that, historically, ''none had produced an equivalent system of liberties. None had so loosened the bonds of station, rank, peonage, and immobility. None so valued the individual.''

As a result of such writings, Novak is often the first person called on to comment when the American clergy confront the Vatican or the government or to challenge the claims of liberation theologians, as he has done in books such as *Will It Liberate?* and articles in the *New Republic* and *National Review*. Stressing economic rather than theological factors, he asks provocatively how, once Latin America rids itself of the evils of capitalism, it will create the seventy-six million new jobs it will need by the turn of the century. ''Revolutionaries in Cuba, Nicaragua and Vietnam, among other Communist countries,'' he said in the *New York Times Magazine*, ''mostly create huge armies. Only economic activists create jobs. Sooner or later, liberation theologians will need to grapple with how new wealth can be created and sustained systematically.''

Novak's listing in *Who's Who* takes up the space normally allotted for three people and includes an astonishing array of current positions with various delegations and task forces, although he spends most of his time at the American Enterprise Institute in Washington, where he holds the George Frederick Jewett Chair in Religion and Public Policy and tends to write, cowrite, or edit several books a year. Given the current surge toward progressivism and independence in the American Catholic Church, Michael Novak is well aware that he once again represents an unpopular viewpoint — which he does in the meticulously reasoned and articulate style that has become his trademark.

MY GRANDPARENTS came to the United States from villages high in the Tatra Mountains in Slovakia, not far south of the Polish border—on a clear day, you can see Poland from the farms just above the village where my mother's family comes from—and they met in the United States. An uncle of mine traced the family back through the records of one of those villages at least to the thirteenth century—it's a very small village indeed—and so the family presumably has been Catholic from pretty far back. Both of my parents were born in 1910 in Johnstown, Pennsylvania, where a good part of the family settled. On my mother's side, about four members of the family remained in Slovakia and four came here. My father's family in Slovakia has pretty much disappeared without a trace.

My father's father died a year or so after my father's birth, so my father never completed school past the fifth or sixth grade. He had an assortment of jobs in Johnstown working for Sanitary Dairy and in the cheese department at Glosser Brothers, but then he joined the Metropolitan Life Insurance Company about the time he was married and worked at that until his retirement. He did set his mind on two things. His first purchase, before he had a home or even a bookcase to put them in, was of the Harvard Classics—he loved to read and at that time to write poetry, too—and he wanted to build a family around that. So one thing we all grew up with was a set of the red Harvard Classics in the house. Various bribes were offered to us if we would read all of them, but none of us ever quite did so.

We lived in Morrellville, the part of Johnstown where the ethnic immigrant families lived, and he wanted to move up on the hill in a borough called Southmont. He had pointed out to my mother before they were married the house he wanted to live in. By the time I was seven years old, we did in fact move there, and we were one of the first Slovak families to make the move. We didn't think Morrellville was a ghetto, but it was where my mother's father ran a butcher shop which, by the way, was not altogether different from a shop which his cousins still operate in Slovakia today. But Johnstown was a flood city, and one of my first memories was of one such night in 1936. My father hadn't come home from work—he was working in the downtown area right in the flood district. He had managed to walk through the water up to his neck to the high school building, where he spent the night on the second floor. I must have been about three, but I remember the fear and the candles on the back porch in the falling rain. I say this because being "up on the hill" had a special meaning then. Morrellville was higher up a bit, so we were fairly safe, but moving up on the hill had something of that sense of safety, too. Yet above all, it meant moving where the "Americans" lived. I don't think I ever heard the word *WASP*, but I remember being asked, "What sort of a name is Novak?" I must have brought it up to my father, because I remember him saying, "Just keep your chin up and say, 'American.' "

I was instructed that we must be more careful with our clothes, wear clean overalls, be a little more careful, more responsible, neater, work a little harder than others. There would be some penalties to come along that I shouldn't be surprised at — not being chosen for this or that. There were a number of Catholic families in Southmont, but not more than three or four in a class of thirty. The nearest Catholic church was a mile and a half away in the next borough, Westmont, which was more exclusive. I used to have to get excuses from school to serve Mass at funerals on weekdays. I can also remember pointing out to a fifth grade teacher that she had spelled the name of Pope Pius wrong on the blackboard (with an *o*).

My parents were childhood sweethearts. We moved around a good deal after I was born, but in the same general area of western Pennsylvania. My father was working for the Metropolitan Life Insurance Company, and we moved along with his several promotions. But we then came back when I was about fourteen to settle in Johnstown, where my parents still live. I had four brothers, of whom I was the oldest, and — the baby of the family and its favorite — a sister. Through sixth grade I went to public school but used to walk to our church to serve Mass early in the morning before school, and I sang in the choir there as well.

My grandfather was a very devout, pious man. One would even catch him on his knees in the corner, saying his prayers at certain hours, but that was uncommon. My mother was also devout. My father went to Mass regularly and encouraged me to be an altar boy and a choir boy. He had been both — he has a lovely tenor voice, which I don't. But I would've said my father was *not* very devout and was rather anticlerical when we were young. My younger brother attended the University of Notre Dame, decided to become a priest, and, going on to become ordained in France for the foreign missions, was later murdered in what was then Pakistan (it's now Bangladesh). That was in 1964. Since that time my father has become noticeably more devout. But in those years, it wasn't so. In 1947, my father very much opposed my going to the seminary when I completed the eighth grade and told me I'd regret it.

By that time I was in my second year at Catholic school, and the nuns and parish priests were also opposed to my going in. But I wanted to go, and I went. I was very good in football. I had unusually large hands and

I was very quick on my feet. The local high school coach had seen us play — we played all comers, losing only three of nineteen games, and those to much bigger kids. But I thought, If I go on into high school, I'm going to get so caught up in football and girls, I'll never go on to the priesthood. I applied for the Jesuits, but they wouldn't take you until after high school. That's what the nuns and priests thought, too — that the more you saw of the world and the more experience you got under your belt, the better priest you'd be. I thought that was good advice in the normal case, but not for me. I was not certain God wanted me to be a priest, but I somehow felt certain I should at least try to give it my best. The only question in my mind was when.

So in ninth grade, I went out to Holy Cross Seminary at the University of Notre Dame and began studying for the priesthood. As my father had predicted, I almost left after one year. I didn't have an easy time. I was very much attracted to girls and hated giving up dating and all that. But whatever came up, I managed to stay in. I loved study, I loved my friends, and I loved the sports and everything about it. In a quiet part of myself, it seemed to me I was doing God's will. I was really very happy. After high school, as much as I loved Notre Dame, I chose to go to Stonehill College in Massachusetts to join the eastern province, which was the more pioneering thing to do, and I spent the next four years there. I was then chosen to go to study in Rome in 1956 and spent two happy years there. On the other hand, I felt more and more drawn to politics and to fiction. My turmoil was more and more pronounced. Chastity was difficult for me; obedience even more so. I didn't think I wanted to go on and be ordained. I told my superiors, and they said that of course I should leave if I wished to leave — but since I had put in so much time, wouldn't it be wise to make sure I wasn't leaving because of Rome or because I wasn't studying literature and American studies, as I wanted to? And so I spent another year and a half at Catholic University, by which time I was sure that I wanted to leave and did leave in January 1960.

By then I'd spent twelve years in the seminary, which is just about as much time as I'd spent outside the seminary. I would have been ordained within the year if I had stayed on, but I was really quite sure that I wanted to go my own way. I didn't want to be in the position of speaking for the Church, which is the role that a priest rightly plays. I also wanted to be more involved in politics than I then thought proper for priests. I recognize now that many priests are much more active in politics, and perhaps if I had continued, that wouldn't have made so much difference today. But I didn't like priests in politics then and I don't like it now. I wanted to write and comment on politics. I wanted to do what I still do now in theology and philosophy—and to be totally engaged with political and cultural movements. I wanted to plunge into everything. I even thought of running for political office. For some years I entertained the possibility of running for the congressional seat in Pennsylvania, and I maintained a residence there for many years through my parents.

When I left the seminary, I moved into a cheap attic room in New York, up near Fordham. I didn't have much money to live on, but I managed to make enough writing book reviews and selling articles to *Commonweal* and *America* and magazines of that sort. I was also finishing a novel that was bought by Doubleday and brought out the following year, *The Tiber Was Silver*, a story about the ordination of a seminarian in Rome who was contemplating leaving but who went on to ordination. I thought the most difficult task would be to make credible the decision to stay rather than the decision to leave. Meanwhile, I applied with considerable innocence to Harvard and Yale *only*—that was the innocent part —and was accepted at both, but I received a fellowship at Harvard that enabled me to go there. So I enrolled at Harvard in the fall of 1960.

Earlier that summer, through a young friend who'd been in the seminary with me at Holy Cross but whom I hadn't seen since 1948, I became involved in the political campaign of a would-be Democratic congressman from New Jersey, who lost, but for whom I coined the phrase "The New Frontier." His staff thought this was a corny idea. But the candidate planned to suggest it to then likely presidential candidate John Kennedy. However, without any help from us, Kennedy used this theme in his acceptance speech at the convention, and then, of course, his staff thought it was a wonderful phrase. I did send speech material on to the Kennedy team. I was very excited by the Kennedy campaign in the fall of that year and very moved by his presidency throughout.

I was at Harvard when Vatican II began in 1962, and in some ways I had been predisposed to it by my years spent with the Holy Cross Fathers. First of all, they have always been, in recent times anyway, a very enlightened order—very serious about scholarship, pretty much like the Jesuits, but with a stronger sense of community that derives from a more monastic tradition. As with the Jesuits, almost all fields of work were open to us: Father Payton was the movie priest out in Hollywood; there were the missionaries, who attracted my brother; there were scientists, writers, and editors; people like [former Notre Dame President] Father Hesburgh; and so on. One reason I had turned to Holy Cross in 1947 was that I had many ambitions and didn't know precisely what I wanted to do. Holy Cross had roots in France, and its priests were very close to the liturgical movement that had been going on in Europe for about a century and that turned out to be very influential at the Vatican Council. We had priests who were very much involved in the *nouvelle théologie*. So, as I discovered in Rome, Holy Cross was probably ahead of anybody. We were eager for the reforms. In fact, with a couple of my friends in my first year in Rome back in fifty-six, we started an international organization of seminarians, and part of the idea was to deal with all the new ideas and possibilities in the Church. It was designed to attract those seminarians who were interested specifically in renewing the Church. So, far from being surprised by the Vatican Council, my friends and I thought it fulfilled our own hopes.

I met my wife, Karen, in 1962 while I was studying at Harvard, and we were married in June 1963. We determined to go on our honeymoon to Rome, and I took a leave of absence from Harvard so that we could be there for the second session of the Vatican Council that fall. I figured we could make a start from our wedding gifts, and I could earn enough writing about the council to get us through until January. The January day when we arrived back in New York, I learned that my brother had been killed during riots in Dacca. This news threw me into great darkness. Following by less than two months the assassination of Kennedy, it taught me that whatever one loved could be taken away instantly, that life is far more cruel than one wishes to believe. The genesis of *The Experience of Nothingness* lies here — but also in the long darkness I experienced in the seminary.

I was at Harvard with Daniel Callahan, who had completed his course work in the philosophy department, which I was just beginning; we became fast friends. He was also a teaching assistant over at the divinity school, one of the first Catholics there, under Christopher Dawson. Harvey Cox, of course, was there as well, and later Bryan Hehir. That was a good and stimulating period of my life. Karen and I were away at the council for half a year and then again the next fall, this time for *Time* magazine for six weeks. She completed a set of six prints on T. S. Eliot's "Ash Wednesday," just as the year before she had completed a series of seventeen on the Apocalypse. (She shares my dark vision.) We ate much better on *Time*'s expense account. They kept pressing more money on me and telling me I wasn't spending enough and insisting I take more people out to whatever restaurants I wanted. It was the only time in my life I've eaten in the best restaurants in Rome. Saying I was from *Time* also opened many more doors for interviews — in the Vatican and in the Italian government — than freelancing had. The power of journalism over other elites is immense.

Robert McAfee Brown was in Rome as a Presbyterian observer of the council, and we became good friends. So, through him, Stanford invited me to take a position on their soon-to-be religion department, then called Special Program in Humanities. I had early formed the idea of spending my life in non-Catholic environments. Stanford had not had a Catholic before, and they invited me, even though I hadn't completed my work for a degree, to an assistant professorship. Karen and I moved out to Palo Alto in 1965, and it turned out to be an unusually fruitful and exciting period of time. Two of our children were born there; our older daughter returned to Stanford as a freshman last year. Stanford was an extraordinary place to teach, not only because the Vatican Council had put Catholics in the news and because the ecumenical movement was taking off but also because politically the California campuses were in turmoil. So often in my life it has happened that what I wanted to do and what I had prepared myself for, I was *invited* to do: the invitation came from Stanford, as the acceptance had come from Harvard, and so on. Reluctantly at first, I became persuaded that the war in Vietnam, although moral in its purposes, was becoming less than moral in its execution and in its likely outcome. I became involved in radical politics, opposing liberals from the left. I went to South Vietnam for the presidential election in 1967, visiting several Stanford students who were there as civilian volunteers. One of them, Dwight Owen, was slain in a night ambush; I was to have been with him but was bounced off the plane list at the last moment and arrived to find him dead.

Around that time Daniel Callahan wrote a book called *Honesty in the Church*, and one of his points was that some Catholic progressives were deceiving themselves because what they were interpreting as problems of renewal and reform were actually fundamental problems of belief. I re-member disagreeing with him at the time, although not on the point that there was a crisis of belief — about that I was so sure that I had written my own book, *Belief and Unbelief*. His thesis seemed to me too cynical. Dan would always look more carefully at the down side of things. He would resist enthusiasm and look at the probable ways that things could go wrong, and we often had arguments on those grounds. He applied to me James's description ''tender-minded,'' while he was naturally ''tough-minded.'' Though I didn't like it at the time, there turns out to have been a lot of truth in that. Many conservatives were predicting that the Vatican II reforms would go badly, and we called them ''the prophets of doom,'' after a phrase that Pope John XXIII had used. I kept thinking that the time was ripe and that, done well and with wisdom, the reforms would be very popular and revitalizing. I did not anticipate that so many priests and nuns would leave and that institutionally there would be so many disruptions. I did not think that there would be so many challenges to the core of the faith itself, although I do remember using as the frontispiece of *The Open Church* "All things human, given enough time, go badly." And I opened and closed the book with the image of the jesters in the fountains of Rome, who had been there so many centuries that they seemed to be laughing at the passing generations.

I used to resent Evelyn Waugh's complaints about the bad English translations from the Latin that resulted from council reforms. But now I must say that, regarding many of the new songs and hymns, what he spotted early has grown even worse. Now we endure the Liturgy of Happy Talk and Forced Cheerfulness. It's worse than television, and as I grow older, it affects me badly. Even the new formal liturgy, which I didn't find so bad at first, wears worse on me each time I realize what was done. I am often depressed that I didn't notice it sooner and fight against it harder. The reformers took out all sense of mystery, all sense of real adoration, and all sense of real humility. They took the solitary and the personal out of religion, making it group-think. They also took out the sense of—I almost want to say "soul," in defiance of present talk about "person." The sense of soul before God. You don't feel that sense of being on your knees before the Almighty and before all the angels and saints—we've lost that connection with the past history of the Church. We've lost the sense both of solitude and of community, a marvelous sense of solitude and yet a marvelous sense of praying together with a community that went down through all the ages. What we now have is a *modern* sense of "community," as in reach over and shake hands. It feels more like a meeting of the Lions Club. The liturgy has been made over into a celebration of our being together—how lucky we are to be together with one another! It's awful.

But I don't think it's precisely through translations that all that has been lost. The whole design of the liturgy has been altered. And I don't believe that the liturgists have fulfilled the intentions of the liturgical reform movement stretching from the nineteenth century right on up to the Second Vatican Council itself. It's something quite other than what that first reform movement envisaged. Enduring it is a crucifixion—in that, at least, it accomplishes its symbolic object.

On the other hand, the folk Mass can be very successful, let me say, at places like Notre Dame, where you have a group of students all the same age, for whom folk music is as informal as they like. In a small room, say a Mass in the dormitory, it's very moving. I've been there on several occasions and, much as I hate it, at least I find it *is* successful: the kids are silent, with a kind of awe. It works for them. But at that age, it's one thing; it's very hard to live on when you're fifty.

A couple of my friends long ago said that I have a conservative tem-

perament and a liberal mind. I interpret that in my own life as meaning
that my sense of roots began to carry more meaning for me as I grew
older and as I encountered various experiences which revolted me or
attracted me in very different ways from the ways in which they were
affecting my colleagues. Some of that difference I could only attribute,
on reflection, to being Catholic and Slovak, having known poverty and
—I don't like the word *class*, but seeing life from the bottom up, as I
felt I had. My uncle worked in the mill, as did other uncles. My grandfather
had been a miner. The sense of being extremely poor was quite real, even
when my father moved up to Southmont.

I wrote a piece for *Harper's* magazine in 1961 called "God in the
Colleges," which was a strong critique of the liberal corporate culture of
America with its technocratic mind and all that. Beneath the smooth, fast
surface, I was saying, questions arise about the meaning of life. What's
the meaning of man? I was describing how at Harvard under analytic
philosophy, such questions were being suppressed. The best colleges were
very rocky soil for a religious sensibility. The things that meant the most
to me in life could scarely be talked about in the terms of analytic philosophy. Well, that article was often reprinted by student radicals. It had
a bit of the Port Huron sensibility. As did many radical statements of that
time, it came in part out of Camus. And incidentally, it's not accidental
that so many of the radicals of that time were Catholic, like Tom Hayden
and Mario Savio, or Jewish. We had a history of existentialist inquiries,
if I can put it that way, which helped us to criticize the merely objective
science that was much the vogue in those days. In a Catholic school,
Mario Savio once said, every day is the feast day of a martyr in some
long-ago age.

That was, perhaps simultaneously, a sign of the conservative and the
radical in me. I rebelled against the two-times-two-equals-four liberal, the
technocrat. On the other hand, I favored Camus, not Sartre. I was drawn
to the radical critique of university liberalism, but both disliked the total
antinomianism of the most radical and drew back from their contempt for
"hard hats" and "pigs" (the lower class: manual workers, policemen,
national guardsmen). I was a strong supporter of John F. Kennedy and
also of Robert Kennedy. In January of 1968, I had supported Eugene
McCarthy for the presidency. But then I switched in May to support Robert
Kennedy. He was, I thought, the only politician who could unite black
and white working-class people, as he showed in Gary and Omaha. Eugene
McCarthy, much as I loved him and as deeply as I respect him, was going
to get more of the college and suburban vote, and I was beginning to
worry about what later came to be called the "new class."

Then in seventy-two I published *The Rise of the Unmeltable Ethnics*, arguing that the Democrats were too much forgetting the politics of family and neighborhood, and they were very much forgetting the ethnic, largely non-college-educated population, which was becoming more and more important. The young Mario Cuomo was the sort of person I had in mind. I didn't have Cuomo in the book, although I did have Barbara Mikulski in it. I knew of Cuomo from Italian Americans I was going around with in New York at that time. Today there are Deukmejian, DeConcini, Celeste, Dukakis, Sarbanes, and dozens of others. But that book was quite heavily criticized as too conservative, if not reactionary. I had written it as a book which I thought would lead the Left in a somewhat new direction. Yet I found myself being excommunicated.

Theologically, I don't think I've changed much. I have roughly the same theological views I had in the nineteen sixties. Many of my old friends, though, have moved theologically much farther in what's called the "progressive" direction. I don't very much admire that direction. *Politically*, I don't think I've changed that much, either. I still cherish the ideas and the kind of presidency that John Kennedy had and the ideas that Robert Kennedy championed, although I would say that the Republicans have taken over those ideas, while Democrats like Teddy Kennedy have moved ever farther left. John and Bobby Kennedy were internationalists. They believed in a strong military, and they didn't get into Vietnam by accident. Vietnam might have been a mistake — I think it *was* a mistake, a *double* mistake, how we got in and how we got out — but it was the sort of stand that Democrats then took and Democrats now don't. The leading lights of the Democratic party are today much more isolationist and much less willing to strengthen the American military. They've lost sight of the importance of military power as a form of influence and a deterrent to larger war. I learned from the war the opposite of what most others did. I still feel guilty about the boat people, for what we abandoned the Vietnamese to, where the Russians now sail their fleet from, preparing for the next war. Reading memoirs of those who were in the Viet Cong and the like, I believe now that I was a sucker for Communist propaganda.

Where I *have* changed most is that I had been brought up to think of *capitalism* as a word to be used pejoratively, of corporations as institutions to be despised, and of profits, markets, and entrepreneurship as morally inferior mechanisms, if not mere expressions of greed or, in the polite socialist word, "acquisitiveness." Without declaring myself, I took care to be leaning in a democratic socialist direction. I was afraid to call myself a socialist outright because of the history of socialism in Eastern Europe. But I had a sense that I had to clarify in my mind whether I was a socialist or not. I thought like a social democrat. Everything I wrote about capitalism had a negative edge to it. That's normal for those trained in the humanities. It was also, superficially at least, very ethnic. It matched my early memory of the managers of the mills — the dam of their rural retreat burst in 1889, engulfing the city in the first Johnstown flood. And it seemed to match the experience of my family in Europe, where the nobility lived in great castles, the serfs in rural sheds. To say "capitalist" was, in one dimension, to say "people not like us" — Protestant, upper class, Anglo-Saxon.

Nonetheless, as I began to read more in economics and to look at what was happening in the world, I found to my surprise around 1977 that I really could not call myself a socialist. I was afraid to publish this, didn't want to admit it publicly, hesitated to tell anyone (even my wife). But even when I held up to myself pictures of Sweden, it didn't help. It took me a while to come out, but I finally wrote a piece that appeared first in the *Washington Post*, "A Closet Capitalist Confesses." Then I began, reluctantly at first, to study the literature of capitalism, by which I became more and more persuaded. A form of false consciousness began to fall away. I recognized *why* my family had found such opportunity in this nation but also why so much education is anticapitalist. Capitalism had been relegated to the economists. The moral and philosophical dimensions had never been spelled out. And so I set out to explain for myself, in my own terms, the meaning of a capitalist economy embedded in a democratic polity. I had always loved America, but why? What was it about its political economy that rang true, as a moral statement? Most of my education gave some good answers concerning democracy, but not concerning capitalism. It was all right for theologians to be socialists — Paul Tillich said any Christian had to be. But in favor of capitalism? That was held in contempt. Having learned to ask the famous question "Compared to what?," the more I looked at the U.S. economy, the less I had contempt for it. The more I thought, I'm awfully glad my grandparents didn't migrate to Brazil.

In economic contexts the Popes always used the word *liberal* pejoratively. For many years, so had I. Now I began to think that what we were looking for, in order to lift the poor of the world, was a combination of bottom-up enterprise and democracy in the framework of the Jewish-Christian ethic.

What's attractive about capitalism is that it doesn't demand enthusiasm. Two cheers are quite enough. Maybe even excessive. It's a system intended to work, not to breed enthusiasm. You can't expect it to be terribly romantic, but it's going to raise up more of the poor and incidentally reveal something important about Christianity and Judaism, too. Namely, that man most imitates God by being a creator. A sustained institutional focus upon wit, discovery, invention, and enterprise makes capitalism different from traditional economies, which are based solely on markets, property, and profit. Jerusalem in biblical times had the latter. It did not have the former.

I used to argue, from the time I was very young, that we need a better theology of the world, of work, and of the laity. If we're going to achieve that, I thought, we're going to have to study comparative economic systems. I just didn't expect when I was young that I would find capitalism of the American sort the best of the existing lot.

Let me put it another way. My life's ambition, as I wrote in my first nonfiction book, was to interpret the American experience in a new philosophical and theological way. For a long time, I thought that meant rejecting "capitalism" and "liberalism." Everything I've learned about the world has shown me that was wrong. So I've changed, and I don't understand why others haven't.

My critics call me, when they are being nice, a "neoconservative." How can anyone who is in favor of democracy, capitalism—which is so dynamic—and pluralism of conscience be called a conservative? That was Hayek's question. The tradition I like best is that of the Whigs, from Thomas Aquinas right through the Americans of 1776, of whom George Washington said they were *all* Whigs. But how can anyone today call himself a Whig? Lord Acton was lonely, being Catholic and liberal, but it is a loneliness I would not surrender for the world.

One thing that struck me as I reflected on the Nicene Creed for *Confession of a Catholic* was the central importance to Christianity of the symbols for male and female. The creed affirms: "I believe in God the Father." Why not "God the Mother"? You could not express the Incarnation in that way. Mary the mother of Jesus, Bethlehem—this is one of the most powerful sets of images in history. If God were to be imagined as a woman, that story could not be told. The offspring of a goddess could not be imagined as *human* in the way Jesus was—no nine months in the womb, no birth in Bethlehem. As C. S. Lewis said, if you change the sex of the Christian God, you change the whole nature of the religion; you no longer have Christianity, you have something else.

Some feminists today write about "post-Christian" religion. They have grasped the essential logic. Between feminism of a radical type and the real, historical Christianity there is radical incompatibility.

Women priests? Protestants do not see the priesthood as Catholics do.

If one thinks of priests solely as ministers, servants of the people, counselors, preachers, and the like, well, women can do all those things as well as, even better than, men. If that is all a priest is, of course women can be priests.

But the Catholic vision of the priesthood — and of the Church — is very different from that. There is no other vision of priesthood or of church quite like it. You cannot explain the Church in human categories. It is *not* just "the people of God," a sociological community held together by certain common beliefs or a common culture. It involves a special mode of being, a participation in the life of God. Otherwise, there is no real point in belonging to it. As a sociological reality, it is not terribly attractive. There is an immense amount to rebel against in it. Personally, I don't like the pre-Vatican traditionalists any better than I did in 1964, but I have come in recent years to dislike the Church of the progressives even more. Probably because they think they are so superior. I dislike their new liturgy, their mode of enforcing authority, the hymns they sing, their sentimentality, their politics. If that were all the Church were — the Church of the progressives — I would not wish to belong to it. Because it is much more than that, I am glad they are part of it. I like the variety, the turmoil, the struggle, the rivalries and cliques in the Church — they are proofs of its human, conflicted, turbulent reality. I don't like those conservatives who would want to drive the progressives *out* of the Church. Not at all.

Still, maturity means making decisions and having edges, taking on a clear identity. It means saying no. As persons grow older, they have more angles, more sharp edges, more definition. So it is with the Church. I hate the idea of "sandbox Catholicism," in which persons of our generation play amid the treasures of tradition, throw them about, discard them, as the whim seizes them. No. We are carrying forward a tradition, which has its own identity and makes clear and distinct and troublesome demands. Demands we often don't like. Many years ago someone taught me, in reading the missal at Mass, *not* to pick and choose but to listen especially to those passages one doesn't at first like. To allow one's soul to be shaped by the ancient Church, in her wisdom.

Let me give you an example. I used to be troubled by passages about the wrath of God, the jealousy of God, the vindictiveness of God. Passages about hell, plagues, sufferings, the cruelties endured by Job, and that sort of thing. Those didn't sound to me like the way I was being raised — to be tolerant, nice, forgiving, kind, soft. Sometimes I would look at Christ on the cross (Rouault's paintings touched me in this way) and wonder what kind of God it is who could do this to His Son? His own *Son*. Later I learned in life how cruel God can be, how cruel and barbarous history is. Actually, I could see this even among young boys at play. We *were* mean to each other. Sometimes I was. The point is, the God of Christianity isn't "nice." The God of Christianity and of Judaism (He is the same God) is *not* what we would like God to be.

Orthodoxy is also like that. It is a horrible waste to make the Church suit our image. Who would want to belong to a church like that? The Church is outside us, bigger than us, telling us we're wrong. We wrestle against it and fight it. There's no point in going to the Church for peace and serenity, security or comfort. It's a place of battle. I can tell you I normally leave the contemporary liturgy in a state of numbness. What a mockery the new liturgists have made of the ancient tradition! I am not as old or crotchety as Jacques Maritain was when he wrote *The Peasant of the Garonne*, and I didn't and still don't like that book, but I have come to experience emptiness in the Church of the progressives. If the progressives succeed in making the Church fit their self-image, I probably would not leave the Church — my motive for belonging to it is not its contemporary sociological order — but for me it would be a long agony, a Gethsemane, a desert. I think of the progressive Church as "progressive bourgeois Christianity," and its sentiments of peace, love, community, solidarity, and the like remind me of the saccharine holy cards of an earlier form of bourgeois Christianity, which I also did not like. "This place stinks of God!" When I hear progressive sermons I think of another line of Bloy's, about preachers whose lips are like a hen's ass blowing air. That makes me smile, and sermons become tolerable.

Really, to read the letters columns in the *National Catholic Reporter*, the flagship of progressive bourgeois Christianity, is to overhear spoiled children.

No, the Church means participating in God's life, no matter what, believing in *God*, and not in nonsense. The Creator of this whole blue-brown ball in space and the vastnesses beyond — a Majesty whose viewpoint dwarfs what each of us must live through day to day.

The priest is not just a social worker, teacher, nurse, counselor, minister. The priest is Christ, in a special way. I have friends who make fun of the way, when we were younger, before Vatican II, we were taught that the priest's hands were holy because they held the Body of Christ, brought Christ down within our sight and placed Him on our tongues. What a "magical" view, they said. We have now seen the priesthood demythologized. So what is it now, a club of political activists? No, the priest is "set aside." Celibacy is a sign of this being "set apart." Of course, such signs can change. Celibacy is not a metaphysical thing, absolutely necessary. But why would one change it, in an age itching to make everything over into its own self-image? Celibacy *contradicts* the spirit of our time. That is its power. Of course, the demands it makes upon the young who accept it are furious and terrible. But it is not wrong to tremble in the sight of the Lord.

You are thinking that I am terribly old-fashioned. Is it better to be new-fashioned? Celibacy is now a thousand years old and has seen many fashions come and go.

Women priests? Maybe. My two daughters would make excellent priests — bright, sympathetic, reflective, outgoing. My wife would make an extraordinary priest; all who know her love her for her gentleness, her perception, her strength. But the priest is an in-the-flesh image of God, and we ''believe in God the Father'' and pray ''Our Father who art in heaven.'' If you wish to argue that there is no difference between male and female, you face two possible conclusions. One is that females may also be in-the-flesh images of God. That violates the constant, traditional imagery of Judaism and Christianity; metaphorically, it jangles, is discordant, alters the entire symbolic network. The other conclusion is that then it really doesn't matter that all priests are male; if there is no essential difference, males may represent females quite adequately. No, you say, but then males have all the *power*. Is Christianity a competition for power?

The Catholic faith is not based upon the Scriptures; the Scriptures are based upon the Catholic faith. It was the Church that decided which books represent the true canon of Scripture, excluding many and including those that have come down to us. The Church does not overthrow Scripture, on the contrary is faithful to it, but it is certainly larger than the Scripture. Those Catholics who base their faith upon contemporary biblical scholarship soon have great difficulties telling you why they bother to be Catholic at all or even to believe in God. Subtly, their center of gravity shifts to fidelity to the critical examination of texts, and they become masters of texts and masters of all they survey. Intellectually, their god seems remarkably like a modern bourgeois man of the Left.

There is an orthodoxy in progressive bourgeois Christianity, too. I know, because I have been excommunicated from it. Friends report to me (and crank letters sometimes give me firsthand evidence) in what low regard I am now held by the Catholic Left, as if I were an apostate or an infidel. According to this orthodoxy, I ought to hold that celibacy should be abolished; that women should be priests; that the Pope should be a colleague — one bishop among bishops, one theologian among others, one conscience equal to all others, one of the happy crowd of progressive bourgeois Christians, all alike; that in Central America, God is on the side of the Sandinistas and the guerrillas in El Salvador, etc. There is a progressive bourgeois Christian credo and agenda. Here, it is true, I am a heretic.

The Catholic Church also has its own defined character. Like all things human, this character is flawed, angular, deserving of criticism, and always in need of vigilance and reform. But those who choose to belong (no one has to) incur an obligation to carry forward to our children its wisdom and its treasures. These are, I think, indispensable to the humanism of the world—not only to the West in a geographical or geopolitical sense, but to all who share the vision of human personality and voluntary community that we mean when we say "the West," a heritage of ideas, symbols, stories, and values.

The Catholic Church has its own political economy, so to speak, disguising the mystery at its heart. In its human workings, it is not a nation, but it is a multinational, multicultural worldly institution. It, too, is built on checks and balances. When the U.S. Catholic bishops met in Washington in 1986, the newsmagazines suggested that they might break from Rome over Rome's decision to divide episcopal authority in Seattle, that the U.S. bishops would set themselves up as a kind of Supreme Court, with jurisdiction over Archbishop Hunthausen and the papacy. Thank God, they saw that this was absurd. A Catholic bishop would be pretty ridiculous independent of Rome.

The Catholic system of checks and balances is more complex than that of any other religious institution, or secular for that matter. What the people believe is one check. Not that the people are always right—that a majority once tolerated slavery did not make slavery right. Another check is the faith of all the bishops, in communion with one another, a kind of Quaker test by consensus. A third is the communion of all with the Pope. Each of these three challenges the others. Yet the benefit of the doubt lies with the mystery of the papacy. If you do not believe that God in a special way protects the teaching of the Pope, at least within certain carefully drawn boundaries, calling yourself a Roman Catholic is a little absurd. A curious belief, to be sure, this Roman Catholic allegiance to the papacy. It contradicts the spirit of virtually every age—struggles against the papacy are a fixture of history.

For myself, I have a special love of Pope John Paul II, perhaps because he is a Slav—but I would like to think for deeper reasons—and because he represents so many of the ideals I have tried to pursue in my own life, a love for poetry (in my case fiction), for St. Thomas Aquinas, St. John of the Cross, for twentieth-century existentialism and phenomenology, even for athletics. I wish he understood the American system better; he would make a wonderful American; he has all the right moves. He is certainly *not* a progressive bourgeois Christian, and I wish him well, urgently well, in his struggle against such. The history of the next hundred years depends on how well he succeeds in his project — to strengthen the deepest resources of Catholic faith and discipline, for terrible, dark days ahead. Sometimes I am very pessimistic about the success of Soviet power and duplicity in the world and about the complacence of progressive bourgeois cultural leaders elsewhere, the "children of light." Perhaps such pessimism is only a reflection of dark Slavic brooding, undiminished in my case by growing up in optimistic America. Still, "get ready for dark times" is what my heart keeps telling me.

BOB GUCCIONE

Art and Pornography

Perhaps one of the great differences between Roman Catholicism and Protestantism is that the Church can see that an image or a book can be both artistic and pornographic at the same time, that there are extradimensional values that give one a sufficient reason to preserve it. With the other religions, it's either artistic or pornographic, but it can't be both at the same time.

—Bob Guccione

The image of Bob Guccione that has appeared in the media in recent years, particularly as he has debated both fundamentalists and feminists on the subject of pornography, should be familiar enough by now: the tan skin setting off layers of gold chains (from one of which dangles a miniature gold phallus), the Italian silk shirt open to reveal the solar plexus, the gold chain-link watchband that (minus the timepiece) might have adorned the wrist of a Roman pontifex, the leather trousers stuffed into the kind of luxe cowboy boots Marlboro men only dream of. It may seem, at first blush, like a visual cliché borrowed from the board rooms and kidney-shaped pools of Hollywood, but its true provenance lies, I think, in other provinces.

It's a matter of record that Guccione once began study to become a Roman Catholic priest and that he is a painter manqué. Those influences show their hand in a curious asceticism and a kind of priestly demeanor and in a lavish art collection. But is it too much to ask the reader to see in Guccione's elaborate yet meticulous grooming—the hair coiffed just so, a Kleenex tucked neatly into his shirtsleeve—the picture of a Man Who Would Be a Renaissance Prince?

The outspoken publisher of *Penthouse* who made national headlines in the summer of 1984 by running nude photos of the country's first black

Miss America, Vanessa Williams, and so set the stage for her dethrone-
ment, lives in a renovated seven-story townhouse just off Central Park—
a princely pad that is a curious blend of period and modern and that has
been featured in the leads of almost every article written about Guccione
in the last five years. The multimillion-dollar collection of paintings and
antiques, the bathrooms of solid Carrara marble with gold fixtures, the
silver-lined indoor pool, and killer Rhodesian ridgeback dogs have all
been documented. Somewhat less attention has been given to the fact that
apart from these luxuries—paid for by profits from *Penthouse* and *Omni*,
which he also publishes, and investments in various films—Guccione
lives a life that by New York standards might be considered rather low
profile, semi-ascetic. He is rarely if ever photographed, for instance, at
nightclubs, discos, galas, or the other perks of prominence, although he
has been known to throw the odd dinner party for the likes of Mike Tyson
and Yitzhak Rabin. He doesn't own a private jet, cars, or boats and says
he doesn't smoke, drink, or take drugs. A writer for *Money* magazine
was moved by all this to refer to Guccione's "almost monklike austerity."

His office, dimly lit and almost gloomy, is paneled with wood imported
from England. Over his shoulder on the day we spoke was a Holbein
portrait of Henry VIII which may have been responsible for casting a
Renaissance penumbra upon things. Of course, in the same room—dubbed,
perhaps because of the expensive woodwork, the Georgian Room—hang
works by Vlaminck, Léger, Vuillard, Gauguin, Pissarro, and de Chirico.
But it was the Holbein that kept looming.

The monachist epithets may ultimately be misleading, though. By all
accounts, Guccione does work eighteen-hour days and rarely leaves his
feste Burg on Sixty-seventh Street. And he is fastidious: in the course of
our conversation, when a can of diet soda was brought to him, he spent
an inordinate amount of time wiping and rewiping its rim with his Kleenex.
("God knows what these things carry," he exclaimed to one interviewer.
"They sit in warehouses. Cockroaches and rats scrabble over them, and
all kinds of people touch them.") But he appears to be a man who
appreciates power and seeks it out. Speaking to the *London Times* not
long ago about his investment in research to build the world's first fusion
reactor, he said that if it worked, "I would be worth the equivalent of
Exxon, Getty Oil, British Petroleum and all the other oil companies rolled
into one." If Bob Guccione had gone on to become a man of the cloth,
one can't help feeling that he would have settled for nothing less than the
red hat.

Granted that the tangle of arguments concerning pornography and First
Amendment rights is complicated enough to have led certain feminists to

get into bed, so to speak, with Christian fundamentalists, Guccione manages to apply an almost Thomistic logic to the issue. Whatever one feels about the man — and his exposé of Vanessa Williams, for instance, has made him rankly unpopular in the arts community for dubious reasons — his explanations deserve to be heard. After all, anybody who is reviled by Jerry Falwell, Gloria Steinem, and Ed Meese must have something interesting to say.

I WAS BORN in Flatbush [Brooklyn] and raised in New Jersey. I never went to parochial school, but I did go to church at St. John's in Bergenfield, New Jersey. I went to Sunday school for a number of years as I was growing up. But I think that by the time I was twelve or thirteen I started to drift away from the Church. I was strongly attracted to the Church when I was younger because I was attracted to the metaphysics. It wasn't until I was twelve or thirteen that I began to question things. Just prior to quitting the Church physically — I didn't ever quit it emotionally or even psychically — I got so interested that I wanted to become a priest. Just before the fall, as it were, I was very devout, very much caught up in the religion, and I went to a seminary for a while. I liked it. I was pretty dedicated.

But I really left the Church because it failed to explain a lot of questions that I had as a kid. The Catholic dogma just didn't gel to that young mind, that young boy that I was. But a lot of the things that I learned as a kid or took from my religious training really have remained with me to this day. One of them was an appreciation for other people. Bear in mind that I came from a big Italian family, lots and lots of cousins and uncles. We were all very close because, of course, the whole family was Roman Catholic, so there was a kind of pervasive effect. We had cousins who became nuns, others who became priests. One thing I learned and maintain to this day — even though most people wouldn't understand and don't agree because they don't understand — is that I developed a great respect for women. Now this is a bone of contention between me and the feminists, who are, for all practical purposes, my enemies. They would have it that *Penthouse* demeans women and that the work I do is degrading to women. I don't believe that at all, and if anybody were to follow the magazine closely, to look at it over a period of time and in some depth, they would never be able to come to that conclusion. I have great respect for women, all kinds of women. When I was going to Sunday school, there was a great emphasis on the family, on sisters, on marriage — and coming from a large family, I guess that all made a great deal of sense to me. We all had friends outside, but our deepest friendships and our most profound alliances were within the family.

I still have a lot of respect for the Church, and to some extent I support it. That is to say, I support it philosophically, even though I am not in agreement with much of what they believe and teach. And some aspects of it I support financially because I think they're doing good work. As a private individual I have several personal charities. Two of them involve nuns: one set up a halfway house for alcoholics and the children of alcoholics, and I am almost the sole source of support for this woman's work; and I support another nun who teaches wayward children. I get beautiful letters several times a year from these nuns who pour their hearts out and thank me profusely for what I'm doing for them. That gives me a great deal of satisfaction.

When I brought out my film *Caligula*, which was very controversial and created chaos all over the world, I had three obscenity actions brought against me. When you fight an obscenity action, you introduce expert witnesses because they're always very impressive to juries — juries have little or no savvy of these esoteric affairs. I reached out to a friend of mine in Rome who is one of the senior Franciscan priests in the world. He works at the Vatican and broadcasts nationally on behalf of the Vatican three times a week; at the same time, he's a very reasonable, intellectual man who has been intimately associated with the Italian motion picture industry for thirty-seven years. There are people like Fellini who will not shoot a single frame of film unless this particular priest blesses the set and goes through the script. He's baptized the children of many very famous Italian directors, producers, actresses, and so on. He knew about *Caligula* and I asked him if he would give evidence for us. He agreed, which was extraordinary, given who he was.

In his deposition, which took over nine hours, he said that he would like to have a film like *Caligula* as a teaching tool for his students. This really cracked the other side up, and they asked how he could say such a thing about a blatantly pornographic film. His response was "How better could I describe to my students the reasons why Catholicism and Christianity had to come into being during the paganism of ancient Rome?" Coming from a man like that, who was also an orator, it came across like gangbusters. So that established once again in my mind the fact that many higher-ranking priests are invariably much more flexible and liberal than one normally expects. As tough as the Catholic Church is, as dogmatic as their public image appears to be, they're much more liberal than a lot of people think.

I've been married twice, and on neither occasion was I married in the Church. Neither of my former wives was Catholic, and although I was not religious at all, I encouraged my second wife to change from the Church of England to Catholicism. There's not that big a gap, but I thought the Church of England was nowhere. If I was going to have children, I wanted them to have a somewhat more serious religion to fall back on. The Anglican Church is, in my opinion, a bed of pseudo-religious nonsense.

Although I've drifted away from the Church, I haven't become interested in any aspect of any other religion. I have not become an atheist; I am really an agnostic. So the Church has had that kind of impact on my life. It's very easy to be an atheist in this age of ours, especially when one is interested in science as I have always been. My children, who are all grown up and range in age from twenty to thirty-six, all still go to church from time to time. My son Bob Jr. [editor of *Spin* magazine], who is thirty, goes to church every Sunday. I sent several of my children to parochial school in England. I've always encouraged them, because I wanted them to have the same kind of background that I did—then, ultimately, they could make up their own minds. I did not want to infect their attitude in any way with *my* lack of belief.

I was very taken with the concept that life could endure forever and that there was something very special after death. This is probably part of an attitude that one develops in a family like mine which is very close, where there's always somebody dying, an aunt or an older uncle. Their funerals are attended en masse by the whole family, and it's an important family experience. To this day, when a member of the family dies, wherever it may be, I go to the funeral; and every funeral is attended by religious ceremonies which I participate in.

About four or five months ago I took my girlfriend to Venice. We were going around looking at the art in some of the old churches, and I found myself lighting a candle, which is something that an irreligious person simply doesn't do. It would probably have come as a great shock to a lot of people who know me if they had seen that scene; but it never really entirely leaves you. There's always something that stays with you. It's like with Jews: even if they reach a point where they're no longer religious, there are nonetheless certain things that remain with them. As with Catholicism, Judaism is a big, formal, ritualistic religion—whereas I see the others as pale imitations.

I don't think there was any special moment when I came to the final decision to leave the Church. It was something that took place over a period of time. I began to feel less involved, less receptive to the teachings of the Church, less inclined physically to go to church. I was becoming more aware of the rest of the world, and I just found that the Church couldn't answer questions that I was asking myself. I was very concerned about evolution as a kid, and the Catholic perspective made absolutely no sense to me at all.

Confession was probably the last aspect of ceremonial Catholicism that bothered me. I didn't enjoy it, but it made sense to me that if you did something wrong at least you had somebody to talk to. And none of the actual ceremony of the Mass bothered me. I thought it was all very beautiful, and I still do. The problem really was that I had questions and more questions, and I wasn't getting answers that satisfied me. But, in fact, for many years I was an altar boy. I once served Mass on Christmas Eve, and that was the high moment of my life in the Church—I was chosen by our priest and I felt very privileged, very special. It was around that time that I felt I wanted to *be* a priest. I was about eleven. I went to a retreat in, I think, New Jersey or Pennsylvania, and I lived with this Salesian brotherhood for about six months. I was very serious and talked my parents into letting me do it. Then when I came back home, I developed a different attitude. I'd had a friend there with whom I became involved in very deep metaphysical discussions, and I found that I wasn't agreeing with him. My sense of logic as a kid would not allow me to accept much of what I was being told.

On the other hand, I was always encouraged by people in the Church to be an artist; I was never discouraged. I was told that it was a special gift, given to me for a very good reason, and I believed that. I was drawing from the time I could hold a crayon in my hand, and I started painting when I was seventeen. I feel that it's inevitable that I will eventually take myself more and more out of this business, turn over more and more control to my kids, and go back to painting.

I was a heavy smoker and I quit smoking. I was never a gambler in the casino sense. I never used or was attracted to drugs. And to my knowledge I've never taken advantage of any individual under any circumstances. The opposite would be true. Those were the kinds of things I was taught when I was growing up, and maybe this is a carry-over from the way I was trained. But as I say, I was brought up in a large family where issues like these were a part of our training, so I'm sure there was some kind of religious and familial effect that was carried forward into my life. If, for example, one of my children were to tell me tomorrow that he or she wanted to get married, I would hope that they would marry in the Church—even though I didn't on two separate occasions. And I didn't seek to marry a Roman Catholic: the first woman I married was a

Jewess, the second was an Anglican. But I would suggest to my own children that the ceremony and the experience give something that's more durable and make it more important.

I have a strange kind of dichotomy with respect to the Church. For instance, I feel that the Church is making a serious mistake by not updating itself, by not evolving as society evolves and knowledge and experience develop. On one hand, I feel that the Church should be much more flexible, and on the other. . . . Just recently I met a group of nuns who were dressed in ordinary day-to-day clothing, whom you could never identify as nuns. I was enrolling one of my children in a Catholic school in England, and I was shocked. I said, "Who are all these women running around? I thought that nuns taught here." Well, they were all nuns — they were wearing *miniskirts!* I thought that was a disaster; I really rebelled against it. I wanted to see them dressed as penguins.

I don't know quite what that means, but it did impress me. I find that with sexual issues the Church is much more expansive and tolerant than, say, the Protestant, Baptist, and fundamentalist religions in America. For instance, we're getting a lot of static, as a company, from the Baptist and American fundamentalist movements, and *never* from the Roman Catholic Church. Catholicism is older, wiser, and much more worldly, and they don't really need what are essentially political rather than religious devices to take more money from the public.

Even the Church's attitude on masturbation has a very logical rationale behind it, whereas the Lutheran and Baptist attitude has no redeeming qualities at all. The Catholic rationale is that masturbation is an inconclusive act and that it has no greater meaning than to give some pleasure to the senses. The other religions — if you'll forgive the term, the *lesser* religions — don't go that far. They just say that it's wrong, that all sex outside of marriage is wrong. It's as if they pick up pieces of more serious religions and apply them without really knowing what they mean.

My reading of the Catholic dogma is that sex in the right circumstances, within marriage and for the purpose of producing children, is perfectly acceptable. There's nothing wrong with sex per se or with deriving pleasure from it, but there's something wrong with sex that has no dimension other than the simple giving of pleasure. Once again, that makes *some* kind of logic. After all, the Vatican has a wonderful collection of pornography because they recognize the artistic value of what they've collected. It may be pornographic in general terms, and it's not on display for everyone to see, but nonetheless they have appreciated and understood art sufficiently well to say that we must hold on to this because it has a value for those who are informed or worldly enough to understand it. It must be preserved. You would never find that attitude in Protestantism at all: It's pornographic? It should be destroyed. There is no redeeming value to pornography at all for the Protestants.

Perhaps one of the great differences between Roman Catholicism and Protestantism is that the Church can see that an image or a book can be both artistic and pornographic at the same time, that there are extradimensional values that give one a sufficient reason to preserve it. With the other religions, it's either artistic or pornographic, but it can't be both at the same time. I've found this through hard, practical experience in having to deal with them.

Although my personal morality may be quite different from the establishment morality of the Catholic Church, the dynamics are not so far apart. My attitude toward sex is very definitely a moral attitude. It's not a freewheeling attitude that says, "If it gives me pleasure, that's all that matters" — it's not that at all. I think that one can be to some extent sexually promiscuous — which is to say, having sex with people to whom one is not married or has no intention of marrying. But I have never made love to a woman whom I didn't respect, whom I didn't have genuine feelings for. I'm not a pushover that way. There are all kinds of temptations in my life — a *thousand* times more than the average guy experiences — and I will bet that the average guy is more promiscuous in actual practice than I am, than I have been. So I think of my own personal sexuality as being controlled by a kind of morality which may not fit in with any church's attitude, but nonetheless is an ethical code that I follow.

That can only be as a result of my training as a kid, learning that there is such a thing as morality. And the fact that one can live according to a code of morality in today's world is saying a great deal because there is, with respect to sex, virtually no code of ethics or no morality that I know of. It's just "If it feels good, do it." That's the common expression. I don't accept that, I don't believe in that.

Did I ever get drunk and just sleep with someone without real feelings? I can't say I've never done that — of course I have — but those would be very rare exceptions in my life. First of all, I never drink like that. I drink only when I feel I really must to keep up with everyone else socially. We give a lot of parties, and sometimes I feel that everyone is drinking so I really should take a drink. I take two drinks and I'm smashed. I look like a falling-down drunk. But that's rare.

There was a very tempestuous period of my life, when I had separated from my first wife and I was living alone in Italy. I think at that time I'd been undergoing a lot of very deep psychological changes, and I was extremely promiscuous for a period. And then I paid for it. I went through about three or four years, as a very young man, of impotency. I was utterly unable to have sex. I was paying for the promiscuity; I was punishing myself.

I never talked to anybody about it. I just went through it, and, happily, eventually emerged from it. But for a number of years I was in a very bad state — I really couldn't consummate a sexual relationship with anybody. And I attributed it to the way I was conducting myself a few years earlier when I was extremely promiscuous. During that period I picked up a very minor venereal disease. It wasn't even a venereal disease — I picked up a case of crabs. I was twenty-one years old, and I was so knocked out by what had happened to me. I've always been personally very clean and am to this day. I'm sure I get this from my mother, who is *fanatically* clean. And to have carried these lice. . . . To most people it's unimportant — you go through all kinds of things, particularly when you're in the service. They come up with all kinds of diseases and they don't care about it. But I was so impressed by the fact that I was so physically dirtied by these lice that I had picked up.

Bear in mind that I'm talking about moving to Italy five years after the war was over, when you still couldn't get a piece of meat. It was still tough times; the economy was in terrible shape. There were a lot of prostitutes around, and love was very free and very available, so it was easy to do what I had done. But as I say, it so impressed me that for four years I was unable to have sex, I must've been so frightened. Not frightened of the lice itself, but morally frightened.

I don't think that sex is ever dirty if it is practiced by consenting adults. If two people like to beat each other to death, if that's their bag and they enjoy it and that's how they conduct their sex lives and that's meaningful to them, then to me that's perfectly acceptable. It may not be what *I* want, but that's not important. As long as what I am doing is not offensive to the person that I'm with, that anything I want or they want is acceptable to them or to me, then it's fine. Its practice may be difficult in certain circumstances because of an unwilling partner, but I don't see that I would ever describe it as dirty.

When feminists say that we're exploiting women, the immediate answer that comes to mind is How can you be exploiting someone who, first, wants to do it; second, is paid a great deal of money to do it; third, wouldn't have it any other way and has no regrets? As opposed to the man who buys the magazine, the consumer who has to pay for the privilege of looking at a girl who is being paid to expose herself. I take a very basic biological view in that, generally, men are voyeurs and women are exhibitionists. There's no way around this: women are predisposed to

undress themselves, to exhibit themselves sexually for the primitive purpose of attracting a mate. And men, who have this much more protective
attitude and are really spectators, are impelled to look and appreciate and
be attracted by women. It's like the petals of a flower that attract an insect
to pollinate it. It's a kind of exhibitionism on the part of the flower and
a kind of voyeurism on the part of the bee which is attracted to the flower's
exhibitionist tendencies, if I can use this bizarre analogy. But that's the
way it is with men and women.

So I feel that *Penthouse* is fulfilling a very basic function in society,
in that it's giving men something that they all want and are biologically
impelled to seek. It is not hurting women, and it is probably helping a
lot of guys who, if they didn't have another valve to let steam off, might
in fact go out and commit an antisocial act. One of the criticisms of
Penthouse and magazines like ours is that there's a causal relationship
between exposure to our kind of eroticism, or hard-core pornography, and
the commission of antisocial acts — which is, of course, utterly ridiculous.
Nor is there a scintilla of scientific evidence anywhere to support it. On
the contrary, there's ample evidence that exposure to pornography in
general has a therapeutic effect on the viewers because it keeps them from
going out and doing something that may be harmful to society at large.

Just look at the example of Sweden or any one of the Scandinavian
countries where they eliminated censorship years ago. The *whole* crime
rate, not just rape or criminal acts with a sexual basis, has dropped dra-
matically. By comparison, we are a very uptight society. There are more
churches of every denomination per capita in this country than anywhere
in the rest of the world. We have churches here that nobody ever heard
of. We've all been made to feel very guilty about our sexuality; and this
guilt, induced by churches and religion, is responsible to the greatest
possible extent for the breakdown in marriage. Because the lines of communication between men and women, especially on a sexual level, have
broken down. People are simply afraid to communicate. There are men
who would *love* to say things to their wives, to say what they really want,
what really concerns and interests them, and vice versa. But they can't
communicate because they think it's dirty: "If I say this to my wife, she'll
think I'm crazy, she'll think I'm sick." There is not the openness that
European and Eastern societies have. We're the worst; we are sexually
the most guilt-ridden society in the world.

I honestly feel, and I say this with my hand on my heart, I genuinely
believe that *Penthouse* has done more good in this country for its readership
than any other force within the communications industry that I can think
of. Because it makes people think, makes them talk, opens up lines of

communication. Some very sheltered or naive individual sitting out there in never-never land may feel that his personal predilections are sick, that *he* is sick, and that because he has a propensity for a particular kind of lovemaking that isn't brought up in conversation he cannot have a normal sex life. When he looks at a magazine like ours and reads the letters column and sees the topics that we discuss, he will suddenly realize that he is not all alone in the world, is not sick, that there isn't anything wrong with him sexually, that he is simply different, and that there are millions of people who share his difference. So he will find someone who is more suitable for a relationship for him. I think this is an extremely positive force because it is taking something out of the wilderness of our conscience and making all the information available to everyone. It's educational, and no one can persuade me that the dissemination of information as important to our lives as sexual behavior is wrong.

Sometimes the question is asked of me, Would I allow my daughter to appear nude in *Penthouse* or in another magazine? The answer is, obviously, No, I wouldn't allow her to appear in another magazine — not because of any moral stand I would take, but because it would be extremely embarrassing to me as publisher of a magazine like *Penthouse* to have my daughter appear in somebody else's magazine. The press would have a field day with that. If I thought my daughter were really beautiful and that she could be photographed very artistically, would I allow her to appear in *Penthouse?* Possibly, depending on the way she was photographed. If it were indeed something that I regarded as artistic, yes, I would find it acceptable. Because to me, art overcomes all, it has its own morality, its own *raison d'être*.

There is another category of answers to this question, based on the premise that I did not have a magazine like *Penthouse*. If I had continued just to paint pictures, and my daughter came to me one day and said, "I've been invited to appear nude in a magazine," I would make a different kind of judgment, probably more an esthetic than a moral judgment. I'd want to know who the photographer was and if he was a really good, class photographer. And if I thought my daughter was genuinely beautiful and I could see this as a work of art, then I would agree to it.

Ultimately, though, my daughters have the same kind of mind that I do, the same character. They're very strong-willed, very determined in their way. If one of my daughters came to me and she was determined to do this, nothing I could do would stop her. And in the end I would respect her determination, whether she succeeded or not. The fact that she was determined to do something and did it despite the fact that I didn't like it would be a quality that I would have to respect.

TERRANCE SWEENEY

The Crisis of Authority

Heresy is the lifeblood of religions. It is faith that begets heretics. There
are no heresies in a dead religion.

— André Suarès
   Péguy

But this is the covenant which I will make with the house of Israel, says
the Lord: I will put my law within them, and I will write it upon their
hearts; and I will be their God, and they shall be my people. And no longer
shall each man teach his neighbor and each his brother, saying, "Know
the Lord," for they shall all know me, from the least of them to the greatest,
says the Lord; for I will forgive their iniquity, and I will remember their
sin no more.

— Jeremiah 31:33–34

With his rather long, swept-back hair and young good looks, Father Terrance Sweeney seems like the kind of worldly Jesuit Hollywood would
be happy to cast as the embattled priest who stands by his convictions
even though it means suffering the contumely of the Vatican itself. Father
Sweeney is at pains to enunciate each syllable as clearly and lovingly as
if it were part of a crucial liturgy — perhaps a sacramental sign of the
inner conviction that informs his course of action. It's the sort of detail
that the critics — particularly those who had lived through the Vatican
Council and had known young priests straining to make their knowledge
of God *relevant* — would hail as honest and empathic.

As it turns out, neither Hollywood nor the critics would be far off the
mark. In the film, of course, the Jesuit would somehow be proven right
in the end and would humbly accept a new position as head of some
glamorous Southern California parish, to serve out his days as Confessor

to the Stars. At the very least, some amiable compromise would be worked out with older and wiser hierarchs that would allow both sides to pursue the gospel teachings in their own way.

In real life, no compromise has been proposed or accepted. Terrance Sweeney does indeed live in Beverly Hills and continues to work in the film and television industries, but there the scenario begins to resemble Frank Capra less than Ken Russell. On August 15, 1986, Father Sweeney resigned from the Jesuit order rather than destroy research that he had been conducting for some time. It's a complicated story.

The Society of Jesus, founded in 1540, is the largest order of priests and brothers in Roman Catholicism. It has traditionally been perceived as being the advance guard of Catholic thought, represented in recent times by renowned Jesuit writers such as Teilhard de Chardin and John Courtney Murray. But even within the context of that intellectually challenging tradition, Terrance Sweeney is somewhat anomalous. In his twenty-four years as a Jesuit, he worked as a producer, writer, and director of more than forty films and television programs, for which he has won five Emmy Awards. The forty-two-year-old priest has served as consultant and technical adviser to major productions dealing with clerical characters or religious subjects, from the television miniseries *The Thorn Birds* to the feature film *The Mission*. He has written several books, including *God &* (a series of interviews about the perception of God that he conducted with public figures ranging from Richard Chamberlain and Martin Sheen to Father Theodore Hesburgh and Dorothy Day) and *Streets of Anger, Streets of Hope* (a book about gang violence in East Los Angeles that was made into a television movie which he directed).

In November 1985, as part of research he was conducting on the vocation crisis confronting the Church, Father Sweeney sent out questionnaires to 312 American Catholic bishops. They read: "In light of the mission of the Church and the pastoral needs of the faithful, I would approve or disapprove of: optional celibacy for priests, ordaining women to the priesthood, ordaining women as deacons, and inviting married and resigned priests to return to active ministry." The responses and their significance are explored toward the end of this interview, but fascinating in its own way was the Order's response. Although the Jesuit Provincial of California, John W. Clark, initially approved of Sweeney's work and encouraged him to continue, Father Clark reversed himself after hearing objections from Cardinal Joseph Ratzinger in the Vatican. Even to have asked the four questions was apparently considered a breach of faith, and Father Sweeney was ordered either to discontinue the survey and destroy his results or to resign from the Jesuit order. For reasons he explains here,

Father Sweeney felt he had no choice but to continue his work, even if it meant facing the possibility of never again saying Mass or hearing confession.

Father Sweeney remains a priest for life, but he cannot actually practice any of his clerical functions without an invitation from a bishop to serve in his diocese. Considering the severe and escalating shortage of Roman Catholic clergy in the nation, it is at least ironic that he hasn't been actively recruited. Among the unique insights he discusses are his understanding of the great wrenching changes wrought on the clerical world by Vatican II and his ultimate vision of the Church's survival beyond the immediate crisis of authority which has put him at odds with the hierarchy.

BOTH OF MY PARENTS are of Irish descent. My father, George Sweeney, was born in Brooklyn and moved out to California many years ago. My mother, whose maiden name was Angeline Cullen, was born on a farm in Minnesota, one of nine children. She had also come out to California, and for many years they were both involved in the movie studios, working in the film labs as optical printers, cutters, and that sort of thing. Both were Catholic, although I'd have to say that my father was not really a practicing Catholic. My mother was very much so and felt it was extremely important that all five children have a Catholic education, and she sacrificed a great deal in order to ensure that.

I was born in Los Angeles in 1945, the third of five children. One of my brothers died last year—before his death I had two older brothers, and I have a younger sister and younger brother. All of us went to Catholic grade schools and Catholic high schools. We moved several times, but I spent the first four years of grade school at Our Lady of Lourdes in Tujunga, which is in the Valley. In the middle of the fourth grade, my mother moved the three oldest of us to a military boarding school in Anaheim run by Dominican sisters. Then I went to Loyola High School with my older brothers, and that was taught by Jesuits. I entered the Jesuit order after I graduated from high school in 1962. So I was a Jesuit from September 7, 1962, until August 15, 1986.

The two distinctive things that I remember around the house during the first four years of grade school—since after that I was in military boarding school—were, first, that my mother would try to have us say the rosary as a family. And I remember her insisting that we go to Mass and really encouraging us to serve Mass as altar boys. Other than that, I don't remember any kind of specific religious instructions coming from my parents.

My father was very heavily involved in the horse races as a gambler, and unfortunately his Irish luck was not that extensive. Because he started incurring enormous debts through his gambling, he put tremendous pressure on the marriage. In essence, my mother asked him either to give up the horses or to leave. So he left, and because she had to have money to support the kids, she started working two jobs and put the three oldest boys into the military boarding school. For the most part she worked at the studio called Technicolor, although she has also worked for MGM and others.

It was a pretty big shock for me as a young boy to go from a home environment to a boarding school where there was a tremendous emphasis on order and discipline. I recognized in that environment, even that young, a sense of loneliness and a sense of being unhappy because of the situation. I also recognized very early — probably as early as the fifth grade — that it was very important for me to help other people find happiness. It sounds simple, but at that time I started thinking how important it was for a person to be happy in his life and to try to make other people happy. I started thinking in that same context that maybe I was supposed to be a priest. Very vague, very indefinite, but the two ideas were distinct as early as the fifth grade.

I think the reason I associated the priesthood with happiness and helping people be happy was that I recognized that God was a Being who — no matter where you went, how old you were, or whether you were alone or not — was there with you. It seemed to me that a priest was someone who was in touch with or striving to be in touch with God and who was aware of God and who could make other people aware of God. At that very early age, it seemed to me that when you were in the presence of God, you had your best shot at happiness. Boy, was I naive!

The priests that I had through grade school were always off in their offices and I rarely saw them. Even when I was serving Mass it was very in and out. But I did meet some very happy Jesuits during high school, and there was much more that sense of camaraderie and fun and excitement about being alive — working hard yet having a good time doing it. In that sense, the specific association of priests and religious people being happy came in my experience of the Jesuits at Loyola.

Those Jesuits also seemed to have a wide range of interests and talent. More important, I sensed that for the most part they really liked the students. And even today that's still true — they like their work, they like the students, they'll go the extra mile. When a student is in need regarding personal things, conflicts at home, or real problems with particular courses of study, if a Jesuit can help he will indeed help. That sense of interest and care and commitment to the students was a huge plus.

Since I hadn't been through the training yet, I didn't know how extensive and rigorous it was. I didn't know the international and historical reputation the Jesuits had and the impact they had made at various very critical points in history in a wide variety of fields. So when I entered the Jesuits and started reading history and doing more in-depth studies on a number of subjects, I began to appreciate even more what some great Jesuits had contributed to the advance of civilization and culture and human thirst for God and for a better society. I think that the image that most people have of Jesuits is that they're scholars and that they're frequently on the cutting edge of change within the Catholic Church. Those impressions, even though they don't apply to all Jesuits, are quite accurate with respect to a few great Jesuits in history who have made an enormous difference in the shape of things. I'm thinking of Francis Xavier, of Matteo Ricci in China, of Teilhard de Chardin and John Courtney Murray in this century, Ignatius Loyola himself, Robert Bellarmine, and Athanasius Kircher the scientist. Yet while individual great Jesuits have shaped the outstanding reputation, it's the yeoman, the ordinary, hard-working Jesuit that has kept the Order going for four hundred years.

Entering the Jesuits in 1962, at the beginning of Vatican II, in essence I got both sides of the transition. When I went into the Jesuit order, it was still structured around the pre–Vatican II concept of religious life, which, if I can summarize it, was that imitation of Christ is the goal of all Jesuits and people in religious life and that asceticism and denial of self are some of the outstanding ways by which a religious can achieve that and therefore become a better person and more effective preacher, apostle, priest, sister. There was an enormous emphasis on asceticism. Thirty-five bells a day — every single minute of the day was ordered and structured. You spoke only Latin if you spoke at all, except for occasions when you could converse in English for recreation. There was a tremendous emphasis on discipline of the will and on learning through practice the great spiritual doctrines of the ascetics throughout history, who by their vows of poverty, chastity, and obedience learned how to deny themselves in order to become more Christ-like. The myriad ways which that particular philosophy can be embodied through ascetic practices was what I walked into in 1962. And, of course, with Vatican II finishing in 1965, there were incredible changes at the very foundations of religious life: Is it principally asceticism, or is it principally an expression of community and fraternity and love? There were major changes that took place all the way along as I was going through my Jesuit training, and I'm glad that I saw both. Because if I had not seen the former ascetic way, I would not have understood why a lot of people were disillusioned with the changes of Vatican II.

What I have found in terms of the response of the laity to Vatican II is that you have two ends of a highly nuanced spectrum. At one end are the people who felt really cheated and disillusioned by Vatican II because it took away what they felt was sacred. It changed too many things that had too many psychological, emotional, and intellectual overtones with individual Catholics. For example, a lot of Catholics felt that the Vatican Council cheated them because it took away Latin, it took away that experience of Mass as being sacred and mysterious, and instead presented an experience of Mass as participating and acting as a community and no longer giving those people who were so inclined the opportunity to say their rosary or to be there with their private thoughts and devotions. The priest had been saying Mass in a language that they could not understand; therefore, they would fall into their own interior thoughts and devotions. A lot of people who identified religion with the forms felt that Vatican II took away their religion and their devotion because they were no longer able to experience what they experienced in the past.

On the other end of the spectrum were the people who felt that Vatican II had not gone far enough. They felt that society had undergone massive changes and that there should be far more experimentation in the religion, far more openness and dialogue. They felt that Vatican II was going in the right direction but that it wasn't going fast enough and they were disillusioned because the changes did not measure up to their own conviction of what should happen. So people on both ends of the spectrum were disenchanted.

In religious life, you can just accent that even more — because in religious life, a person lives what he thinks and believes and prays. A person gets up at five A.M. and works all day long with all the pressures, all the intentions to be a better and more Christ-like person. Then, all of a sudden over a period of three or four years, he's told, "Hey, you don't have to get up at five o'clock in the morning. You don't have to discipline your will — you're supposed to *love* yourself." For thirty-five years you were told *not* to love yourself and to give up your will and always pass the best food along to your neighbor. And now they're telling you that you can't go around with your eyes downcast when creation itself is a gift of God. You can imagine what a shock that was when it finally dawned on people. The business about habit and clothes is a very good example: the habit of a nun or the clothes of a priest, for those who were steeped in that tradition, was another manifestation of modesty and commitment to religious life. Then someone comes along and says, "Your clothes are setting up a barrier between you and the people. If you really want to be effective, dress like everyone else and forget this modesty stuff — virtue is not measured in terms of modesty but in terms of love."

So vocabulary changed, philosophy changed. It was too much of a shock, and older people as well as younger people left religious life. There was an enormous rate of departure from religious life. We're starting to add up data, and since 1965 over a hundred thousand priests and over three hundred thousand nuns have left. And even though it has tapered off somewhat, still the entrance rate in most parts of the world has not increased. So we're talking about religious life and priestly life in its very structure going through a crisis, and Vatican II was right at the heart of that crisis, as were the larger societal changes.

Most Jesuits have two years of novitiate, and then if they haven't already, they go through a collegiate program in which they get a bachelor's degree in philosophy. They teach for two or three years in a Jesuit high school or university, and that's called the regency period. Subsequent to that they go on to theology for four years and get at least a master's degree. Generally speaking, they're ordained a priest somewhere from eleven to thirteen years after they enter the Order. That was basically my training, except that I did master's work in communication arts and Ph.D. work in theology of the arts. I did that with the intention of working professionally in mass media. As I was going through my training, I realized more and more that the pulpit and the traditional ways of spreading the gospel in its broadest sense — as an enormous fund for social justice and questions of faith and healing — would not really communicate to the masses of people who are longing for knowledge and inspiration. I felt that it would be important to help translate and communicate those values to large numbers of people rather than to just a few, and to that end I started doing work in mass media.

It wasn't so much that my parents made contacts for me in the film industry. That was never the issue. It was simply that they were there working in it. I grew up with that kind of intuition and love for filmmaking and what it can achieve in stirring up human emotions and thoughts. But the particular impetus for my going into it was a Jesuit by the name of Father Phil Bourret. Way back in 1963, he gave a talk to a group of us young Jesuits, saying how important it was for Jesuits to get involved in radio and television and film and mass media, particularly in mission countries. Prior to his giving that talk, I had not heard of any Jesuit anywhere in the United States being involved full time in the mass media. As a matter of fact, I don't think there were any. Father Bourret was from the Far East, from Taiwan.

Having heard that it was possible for a Jesuit to be in mass media, even though there was no precedent that I was aware of, I asked my superiors for permission to do special course work in this field. I started in sixty-six taking electives in television production, eventually getting the OK to do master's work in communication arts and a Ph.D. in theology of the arts. After I finished that training and was ordained, on June 15, 1973, I moved to Loyola Marymount University campus. For three years following that, I worked professionally for a company called Paulist Productions. I started off as a consultant, then as a writer, and later as a producer. Then I freelanced, did a lot of work in East L.A. with street gangs, and lobbied to set up a community youth gang services project for gangs throughout L.A. Around 1979 I went back and spent three more years at Paulist Productions as a producer and then started freelancing again.

I've produced about forty different television shows and films, and three of the five Emmys I won were for the "Insight" series that I produced for Paulist Productions. One Emmy was for a Christmas special that I produced, called "The Juggler of Notre Dame," and the fifth was for a one-hour documentary that I wrote and produced on the Chicano gangs in East Los Angeles. I have also acted as consultant to a lot of projects. The two I enjoyed the most and am most proud of were a miniseries called *The Thorn Birds* and a film called *The Mission*. I had been asked to read the drafts of the scripts and in an informal and nonofficial way give my input.

On *The Thorn Birds*, the producer wanted me to be available to Richard Chamberlain both prior to and throughout the film on any question that he might have pertaining to the character of Father Ralph. He also wanted me to read and critique every draft of the script with special emphasis on matters pertaining to the Church and the religious characters. When it came to the actual filming, he asked me to be available to anyone who had questions regarding costumes, authenticity, ritual, gesture, you name it. Christopher Plummer, who played the cardinal, had those kinds of questions: How would a cardinal say this? Where would the book be placed? Where would an anointing of a bishop's hands be? What would a priest feel like if he falls in love and recognizes that he has a conflict with a vow? Where do the vows come from? That kind of thing.

Much to the credit of both Stan Margulies, the producer, and Carmen Culver, the writer, they were very conscientious about having me critique the script and point out things that were erroneous or historically inaccurate. For instance, they had Father Ralph having three vows and being a parish priest. Well, diocesan priests don't have three vows, that's just wrong information. I have to say that on the level of historical and "religious" inaccuracies, they changed every one of them. On the things that they could get away with but that would raise some eyebrows, they changed seventy-five to eighty percent.

I wrote an episode of "Barnaby Jones" that was the story of a Chicano

gang member who got framed for murder and a street priest who helps
Barnaby prove his innocence. In another instance, I was approached to
be the consultant on Ulu Grosbard's *True Confessions*, which I thought
was an outstanding film when it was finally released. But the draft of the
script that I read was so philosophically fatalistic for me that I declined
to work on it. Believe me, I really wanted to work with De Niro and
Duvall on it because I have great respect for their talent — but it was just
one of those situations where you have to make a decision. So they went
to another Jesuit. He worked as consultant, got a small part in the opening
of the film, gave them a great critique, probably contributed significantly
to the betterment of the script — and about a year and a half later put up
a notice on the board saying that he had left the Jesuits and was married.

But there are very few priests who work professionally in the media
and have enough experience in it that producers will automatically turn
to them. There should be a lot more because the potential for good is
substantial.

The work I did on the gang situation was very important for the gangs
and enhanced safety on the streets, but it taught me something else as
well. In the process of lobbying to try to set up the community youth
gang services project, I spent two or three years going to the cardinal,
going to the assemblyman's office, to the local congressman and the
mayor, having meetings with the governor's representatives. In the course
of lobbying, I learned a lot about authority — both political and religious
authority. As disgusting as this is to have to say, I learned that a lot of
people in authority and positions of leadership do not respond to the truth
of a situation, but rather to the public image of the situation and how that
might affect *their* image. For three years of my life I was literally burying
gang kids and talking to other gang kids trying to keep them from starting
gang wars. I was aware that East Los Angeles had become the violent
gang capital of the United States, that there were more gang-related killings
in Los Angeles than in any other ten cities combined.

There I was, banging on the doors of the community leaders — and I
have to say that it was more frustrating and more an occasion for despair
to talk to well-dressed politicians and well-heeled community leaders and
have them smile and shake my hand and do nothing than it was for me
to hear of another horrible gang incident. I recognized that for a lot of
the gang members who were uneducated and struggling for food, dealing
in dope just so they could have clothes on their back and a place to sleep,
there were any number of reasons why they were messed up or why some
of their actions were destructive to society. But people who were well

fed and well housed, who had the respect of the community, when push came to shove didn't care whether people were dying. That, to me, was disgusting.

With that little prelude regarding my awakening concerning authority, I'll explain the course of events that led to my resigning from the Jesuit order. As far back as 1978, I had started reading and reflecting very seriously on the issue of authority in the Catholic Church because I was eligible for final vows as a Jesuit as of that time. The number one unresolved question in my mind was What will I do if I am ever ordered to do something I think I shouldn't do or ordered not to do something I think I must do? In the course of doing the larger research on that question, I found out from various sociological data and from the writings of priests who had left the priesthood that one of their major problems with the priesthood was precisely the problem of conflict with authority. In 1970, the National Opinion Research Center did a survey of resigned priests throughout the United States, and the leading reason for priests' leaving the priesthood was conflict with authority. (The second reason was problems with celibacy.) And I thought, My God, I'm not alone — a lot of people are asking this question. There were ongoing efforts by sociologists and other people in the know to inform the Church that we were headed for a massive vocation crisis, with all the attendant things that would come with a shortage of priests and religious: schools close down, churches close down, people go without the sacraments and without counseling, people contemplating suicide don't have a priest to call. The impact on the Catholic population worldwide is staggering.

I wondered why nothing was happening with this information: statistics that said, for instance, that in 1970 there were thirty-seven thousand diocesan priests and by the year 2000 there will be fifteen thousand left in the United States. In 1965 there were forty-eight thousand seminarians; in 1985 there are only ten thousand. I started to say, What's going on here? Why aren't bishops and people in authority addressing this? In my research, I found that the most frequently proposed solutions to this dilemma were precisely the four questions that I put into my survey. Although I knew that a survey of the American hierarchy had been conducted back in 1970 on two of the four issues, that data seemed to be buried in the massive study that came out at the time. So I thought, Why not address only these four issues — not a long questionnaire that the bishops wouldn't answer — and why not send it out only to the policymakers?

I sent my survey out to 312 U.S. bishops, of whom 145 responded, a forty-six percent response. The results, I thought, were very interesting: twenty-four percent of American bishops would approve optional celibacy for priests, eighteen percent would approve inviting married and resigned priests to return to active ministry, twenty-eight percent would approve ordaining women to the diaconate, and seven percent would approve ordaining women to the priesthood. The four questions were introduced with these words: "In light of the mission of the Church and the pastoral needs of the faithful, I would. . . ." So the bases for decision were extremely serious pastoral and theological criteria. It's my sense that certain people in the Vatican were very threatened by this because if the magisterium themselves feel that there should be change in these matters, it calls into question those who defend the current policy.

Even though the majority of the bishops did not want changes on any of the four issues, I recognized that the criteria for approving or not approving were so serious that a larger question arose. If people close to you need something vitally, why should a policy set eight thousand miles away inhibit those needs? If one bishop in one diocese is saying, My people need a married clergy, my people need women deacons, then what is so serious about the universal policy that it can deny the needs of people right here at home? I started feeling more empathy with those bishops who are struggling with having to close down their grade schools, struggling with having to have one priest take care of three or four different parishes on a weekend, struggling with the fact that their priests are dying on average five years before the general population, that priests are turning into alcoholics because of the stress they're under. Comparing my figures with the 1970 survey, I found that the number of bishops wanting changes in optional celibacy and married or resigned clergy had doubled, showing that there had been a movement toward facing the inevitable.

At that point, the Jesuit Provincial of the California province had received a directive from the Superior General of the Jesuit order in Rome, Peter Hans Kolvenbach, who explicitly asked that I cease and desist all work on this matter and that I destroy the material that I had gathered so far. Father Clark, the Provincial, explained to me that the Superior General in Rome had been approached by people in the Vatican. There was no middle ground. He said: "If you do not do what I'm asking you to do under holy obedience, then I will have to ask you to leave the Jesuit order." And that stunned me. I knew that I was working on sensitive material, but I had no idea that there would be that kind of ultimatum, that swift, that definitive, with no room for compromise.

My next course of action, of necessity, will be to find work very soon in mass media on one of my projects. When you ask me how I felt upon being asked to leave the Order, realizing that I was also leaving behind my community and my source of livelihood and financial support—well, you name a feeling, I probably have felt it. Tension, disillusionment, heartbreak, anger, rage, hurt, confusion — and, as time goes on, the interior recognition that not to abandon or destroy the research was the right decision. At least, in the midst of all these other elements, as difficult and confusing as they have been, I know in my heart that what I did was the right thing. At least from that perspective, I feel inner peace. I can live with myself. I know that if I had destroyed that research or put it aside, I would have compromised something very important in my soul and that I would be a very unhappy man right now. I've had stomach problems and headaches, all of that, but fortunately it hasn't been crushing or overwhelming.

Two things have pulled me through. One is the realization I just mentioned that I know what I did was right. The other source of support and encouragement and sometimes humbling realization is how good people have been to me in the wake of this. Friends, strangers, Jesuits themselves — anything from postcards or letters to sending checks or calling. The support that I've received from a wide variety of people concerning my situation is really touching. Of course, included in the first realization is that peace of conscience to me is a sign of the presence of God. I certainly don't rule out the possibility that the hand of God is in this. With God there's not always happiness; I know that sometimes Christianity and doing what is right *costs*. It doesn't mean that God isn't there, it just means that you've got to take the good times with the bad.

Ultimately, my faith has been strengthened by all this. I have been in religious life long enough to know that a few people in authority who exercise their authority in a destructive manner are not the Church. They may have exceptional power that can radically alter my life, but they are not the Church. They are one aspect of the Church, indicative of its weakness. Because I recognize weakness in myself and recognize that society is not perfect and the Church is not perfect, I can then know that simply because perfection isn't there doesn't mean that God isn't there or that I should leave. The fact that I have been asked to leave the Jesuit order, and have in fact resigned, has not diminished my love for the Jesuit order, nor has it diminished my love for the priesthood. I recognize that it is extremely difficult for me to function as a priest now, and it probably will be extremely difficult in the future. That I am fully aware of — along with, as we speak, the stark possibility that I will never be able to say Mass again or to hear confessions again or to counsel in a sacramental way through baptism, marriage, and anointing, helping people that way. I'm aware that that may not happen again, and that's very hard.

I think the number one problem facing the Catholic Church right now is a crisis of authority of worldwide proportions, and either an intellectual or emotional separation from current policy that permeates all levels of the Church, from the hierarchy down through the clergy and into the laity. The potential schism that I see is not so much the schism of the American Church breaking off from the Roman Catholic Church. What I see as much more likely is an interior intellectual and emotional schism from the so-called magisterium, the authorities of the Church. The authorities are talking a language that they and maybe a few million other people hear on specific issues, but large sectors of the Church have written them off either as being out of touch or not themselves guided by a spirit of God or as somehow making pronouncements too difficult to bear or somehow expressing things that do not express *their* own experience and conclusions. And given the current tenor of unanimity of opinion and of squelching dissent and of ruling with power and authority rather than with truth and the spirit of God, I think this kind of interior schism is much more likely to happen and in fact *has* happened to a lot of people already.

The Catholic Church is on the verge of a major change and a major re-evaluation of how it exercises authority, what its attitudes are toward women and particularly women in ministry, and what authority it has to lay down disciplines or laws for the bedroom and for couples and priests. Until some of these major issues are properly addressed, the confusion is going to mount, the polarization is going to become more aggravated, and the credibility of people in authority is going to be more substantially questioned. Within fifteen years, I think there will be a major turning point in the Church. Either the magisterium will be able to weather this crisis of authority with a renewed sense of the spirit of God being written in the hearts of all people or they will define authority as essentially coming from God through the Pope and cardinals and bishops, down to the priests and the people. And if that model of authority continues to exercise itself, it's going to cause great damage to the Church.

If you start with the premise that the spirit of God is written in the hearts of all, rather than the premise that the spirit of God is found only through the teachings of the magisterium to which everyone else must assent, and if people themselves had a sense that their voice was shaping policy or that their voice was listened to going back to Vatican II, we would not have this crisis. But the reality is that the Catholic Church as an institution does not listen to the voice of the laity, which happens to be its 855 million people. Given current technology and given something as basic as the microchip, where one little disk can store hundreds of thousands of bits of information, there's no excuse for why we cannot have unity with incredible diversity. There is no excuse for denying a fundamental biblical truth that the spirit of God is written in the hearts of all.

I have a radical optimism that God and the spirit of God is present in the hearts of the faithful, and my optimism also extends to the hope and conviction that eventually people in authority either will be forced by circumstances or will be led by honest prayer and honest attention to truth rather than to politics and that eventually they will recognize that the Church has to make a major change in the way it exercises authority and the way it listens to the laity. Whether that's going to happen with this particular administration, I'm not so optimistic. Until we are willing to take an honest and searing look at where God is found and realign the way authority is exercised based on that examination, then we're fooling ourselves. We're doing patchwork. I think, personally, the spirit of God is leading the Church, and the laity will eventually have a substantial voice in the shaping of Church policy, in determining morality, in determining what is appropriate and inappropriate sexual behavior, how liturgies are to be expressed, whether to have a married clergy or women in ministry. And when we get to that level, where the people who are most affected can themselves shape the policy, we'll have a more honest and promising and healthy Church. And I think there's a possibility we might get there.

My optimism doesn't stem from any conviction that the current administration is making great decisions. It stems from the fact that I really believe that God triumphs and that people are basically good. Sure, we're all capable of destruction, but people are basically good. And if you give them an opportunity to shape their spiritual future — instead of looking at them as uneducated and uninformed and not having sufficient knowledge to deal with these complex questions — then they'll do a very good job with it because they recognize that everything is at stake.

PATRICIA HEIDT

A Life of Service

I think my Catholic education was a great gift, in that it did start me on a
path.
—Patricia Heidt

I met Patricia Heidt four years ago when, through a friend of a friend, I
housesat for her home and her three cats in Stone Ridge in upstate New
York. For two weeks at the end of the summer, my girlfriend and I had
the run of a lovely old frame house with a wonderful garden, just far
enough off the main road to be quiet and somewhat secluded. We ate
tomatoes and broccoli and cabbage and cauliflower from the garden, rum-
maged through the larder, and browsed in a library of books heavy on
healing and spiritualism, including a volume of poems by Patricia's husband, Samuel Exler. On the kitchen wall were photographs of Patricia
with enormous cabbages from the garden; their wedding picture hung over
the Sony Trinitron. I had no idea she had once been a nun until I came
across a hand-knitted black wool shawl with her religious name on it. I
did my best to make nothing of it, to joke it off, but the die was cast.
I knew that I had to find out more about this woman who now had a
successful private practice in psychotherapy. The fact that Sister was now
Dr. Heidt, codirector of the New York Center for Psychotherapy and the
Healing Arts, where she teaches courses on therapeutic touch and holistic
health care, clearly bore some looking into.

But curiosity is one thing; vestigial fear is something else. One never
knew what to expect from the nuns: an innocent question could trigger
an entertaining anecdote about Sister's family or a baffling torrent of rage
directed at the questioner. On the whole, it was a lot safer to wait till you
were called on. Accordingly, I became friendly with Patricia, but I was

careful not to ask too many questions. When I got the go-ahead to write my book, though, she was one of the first people I called. On the day of the interview, which took place in her Stone Ridge home, I arrived to find that she had prepared pages of detailed notes to help guide us through her recollections. In years of interviewing people for newspapers and magazines, I've never known anyone else to do that. Maybe there was something after all to the neatness and precision that the nuns had always harped on. As it turned out, the notes came in handy, for her story took turn after turn and was filled with detail. But in reading it over, I keep coming back to the path that led from her home to the church to the school to the parish hall and back again and to the image of a little girl sitting in the dark watching Jennifer Jones play Bernadette of Lourdes. Everything else seems small beside that.

◄§ MY FATHER WAS BORN in this country of German parents in Erie, Pennsylvania, on the lake. My mother was also born here, of English parents, up around Union Springs, Saratoga, New York. She was born on a farm, the youngest girl in a family of six children, and later she came to Erie and met my father. She was raised Protestant, although I don't think she was practicing *anything*. My father was born into a Catholic family. When they married, my mother turned Catholic for my father, as you had to do in those days. That may have been hard for her since it meant being different from the rest of her family. Being Catholic was different, and anti-Catholic sentiment was rampant in the country back then.

My father left school early when his own father died, and he took over the support of the family. In fact, both of my parents worked full time to support their families. That may seem extraordinary by today's standards, but it was the kind of everyday heroism that was quite commonplace and taken for granted at the time. They settled in Erie, lived there and never moved. They are still living in the house in which I grew up and where they celebrated their fiftieth wedding anniversary last year.

They had four children, of which I am the oldest. We went to Blessed Sacrament Church and School. The parish was run by a rather extraordinary priest who was a bit of a maverick for his time. He was a free-thinking individual who was somewhat at odds with the bishop of the diocese. It was always considered rather a distinction that we belonged to Blessed Sacrament because we had the shortest Masses. Everybody would flock to Blessed Sacrament for the short sermons. But he was a very loving human being, and I think my father found in him the father he had lost, and he assumed a great importance in our lives.

My father was one of the founding members of that parish, and he belonged to the ushers. To be an usher every Sunday at eleven o'clock Mass was a symbolic thing for him. As I noted, our pastor was short on words, but what he said seemed to come from direct experience. He wasn't a lettered person but was more emotional — so he appealed to my father who was a rough laborer, and he appealed to the people in the parish. And so the parish prospered. It started out from a little tiny church, then they built a new church, and my father was a part of all that. It was a very important thing in our lives.

Actually, I recall that in my early childhood the Catholic Church was the pivot of our lives. My education was there, I went to church there, had Girl Scouts after school there, church work on Saturdays cleaning the rug there, choir practice — I mean, our whole lives wound around the Church. That was the path you made, from your house to the school to the church. That was the social focus for us and the people we knew.

We were taught by the Sisters of St. Joseph. They had their motherhouse in Erie and taught in the diocese of Erie, which encompassed a large number of people. At that time maybe sixty-five to seventy-five percent of the city of Erie was Catholic — German, Polish, Italian. Most of the schools, the hospital, the orphanage, and the social work agencies were all run by the Order. In those days there were enough nuns so that every year our classroom teacher was a nun. And, at the time, I thought they were the most exciting people that I knew.

Your teachers do shape you a great deal. Because of the economic situation in Erie, I received my cultural education through the Church — *totally*. From 1940 through 1948 I was at Blessed Sacrament grade school, and that was during the Second World War. I remember that because the janitor of the school went off to the war and we all sent him little CARE packages.

When I graduated from Blessed Sacrament, I went to Villa Maria Academy, which was run by the same nuns, and there I was exposed to a wider framework. It was 1950, which was called the Marian Year, and everybody joined the Blue Army of the Blessed Mother to combat communism. I didn't understand any of that, I just had the instinctive feeling that communism was a bad thing because it was opposed to the Catholic religion. As much as I feel that my Catholic education was priceless, the deficit was that it made it hard to develop a critical faculty.

I think our nuns were themselves the product of this kind of education. They started out with an absolute truth, and that notion didn't encourage

a great deal of thinking. I felt that to be a lack when it came to literature and history particularly. The rest of my education I thought was
excellent—Latin, science, biology, chemistry, all equipped me very well.
When it got into the social sciences, though, I didn't have an equivalent
background.

Most of my education was geared toward the role of women in that
day, which was a life of service. After all, that was the nuns' philosophy,
and so that's pretty much how they taught us. And they sure did a good
job of it. They really did teach a person how to serve in the world, which
is not a bad idea. It has a very important dimension which I think is
somewhat lacking today, unfortunately.

Probably the first person who impressed me strongly was Sister Eleanor
in sixth grade, an older nun. She told stories about the French Revolution
that I still remember. Instead of reading the history book, she simply told
the story. Spelling bees, how to diagram sentences—I tell you, I can
diagram anything. Give me a book and I can go through the parts of
speech—she really made that come alive. We were all experts at dia-
gramming, spelling, and the French Revolution. It was a wonderful year.
And the next year I had a young teacher, Sister Gertrude Marie, and I
was just absolutely certain I was going to be a nun by then because I
adored her. You become very idealistic around seventh and eighth grade
and you want to emulate the adults that are in your life. So I started reading
all the lives of the saints: Saint Teresa, Joan of Arc, and Bernadette of
Lourdes, who was very popular.

There was a movie out around that time, *The Song of Bernadette*, with
Jennifer Jones. Oh, I tell you, that was extraordinary! I remember the
scenes, I can remember the whole movie. At that time I was certain that
the most important thing was to love God and go to heaven and that I
was going to give my whole life to doing that. My mother took me to
The Song of Bernadette, and the idea of the Blessed Mother appearing to
someone in our lifetime was just extraordinary.

Of course, there was a lot of talk about Lourdes at the time, people
going off to the miraculous waters and getting healed. I didn't understand
all those things, but they had a great influence in my later life. That's the
interesting thing, because I'm very much involved in healing now. I
thought about that much later when I got my Ph.D. at NYU and wrote
my dissertation on therapeutic touch. I came back to that. Therapeutic
touch is a more secular term for laying on of hands. It's a healing modality
in which you work with the energy fields that surround the body. I did
research on the use of therapeutic touch with cardiac patients, and I've
actually devoted a lot of my life to teaching people that.

Bernadette of Lourdes was a little girl to whom the Blessed Mother appeared fourteen or fifteen times. On her last appearance, she told Bernadette to dig into the earth. And when she did, she found a stream of water. Eventually the Basilica of Lourdes was built on that spot and pilgrims came from all over the world. There were many miraculous healings which took place, and some were documented medically.

I think there *are* holy spots on the earth, places that are very sacred. We know more about placebo now, about what the ill person brings to healing. In that regard, the pilgrimage to Lourdes would be as important as the moment of being there. I didn't understand it then, but now we know that the yearning to be well is as important as anything — the faith that you bring to that healing act is the vital part. So it wouldn't surprise me at all, looking back now, that people could be healed when they'd get there. That in itself is part of what it's about, and it doesn't diminish the holy waters or the shrine at all. When people come to me as a healer or a caretaker, they bring a great yearning inside themselves. So anybody who's a healer or who cares for other people knows that he or she never heals them — the person always heals himself. If they come without any hope or belief, it's very hard for them to be healed.

Did the Blessed Mother really appear to the children at Lourdes and Fatima? I don't know; it's a puzzle to me. I thought that I had certain apparitions throughout my life, really thought that I talked to God or had the experience of God. It seemed very real to me. I remember once being in church and I was certain that I saw the Blessed Mother. But it's hard for me to know if that really *was*, or if that was my wonderful, emotional imagination taking over. So I don't know if Bernadette was like that, but it's hard to believe that she would have fabricated that all those times.

Strangely enough, I first felt that I might want to be a nun in first grade. I think it disappeared on and off. Compared to life in the neighborhood in which I grew up, the nuns and the Church seemed really different. I gravitated more toward the example of my teachers and Mrs. Mac, as we called her, the Girl Scout leader, who was quite influential in my life. I saw the world of the nuns as the more exciting path. There was simply something mysterious about the nuns, something that appealed to me.

I had a very deep emotional experience of God when I was six, around my first communion. I remember writing a letter in which I had a very personal relationship with God, and that never left me. It made a very deep impression, and I suppose in some ways I recognized my soul at that point. That didn't seem strange to me because I was always talking to God, always praying — before meals, after meals, and late at night. I think that a lot of children have that experience of God, but what may happen is that things interfere with it later. Yet nothing interfered with it in my life — not my family, nothing. I really had a childhood. I didn't get involved in early sex or things that might draw me away from that early imprint, so it stayed very deep inside me. That experience is unique and somewhat missing in today's society. And I was not alone in that. When I entered the convent in tiny Erie, Pennsylvania, there were twenty-three other girls who entered with me.

The interesting thing about growing up in Erie was that our lives pivoted around the liturgical cycle. You have Advent leading up to Christmas, then that long celebration of Christmas and Epiphany. After Epiphany there's a whole quiet period, but then soon comes Lent and getting ready for Easter. Then you have another long period, the octave of Easter. So you had two major poles in what they call the liturgical year, and your life wound around them. We don't have that in today's society.

And it was there in terms of color: the purple of Advent and the statues all being draped. Fantastic experience to go into church and see everything mysterious, all covered with purple! Then there'd be that one Sunday, Laetare Sunday, when you'd have *pink*, meaning some anticipation of the Divine Child coming. It's hard to explain, but that *was* the excitement in your life. Nothing else was that exciting. And then there were the May Day ceremonies, and Palm Sunday, and all those processions with the Blessed Sacrament being carried. I'll never forget those experiences. They were very exciting because you would dress up in your white dress and you would carry flowers and you would pray through the church. It's as if you were transported out of yourself.

That is something that we don't experience today: something that's bigger than ourselves. The other side of that, unfortunately, is that you didn't *have* a self. But you did develop a sense of the transcendent, the cosmic, like a vision that was so big it was all-encompassing. What did they call that? The communion of saints: the people in heaven, the people in purgatory, and the people on earth, all one. So isn't it interesting how important that became for me?

I was in the choir in church — in fact, I feel as though I ran the choir. I substituted for our organist when she was on vacation. So, from the time I was six until I left the Church when I was forty, I sang all my life. And the singing made it very alive: "Tantum Ergo," "O Sacrament Most Holy."

In those days you made plans. You didn't expect to stay with your mother and father like kids do today. The message was pretty much that you would seek your own path in life as your parents before you had done. So around my junior year in high school it became a question of

What was I gonna do? And the thought of entering the Community came up. By my senior year I was pretty definite on that. You had to make application and be interviewed by a priest and the Mother Superior, but in my case it wasn't very hard because they'd known me all my life.

The Sisters of St. Joseph were a semicloistered order. Cloistered orders didn't have any interface with the public, whereas the semicloistered orders were active. The Sisters of St. Joseph interacted with the public a great deal. Little did I know what I was getting into. From morning to night you were out either teaching or nursing or doing something. It was very active work and was called "a life of service and devotion."

And prayer. We would rise in the morning early — five o'clock — and would have prayers and Mass and meditation until seven. Then we would have breakfast and go out to work — my work in those first days was teaching grade school — and we wouldn't arrive back home until six in the evening. Then prayer and meditation, dinner, perhaps some recreation, and preparation for classes the next day. Then there was the washing of those black wool habits with all that starch in the bands, and the gimp, which was like a bib.

We wore the dress of the seventeenth-century women who cared for sick people. In that century, women covered their heads and wore long veils and dresses to their feet. We retained that habit until 1967 when the Order changed to a simple black dress. By 1970, when I was leaving, you had the option of not wearing the habit at all. People were wearing black suits or red suits or whatever.

In addition to working outside the Community, you also worked *in* the Community, and that was known as your "charge." Our Order had five hundred nuns, of whom maybe two to three hundred were based in Erie. At the time, my "charge" was to take care of the sick nuns. That actually was how I ended up being in nursing, since I had a knack for taking care of the sick sisters. It was very inspiring work — we had one nun who was completely paralyzed and I would take care of her and feed her and turn her and bathe her.

As a result of that, when I had been in the Order for about five years — I was at the end of my novitiate and was about ready to become professed — my novice mistress came to me and said, "We're starting a nursing program in the college, and we're going to need nurses who have a baccalaureate degree. And we would like you to go off and get your baccalaureate degree." I said, "My God, I can't stand the sight of blood." And she said, "I'm sure you'll get over that." That was it! Never did I think of protesting or saying anything different.

I went to Catholic University in Washington, D.C., for three years and got my baccalaureate. I lived with nuns from all over the country who were studying there, and it was a very broadening experience for me, a girl from Erie who didn't have much of a cultural background or world view. I took metaphysics from Jesuits — what an eye opener!

I think entering the Order was a very interesting thing for many girls. Number one, it was a way of getting away from their families if they didn't want marriage. It was a way of getting a good education. Nuns were wonderful people, the most educated people that I knew. Not a lot of women in the city of Erie were educated like that. And this was before the Peace Corps — if you wanted to enter a life of service without getting married, what else was there?

Life in the Order also provided a discipline and purpose and meaning that was very valuable for me. To the day I left, I felt very strongly committed to that. As I grew older in the Order, though, I began to experience an internal shift. My ability to think critically developed. What I had accepted naively and fully at seventeen I began to be at odds with by the time I was thirty-seven — issues such as divorce and birth control.

I began to see people around me getting divorces for what seemed like very good reasons. It didn't make sense to me that these people should be denied the sacraments simply because of that. Other Catholics I was very close to were having one child after another, and the idea of their not being able to practice birth control seemed ridiculous to me as well.

I questioned the doctrine of papal infallibility in my mind. I didn't see the Church growing. I was growing, but the Church wasn't, and that bothered me. My consciousness was shifting, and there simply wasn't any room within the Church for that shift — so I had nothing to do but to move outside of it.

Furthermore, I wasn't certain that I wanted to live a life of chastity any longer. The two came together and I had to make some decisions. I decided to go away for my Ph.D., and I came to NYU. Within a year I had left the Order. I needed that time away from them to make that decision. It was obvious that there was a different consciousness in the world at that time, that there was more support for leaving the orders. Many nuns were leaving, and priests were leaving. There wasn't that same stigma attached anymore.

I left the Order in 1971, and over a period of years after I left I stopped practicing my faith. I stopped going to church, my yearly confession, and things like that. As I began to study and search out other spiritual paths, one gave way to the other.

What began to take hold of me was my own personal experience. All of my life I had focused on the divine or the transcendent and I hadn't

developed myself. When all of your growth is in one dimension, the other
dimension is pretty small. I had some catching up to do on the personal
level. I had to leave all that, and I left it good. I had to find myself and
I wanted nothing to do with the Church; I really closed the door. At that
time, my own personal experience was all that mattered — my own sexuality, my own intellect, my own growth.

I went into psychotherapy for a long period. I began to create my own
personal God, my own idea of God. I was depressed for quite a while
following that. I got my Ph.D., and I met my future husband, which was
quite wonderful. I became a psychotherapist myself. I was at the height
of my career: teaching, nursing, writing, working as a therapist. But I
felt very empty inside. Once you have experienced your soul or have
experienced some transcendent dimension of the world, you simply can't
leave it — you know what I mean? It haunts you. God haunts you. You
know that it's there; you cannot turn your back on it; you have to come
to grips with it.

Looking back, I think my experience of psychotherapy was a very full
one. The focus was on the development of the ego, which was very
important because I didn't have that dimension at the time — my sense of
myself was undeveloped. On the other hand, therapy is just one-dimensional: you have a very rich, full ego, but so what? If it's not connected
to something beyond yourself, so what? And that's the existential dilemma
of our present generation. We have all these people who are very well
developed in terms of self. Their emotions and their minds are highly
developed, but they're saying, "What is it all for?"

We not only have an ego, but we also have a soul. Therapy is directed
toward ego development, and that's very important. However, our souls
yearn to be united with the larger vision. If that doesn't happen, you can
walk around with a very well developed ego yet be ready to kill yourself
because there's no purpose to your life.

And so I started searching once again for what was the meaning and
purpose of my life. I studied Buddhism, but that seemed so empty — their
idea of sitting in the Void, that nothingness. It was a terrible experience,
and it made me depressed. Then I looked into the Gurdjieff system. I
tremendously admired Mr. Gurdjieff and I studied for nine months in a
Gurdjieff group and learned a great deal from that system. But I felt there
was something lacking because Mr. Gurdjieff never thought there was a
soul, so I never felt I could stay with that. Then I had a very wonderful
experience recently, around my fiftieth birthday, when a friend introduced
me to the books of Patrizia Norelli-Bachelet. She is continuing the work
of Sri Aurobindo and the Mother of Pondicherry, India. It was as if all I

had closed out spiritually opened up again. But this time it wasn't attached to a religious system. I experienced something — it was as if I got back in touch with my soul again.

There had been no pressure when I decided to leave the religious order. No one had said I shouldn't go or anything like that. I think the Order may have seen that I needed to go. Some of my friends and people in the Order thought that I should leave, quite frankly. They saw something in me that wasn't fitting in any longer that I didn't want to see. I think they were a little wiser than me. Over the years, the people who needed to leave have left, and the ones who have wanted to remain have drawn meaning from *that* — as it should be.

What I've begun to see since then, in putting the Church in perspective, is that the place and time of the Catholic religion — that long span of years that was focused around the person of Jesus — was a very important time. It was a very important dimension in terms of spiritual consciousness of the world. However, it is a step in a long series of steps that make up the journey of our spiritual consciousness. I see it as a long spiral. The world was created by a divine or transcendent Being, and there is a purpose to it all. Christianity is a segment of that spiral of consciousness, and Catholicism is a very important part of that spiral. But the very nature of evolution implies change and growth. From what I see around me, the era of religions, of Catholicism, is ending — as I feel it *should*. There *should* be a dissolution of the role of the churches and Catholicism. We are in a period of transition, and for those persons like my parents who still find meaning in church services, I'm glad. That's the way it should be, too.

By the same token, the idea of taking bits and pieces from the Catholic experience and trying to renew it, to make it something new, seems awful to me. I think the Church in its essence was exactly the way it was supposed to be. I'm not so certain that we were meant to carry the Catholic religion into the next century. I had hopes at one point that things would change, that the Church would change, and I could still remain Catholic — but I now realize that *any* religion is divisive. What's got to happen to save the earth is something entirely new, something unifying. Religions by their very nature tend to divide people. A new spirituality is in ferment; the seeds are planted. But people want to hang on to the old paths of spirituality rather than letting their souls be open to the new way.

All my life I've been searching for some meaning and connectedness, for some vision beyond myself. I do believe in a series of lifetimes, and I think I must have entered this lifetime with a desire to search for the transcendent or the divine, since that began so early in my life. That's been the theme of my life, and it's becoming stronger as I get older. My life as a religious, my work with nursing, my research in healing, and going on to be a psychotherapist can all be seen within the context of giving some sort of meaning to that vision—having the vision and then being of service to others. As a therapist I don't impose my belief system on anybody, but it's what gives me meaning. And as a result, I feel as if I'm a channel of that energy which goes to my patients.

It's very exciting to witness a new spirituality descending on the earth and to be a part of that. I'm not certain just how I *will* be a part of it, I'm simply praying that I will be open to some sort of a life of service again, whether it's as a healer or a therapist—or as a gardener! There's a sadness dwelling in a lot of people because they have lost their Catholic vision and have not been able to put that loss into a broader context. Having been Catholic, they feel they've been duped, and now they're disillusioned. But it's important to realize that we're at the very end of a long phase, the phase in which religions like Catholicism were important.

In the Hindu belief there is a triad: creation, preservation, dissolution. Something starts, something takes hold, and something gives way. It's the opposite in the Catholic or Western experience—you get a hold and you keep it forever. God forbid that it should change. But in the Hindu system, that letting go occurs so that the cycle can continue, so that a new consciousness or awareness can come. People can take hope from the fact that we're at the end of a cycle, but only because another one is beginning. Now, Sri Aurobindo says, it's in the seed stage.

Today, scientists are engaged in a spiritual pursuit. Bohm talks about the "implicate order," the energy or fabric of the universe, a oneness of all being. The forms of energy are different, but the fabric from which we were created is one. That sounds almost divine, like the Mystical Body of Christ, doesn't it?

JIMMY BRESLIN

Grammar and Religion

There is no reason for the Catholic Church to continue the policy of sexual disorder that it now pursues. There is no basis anywhere in its body of faith for priests to be celibate and women to be excluded from ordination as priests. . . . It was Brendan Behan, rolling down Dublin's Grafton Street, who was so much ahead of everybody. "Ah, Sister," he bellowed at a nun, "may all your children be bishops." The man meant no blasphemy; he was simply a delightful human being telling a woman he was rooting for her.

—Jimmy Breslin
  New York Daily News, September 1981

The president and Haig the General somehow might be able to get their small war going in El Salvador, but it won't be a real good one. This is because American Catholics, who used to erupt with joy at the notion of drawing blood, are against it. . . . The peace movement of the eighties, if one is needed, will come out of the Catholic parishes. You can't drop very much napalm on children with this kind of opposition at home.

—Jimmy Breslin
  New York Daily News, January 1981

Having won a Pulitzer Prize for his newspaper work, Jimmy Breslin makes a point of talking more like a cabbie than a professional writer, but that's only part of a rather transparent disinformation program. *Who's Who* lists his birthplace as Jamaica, Queens (it isn't); he says he can't remember most of the details of his early childhood. He has claimed to have a doctorate from Cambridge, to have attended Elmira Reformatory, and to have spent five years in high school without graduating—though he readily admits that none of that may be true. Strange lapses on the part of a seasoned reporter who takes few notes yet remembers street conversations verbatim, and in a variety of dialects.

"I try to write people the way they talk," Breslin once told *People* magazine, and his ear for speech is more legitimately that of the novelist than the journalist. It comes, in part, from the eerie willingness of a man well over two hundred pounds to go in search of his stories to areas of New York City that don't feature four-star restaurants—or elevators. "They never live on the first floor," Breslin said of his subjects after accepting his Pulitzer.

Some of Jimmy Breslin's accomplishments are as serious as his breaking the story of the massive corruption case in his home borough or of having written the most effective firsthand account of the assassination of Robert Kennedy. Yet his best work evinces a sense of humor native to New York.

"If I wasn't a journalist," Breslin once said, "I'd probably be an unhappy cop." And he has been unrelenting in his fury at a police force he often characterizes as "racist" and composed of "aging Irish Catholics." His columns attacking the actions of Bernhard Goetz on a subway train in Manhattan or the New York Police Department's firing of a female cop who had posed for a skin magazine drew return fire from the mayor and the Patrolmen's Benevolent Association. An interview in which he said of his fellow Irish Americans, "They yearn for fascism. They love it. . . . The Irish hate an underdog. They only want big winners," did not endear him to the Ancient Order of Hibernians.

Breslin has worked brief stints on television, has written novels and a musical, has acted in the movies, and has been featured in beer commercials. But one assumes he will always be identified with the succinct style in which he writes his columns—something he has been doing for twenty-four years. That deceptively simple technique encompasses going to the scene, listening to the people tell their stories, and putting it all together in the clearest way possible so that it tells the reader more than merely what happened. "He reinvented the column form," his friend and colleague Pete Hamill has said. "The idea of reporting breaking news as a column didn't exist before him."

José Torres tells the story of getting a call from Jimmy Breslin at 2:00 A.M. asking for the spelling of a Hispanic surname. A groggy Torres obliged and then inquired why Jimmy was writing about that particular person—only to realize that he was talking into a dead line. Breslin had already hung up. As one soon discovers, that can be considered a harangue by Breslin standards. So it was that after a long series of extremely brief phone calls, we agreed to meet at Breslin's office at the Daily News Building on East Forty-second Street in Manhattan. While we talked,

Breslin fielded calls from, among others, a Puerto Rican woman claiming that she was being falsely accused of murder, a white man who'd been mugged by a black man and wanted to know how Breslin could still champion blacks, and a gangster seeking advice on how to lie to the police without incriminating himself. Through the five hours we spent together, the columnist was seen to eat nothing more than a blueberry muffin, fueling himself on half a dozen cups of coffee and a couple of stogies. Maybe they still *do* make newspapermen the way they used to.

Like many Irish intellectuals, Jimmy Breslin has ambivalent feelings about the Roman Catholic Church. It's plain from listening to him that he values the education it gave him above anything in his youth and that he is a regular churchgoer. Beyond that, though, he is acutely unpredictable. As chronicler and supporter of the city's underclass, he finds little reason to be sanguine over Rome's attitude toward race or organized crime. Then again, he has only good things to say about the seven deadly sins.

I WAS BORN in Ozone Park, 134–02 131st Avenue in Richmond Hill, Queens. My father was a musician and my mother was an English teacher in high school. They both went to Catholic schools — Fordham and the College of New Rochelle, respectively — and both my aunts went to Catholic high schools, along with my uncles and my sister. Everybody in the family went to Catholic school. My grandparents came over from Ireland, but unlike the common conception, I don't know that much about them. I mean, who gives a fuck about your grandparents? They were dead early. In those days, everybody died early.

I went to school at St. Benedict Joseph Labre, on 118th Street in Richmond Hill, Queens. We were taught by the Sisters of St. Joseph. They had rulers and pointers that they hit you with, but they also formed the last bastions of English grammar in the world. Nobody else knows good grammar anymore, except for people who went to schools like that one. One out of five hundred people in the newspaper business knows English grammar. It's a disgraceful fucking business. Look at the Columbia School of Journalism: thirty years of it and I'm still here. That shows what they must be doing — they haven't produced anybody who can replace me. I'll tell you one thing: Columbia School of Journalism ought to concentrate on simple declarative English sentences with verbs in them. In a quarter of a century they haven't produced a person who can write. I find that hard to believe. A quarter of a century and not one writer. Tell that to [former Dean of Columbia Graduate School of Journalism Osborn] Oz Elliott—he can't write either.

In the end, the good aspects of going to Catholic school outweighed the negative for me, and for several reasons. For one thing, I got a knowledge of English grammar out of it; for another thing, it gave me something to talk about—people love to hear those stories; third, it gave me something to believe in, in terms of the religious training. Nobody has anything to believe in anymore. I go to church every Sunday. I don't see how you *can't* believe in it. One day, I was having a cup of coffee in the Harvard Medical School cafeteria in Peter Bent Brigham [now Brigham and Women's] Hospital, and I was listening to four medical students talking. They were saying that the body was so complicated that it could not have just occurred by itself, that it had to come from a higher source. They all agreed on that. I just started laughing because, I mean, they should've just gone to grammar school with me and they would've known as much. I could've told them that.

The religious training that the nuns put into you in grammar school comes back in one instant to everyone who ever had it—no matter how far they get from the Church or how much they laugh about it with their friends. Let a guy have one chest pain, one twinge in the chest, and he goes flying back to the things that he was taught in third or fourth grade. *Nobody leaves the Catholic Church.* Pete Hamill has fallen away—but he'll get a chest pain, he'll be back, don't worry. People like him procrastinate with the religion, they walk away from it. They just don't want to spend the time going to church.

What really got me about the nuns, though, was that they used to go on and on about neatness. I remember once I was writing something about sports: took me a long time to write it but the nun got upset because she thought the penmanship was bad. She held it up and said, "Look at this! Look at this!" I thought she was complimenting me, holding it up like that. Now because of them, I still can't hold a pen right. I can't do it because they made it such a fucking thing to hold the pen a certain way. When it came to things that were really incidental to life, that was the minus side of the nuns. No question about that.

Where I grew up, I never knew any non-Catholics. I thought everybody *else* was in the minority, you know? There were two Jewish families on the block, the Worships and the Goldbergs, but that was it. I don't remember anything else. So I always thought that there was something wrong with the Protestants—I don't know what, but there was something the matter with them. And I never left it. Who the fuck ever leaves it? You don't; that's a lie.

You carry the neighborhood with you wherever you go. I went to a public high school—John Adams High School on Rockaway Boulevard in Ozone Park—and there were as many Catholics there as there were in church. Except there was a big deal made at the time about the Our Father: if you heard someone say "For thine is the kingdom and the power and the glory," then that meant they were dirty Protestants, and you had to beware. And when I hear them say it in church today, when they sing it in the Catholic Mass at St. Jean Baptiste on Seventy-sixth Street where I live now, I still think there's something the matter. I spent most of my life in Queens, and now I live on Central Park West, on the second floor. The one familiar sound I've heard there, except it was at night, was the sound of people walking on Rosh Hashanah to the Stephen Wise Free Synagogue around the corner from me. I could hear their feet on the sidewalk and I said, "Jeez, this is the first sound I've heard in this fucking place that I'm familiar with, people going to worship." It was that Sunday morning sound that I grew up with: high heels on an empty street, once an hour, going to and from church. You know that sound? So that stays with you.

There are two things that you can learn only by rote: grammar and religion. It's the only way, and you must not question it. You can't question English grammar. I had a Puerto Rican kid last year who used to ask me, "What's the difference between 'had went' and 'had gone'?" Right? I said, "Just put 'had gone' and shut up." That's it, and don't ask me why. And it's "between you and me," right? Now, you keep it that way throughout your whole life. And you learn the religion the same way. And at the end of your life you have a person who never makes the mistake of saying "between you and I," who always has the proper object of a preposition, and who, upon feeling the first twinge in his chest, knows that the priest is going to be more important to him than any doctor. That's what you have by rote, and that's the Catholic religion. That's what your upbringing is. You came out of school with the structure of an English sentence and with the mystical structure, the manner in which a religion is held together. I don't think I learned anything else. And they're both based on the same thing: blind obedience. Faith in the sentence and faith in God. I once met a woman who went to Joan of Arc Junior High School here in New York and who, forty years later, can still name all the prepositions in alphabetical order.

And another thing—the Mass should still be in Latin. Why have a secret society if you don't have a secret language? I hate it in English. I once went to Notre Dame in Paris and the guy said the Mass in French.

Who the hell needs it? I want it in Latin—I need an anchor. I think they made a tragic error. Their answer to modern life was to go to another language. I don't understand that.

One thing I learned from the Church is that you do better with the poor than you do with the rich. I don't know where that lesson got away from most of them, but it did. I think that if I had wanted to attack blacks in the paper, I could've been without doubt the single richest person in the history of the American newspaper business. Nobody could've done it in my league. [William F.] Buckley wrote for the whites. Look at the living *he* made, and he's almost illiterate, with *his* sentences. But if, in 1963, I started "nigger-bashing," I'd have to be making a million and a half a year by now. More, because George Will is just a little guy, and I could come over like a neighborhood guy—I know those people; I lived with them. And I'd feel a lot better. For one thing, I could still drink—because you don't have to go anyplace to write the kind of stuff that Buckley and Will write. I've got to go climb fucking tenements to see some mother-fucker freezing five floors up. So does Hamill. If you had to do it straight, you could sit in Key West and just write "Niggers are bad. Don't get on the bus with them. And there was another crime in Harlem last night." Just interview the policemen who made the arrest. But in my case, I have to attribute what I do to the grammar school training, where you kept hearing the word *poor* so much that they made you believe it. The training did it to me; otherwise it would've been lights out.

On the other hand, I have to keep examining my conscience. Am I writing about the poor because it's an easy way to make a living? Am I using them? Because they *are* the best copy, the poor—the rich are boring. The poor are tremendous; they're the greatest. I outdraw Suzy [the *New York Post* society columnist] and all those other columnists in readership three to one. And I get the most money in the history of this building, for Christ's sake. So you could make that charge, that I'm using them to get ahead. But I believe that if the money comes while you're doing your work, if you do well, that's fine. But if you go out of your way and just concentrate on making money out of it, then that's impractical in a way because you're going to be uneasy about it. That sort of thing will go against your training—it has to cause some inner turmoil. And someday you'll be judged. I wouldn't take a fifty thousand dollar bribe to write in favor of some contractor. I could make a lot of money here. But I think there's something wrong with people who are comfortable with doing that kind of thing. The money makes you miserable—you get possession-sick, so what's the difference?

That's not to say that the capital sins can't be fun. Greed, slander, pride, envy . . . envy's delicious. It consumes you; it kills so much time. I think it's the greatest sin, personally. I love being envious. I envy everybody: anybody who's doing good that particular day. The best story on envy I ever heard was about Adolph Green. Green and Betty Comden love to go see their friends fail with a new show. You know, not fail terribly, but just miss, so they could say after it, "Isn't it a shame? They're such nice people, and they just missed." So Adolph Green went to see *My Fair Lady* on opening night. And he says that when it started he thought he had a knife in his side for half an hour. He was in the worst pain he'd ever been in in his life. The envy nearly destroyed him. He said that he wanted everybody on the stage to die. Great sin, envy. Greed, sloth, gluttony—fucking beautiful.

But not lying. I said that I attributed my decision to write about the poor to my Catholic school training, but some of my political beliefs were shaped by other events. The best thing that ever happened to me was in 1951 at La Guardia Field. In those days, you used to cover the airport like it was big news. Tom Poster, who writes the People page now for the *Daily News*, was out there with me, covering for the Associated Press. It was a Sunday, around one o'clock in the afternoon, and there was a big crowd. A plane came in from Milwaukee with Joe McCarthy on it. This was at the height of his career. A crowd gathered around him and they were all saying, "God bless you, Senator McCarthy!" So Poster went up to McCarthy as he had a hundred times before, because he used to cover celebrities arriving on the planes, and he asked, "What brings you into town this time, Senator?" McCarthy said, "Well, Tom, I was flying from Milwaukee to Washington, and the plane was landing here, and I saw I just had time to get off and make Mass. So I got off, and I'll fly on to Washington later. So long!" And you saw the broad at the edge of the crowd that he was gonna go meet—that was obvious.

Now, Poster knew everything about every Mass in the city of New York, of which during that era there was none at one thirty in the afternoon. Today there are Masses at all hours, but in the old days by one o'clock it's all fucking over. The game ended. So I went to the bar that night in Richmond Hill, which was in the heart of God Bless Senator McCarthy country. And I said, "Jeez, I have to tell you one thing: I really and truthfully know that guy McCarthy's a fuckin' liar." And they all went crazy. I said, "I don't care what you say about me. I know the guy's a liar because he lied today, and if he lies once about a thing like that, it means to me the guy must be lyin' all fuckin' day long. I'm very nervous about him." And any other way they proved it to me, I didn't care. That's how I knew McCarthy was full of shit. That took care of me. I forgot everything else I ever knew about him then. That was it—fuck it, forget about it. Next case.

I don't know exactly when the conflict with the Church came, but it did. Writing for the newspapers, you thought you were smarter than they were; and they helped it with some stupidity, too. Holy Jesus, the Church went right wing back then. Cardinal Cooke said he wanted "peace with justice" in Vietnam—that "with justice" part meant "win." So some poor kid from Harlem had to get killed over that word. The Church could have ended that war. Vietnam was a Catholic war—they couldn't have conducted the war in Vietnam without the Catholics' support. It would've ended if the Catholics backed away. They're the dominant religion here —forty million people in this country—and they could've stopped the war dead.

But for all that, I was never tempted to part company with the Church, really. These issues are just temporal things. They're not rules; they're goals as I see them: just *try* to behave, try to attain the goals. The main thing is not to hurt anybody. What the Church's position on the war means is that the people running the Church at this point in history are wrong. It doesn't mean that the whole religion is wrong. Yet if they got as angry about the Mafia killings as they do at a woman getting an abortion, I'd feel much better about them. Cardinal O'Connor didn't allow a funeral Mass for [Mafia capo] Paul Castellano, but he had a bishop say a Mass for the family. That family was living under a roof that was built with narcotics sales—what does he say about that? The family should be told that they're living by ill-gotten gains. I would excommunicate all of them and their families. They built their homes with narcotics money. Did the grandson give back the money from the house he's living in, money that came from drugs? I'm probably wrong. I know you're not supposed to judge.

The Church is supposed to be the one most socially liberal institution on earth, but it's not. There are a million reasons for that, if you look at the history of it. The British wouldn't let the Irish read or have vocations, so the Irish smuggled people over to France to study. But some moron over there was teaching Jansenism, and they brought it back to Ireland as the only religion they had. And from Ireland it came over on the boat to the city of New York and then to Philadelphia and Chicago. The Church is a white institution, and it falls on its face when it tries to deal with the black problem. It's crazy: the Church hates blacks, and yet it doesn't want birth control. That's a crazy position because it means that you're going to end up with more people that you don't like. The Pope's answer to that is to go to Africa and bless a rhinoceros. Race has got the Church completely nuts, and they don't know what to do.

This country is where they should start. The Church should make it plain to this country that Catholics should be for things like busing. But the hierarchy is afraid that Catholics will leave the Church over the race issue. Of course, they could scare the parishioners and say, "If you leave over race you'll die and go to hell"—the way the nuns scared me. Why don't they go back to scaring people? Being scared is fun.

I should add that, at least in the diocese of Brooklyn, they handle race better than they do in Rome. It's the only place where the Lord's word works. Years ago Cardinal Cooke took money from the rich white Westchester parishes and put it all into the South Bronx and Brooklyn and kept them going. But he wouldn't do it publicly. He wouldn't make any noise or announce what he was doing because he was afraid that if he did, all the whites would stop giving money if they knew where it was going. I would criticize him for not making it known that this is the way we're supposed to live, but I'm not practical when it comes to those things. When I sit here at my typewriter, I can be very impractical. But in the politics of religion or temporal life, you've got to be horribly practical. As it stands now, the ethnic breakdown in parochial schools in the diocese of Brooklyn is sixty percent white to forty percent nonwhite, and that's pretty good. Still, if you ask where resistance to blacks is the strongest, the answer is in any decent Catholic neighborhood.

The Church's position on birth control has to be insane. I've got a little headache with abortion myself—I don't like that shit. I'm going to be very consistent on the question of the state tinkering with life. I'm going to be against war, I'm going to be against capital punishment, against euthanasia, and against abortion. But how can they be against birth control when they have to be for it in China, in India? As far as the Catholic Church in Rome is concerned, the entire foundation of their religion seems to be that nothing, *nothing*, must be allowed to stand in the way of the male sperm. Do they want people to be born just so they can starve in Somalia and have twenty-nine-year-old grandmothers in Brooklyn? They spend too much time preaching about sex. How are you going to go to hell over love? But you're gonna go to hell over hate.

ENRIQUE FERNÁNDEZ

Metaphysical Rushes

Besides pain and suffering, the other concept that gets ingrained is the primacy of sex, which is something that all Catholics of a certain age have in common. There *are* ten commandments, but really there are only two that ever get discussed. There's only one kind of sin that I ever worried about and, I think, that most Catholics ever worried about.
—Enrique Fernández

Born and raised in Havana, acculturated in Tampa, Enrique Fernández is qualified to comment on Latin Catholic life from both sides of the Caribbean. Besides that, he's about the only person I know who can discourse knowledgeably and passionately on the writings of Octavio Paz, the films of Buñuel (and just about anyone else), and the best merengue band playing on any given weekend in New York City.

Fernández came to America midway through high school and ultimately earned the first doctorate in comparative literature at Indiana University with his dissertation on the influence of the nineteenth-century Spanish novelist Benito Pérez Galdós on filmmaker Luis Buñuel. After teaching stints at Wesleyan, Purdue, Franklin and Marshall, and Bennington, he came to New York and began writing for a downtown Manhattan arts weekly called the *Soho News*, where I was working as music editor. Going on to write for *Latin New York* and to serve as managing editor of *Billboard en Español* (the Spanish-language edition of the country's leading music trade publication) and as senior editor and staff writer for the *Village Voice*, Fernández has become known as one of the country's leading commentators on Latin culture, film, music, and literature.

He is at work on a book chronicling his travels through the great Latin communities of the United States, from Miami to L.A. "It's about a country within a country," he says, "which is what I've been writing about for a while now. What Latin culture is about in this country is Catholic culture, but of a different kind from other American Catholic cultures. It's more like Old European peasant Catholicism, which is fused with all kinds of beliefs other than Catholic dogma—what we call superstition but what are actually pagan beliefs interwoven with Catholicism." Fernández likens the mixture of African religious practices and Catholicism that exists in certain Latin communities to the "magical realism" of Latin American literature. With customary élan, he refers to his own writing as " 'magical journalism,' because I make up a lot of stuff."

✑ I GREW UP in Havana, Cuba, and as a young boy I went to two different schools there that were run by the Christian Brothers. One was called the Academia de La Salle—after the founder of the Christian Brothers, the French saint Jean Baptiste de La Salle—and went from first to fourth grade. The other was the Colegio de La Salle, which went from the fifth to ninth grade. Religion courses were divided in two. Catechism was set up in a series of questions and answers which one simply memorized and gave back. Then there was another course, called Sacred History, which I later found out meant the Bible. But since Catholics have traditionally been encouraged not to get too involved in the Bible—after all, the whole question of personal interpretation was one of the reasons for the Reformation to begin with—that wasn't really made clear to us at the time.

I was good at catechism, although I liked Sacred History better for the obvious reason that it dealt with narrative and told stories. And I always preferred the Old Testament because the Old Testament is full of blood and gore and the New Testament is just very bland—until the end, when it gets very gory. For the same reason, I like movies based on the Bible because there are great battle scenes, people dressed in weird costumes, brandishing swords and riding horses.

To me, religion was always bound up with school. My parents sent me there in part because they were relatively pious, but primarily because the Christian Brothers were supposed to be good educators. Public schooling in Cuba when I started going to school in the late forties was, at least in my parents' eyes, not all that great. If you could afford to, you would send your kids to private school, which my parents did—at great sacrifice, I think. The schools were divided. They all started out the same, but in

Academia, for instance, by the time you got to the junior high level, you were basically taught practical trades. It became a business school at that point, while the Colegio was a college preparatory school.

When I started first grade, a funny thing happened. I already knew how to read because I had taught myself to read at a very early age, and to write. When I got there the brother in charge of first grade put up a blackboard with some words on it and asked us to read it. And I blew it. I hesitated — I've done this all my life — I asked him which line he wanted me to read or whether I should read the whole thing, or something like that, and he assumed that I didn't know how to read it. I don't know what injustice got committed because of that — probably none. But somehow I thought it was very unfair because I never got a chance to show off my skills.

One experience I never had, though, was going to school with nuns, which is something that a lot of Catholics experienced elsewhere. Catholic schools in Havana were segregated at the time by gender: boys went to schools taught by priests or brothers, and girls were taught by nuns. Another thing I missed was something that a lot of famous people had, a Jesuit education. The Christian Brothers school competed with the Jesuit school in Havana, called Belén, which means Bethlehem. Fidel Castro went there, and look where he wound up. Those two schools were the two best Catholic schools in the country.

Like the Jesuits, the Christian Brothers were dedicated to pedagogy, but they were not priests — even though we used to call them priests, or at least the slang word for priest, which is *cura*, like *curé* in French, a disrespectful term which we would not use to their faces. And even though they were dedicated exclusively to teaching and making wine, they were not as strict as the Jesuits and not as high-powered intellectually, at least in my opinion. They certainly had no equivalent of Teilhard de Chardin that I'm aware of. The statues of their founder, San Juan Bautista, always showed a rather kind-looking man in a seventeenth-century French outfit surrounded by children. So they had an image of the kindly teacher, whereas Jesuits, as you know, are soldiers — they are a military order.

There were always moral teachings in class, everything was very morally oriented — you were supposed to develop character. I don't remember much emphasis put on the *practical* aspects of learning. I got *that* from my parents at home. But for the teachers it was all supposed to be some kind of higher order. Some of the brothers were real monsters who could intimidate the hell out of the students. They were more psychological than physical in this regard. I don't recall that many instances of physical violence. They were great at throwing erasers and chalk — they had killer aim at that. They would sometimes bang you on the head with their knuckles and maybe *occasionally* take a ruler to someone. But it was never like that sadistic English public school kind of thing where someone would come in and cane you. It was never a kind of ritualistic punishment, anyway; it was simply instant retribution.

Yet psychologically they managed to scare the shit out of us. When I think back about it, I say, "Well, what did they do?" But for some reason, we were scared of some horrible physical violence that *might* befall us, especially at the hands of some of them who had bad reputations. I still remember seeing one particular brother who was known for being very mean and brutal — although I never saw him do anything violent — just *look* at a kid who was cutting up in line before school. The kid was a real bad-ass, must have been fifth or sixth grade, yet as soon as this brother stared at him the kid broke down and started crying. I was amazed because this kid was the terror of at least my age group, and . . . just with a stare.

I think probably all those stories of hellfire and damnation, which were really, *really* lurid, had something to do with it. There was a whole ambiance of violence that existed around the teaching of religion in Catholic schools. I think probably that stuff is gone now with all the changes in the Church. But I certainly grew up with my head filled with stories of two kinds of violence. One kind was the stories of martyrs, which were simply stories of very interesting forms of torture. And the other was stories of eternal damnation, which were *also* stories of very lurid forms of torture. God knows I internalized those. One day, I forget how old I was, the class in sacred history dealt with martyrs, and the brother got carried away. Sometimes the classes were relaxed enough that the teacher would just start to ramble on, and this time it degenerated into everyone just telling horror stories — not of martyrdom anymore, just gross things that had happened to people. This included a story about some farmer who was out in the field with a scythe and opened himself up accidentally and his guts spilled out and he had to pull them back in — things like that. Now, I'm very susceptible to that shit. So all these stories of gross martyrdoms and then just plain gross stories grossed me out so much that I started to feel faint.

So we were all reveling in the details of horror, which kids love anyway. It sure scared the hell out of me. The stories of damnation, of course, had to do with the fact that all Catholics who grew up when I did have had the experience of being afraid of dying in mortal sin. Especially if you go to a school where it's taught so thoroughly, and you know exactly what mortal sin is and what dying in a state of mortal sin is. Then if you are told the horrible things that are going to happen to you, and you know it could happen at any moment, well this just petrifies you.

When I read *A Portrait of the Artist as a Young Man*, I realized that my experience wasn't all that original, that it had all been codified. But it does fill you with a strange drive toward self-immolation, a sense of a need to be hurt in order for some kind of transcendence or something higher to happen. There were lots of stories about people who were hurt in some ways because of their faith and their devotion, and the notion is that there is something worth suffering for. We also learned the concept of sacrifice, that you have to sacrifice yourself in some way because this will help you to take time off purgatory or, if nothing else, bring you closer to God. So that concept of suffering and pain really gets ingrained.

And the other concept that gets ingrained is the primacy of sex, which is something that all Catholics of a certain age have in common. There *are* ten commandments, but really there are only two that ever get discussed. There's only one kind of sin that I ever worried about and, I think, that most Catholics ever worried about. We didn't worry that much about lying or even murder. But there's always this harping on sexuality that makes Catholics very sexual people because they're so conscious of it. You become conscious of this sin before you even know what the hell the sin is about or how you commit it. You know it's bad, but you don't know what it is. There was quite a span of years between the time that I knew there were sexual sins and the time I knew exactly how you went about committing them — never mind *actually* committing them. It's very titillating.

All this teaches you that sex is a mystery because of the language that it's couched in. No one says, "Don't fuck." No one tells you what fucking is: "Don't put your cock in somebody's cunt," don't do this, don't do that. They just talk about it in a roundabout way, and you are at that polymorphously perverse age anyway, during which you don't know what's going on. You don't know what *sex* is, never mind straight sex, gay sex, weird sex. So it does fill you with a sense of the mystery of sexuality, the evil of it, and the titillation of it. And then you play, or at least I played, a kind of existential game that is the ultimate game you can play with sex.

It's very simple. You know that you can sin in thought, so that if you think sexual thoughts you will be committing a mortal sin. And if you commit a mortal sin and lightning strikes you right there and you die, you go to hell for ever and ever. So you are actually gambling with your eternal soul every time you do this. I'm talking about a little kid who doesn't even know what sex is about but who has sexual feelings in his body and wants to think sexual thoughts. In my case, growing up in Cuba, the Caribbean itself is a very sexualized place just because of the heat and the fact that you can't wear many clothes and because of the culture. So there's a kind of eroticism all around anyway. Little kids are always talking about sex, trying to see things, say things, and it's in your mind. There's a kind of premasturbatory age at which you can feel certain pleasurable sensations in your penis or balls or somewhere while thinking about sex, but you can't masturbate, either because you're not old enough or it doesn't occur to you. And yet you know you feel good there when you think these things, so you titillate yourself with that. But you know that if you allow yourself to dwell on them, you will be committing a mortal sin and that if you die in a state of mortal sin you will go to hell forever.

Now, there are specific rules about what a mortal sin in thought consists of. First of all, you have to *allow* yourself to think it. Just because the thought crosses your mind, that's not a mortal sin — that's the devil tempting you. In that case, you have to fight it back. Well, how far can you go? And that's the game. It's a very sexy game that you play all by yourself. And what's at stake is eternity, is *everything*. The only everything you can ever conceive. It's not even an existential game — it's a transcendental game, because it goes beyond existence. It's after you die that you're going to be suffering.

The other thing that teaching of this kind does, particularly if you were a susceptible person as I was and still am, is to get you hooked on those metaphysical rushes. This is why Catholics can't be Protestants or why Protestants and Catholics really basically don't understand one another, because to a Catholic, Protestantism is very dry and has nothing sensuous about it. In Catholicism, everything is sensuous — sinning, suffering, everything. Protestantism is very abstract — the cross without the bloody body of Christ hanging on it — and it's very hard to relate to it if you were raised a Catholic. There's no way you can understand it or get close to it or feel anything.

I don't remember the specific martyrs, but I remember a variety of punishments that were assigned to them: getting stretched on the rack, being burned at the stake, having limbs chopped off. The trouble is, I get all of that confused with things that I learned later. For instance, there's that wonderful story of St. Lawrence being roasted alive on a grill and saying at one point to his executioners, "I'm done on this side, you can turn me over now." I read and talked about that story much later on when I studied Spanish literature because St. Lawrence is so essential to the development of Spanish culture. Among other things, there was the famous castle, monastery, and mausoleum in the shape of St. Lawrence's grill that Philip II built for himself at L'Escorial.

These rather familiar stories have become even further confused in my mind because I then studied the history of Latin America, which is also filled with all kinds of martyrs, except there it's the poor Indians who are being hacked around. So I confuse them. There were a number of Indians who were martyred by the Spaniards, for example. There were horrors back and forth, and there was less of an effort to hide the horrors than there is in the teaching of American history. When you're a kid, you have a very vague notion of the past before you actually start compartmentalizing it in your mind. The sense you get is of a past where people were constantly grilling other people and barbecuing them and roasting them and stretching them and chopping them up. Exactly where it all took place gets blurred in your mind, but the lurid details of the martyrdom are very sharp.

The worst part about all this is that at some point in my life I learned that these things were not taking place somewhere in the mythical past but were actually happening right there in my own country. I lived in Cuba in the late fifties when the Batista government turned very repressive and very brutal, and there was a lot of torture, and a lot of people disappeared. So it all kind of came together in a horrible way. By then I was in my teens and knew that this was going on, so it all made a kind of terrible sense at the time.

I liked the Old Testament and all the stories of the Christian martyrs, but the New Testament I never liked. I guess kids are pagans, and they like all that blood and gore and savagery and lust and the orgies and everything else that one finds in both the Old Testament and the lives of the saints. But the New Testament seemed like a kind of boring story, until the end, the time of the Passion. And then it's really pathetic — this poor Man who's done only good things and then gets martyred. But it wasn't exciting in the same way that the stories of all the old Hebrew kings and prophets were. It didn't grab me, it seemed sort of small and dull. Which is strange in a way, because when I read about the Protestant Reformation I thought it seemed closer to the spirit of the story of Christ than Catholicism does. Catholics are rather pagan — there's all this sensuality and sumptuousness around the religion that doesn't seem to have very much to do with the story of a simple carpenter who goes out with some simple fishermen and tells simple stories.

The way I look at world religions, I put Zen Buddhism at one end of the spectrum and Hinduism at the other. Buddhism is almost beyond abstraction. It's pure simplicity, almost ineffable. Hinduism is the opposite, with all its millions of gods and monkeys. To my way of thinking, Catholicism is closer to Hinduism. Catholic religious art looks a lot like Hindu religious art, full of color and life and action. And Protestantism is more like Zen Buddhism in that it's simple. " 'Tis a gift to be simple," as the Shakers said. By comparison, Catholicism is baroque.

Catholicism is full of stories, too, filled and filled with stories. I think it's in part from those kinds of stories that I got interested in narrative. And it wasn't only the Old Testament. I seem to recall that when the Christian Brothers lectured to us, they told stories to illustrate. Sometimes they told stories from the Order, and I don't think it was planned at all. What you had was a narrator with a captive audience, and the more interesting the stories, the more you'll sit up and listen. So they would start to embellish. It took me a long time to learn that most Catholic notions of hell come not from Catholic dogma, which I think says very little about it, but from Dante.

I still remember the time that, in our religion class, a brother came to talk to us about sex, which was one of the weirdest experiences of my education. I think I must have been twelve, and the whole lecture was obviously programmed. We were the right age to be given a lesson on sex — and it was *a* lesson. It was a very special thing. This was an all-boys school, from first grade through high school, so there was a lot of talk about sex in the air all the time. At that age, I was already hearing stories from my peers about their visits to whorehouses — Havana in the fifties was filled with very delicious whorehouses that I never had the pleasure to visit because I was too young. Thinking back, the kids were probably just bullshitting because they weren't old enough either. But they were telling stories about it.

We were all coming into puberty and, for reasons I've already explained, it was a very sexualized atmosphere. There was also a great awareness of homosexuality. Certain kids in the school were somewhat effeminate and we therefore thought of them as "queer." I always worried about myself because I wasn't real macho and I was always terrible at sports. I wasn't so much scornful of these kids, viewing them instead as a troubling presence. So into this setting walked the brother — a prefect, I believe — whose talk was heralded by "Now you're old enough to hear this stuff." And he gave the most roundabout talk about sex you could imagine. He never really mentioned sex, but everything was filled with innuendo. It left me more confused than I was when I started. He never made anything explicit. He alluded to it, whereas we sensed a lot of drama around it, and were waiting to hear specifics. The only thing that really stood out was that he was trying to convince us that Jesus Christ was not a faggot. That was an outrageous notion in any event and one that never had occurred to any of us, I think. But he was talking about masculinity in some strange way, and the idea was that Jesus was macho. Since He was a carpenter, He was probably strong . . . and that was it.

It left me completely confused, as I said, because I expected the classic talk about sex, how it's done, and the dangers. And they did *allude* to dangers — I think he alluded to the dangers of masturbation, for example. That was the talk, in fact, in which he informed us that the penis is not a muscle and therefore you don't really have to exercise it to get strong.

The funny thing about it was that, as I recall, we always thought this particular brother was a little effeminate himself, as indeed a number of them seemed to us. And so it was doubly confusing to us to have this guy who we thought was *maybe* queer come and talk to us about masculinity and sex.

Growing up Catholic, at least the old-fashioned way that I did, is not something that I would wish on anyone. But once you've been through it, it sure is interesting. Your head is filled with all kinds of notions and ideas and possibilities for pleasure that someone who's grown up in a Protestant tradition, for example, doesn't have. The perversity of this kind of teaching can then be transferred into ways of having fun and possibilities for jokes and sexual scenarios you can come up with in your mind. I don't know if it's worth it, but once it's done it's done, and I feel privileged, as an adult, because of it. As a child, it's just a little too rough. Of course, not everybody's as susceptible as I was. I don't think anybody I went to school with paid much attention to that stuff, but I did. It interested me and I was drawn to it. Probably most of them just laughed at it.

After leaving the Church I had a chance, many years later, to reassess my rejection of it just as I've reassessed a lot of other rejections that formed a sort of normal adolescent reaction. But the problem in this case was that the Church had changed, too. The Church has become much more liberal, sometimes in ways that I don't like. I believe, for instance, in theological radicalism, but liturgically I'm a hard-core reactionary. I would rather the Mass were in Latin and the priest didn't face the audience.

In some ways this seems very unfair to me, because I still have some anger pent up inside but it's not focused on anything. Now they come and say, "Hey, you wanna confess? So, confess. Come and talk to me for a while and we'll just rap." They leave you nothing to rail against. It's very annoying.

You see, I do believe in mystery and I believe that there are reasons for having sacred rituals that are different from other rituals. A lot of the current problem has to do with the fact that the Church has become more democratic, and unfortunately that means that a kind of middle-level thinking has been enforced. Before, the Church was ruled from above — and they may have been schmucks, but God knows they've been guardians of some of the world's great art for centuries. Now everything is kind of flat. All you have to do is compare some of the modern translations of the Bible and the liturgy with something like the King James version.

In an ironic way, though, the Church has also become more Protestantized because the Protestant religion is a middle-class religion. Historically, it comes from those countries that developed a bourgeoisie. The Catholic Church was the church of a feudal society that had big divisions between high and low. Now, what I think gets lost in the new liturgy is the specialness of the ritual and the sense that there is a realm called the sacred that is different from the profane. For that, you need a special language — which in the case of the Catholic Church is Latin — and special clothing. All cultures have this. The poorest tribe in the world has someone who puts on some special feathers to produce some kind of enchantment. There's nothing wrong with that — in fact, that is how human beings deal with the sacred, and if you flatten it out, then you run the risk of leaving the sacred out altogether.

Behind all this flight from the sacred is a silly middle-class notion that you need to understand things in order to feel them. Well, if you hear Latin, even if you don't understand it, that sound works through you. Here it's important to look at another religion, say the Hindus and their mantras. The mantra is a holy phrase that is repeated over and over again to help induce the correct spiritual state for meditation. It's not the sense of those words as much as the sound of them and the repetitiveness of them. That is exactly what we call poetry. Poetry is language that sounds different and has different rhythms from everyday speech. That's what takes you into the other sphere — and where the new Catholic liturgy misses out is in not understanding that the sacred is an *altered state* that you need to get to through some kind of process.

I know — although I'm no longer practicing the religion — that I will be a Catholic all my life, like most Catholics. I would feel silly as anything else, including the Eastern religions such as Buddhism and Hinduism. The only religion that could ever tempt me would be one of the Nigerian religions that were, and still are, so prevalent among Cubans and Caribbean peoples, because I also grew up with them. Although they were not a part of my life but were sort of on the side, the rhythms and music and everything else that I heard really moved me. If I ever considered changing to another religion, it could only be one of those. I would feel silly putting on saffron robes. Going into a Protestant church would do nothing for me at all. I still think of myself as a Catholic, in part because it's part of my culture, the way I was shaped. And it's something I have in common with a lot of other people, a way we can communicate with each other because we understand a series of codes.

I never really rejected the Church completely, and now having outgrown that period of adolescent rebellion, I admit that it is a route toward enlightenment, transcendence, spirituality, God, or whatever you want to call it. Whatever that other thing is that religion is all about, the Catholic Church is a fine, legitimate route, and it's a way that is available to me. I've already gone through its rites of passage and everything else. Remember the sixties when everybody was very hip on Hinduism and Buddhism and that stuff? Boy, whenever I started reading one of those books and started seeing the Fivefold Path Toward the Seventh Stage of the Third Mind of the Fifth Buddha or something like that, I would just say, "How am I gonna get through all this shit?" It took me so long just to learn about perfect and imperfect contrition, and then they pulled the rug out from under me by saying that those things don't matter, everything's groovy!

No, I won't learn anything else — this is it. If I'm gonna be saved, I'm gonna be saved as a Catholic. More recently, I've thought that since the Catholic Church has been evolving so rapidly in my lifetime, we would meet again. And indeed, in at least one respect, we have. I got married a few months ago, and I got married in a Catholic church. It was my second marriage. The first was in a Protestant church, although at the time neither my first wife nor I cared much about religion — it just happened to be her parents' church. There is still the chance that the Church and I might meet again on a more substantial level, but I'm not sure how since it still doesn't look very appealing to me. If somebody came now, however, and offered to make me a cardinal, I would take him up on it. As the life that we lead gets progressively more modern, and all that gold and silver and alabaster recedes into the past, what other access is there to it aside from becoming an art historian? Well, the Catholic Church is another route to that receding culture — and to me, culture and spirituality are intertwined in a very important way.

I don't think that I ever dismissed the spirituality along with the authority of the Church, although there were times when that spirituality wasn't quite so available to me. When I first read Aldous Huxley's *The Doors of Perception*, it made perfect sense to me. I said, Of course, that's why people drink, that's why people take drugs, that's why I ever got bombed or smoked a joint, because I want somehow to get into another plane that is appealing to me. Some kind of transcendence. It's also perhaps one of the reasons that, although Marxism is appealing to me as a theory, I can't subscribe to it completely — because Marxism is materialistic, and transcendence seems to be out of the question in any materialistic philosophy.

What about the almost physical need for transcendence? Every time you take a drink or a joint or anything like that, you want to get "high," you want to get somewhere else. But what is that somewhere else and, more important, why do you want to get there? The same goes for sex — it's not enough just to say that it feels good. You want to get into some other state. And religion is the best organized methodology for reaching those areas. Catholicism sure is organized, it's of a piece. It also has built into it mechanisms for change, and so it's not a bad methodology. Even the intransigence of the Pope on the question of birth control is nothing more than that: the intransigence of the Pope, of the mortal Pope. It doesn't mean that the guy who comes along tomorrow can't turn all that around.

MARLENE ELWELL

Baptized in the Spirit

There is almost a desperate feeling out there as hope has lessened. With the suicides, drugs, alcohol, illegitimate children and abortion, we are all feeling pain. We don't know how we got here. We don't know what to do about it.
— Marlene Elwell
   Farmington Observer, October 1986

In 1972, a Michigan mother of five named Marlene Elwell became upset over what the nuns were doing to her children in parochial school. Not that the sisters were bopping the kids on the head or making them execute cruel and unusual punishment as homework. Instead, they were assigning Kate Millett's *Sexual Politics* as required high school reading. Elwell decided to get involved. Earlier in the same year, when a proposition to legalize abortion was put on the state ballot, she had gone into action, successfully fighting to oppose the measure. After the Supreme Court reversed that law the following year, Elwell helped organize the National Right to Life movement to fight for the repeal of abortion laws across the country.

That was the beginning of an odyssey which would take Marlene Elwell from her role as housewife and mother to that of a leading voice in establishing the abortion issue as a plank in the 1980 Republican party platform and in aiding the Reagan re-election campaign of 1984. In 1986, Elwell served as Michigan coordinator of the Freedom Council, brainchild of television evangelist Marion "Pat" Robertson, in an attempt to win him precinct delegates. That job put her in the unenviable position of working side by side with religious sects — namely, the Christian fundamentalists and Evangelicals — to whom Roman Catholics are anathema.

It might have been an insurmountable obstacle except that some years before, Elwell herself had embraced a little-known Catholic movement called Charismatic Renewal, which shares many of the principles of the Evangelical and Pentecostalist sects — giving her a credibility among the fundamentalists that few other Catholics have.

Not much is widely known about the Catholic Charismatic Renewal, although it is orthodox. (Pope John Paul II has commended the renewal to Catholic priests, and the International Catholic Charismatic Renewal Office occupies an office in the Vatican.) The movement originated at Duquesne University around 1966 and migrated to other campuses in the United States and Canada and eventually spread around the world. It is now thought to have over a million members worldwide. Like the Protestant Evangelicals and Pentecostalists, charismatic Catholics base their form of belief on certain scriptural keys, among them Christ's promise to send the Holy Spirit upon the Apostles, the description in the Acts of the Apostles of that first Pentecost, and St. Paul's explanation of the charismatic gifts the Spirit would bestow on all Christians.

In fact, the very style and language of the charismatics mirror that of Evangelical Protestants, right down to the weekly prayer meeting — a gathering that is likely to include hand-clapping, spontaneous prayer, testimony, song in tongues, upraised arms, and shouts of "Praise the Lord!" Charismatic Christians further believe that through their faith they are empowered by the Holy Spirit to perform supernatural acts such as healing the sick and uttering prophecies, although not all charismatics claim to have those powers. But like the born-again sects, the charismatics emphasize the importance of a personal relationship with Jesus.

The very notion of charismatic Catholics embracing a form of worship so close to that of the "Spirit-filled" or born-again sects tends to make many mainstream Catholics nervous. Perhaps more so since, as Elwell is at pains to point out, many fallen away Catholics migrate to Evangelical churches in search of a more emotionally gratifying religion.

Quite apart from her religion, Elwell sees herself as representative of a growing number of embattled Catholic parents dismayed with the liberal values professed by a new generation of American clergy. Willing to join forces with conservative fundamentalists, they are demanding a return to traditional family and social values. Elwell blames much of the current problem on increased materialism. "We judge success by material gains," she told one local newspaper. "What about being a good person? I'm from the school that says you can be a successful bus driver."

Marlene Elwell lives in a quintessentially suburban home with a white fence in Farmington Hills, about thirty-five miles from downtown Detroit.

The almost spartan living room is furnished with only the mandatory sofas and a bookcase where a framed portrait of the Pope stands between copies of the Jerusalem Bible and *Women Who Love Too Much*, where *Native Son* and *The Autobiography of Malcolm X* vie for space with *The Wizard of Oz* and *Treasure Island* and volumes by Malcolm Muggeridge, C. S. Lewis, and Thomas Merton. I sat down to speak with Elwell two days after the 1986 election in which the Democrats had retaken the Senate and in which Pat Robertson had not done as well as expected. As a result, our interview was initially interrupted several times by telephone calls from local reporters asking for Elwell's reaction to the election. But when she decided to settle in and ignore the constant ringing of the phone, the words poured out until we finally had to stop, five hours later.

BOTH OF MY PARENTS were born and raised in Detroit. My dad was a truck driver who delivered ice and coal and then went into bigger trucks and became part of the union. Jimmy Hoffa was his hero. We lived in an ethnic area in Detroit — you name it, it was down there. If anyone voted Republican, it would be like committing a sin and having to go to confession. Working class — my mom did not work. There were five of us, all girls, of which I was the oldest. We all attended public schools.

My dad was French — my maiden name is Beaubien — and my mother was Polish and German. Unfortunately she didn't teach us the languages, yet she spoke about five languages fluently, growing up in that neighborhood. A lot of our generation didn't speak the language of our parents, but we were exposed to different languages, which was kind of interesting. It was at a time when we still had students who spoke no English come to our school straight from Poland and Germany. I think it was a great way to grow up because we were going to school with black and Jewish and Mexican and Spanish kids, so we had a really wonderful mix of everybody.

I married young. I was twenty years old and my husband was twenty-one. I was teaching school, but I got pregnant right away. Of course, you didn't use birth control or anything. We began our family while my husband was going to college and, after seven years of marriage, he graduated as an engineer. I had five children, seven pregnancies. We had our first child nine months after I was married and the second child in less than two years, and then we continued to have our children very quickly. I thought that motherhood was the greatest thing in the world. I wanted to be the best wife in the world and the best mother in the world and didn't really know how to be either. It's not an automatic thing. I also got involved in the Church. We were going to send our kids to the parochial school, and we were going to do everything perfectly right. But then the eggs hit the fan because there were so many changes. The change between my generation and my kids' created two different worlds and we were not prepared for it.

I think this has been probably the most difficult generation of parenting there'll ever be. It's been a nightmare for many parents. We started out thinking we were going to raise our kids the way we were raised, and then the changes came so fast. When we were young and just married, we were idealists, I think. We would have liked to change the world. We were active in the civil rights movement. We marched, we boycotted the grapes and the lettuce. I can still remember us picketing Farmer Jack's grocery store in Michigan and my husband carrying my son on his shoulders. So the social action part of the Church was strong at that time. I think we went into raising our children thinking we were going to do it the same way. And then came this new belief, what I would call a humanistic value system. The only way I can describe it is to say that you knew something was happening but you couldn't put your finger on it.

We got our kids into the parochial school and we got into the Christian Family Movement, which was a Catholic organization created in the late fifties to help strengthen families. We met in homes with other couples who were trying to raise their families with Christian values. We knew that our responsibility as Christians would be to respond to whatever came to us. My husband and I both feel that once you meet Jesus, really know what Jesus is and what He stands for and understand the gospel, then you can never be the same because you respond to things differently.

So we began to try to live the life that we felt the gospel called us to — grape boycotts and civil rights marches. We lived in an all-white community in Dearborn at the time and had our children there. Then we had an encounter with a little girl and, to make a long story short, we ended up being foster parents. We hadn't planned on it, but circumstances caused us to become foster parents. There was an Asian flu epidemic and the Catholic social service asked us to take in a newborn baby that was black. The baby was only three days old when we took him, and that baby caused us to realize the attitude of the people toward blacks — it didn't matter what age. We had neighbors who didn't speak to us because of that. That was living out our faith.

And then we got into Vatican II. Those changes had such a great impact, and on many families our age it was a very negative impact. You still wanted the old, traditional things. And I felt that the change was absolute.

If the Church said you were to do it this way, I felt that was the way to do it. I began, as a result of that, to have a personal struggle. Vatican II made drastic changes in our lives. My life, mainly. Not my husband's so much because he was in the world and going to work and so on. But when those changes came with Vatican II, I began to study them. And in 1967 I discovered Charismatic Renewal.

So I began to study the Charismatic Renewal: the Holy Spirit, being baptized in the Spirit, speaking in tongues, and all that. I was searching for myself. The changes of Vatican II really threw me because now we were talking about a God that loved you. I mean, all you could talk about was love. My husband used to say, "Love, love, love, love." You suddenly began to see God in a different way.

Now, my own experience with my father being a trucker and being a union person was not harsh, but he just wasn't there a lot. He worked, and in that era fathers were not really involved with their kids so much. They went out and earned the money and maybe went to the bar and had their beers and went home. The paycheck was there, you ate, but that was about it. I think you identified God the Father with your own father. So now I began to look at God in a new way. Here was a God who loved me. I looked into the Charismatic Renewal and embraced it, became active in it, began to study Scripture, which I had never done before, and began to see things in a different light. Suddenly, I saw that there was some freedom to be what you could be, that God loved you regardless. You didn't have to be a perfect child to be loved. It was kind of an exciting new thing that I had met a wonderful, warm Man; Jesus became a new Person. I had a personal relationship with Jesus now, and I began to look at everything differently.

At the same time, my kids were growing up. I had fostered the children and I was very busy with my life. Because of my husband's job, we had to transfer to Ohio and a lot of other things happened: my father had just died, I had a miscarriage, but in addition to that I had experienced a couple of miracles within myself, physical things. My husband was out of town, and I was about four months pregnant with our sixth child when I experienced horrible headaches and was rushed to the hospital. They found blood in my spine from a hemorrhage. They expected me to die, and I knew it. Three priests who were active in our church came and gave me the last rites and the whole thing. But I knew I wasn't going to die. I don't know how to describe it, but I just knew that I wasn't going to. It was a very profound experience because I was in tremendous pain. I said to the priest who was leaning over me, "I'm going to tell you guys. I know you're here to give me the last rites, but I'm not dying. I know

God's not going to let me die. I've got five children. I'm pregnant. I've got Joey, who is black.'' Joey was now eleven months old and we had to find a home for him because we couldn't move him to Ohio. I said, "There's no way He's going to allow me to die.'' I called the Christian Family Movement and asked them to pray around the clock. They began to pray and say their rosaries and, after about twenty-four hours of intense pain, all of a sudden it was gone. I remember buzzing the nurse and saying, "Quick, come.'' I told her, "My pain is gone. There's no more pain in my head.'' She called the doctor and had everybody come in and look me over. They had a little conference and did some tests and came back and said they must have made an error because everything was clear. And my obstetrician at the time — who happened to be a Catholic — came in and said, "They just don't know how to explain this, but I'm telling you it's a miracle. I saw the tests, saw the blood that came out of your spine, and clearly it's a miracle. That's all.'' They sent me home and I accepted that miracle.

So that strengthened and increased my faith. I had a lot of experiences like that where I just knew God's presence and He was very much a part of my life. I embraced the Charismatic Renewal and we moved to Michigan in 1972. There was a referendum to legalize abortion in Michigan in 1972, called Proposition B. My boxes weren't even unpacked when I got involved in opposing the referendum. I think the experience of losing my child in the sixth month was so profound that I just knew that it was not God's way to have an abortion. We were expected to lose that proposal by a two-to-one vote, but with a lot of effort and the Catholic Church being actively involved, we switched that around and defeated the proposal by two to one — only to have *Roe v. Wade* change that in seventy-three. That was my first involvement in the political arena.

My participation in the Charismatic Renewal led me to look at how I was raising my children in a different way. Everything that I believed, society seemed to disagree with, so I was constantly in turmoil. I didn't want my children to grow up fearing God as I had. I felt how wonderful it was to love Him. But little did I realize that fear comes first and then love. I was trying to teach them of this loving Father and not fear. And the Church also wanted the people to know that God is a loving Father. They just about wiped out sin, and pretty soon there was really nothing wrong with anything. I sent my kids to parochial school, expecting the teachers to enforce everything I was teaching them.

Being active in Right to Life, I was also fighting the feminist movement. I was the minority voice in the International Women's Year, opposing legalized abortion and everything else. I felt that being a mother was something to be proud of, yet the feminist movement made it something like swearing. I found my peer group feeling inadequate, as if something was wrong with them. I'd hear them saying, "Well, I'm just a mother," kind of apologizing for the fact. I was offended by that. "What do you mean you're *just* a mother?" I would say. "The greatest vocation in the *world* is being a mother. You're giving life to people." But I was like a voice in the wilderness. No one took that position because it was a popular thing to be a feminist.

There I was struggling with all those things on the outside and my children were going to school and my husband was busy with his job. My daughter was in the tenth grade at Mercy High School, an all-girls school. We sent our kids to parochial school at a great sacrifice. We bought homes close to the schools. Education became the important thing. But one day, I was going through her reading and found out that one of her required readings was Kate Millett's *Sexual Politics*. I really came unglued over it. I went to the school and wanted to know why in the world my daughter in the tenth grade was required to read that and what good would come from it — it was putting down women and motherhood and everything I believed in. For the first time, I began to look at the school and I found that everything that I was trying to teach my daughter was the opposite of what was being taught. The nuns had become feminists themselves. Planned Parenthood, for example, could not get in the back door of the public high schools at that time, but the nuns were bringing it in through the front door. When I began to look into this, it was right at a time when they were having a full day honoring the National Organization for Women — in a Catholic high school. I went to participate and was told that it wasn't for the parents, it was for the girls. I said, "Well, I happen to be paying tuition, so I'd like to see what's going on." And I was shocked at what was going on. Every class opposed everything that I stood for, and there were twelve hundred girls at that school. They had a class in which lesbianism was presented as "a lifestyle choice." I'm standing there and girls are saying, "But isn't homosexuality a sin?" And they were being told, "No, there are no longer absolutes in the Church." A *nun* was saying this. Class after class put down motherhood. It was like going through a nightmare. Everything I was fighting on the outside, my daughter and twelve hundred girls were being indoctrinated in. Feminist thinking was being taught by nuns who I thought were going to be teaching them my values.

I think that's the first time I was shocked into realizing that what I was struggling with wasn't just in the outside world but was in the Church and everywhere. I went to the principal, thinking that she was just naive. And of course, I was in awe of nuns because I wasn't raised with them. I just held them in esteem. So I went to her and said, "Do you realize that one of the goals in the by-laws of NOW is to take away the tax-exempt status of the Catholic Church?" It turned out that she was very much aware of it. Now I was absolutely horrified. And then she said, "The Catholic Church won't be what it ought to be until the Pope is a woman." I felt like I was the only one in the whole world who knew this was going on and that somehow I had to get the message to the parents.

So I decided then to call together a parents' group. I called parents who I thought would be concerned and said, "This is what's going on at Mercy High School. They're teaching homosexuality as a lifestyle choice." I described a film that they were showing of two lesbians having an affair, in which they were told that it was acceptable as long as it wasn't hurting anybody. I went to the school and demanded to have a parents' meeting.

After getting an enormous runaround from everyone, including the parish priests, I forced them to hold a parents' meeting at the school. I trusted the principal when she told me that there would be two panels, parents and teachers, who would offer opposing views. But when I got there, I was amazed to find out that everything was the opposite of what we had planned. There was a panel of only teachers and nothing for the parents. I went to her and she just smiled at me and said, "Well, we changed the program." Little did I realize how, when Sister said something, the other parents took the attitude that there was no questioning it. That was the mentality of those parents: "Sister says." We began the meeting and the principal presented her beliefs about how they're making every effort to bring these girls into the world, that they're going to be women of tomorrow, how they had to be educated to what was going on in the world — and giving us no opportunity to speak. Finally, I had to go up there and literally take over the microphone to try to present our point of view. And when I did, I found that none of the parents who had gone with me would stand up. I almost couldn't believe what was going on. Their eyes were closed and they didn't want to know. I presented the types of books, the film and so on, and all that happened was that I began to be questioned by the people. One of the fathers stood up and said, "Marlene, isn't it a fact that you're active in Right to Life? And isn't it a fact that Right to Life opposes the National Organization for Women?" And I said, "Why am I being challenged? I am a Catholic. Aren't all Catholics opposed to abortion, or should be? Why am I defending my faith among Catholics?" Because that's what I was doing.

I left there completely broken. As a result of that meeting, I was banned from the school. The principal asked me never to come into the school again. And I said, "Well, I'm going to come anyway. My daughter goes here." So I raised a lot of fuss in the school. When I learned that Planned Parenthood was there, I would sit in on the class and object to what they were teaching. They were not only teaching the girls different methods of birth control but also where they could get free contraceptives. I finally went to the principal and said, "Look, this is war between you and me. My daughter goes to the school. She chooses not to leave the school. If anything happens between you and her, then you'll realize that you haven't seen anything yet." So, as a result of that, they wouldn't allow her to take any class that was controversial. And she didn't tell me, so there was anger toward me on my daughter's side. She came to me one time and said, "Why can't you be like the rest of the mothers?" I said, "I hope one day you'll understand, but right now you don't." I had to finish her high school days with her being angry at me most of the time.

That was the beginning of the struggle within myself between the values that I held on to and the Church that I counted on to stand up for them but was no more. I began to question my own values and kept thinking there was something wrong with me: I'm being too rigid. Because now you had this whole new wave of thinking, very liberal, very fast. It was a disastrous experience for me, a very frightening experience.

I should also point out that one of our foster children, the oldest, had a horrendous background. We had moved here in August, and in February the following year, she would have been sixteen. When we moved from Ohio, she chose to go to the public school, and that was a shock. I was used to my girls going to school in uniform. Here at the high school, the girls were going to school with no bras and pants so tight you couldn't figure out how they sat in them. And the drug scene was big. I went to the school and saw that it wasn't a learning environment at all. You didn't even know if a teacher was there, with the noise and the spitballs. My foster child and I were at odds because I was always saying, "You're not going to school in those pants." That was a struggle, but the struggle didn't last long because she ended up getting into drugs and leaving. I was really torn up over that. She went back to Ohio and got into all kinds of trouble. We had been one week short of adopting her, but because we were not legally her parents, we couldn't do anything.

I began to realize that the legalistic way of raising kids was not compatible with the world anymore. It was an absolute crisis, and it caused a lot of conflict in our family. My husband, not being exposed to all this stuff day after day, wanted to know why I couldn't just keep the kids in line.

I tried to tell him that it wasn't like it was in the fifties. "No one supports what we're thinking anymore," I said, "and they're being indoctrinated with the new thinking. In order to have any relationship with your kids, or at least to get along with them, you have to understand a little bit of their world, their culture." The boys were wearing long hair and I wanted my son to have a crew cut—but that didn't jibe. You can't just buzz his hair and make him an oddball. So you kind of look at your kid with a sick stomach when his hair is hanging down. But I knew that I had to let that go because I was struggling with other stuff.

I feel like I've been in a battle all my life. My son was going to an all-boys school, but I was busy fighting the feminists and I thought everything was fine there. Yet in my son's senior year, he began asking questions and acting strange and I thought, Boy, that's kind of weird coming from him—he must be reading stuff. He took a marriage course, and I found a sheet of paper with sixteen positions for sexual intercourse. I said, "Where did this come from?" And he said, "Part of my marriage course." He was in a Catholic high school, okay? I went over to talk to the priest and I was in for another shock. I said to him, "Sixteen years old is the hardest time in a boy's life, a real struggle. It's hardly the time to give them all these pictures. Why is that necessary?" His answer was "Well, if they're doing it, they ought to know how." This was the *priest*. Where were the days gone when, in a senior class, you teach him that he shouldn't be doing it? I found that totally devastating.

Meanwhile, I was sitting there thinking, Oh God, what is happening? It's like a bomb's being dropped all the time in the middle of your household. I began to notice that, during my son's sophomore year in college, there was something different about him. He wasn't quite the same. When I pressed him on what was going on in his life, he finally admitted, "Well, I don't believe in God anymore. In fact, I'm an atheist." Oh, my God. First of all, I started to cry. I acted like a silly kid. He said, "Now, Mom, it's not you. You didn't fail as a mother. You're a great mother." He tried to assure me it wasn't me, but it was his choice, and I was devastated by that.

I had never been exposed to someone who struggled with his faith. I just thought that you grew up with it and it was there. And I hadn't talked to people who were atheists. My husband had been, I knew, but I thought that was because he was a Methodist. Now here I had this atheist and it devastated me, so I sought out priests. I thought, Here's this kid who's got one foot on a banana peel and the other in hell because he doesn't believe in God. So I had to go through a whole other struggle.

My kids began to question me on things like "What if we brought a homosexual home? What would you do?'' ''Well, is he going to make advances at Bob [the youngest son]?'' ''No, he's just going to come in and you won't even know it.'' I was trying to embrace this love, accept the whole thing. I'd say, ''Yes, he can come home for dinner, but as long as he keeps his hands off Bob.'' They were always questioning me like that. Then they'd say they wanted to bring home some guy who practiced a different religion. And I'd say, ''Well, is he going to try to get one of the younger kids to become like him?'' ''No. What he practices is he stands on his head and he'll do it in the bedroom with the door closed.'' ''Well, that's all right as long as I don't see it and he doesn't try to influence our kids.'' My husband didn't understand this at all because he was on the work force and he wasn't tuned in to this kid stuff. He saw me as acquiescing to that type of thinking and giving up my values. He said, ''You're just like one of the kids.''

Also, I should point out, there were a lot of parents who'd say, ''Absolutely not. You're getting your hair cut. This is the way it is.'' That was okay when we did that in the fifties because that was the norm, but it wasn't anymore. I attended six funerals of suicides, kids who were friends of my own children. When you couldn't hope, you just put the lights out, you might say. So I didn't want my kids to commit suicide or run away and end up as drug addicts. My husband never went to a funeral. He didn't hear the cries of the kids. And so I tried to be sensitive to them. For example, one of the kids committed suicide and it affected all the kids. He hanged himself and, following him, his friend hanged himself. I can't even describe it. There was a wave of depression.

I had talked to my son about maybe getting the kids together. I said, ''We're going to have a party, so you just tell them all to come on over to our house and we'll have a party.'' I bought all the hot dogs I could so they could have a bonfire in the backyard. My son was very grateful because all they needed was a place to cry, a place to share ideas and talk about it collectively. So he came back and said, ''Well, I don't know if anyone's going to come, Mom.'' But he went to the corner and about ten minutes later he came back and he said, ''Oh my gosh, Mom. There are lights from the hill.'' We had over three hundred kids — they were like ants all over the place. And it probably was, psychologically, the best healing thing that could be, because they cried. They were in corners, weeping. That was something that was needed in the faith, but something, of course, I never experienced growing up myself. When I grew up in high school, I never knew of drugs. No one ever smoked pot even. Drinking, the guys maybe would go off to the park, but girls didn't drink. Girls didn't swear. But they started coming into my house, and the girls were drinking at least as much and maybe more. The guys were using language twice as bad. I'm sure that sometimes to parents, it looked as though I was accepting it all.

Even prior to my experience of the Charismatic Renewal, the Holy Spirit was always a real person to me. It influenced my life. When I first heard about the Charismatic Renewal, I began to read about it and question it because my sister embraced it first. My sister was a nun who had left the convent after twelve years and joined the Charismatic Renewal, baptized in the Spirit and the whole thing. So I was aware of it and I read everything on it, but I really wanted no part of it. When someone would ask me or invite me, I'd say, "No way." The way I felt, the Holy Spirit had got me in enough trouble without my being part of a movement, so I really stayed away from it.

I did a lot of public speaking for Right to Life, particularly in Evangelical churches. After, people would say, "You're filled with the Spirit." And I'd say, "Yes, I am." Then I went to a parish dance outside of my parish, and the priest there came to me and said, "You're full of the Spirit, aren't you?" And I said, "Yes." So he began to talk and I said, "Father, I'm not charismatic. I mean, I've never been a part of the movement. I don't belong to a group. But I know I'm filled with the Spirit." He said, "Well, come and see me." He had me come to the rectory and he began to tell me about the Charismatic Renewal and said, "I really think you ought to be baptized in the Spirit." So he caused me to have a little more interest in it and I decided that I would go to my sister's prayer group.

They have prayer groups within parishes. The whole parish isn't charismatic, but the church has a prayer group. So I went to her prayer group, very skeptical at first—raising hands and all the stuff that I had never been exposed to. But there was a community, there was a deepness, an awareness of God's presence. It was different: the faith was alive. It was real. They had a personal relationship with God. Jesus was a part of their lives and they didn't shy away from talking about it. So I stayed with it. I probably attended that prayer group weekly for about two years. That became a real part of my life, and I became involved in it on a national level. I attended the National Charismatic Conference. We have a large Word of God community.

Eventually I was baptized in the Spirit. It was hard for me to get into reading Scripture at first, coming from a traditional Catholic background. And yet I'd begin to read it, and as I read it, it would come alive to me. My faith developed a new side. As Catholics, we got the gospel at Mass and that was it. You never picked up your Bible and read it personally.

Protestants did that. That was what separated you. I mean, you knew a Protestant because his religion was the Bible and your religion was built on a rich tradition plus the liturgical year and so on. And the gospel depended on how good a homily the priest gave. But when I got into the Charismatic Renewal, I began to read Scripture and to get books on it and I tried to study it and become really alive. I realized that I was living the gospel but hadn't understood it. It took on a newer meaning, a greater depth. I began to find a trust in God that I didn't have before. It took away the fear of my children leaving the faith and made me understand that God sees the whole picture and I see only a little piece.

So then I really became hungry for the Scripture. I couldn't get enough of it and began an intense prayer life. My prayer time now is one to three hours a day. I get up at five in the morning if I have to and read the Scripture and study it. It's become a part of me. I think the terminology the Evangelicals use is "the Word." You have to take the Word in your spirit. The more you read of it, the more it changes your life. There's an openness, and there's a genuine love for all people that comes from that acceptance.

I think that I probably am more conservative than I was when I started out. I happen to be active in the Republican party now. I started out being a Democrat, I thought, but I never was active in the Democratic party. I fulfilled my duty, I voted, and I thought that was all we had to do. But in 1973, when the *Roe v. Wade* decision was handed down, I was in on the beginning of the National Right to Life Committee. And from then through 1980, I was involved politically with any candidate if he was pro-life. So sometimes I worked for the Democrats and sometimes I worked for Republicans — never as a paid person, but as a volunteer. I recognized that changes in our society come about in the voting booth but that you didn't just vote. If you wanted someone to win, you had to put some effort behind it.

In 1980, the Republican convention was held in Michigan. I was working with Right to Life and became aware that someone was going to have to try to get pro-life language into the Republican party platform. But there was no one to do it. That was March, and the convention was to be in July. The state coordinator called me and asked me if I would put together something for pro-life. I said, "I can't. First of all, I don't know anything about party politics. I've never been to a convention. I hardly know what a delegate is." But because I felt so strongly about it, in March I finally said I would put it together.

Then I assembled what I called the Pro-life Impact Committee. I asked a couple of people from my church if they'd be on my committee. Didn't know what I was doing. I prayed and asked the Lord to show me what to do. It's hard to explain, but you know that you know what to do, but you can't say exactly what it is. I started in my church and invited everyone I could think of to a meeting and said to them, "I need help. I don't know what I'm going to be doing. But I know I'm going to need a lot of people. All I can tell you is I know God's in it and the Holy Spirit's going to show me a plan." We have a Supreme Court justice, Judge Ryan. His wife had attended and she went home and said, "Jim, Marlene has flipped." She never came to another meeting. And that was kind of funny, but I prayed and I was desperate because I didn't know what to do. I went to the library and studied what a delegate was and what happened at conventions. One night after being desperate, I went to bed around midnight. At about three o'clock — I'd never experienced anything quite like this, it was almost like someone had nudged me to wake me up — I woke up just as though I'd had a whole night's sleep and I went to the dining room table and I began to write the plan. And I wrote till morning. I followed that plan to the letter. I just felt that the plan was inspired because I didn't know what I was doing and I put blinders on almost.

I got on track and put the thing together and, by the time I was finished, I'd organized the country. I had all the platform delegates. There were all of these lobbies and I knew where they stood. I got ahold of Carl Anderson, who was then an aide to Jesse Helms and is now in the White House, to help me with the language. I went to the National Right to Life Committee and I got some money from them to put this thing together. I had 110 people working with me by the time I was finished. I had the language written. And by the time the platform committee was formed, we knew who was what and what they were going to do and we got that language in. And I am told by many people that it changed the course of the Republican party. It now had a strong pro-life platform, and Reagan had stood on it. It was the beginning of the Republican party taking on that new position.

As a result of that 1980 language, I decided that I had to become a Republican. Reagan was running, so I felt that I had an obligation to get involved with that election. I was not well received by the Republican party or the rank-and-file people because it was like I was wearing a neon sign: one issue, pro-life. After Reagan was elected, I decided that I would get actively involved in the party at the grass roots level. I quit Right to Life, deciding I could not be seen as a one-issue person. I ran as a precinct delegate in 1982 and got elected. In 1983, the state was in disarray as far as the party went, and I realized that we were going to be electing a new state chairman and we needed to have a good chairman to put the party back on its feet. It was thousands of dollars in the red. I put together an organization called the Republicans for Unity for the purpose of finding a good chairman. We supported Spencer Abraham and he was elected.

As a result of that, I was put on a steering committee and I began to be looked upon differently. I had shown that I had organizational skills. So in 1984, I was named the state field director for the re-election of the president for Michigan. In that eighty-four election, I had a real problem with the Republicans because, first of all, they didn't embrace the blacks. I mean, they just didn't get into the cities. And I thought, if you're going to be the majority party someday, you've got to embrace all people. What I found was that a lot of the people who had always been Democrats could no longer accept the Democratic party in a lot of ways. It was pro-abortion, it was a party for the gays, and right on down the line. A lot of traditional-valued people found that there was no room for them in the Democratic party anymore, but the Republicans didn't have the foresight to say, "Here we are!" I got myself in a lot of trouble in 1984 with the Republican National Committee because I was fighting them and saying, "We've got to go into Detroit." And they'd say, "We don't want to go into Detroit because there aren't any votes there." I'd say, "There are no votes there if you don't go in there and cultivate them, right?"

I left that campaign feeling very discouraged, very disheartened. I felt, when I left, that there was a void in the Republican party and that there was no participation by the Christian community — a community of people who believed in the same traditional values. You have to understand, I didn't embrace the party because of the party, I embraced it to try to get my values heard. So in January of 1985, one of the black pastors in Detroit whom I worked with on Reagan's re-election campaign — he happened to be one of the few Republican blacks, an up-and-coming young man — called me and said, "Marlene, have you ever heard of the Freedom Council?" And I said, "No." And he said, "Well I recommended you for a job with them. Have you ever heard of the 700 Club?" No, I hadn't. "Pat Robertson?" Well, vaguely. I didn't know any of that stuff and I don't watch TV, except for the news.

Shortly after that, they sent someone over from Virginia Beach to interview me. I was very skeptical because my idea was that fundamentalists, Evangelicals — I didn't know there was a difference — were judgmental and narrow, and I didn't want to be a part of that. But when I examined it carefully, I saw that the Freedom Council had exactly my vision — and that was to get the nation with prayer and to educate the Christian community about the importance of getting involved politically. A lot of them, particularly the Evangelicals, don't even vote. If we could educate them to get involved politically, then we could motivate them to act. So they had a three-pronged approach: prayer, education, and action. I thought, Man, this is great! So I really decided that I had to take a serious look at them.

I found out a number of things. For instance, I discovered that there's far more of a wall between the fundamentalist Baptists and the charismatic Evangelicals than between Catholics and Protestants. Fundamentalist Baptists don't believe in tongues and they don't believe in baptism in the Spirit. I proceeded to investigate the Freedom Council as an alternative. The person who had interviewed me for the Council had trouble with Catholics. There's a great deal of anti-Catholic feeling among fundamentalists and so I had two strikes against me: I was a Catholic and I was a woman. I saw him in January and it took them until May to hire me. I wasn't sure, though, and I investigated. I watched Pat Robertson on TV. I read his book *Shout It from the Housetop* and finally I thought, This is for me, and I decided to go with him.

In June of 1985, Pat Robertson came into Michigan to launch a national news program. His idea was to have the Freedom Council in every state in the nation, and Michigan, Florida, and North Carolina were chosen as models. But they didn't have a state coordinator in Michigan, so they asked me if I would put together the visit, which I did. It was successful and Pat Robertson was impressed enough by it that he told them he wanted me to become the state coordinator.

I accepted because I thought it was a great opportunity to witness for my faith and to quiet their misunderstanding of Catholics. A lot of them came from the South where they thought Catholics had two heads. But my position as the state coordinator was a wonderful experience because often I ran into that prejudice where they'd say, "You can't go to Catholic churches." Just as you have Catholics who were taught that Protestants couldn't go to heaven, you have a group in the fundamentalists and the Evangelicals who feel that Catholics won't go to heaven, that they're not "born again." So I'd be in the perfect position, addressing a group and trying to recruit people to run for Christian delegates and telling them, "If you really believe in this stuff, then you've got to get involved in the political arena. You have to go out and educate people." And when they'd say, "Yeah, but you can't go to the Catholics," I'd say, "Why not?" "Well, they aren't Christians." "Why would you say that?" "Well, they don't believe in the Bible." And I'd say, "Yes, they really do." "Oh no they don't."

I should take a moment to explain the terminology of being "born again," which is very much misunderstood. If you are "born again," it signifies that you accept Jesus Christ as your personal savior and you have a personal relationship with Jesus. The Protestants and the fundamentalists don't have the kind of tradition that Catholics have. As a Catholic, you gradually come to the experience of Jesus and God — there's a personal relationship and it grows. In the born-again scenario, typically, they're wayward or they're not really into religion, then suddenly they get introduced to Jesus and they accept Jesus as their personal savior and they are "born again." There's a Scripture line that says unless you're born again of the Spirit, you don't get to heaven. And so they hold on to that Scripture line and don't look at the broader picture that we would. So they would say, "Catholics aren't born again, so they're not Christians." They wouldn't know that I'm Catholic, of course, because there I was addressing them and saying, "Praise God" and using all the same language. I do believe in the baptism of the Spirit because of the Charismatic Renewal and certainly have a deep personal relationship with Jesus. So I'd answer them, "That isn't true. Catholics believe in the gospel." But I'd tell them that there's a little bit more to it. They have the liturgy every Sunday. They read the gospel. There's three different gospel readings every Sunday at Mass.

And I would begin, in a very discreet way, to defend the faith. Pretty soon I was breaking down the walls and they'd be getting perplexed. First of all, why did I have all this knowledge of Catholicism, and why was I defending this group that they've seen as not saved, not Christian? I would point out that Catholics believe in Jesus and that the Catholic Church is based on Romans, that its theology is very scriptural. The average person didn't know that. I'd go through all the arguments for it and, in frustration, I'd finally say, "Well, really, I have to tell you that I understand all this because I happen to be a Catholic." Well, you know, boy! That's really hard. When I first started to say that, they'd say, "You're a Catholic?!" It was like, "You're a Communist!" It was that startling to them. "You mean you're a Catholic and you know the Lord like you do and you love Jesus?" I'd say, "Yes." And they'd say, "Wow!" It was a wonderful education.

On the other hand, I had people quit on me. Sometimes they would just say, "No way. We've got a Catholic heading this thing up?" They thought I was going off in the wrong direction. But that was not so often. More than anything, it became a wonderful ecumenical tool. I began to say, "Look, we're all the Body of Christ and you're going to have to lay down the differences because if you don't, we're divided." They'd begin to understand that. So we began to embrace all religions — Lutheran, Catholic, and everything. Consequently, we became very successful.

. . .

The born-again Christians are really Evangelical and Pentecostalist. We had a Pentecostalist church in my neighborhood when I was growing up, just a block away from us, and on Sundays we'd go down there and peek through the windows. We called them Holy Rollers because their hands were going and they were very emotional. We laughed. We thought that was so hysterical and we'd say, "We're going to go out and watch the Holy Rollers." That was our Sunday entertainment, listening to their loud stuff, shouts of joy. What you have today in the Evangelical movement is the born-again Christian who makes a personal commitment to Jesus. But I have not met an Evangelical who does not believe in the baptism of the Spirit. It's an extension of pentecostalism. The Evangelicals are spirit-filled, born-again Christians, whatever you want to call it.

There's a charismatic revival now — the renewal in the Catholic Church, for example. The Pope has wholeheartedly embraced the Charismatic Renewal. We have spirit-filled Catholics and spirit-filled Evangelicals coming together. I believe the Holy Spirit's doing a great thing. Here in Michigan, we have Duns Scotus Seminary — they are spirit-filled and they're evangelizing like the Evangelicals are, but they're Catholics.

You need to know that a large number of Evangelicals are fallen away Catholics. I went to one church, for example, where eighty-five percent of the people were fallen away Catholics. For the most part, they left the Church following Vatican II. I discovered that was the reason I was so well received in many of the Evangelical churches where I went to speak. The reasons they left the Church for the Evangelical movement are very interesting. They became disillusioned with Catholicism because they believe in principles and values that have disappeared from the Church. In cities like Detroit where you have the liberal element — the archdiocese is very liberal — they're bringing in all this new thinking where sin is not taught anymore and there are no longer absolutes in the Church. Dignity, which is the gay rights movement within the Catholic Church, is very active in Detroit and has been supported by the archdiocese, for instance.

So the Church that they believed in had fallen apart. The traditions that they grew up with were gone. The Church made all those great changes and gave people nothing in their place except confusion. We had priests teaching that premarital sex was fine. So not only was the world confusing to them, but their Church was. When they ran into priests like the ones I was fighting, rather than fight them they left the Church. And then the Evangelical movement came along and said, "We've got the answer for you. It's in the Bible. It's in the Word." And it *is* in the Word. But the heartache for me was to go into those churches and have people come and say, "Oh, this is so great! You're a Catholic? I used to be a Catholic."

So I became a new hope for them. The Church that they had been so down on and so bitter toward had someone in leadership standing up there and saying, "I love the Catholic Church, its richness and tradition."

Despite the Pope's acceptance, the Catholic Charismatic Renewal has not been totally embraced within the Church and certainly is not promoted by the official Church in the diocese of Detroit. It had to come in the back door. Maybe they'd give it room in the basement, but it certainly was not well known. So you had people who experienced this on the side and started their own community. If you go to a charismatic prayer group, there is a boldness about your faith. Whereas for Catholics, if you're talking about your faith to somebody else, you hardly can say the name *Jesus* because you're used to saying "God" instead. You just didn't talk about Jesus in a personal way—we never did that. It's something the Protestants did.

Now, you have as much divorce within the Christian community as you do within any community—an epidemic, even within the Church. When I was being raised in the Catholic Church, divorce was unheard of. Today a priest will probably counsel you to get a divorce if you have problems because you were never really married in the first place. Annulments are being handed out like candy bars. One Sunday I actually counted in my church five families that were divorced: this lady's married to that one's husband, and it looks like Peyton Place in my parish. The Catholic Church still had altar societies and ushers and all that, but because of the large size of the parish, they couldn't attend to the needs of their people who were hurting. But the Evangelicals with their smaller community were able to meet those needs, and they were bold about it.

The National Right to Life Committee, headed by Dr. John Willke, is a one-issue group, and they don't take a stand on capital punishment or nuclear war or anything else. The Right to Life group in the state of Michigan, though, is one of the best organized in the country, and they are strongly anti–capital punishment. But that will differ wherever you go. Pat Robertson and I have disagreed on this issue, and I've let him know up front. He is for capital punishment and uses a Scripture quotation to support his position. I'm opposed to capital punishment, so when I address large audiences of Evangelicals, I tell them that I could not support capital punishment. They'll quote their Scripture and I'll say, "That's fine, but Jesus also says that you cannot take life." Pat Robertson and I have sat down on a plane and argued this issue, and he's come to the point where he understands that he cannot change me. But he's had experiences with prisoners on death row, and he's kind of weakening on his position. Fundamentalists and Evangelicals almost without question are pro–capital punishment. In fact, I haven't found one who's not.

What I say to Pat Robertson is that God is the author of life, and we're only here for a short time. You're on a journey to get to the Kingdom—and if that's your purpose in life, then who are you to judge? Jesus very clearly says, "Judge not that ye be not judged." So how can I judge that man? I don't know his background or why he committed that crime or any of it. But a lot of the fundamentalists look at it as an economic question. They say it costs so much to keep some murderer in jail for the rest of his life that it's better just to put him to the chair and be done with it. It's the same as the argument for abortion: it's cheaper to abort than it is to have the baby and support it. Economics plays a part in everything. But my belief is that God's desire is for all men to get to heaven. I say, it's hard for you to understand it, but He loves the murderer and the rapist as much as He loves you—you're no better. That's hard to accept, but with our Catholic background, we believe that.

It's really interesting to get into conversations with fundamentalists. I'll say, "Jesus tells you clearly not to judge. When He drew the circle with the adulteress, He said, 'Who's going to throw that first stone?'" Every man has the right to conversion the day he dies, but only God's got his life plan and knows when he's going to die—and His desire is to go after His lost sheep. That's the argument I use. I will not take responsibility to take someone's life before he's prepared or before he's had an opportunity for conversion. I'd rather pay my taxes to support him in his cell, hoping he'll have a conversion. And they have to think a little bit about that argument.

As for nuclear arms, I really struggle with that because I believe in a strong defense for the country. I believe that there's no man who wants nuclear war, but we have an obligation and responsibility to have a strong defense. Reading the lives of people who were in Vietnam before there was a Vietnam War, and watching what happened to that country when communism came in, and seeing what's happening in Guatemala and all around the world, it's not unrealistic to see that Russia is trying to take over the world. You can't sit back and let it happen. I find that in a lot of areas the liberal Catholic's thinking is Communist-infiltrated. You see that in a lot of other countries, particularly in Central America.

I think that a lot of the priests and nuns and lay people who have certain liberal beliefs have oftentimes genuinely come to those beliefs through ignorance. It's just because that's the cliché: "Love everybody." That's the new theology of Charles Curran [the Catholic University priest censured by the Vatican over issues of sexual morality], and they swallow it. They don't think things out, they don't see what's happening. One of my great concerns is a statement Russia once made that it will take over America without ever having to raise a gun to us. What it will do is destroy our families. And when I see what's happened to the family today, it's a great concern of mine. I've met priests who are pro-abortion. When I was at the International Women's Year Convention in Texas, I ran into a priest who was wearing a coat hanger and heading up Catholics for Abortion; a Franciscan priest was trying to legalize prostitution. The list goes on.

It seems like only a very small minority of the population are atheists — most people in the mainstream believe in God to some degree. And yet when you stand up and speak for principles, somehow they're afraid of it. Even though they believe in God, a great majority of them believe in abortion, too. They support euthanasia. It's hard for me to understand how somebody could support putting someone to sleep. It's very scary to me — I almost see another Germany. I used to wonder how something like that could happen, but I understand it now. It's because we've become a selfish, self-centered people, and we're trying to find a pure race, a perfect person. A lot of people I speak to see nothing wrong with euthanasia for the handicapped and the aged. When we started fighting the abortion issue back in seventy-two, we were concerned that once you lose respect for life at one end of the spectrum, you'll lose it at the other. We're youth-oriented, fixated on the perfect body and what we look like; we've lost sight of the inner man.

We live in a throwaway society — if something isn't just what you want, you throw it away. You have tests to see if the baby is a boy or a girl, and if it's a boy and you wanted a girl, why, you get rid of it until you get what you wanted. If you want a one-boy, one-girl family, you might go through three pregnancies before you get it right. It's a horrible thing. Organizations like the March of Dimes, for example, which was always apple pie and ice cream in this country, is now on a search and destroy mission for that imperfect child. Although they're not doing the abortions, they're referring people to abortion clinics.

I don't support the idea of women in the priesthood. First of all, I believe that the door is open for a woman in the Church. The days are gone when women had to sit on one side of the church and men on the other. Yet there's a clear distinction between man and woman: we aren't the same. That push for equality of man and woman is coming from the feminist movement and particularly from the nuns within the Church: "If *he* can be a priest, so can I." Or that nun telling me that the Church won't be all it can be until the Pope is a woman. I'm very much opposed to women priests because I don't think that's the role of a woman. God has created us for different things. I do think a man is the head of the household. We respect each other's role, but there certainly has to be an Indian chief.

Even though some people will say that what's written in Scripture is a reflection of the culture of the time, it's God's plan and design. He personally chose twelve men — He could've chosen women. I don't think there's anything wrong with women in leadership. We all have a right to see where God is calling us. There have been women saints in the Church, like Joan of Arc. We're all witnesses. Just because you're a woman doesn't mean you don't speak of God. It so happens that where I am in my life I have the opportunity to have a leadership role. That doesn't mean that because I'm a woman and I have leadership qualities the role of priest has to be mine also. It's just like in the home today — the reason we have households in disarray is that women don't want to be under a man's rule. I don't mean in a subservient way, but I mean being submissive to the point where there is a person making that final decision. The same with the Church. I personally feel there's plenty of place for me in the Church. What happens is that the ego gets in the way. Why can't you serve God by other roles? Why does it have to be the priest? I can be anything I want to be, and it's perfectly fine that I don't have to be number one.

I think my role model in that is Mother Teresa: who will serve God greater than she? And yet she's so humble. She's happy to serve Him where she's at, and there's no way she'd ever want to be a priest. Secular humanism has become our religion. If you go back to the feminist movement, Gloria Steinem was saying that she looked forward to the day when God would no longer be God — humans would be. That's what you're dealing with. As I say, not until today did I ever understand how Germany could happen. You can see the subtle erosion of values creeping up until suddenly it's full-blown.

I believe that the Church will survive, although it has hard times ahead of it. There's going to be a struggle — there's a struggle right now. It's never going to be the same institution that we've known it to be. But I do think that it has to take a new look at itself. That's why you have a movement within the Church for evangelization. They're beginning to recognize that we have to evangelize, we have to preach the gospel. I think we became so comfortable that we weren't sharing that message with anybody. When have *you* talked to someone to try to convert them? The Catholics coming over in the early days of this country were missionaries here — we spoke the faith. We lived the faith. Today, Catholics aren't living their faith. Who is going to become a Catholic because of the way some Catholic lives his life? Not too many.

When you look back at people who have converted to Catholicism, it was usually because of the influence of somebody else. You evangelized or witnessed by the way you lived your life. Because of the liberal thinking that's come into the Church today, Catholics are not practicing their faith and aren't living their lives any differently from anyone else. The reason you have such a great conversion to the Evangelicals is that they're living differently. People say, "That guy, he's giving his money to the Church, and he's not drinking, he doesn't swear." When you're with them, there's a difference. When you're with a Catholic, he swears as good as the next guy and cheats on his income tax. The Church has to re-evaluate its priorities. When you go into the Catholic Church, they spend time planning their bingo games and all that stuff. That era is gone. There are some hurting, bleeding people out there, and unless the Church meets the needs of its people, the people are going to be moving away from the Church.

George Carlin

Backstage

One of the things that bothered me a little about my religion was that conflict between pain and pleasure, you know? Because they were always pushin' for pain, and you were always pullin' *for* pleasure.

—George Carlin
  "The Confessional" on *Class Clown*

Back in the late sixties and early seventies, George Carlin was a loony-looking guy with long hair who would appear on Merv Griffin and Johnny Carson making jokes about drugs and confession and growing up white on 121st Street. I remember being put off by his style, perhaps under the mistaken impression that he was somehow co-opting the hip subculture. Then in 1972, his recording of "The Seven Words You Can Never Say on Television" led to an FCC suit against radio station WBAI in New York for airing it, and I began to change my opinion. The suit created the sort of scandalous furor in which one instantly reveled during those countercultural days. But what I missed at the time was a series of bits on the flip side of the same album under the general heading "I Used to Be Irish Catholic." Playing them back recently I found them to contain, at least to my mind, some of the funniest stuff Carlin has done. One of the liberating aspects of Carlin's humor is that he can turn what for some has been a major source of self-righteous wrath into just another fillip of celestial absurdity. "I've been gone a long time now," he says in referring to his lapsed Catholicism on the record. "It's not even a sin anymore to eat meat on Friday. But I'll betcha there are still some guys in hell doing time on a meat rap."

Anyone who has put in even modest time on the streets can probably come up with five or six of the seven words you couldn't say on television back then (one can, of course, hear them any day of the week on cable now). The particular genius of Carlin's sketch lay in his listing the words in near-clinical fashion, then repeating the list until they had lost some of their shock value, and then turning the whole thing into farce. "I think the word *fuck* is a very important word," Carlin says with didactic sincerity. "It's the beginning of life, and yet it's a word we use to hurt one another quite often. People much wiser than I have said, 'I'd rather have my son watch a film with two people making love than two people trying to kill each other.' I agree, but I'd like to take it a step further. I'd like to substitute the word *fuck* for the word *kill* in all those movie clichés we grew up with: 'Okay, sheriff, we're gonna fuck ya now. . . . But we're gonna fuck ya *slow*.' ''

What's interesting in all this is the significance Carlin now attaches to having one of his grammar school nuns come backstage after a performance and acknowledge that she had been using that record as a teaching aid. Should we be surprised that a guy who leaves the Church in high school is thrilled to find acceptance in its eyes years later? Once a Catholic, indeed.

Carlin is still a somewhat loony-looking character onstage. The only difference now is that he plays not to a hip crowd but to a very large one, lining up more HBO specials in a two-year period than there are words he couldn't have said on them twenty years ago. Carlin's rise to mass acceptance, though, has followed the familiar Hollywood script of the fifties. That scenario usually called for the performer to struggle through initial rejection (in his case, being canned in Vegas for calling out some of the less refined audience members with a word you apparently couldn't say there either), lapse into some form of substance abuse (complicated by a couple of strokes), discover that the idiosyncratic personal material he does best is finally what audiences like most, and ride off into the Sunset Strip.

That, also in true Hollywood fashion, is somewhat oversimplified. For one thing, Carlin continues to be misinterpreted and sold short after all these years. When I mentioned Carlin to an otherwise worldly older friend of mine, he sneered, "Oh, he's the guy who uses all that gutter language. I don't like him at all." Word for word, Carlin's act is probably less salacious than the average Buddy Hackett performance, with none of the leering, but the label has stuck. At least Sister got the point.

Not surprisingly, Carlin in person is one of the least pretentious stars you could meet. Dressed in a sweat suit and a red T-shirt that read "Larry's Place, Doylestown, Pa.," he began by discussing the peril to one's back that comes of driving all night from Elmira to New York City. During the long interview in his room at the Park Lane Hotel, with its sumptuous aerial view of Central Park, he kept stealing glances out the window — not at the greenery of the park but at the faded buildings just north and west of it. That's the location of the old neighborhood Carlin came out of and that has figured prominently in his work (although he lives in California now with his wife and daughter). You could almost hear Carlin's assortment of repressed priests and speech-impaired cops, raunchy Italians, hip blacks, and wise-ass Irish yobbos saunter into the room to check us out while George relived his long journey from 121st Street to Central Park South, a total of sixty-two city blocks in a little over forty-two years.

THE BACKGROUND, OF COURSE, is Irish American. My father was born in Ireland but emigrated here when he was an infant. My mother was born here of Irish immigrant parents. My father was from Philadelphia; my mother's people were all from New York. My mother and father were married in 1930. That was rather late — well, for the Irish it was probably early in their lives. You wait for your parents to die and then you get married. My mother was thirty-five when she was married, and my father was forty-three — he was marrying for the second time. My brother, Patrick, was born in 1931, six years earlier than I was.

Now I've only heard my mother's side of the story, with a few relatives thrown in, but according to her, she spent a lot of time apart from my father because of his alcoholism. He was, if not physically abusive, at least threatening and bullying and hard to get along with. Again, I don't know his side of it — I'm sure she put some fuel on the fire — but they were in and out of living together for five or six years until I was born. Two months after I was born, their final split took place, so I was raised in a home with only my mother. Both of them, by the way, were very successful in advertising. My father was the national advertising manager of the *New York Sun*. He had worked earlier for the *New York Post* back, as my mother would say, when the *Post* was really a newspaper — of course, she was already saying that in the fifties. And she was executive secretary to a number of top advertising people leading up to Paul West, who was the president of the Association of National Advertisers.

My mother earned good money and raised the two of us, but we had another woman in the home who took care of me until first grade, along with my aunt. So I grew up with these three women and my brother in a Catholic home. The religious feeling in the home was nothing like you run into in some homes. There was no votive shrine. We had a palm behind every picture, of course, and an Infant of Prague statue and the Statue of Liberty—I mean the Sacred Heart of Jesus! These icons are all the same after a while. Anyway, the main religious message in the home was that this Catholic stuff was all true and that if you did the wrong things God would send bad children into *your* life to get even with you for what you did to your mother: "I pray that some day God will send you children that will do to you what you did to me!" You know what I mean? So God was an instrument of revenge, as usual.

My mother excused herself from a lot of the duties of the religion because she had a hard life, as she would have put it, and God lets you off on that. You know, you go to the late Mass. And then later on she just stopped going because her knee hurt, even though we lived on the same street as the church. The Catholic grammar school was just three doors from my house. I could literally wake up at twenty to nine, do a quick job on my teeth and hair, and be in class at five to nine. The majority of what I heard about religion came from the school, which was quite a different kind of setting from the average parochial school in New York.

Corpus Christi Church and School were on 121st Street between Broadway and Amsterdam. The school was right on the fringe of Harlem—black and Spanish Harlem and a small Irish working-class neighborhood—and on the other side was the Columbia University institutional domain, which included St. John the Divine, Riverside Church, which we called Rockefeller Church, Juilliard School of Music, Barnard, even Grant's Tomb. Teacher's College was right across the street from our church and the house I lived in. To an outsider, Corpus Christi would have seemed like just another Catholic neighborhood church and school parish. But we had a pastor, Father George B. Ford, who, as I understand it, converted from Protestantism before being ordained. I'll probably state this imperfectly, but the system of education that John Dewey espoused, so-called progressive education, was what was going on at that time at Teacher's College. I think that Father Ford was originally the Catholic chaplain to Columbia and as such was involved in a lot of this ferment and thought rather highly of it.

He somehow convinced the diocese that it would be advantageous to have one parish where the Catholic Church was experimenting with, let's call it, humane treatment of children. That's my version of it: They said, This would be a nice experiment; let's treat them like humans for a change and see what happens here. At any rate, the changes were quite noticeable and, I think, made the difference between my being a relatively adjusted person these days instead of maybe having wound up in some wholly different part of the drama on earth. We had Dominican nuns who, I believe, had some special training other than just a master's degree from Catholic University.

For one thing, there was no corporal punishment in the school; the sexes were not segregated; the desks were not nailed to the floor in a grid formation — they were movable and they were modern looking, and every month they were formed into different groupings so that you had a new bunch of desk partners. On an academic level, we did not have marking periods and grades. And we didn't have to take the New York State Regents Exams because the level at this school was such that we only had to take diocesan tests in each subject at the end of each year. There simply was not the same kind of threatening mood that I could sense in other schools whenever I went to visit friends or to basketball games there. It was somehow more open, more nourishing and nurturing.

I don't know much about the specific curricula at other Catholic grammar schools, but it seemed like there was a special attention to more than just the three Rs and discipline in my school. To a degree there was an encouragement of the individual and the creative spirit. Now, I was a cutup, which is the mild form of class clown. And I was, of course, asked not to do that and to tone it down and so forth. But at the same time, there was a tolerance of it. You pick up a feeling of what other people went through in those schools from all of your reading and all of your listening over the years, and the feeling I have is that it could have gone much worse for me in, for instance, Ascension or Incarnation or St. Raymond's or Our Lady of Victory or Our Lady of Good Clothing — one of *my* favorite parishes.

I'll give you an instance from my eighth grade that's an example of what I'm talking about. I went through the first seven and a third years of grammar school without any worse report than "He's fidgety and he's disruptive to the rest of the class, Mrs. Carlin. And he has a good head but he's not using it" — that famous thing. "If only he would knuckle down," and all that. But I always did well on my tests. On the other hand, I would ignore a lot of homework, and that kept me in trouble. Or if I did turn in homework, the teacher would hold up the homework and say, waving the paper: "*I* can't read the name on this." And then there were the inevitable bacon fat stains when you do your homework at the kitchen table. My handwriting was atrocious, too.

Anyway, around fall of the first semester of eighth grade, while attending a basketball game at our gym, a friend and I went into the visiting locker room and stole money out of the wallets of the visiting players. We were caught, and my mother began to worry that with my father not there and my brother off in the air force, I was suffering from a lack of male supervision. The principal, Sister Richardine, said that maybe I should be sent to a boarding school with the Salesian Fathers in Goshen, New York, and finish the last year of grammar school there. I was more or less kicked out of Corpus Christi and went up to the Salesian Fathers. This was my first encounter with the kind of discipline that the male members of the clergy were used to administering. I got beaten around a few times, which struck me as very strange and inhuman. But I was a good student there and got on the honor roll and was given a speech to deliver at the twenty-fifth anniversary. I always had this bent toward performing, even in the fifth grade, where I would stand up and sing "Mañana."

But by February or March, I was in trouble up there. This is involved but I'll try to tell it to you so you understand it. When you erase with an art gum eraser, the erasure that comes off has a funny kind of consistency. If you color a page with red crayon and then erase with the gum eraser, the erasure will have a red tint. If you do it with green crayon, it'll have a green tint, and so on. I found a little Lucite pillbox with nine compartments and a cap on it, and I put different colored erasures in each of the nine compartments and closed it. It was clear plastic and it was just very nice to look at. It was attractive and interesting and I had made it myself. Some kid asked me what it was and I said, "*Heroin!*" Y'know? I said it was all different kinds of heroin.

A week later, Father Director calls me into his office and asks me about this. I described the whole ridiculous thing to him, and I think I might have even still had it and showed it to him and said it was a joke, you know? He said, "Well, okay, joke, *but.* . . ." He said, "I was asked this by the parents of one of the students. Now if a parent believes that, I can't go around to every parent and show them something like this. All I know is that a parent is out there thinking that a boy in this school had something to do with heroin."

I was on the bus on my way back to the Port Authority Terminal before you could say Jesus, Mary, and Joseph. By then it was March of eighth grade with about three months left before graduation, and my mother and I wound up back with Sister Richardine. My mother said to her, "Look, this is such a ridiculous thing, he's sort of paid his punishment—will you take him back and let him graduate with the people he's been with for eight years?" Sister Richardine said, "Okay, I will, if his eighth grade teacher, Sister Jacqueline, will agree to it, because it's really up to her." So the question was put to Sister Jacqueline, and she said, "I'll take him back—*if* he'll write the graduation play." So do you see the tone I mean about this school? They knew this about me, that I was creative and wanted to do that kind of thing, so they put it to work. That's what I remember from that school.

The play, by the way, was called something like "Leisure Time," I don't know. All I know is that a lot of people forgot their lines and I began ad-libbing. I remember that because it was my play and I was onstage, and Ilda Mulletine didn't give her line, or whatever, and so I said, "Well, whaddaya think about that, Dave?" I just remember that and I remember that we had a lay drama teacher, Miss Kness—who didn't wear any underwear, by the way. We found that out in the seventh grade and a lot of guys would drop an eraser and. . . . So that's sort of the beginning of it all.

High school was different because of the brothers and priests, and I didn't last very long there. You can imagine the sudden change from my grammar school. We had Irish Christian Brothers the first year. Cardinal Hayes was so big that they had three annexes for freshmen, and you didn't go to the main building until sophomore year. The annex I went to was St. Bernard's on Thirteenth Street down off Eighth Avenue. When I got there, it was physical intimidation. You didn't do your history homework or failed history, you might get punched—or if you said the wrong thing or leaned the wrong way. Some of those brothers undoubtedly were sadists in their way, and some of them I think were unbalanced in other ways. One guy used to like to spank the kids in front of the whole class—you know, something's happening there.

I tried out for the band, and I began to play trumpet. Then, when I went to the main building the next year, I was in band there and I got the uniform, and that fall I played at the football games. I quickly found out that it's impossible to play the trumpet and to read music and march intelligently at the same time. So I gave up the first two and decided just to march. Let the other hundred and twenty people play, certainly they know the songs better than I do; I'll march, cool, because that's the only thing people can really see from the stands. I was interested in image, not reality. The point of this is that I wanted to follow the trumpet thing, I wanted to go to Music and Art High School. So I quit Hayes without having been admitted anywhere else first, and I went to Music and Art, where they said I had to start high school all over again because I didn't have theory, conducting, harmony, and arranging. I said fuck that, I'm not giving up a year. I went to the School of Performing Arts and they said the same thing: Well, you don't have fencing and speech and ballet and all that, so you'll have to start over again. That was when I quit high school.

Incidentally, in the air force I only lasted three years and a month,

instead of four years. I had several courts-martial, several Article
Fifteens—that was history. It happened with anything I joined or was a
member of. The choir I was kicked out of because at the end of "Carol
of the Bells," instead of singing "ding dong," I sang "ding dung." I
got kicked out of the Boy Scouts, too—anything organized, even if there
was no implicit threat.

Psychologically, I wasn't a Catholic much after eighth grade. That was
the last year they could tell if you were going to Mass because you were
supposed to go to the nine o'clock Mass. But I had given it up internally
a few years before that. It never took with me. There seemed to be a
hypocrisy, an inconsistency, a stressing of penance and punishment and
pain, and not a celebration of life. It seemed very antihuman. Some of
this is wisdom that comes with hindsight, but there was a feeling that they
weren't really sure of themselves. They would change a rule, for instance,
that you couldn't eat meat on Friday. You may have heard this in some
of my recorded work, but now there are people in hell for eternity for
eating a piece of bologna, and it's no longer a sin. I just sensed that they
weren't really serious. I believed in a God, and I had a strong spiritual
development. But the religious, external stuff didn't take very well.

Yet there definitely is a distinction between the spiritual and the religious. Between the ages of six and twelve, I guess, I used to go into
church and make a visit, as they called it. And while I was in there, I
might say a Hail Mary or two by rote, but mostly I would just talk to
God. I would look around and see that I was the only one in church at
that moment, and I would say things like, "Well, God, I'm not gonna
leave now until someone else comes in. I'll stay here with ya—usually
there's an old lady in here by now; one of these old ladies will probably
be coming along real soon." Almost as soon as I would say that, in would
come an old lady with a little doily on her head, and I would be excused.
God would say, "Ah, you're doin' fine, lad, thank ya. Now the ladies
are here, I can take care of myself." Then I would make one of those
genuflections where your knee doesn't touch the ground, and I'd be out.

I remember having that feeling and that attitude about God, that it was
a personal relationship and that it didn't have a lot to do with formality.
Prayers were for the times of ceremony and all that. The two most famous
words in my internal life were, and still are to some extent, although I've
changed it a little, "Please, God . . . Pleasegod, oh pleasegod." I now
have a thing where I just say, "Pleasegod, thankyougod," and "Pleasegod, thankyougod," because that wraps it up. The person I'm talking to,
I call him Dwen. I feel that this word *God* is emotionally and psychologically loaded; it's got all sorts of historical baggage to it. I like choosing

a name that has none of that. I don't use it when I pray — and I don't know that I pray, I use all these terms advisedly with you — but if I want to talk about whether I believe in something, I say, Let's call it Dwen for the sake of this discussion so that we lose all of that other kind of stuff.

When I had my first heart attack in seventy-eight, it was not an emergency situation. The second heart attack and the auto accident in eighty-one and eighty-two were, and by that time I had reconciled myself with something out there. Originally, as I said, I'd thrown out the spiritualism with the religion, and by this time I'd retrieved the spiritualism. My sense of correctness about my place in the universe was secure at that time. I did find myself once in a while saying, "Pleasegod, let this be all right." This was after the emergency had passed. But I had already made a sort of bargain with myself that "Please, God" really meant "Please, George," and "Please, George" only meant "Please, Universe" because I'm a part of it and it's a part of me, and all that stuff. So the aim of the prayer was more to myself and my connection than for a favor from a judgmental God.

Now it seems as though I believe that there probably is some unifying, harmonizing force or order. I don't know what kind of a thought process it would or does have. I don't know that it has to. Something dictates that the electrons around the nucleus of a hydrogen atom make so many revolutions in me the same as they do on the sun. I'm like everybody else; I can't explain it but I know that something did that, and I feel that I can be in touch with that. I do that through a very limited process called thinking a prayer.

I do believe that the Eastern religions have a better grasp on it because they're internalized. It seems like the Western religions are all external, all showy and "Let's go next door and convert *them*." The Eastern religions are more concerned with the unity of the individual with the universe. I'm pretty inarticulate about this, but I feel it very vividly. Obviously, this is something that one can come to without the help of a Catholic background. All that did for me was to foster the reality of some connection with a bigger thing. And then they had all the wrong labels and all the wrong stories, and, of course, they did terrible things with the original Scriptures, and they never told you about the bad Popes, and they really covered up all their garbage. Then when you get older they tell you, okay, now you're in college, now we can begin to tell you some of the good stuff — but not all of it, just some of it.

Still, there's one thing you have to say for the Church — they sure know how to put on a show. You know, the liturgy. First of all, they nail you before your reasoning powers have been developed, so that once they are

developed, you're afraid to use them! Of course, I loved language, so
Latin was fascinating once I began to learn the vocabulary. I didn't care
to translate Julius Caesar, but I loved knowing the vocabulary and understanding the conjugations. And as I said, there was the great show
they put on, the ritual and *mystery* involved with it. On certain days the
Blessed Sacrament was on display in the monstrance. I don't recall which
days, but He was out — in person, live, on our stage, tonight! That was
weird. And then this whole thing about It's not wafer and it's not wine,
for a little while here it's actually blood. When I was an altar boy, I
always wondered, Does it really turn into blood in the chalice?

Of course, by the time you become an altar boy, I think you're gone
anyway. They wouldn't let me be an altar boy in my parish because I
was a discipline problem, and I think the priest who ran the altar boys,
Father Kelly, didn't like me. But I went away to Catholic summer camp
and became an altar boy there and I loved that, just because of learning
all that Latin and really being able to rattle that stuff off. I'm the only
comedian that does the *Suscipiat* in his act. I don't anymore, but I used
to do that: *Suscipiat Dominus sacrificium de manibus tuis ad laudem et
gloriam nominis sui, ad utilitatem quoque nostram, totiusque Ecclesiae
suae sanctae.* And I'd say, "Ladies and gentlemen, you may not know
what it means, but neither do I."

The Latin was easy for me; the hard part was remembering all the
movements. I've always wondered, say, at a Pope's funeral, how they
remember what to do. Let's face it, these things happen only, what, five
times a century on the average. Lately we've had a spurt; they're trying
to keep up with Russian leaders. But you'll see a Pope's funeral and you'll
say, Now there's four guys with the same vestments, and then come six
groups of three people across with the same vestments, then there's two
on each side and they've got thuribles with them. Who keeps track of it?
"We got the pictures from last time? Show me that overhead shot. Yeah,
you're right, he was standing over there. . . ." I'm waiting, by the way,
for a Pope to choose the name Buster, or Booger, or something like that.
I think that would bring it down to a human level. His Holiness, Pope
Buster I, up on the balcony of St. Peter's. And I want to see the Pope
give the football scores from that balcony: "Miami 27, Green Bay 10."

My experience in adult life was such that I responded negatively not only
to what actually had happened to me but to what I later *suspected* they
were up to. I really became indignant about religion, and I went the other
way. Now I didn't finish high school, and I didn't have a college education,
so I didn't have that sort of fashionable atheism or agnosticism that seems

to go on at some point with higher education for certain classes. I didn't have that kind of sitting around with the other college students and questioning the universe. Mine was sort of homegrown and came from whatever reading and bar conversations I got into. So it was primitive but nonetheless genuine. My reaction to what had happened was to go completely the other way from religion to severe agnosticism bordering on atheism. Except that I could never really buy the atheism thing because that was as slavish as monotheism.

So agnosticism appealed to me and went great with all sorts of other attractions. I was a pothead most of my adult life. Thanks to my neighborhood, we got into that kind of young — in the fifties, when white kids weren't supposed to do that. And that opens up all these channels of thought. At least it seems at the time like they are; I don't know what they really are, but they're windows, and you can look through them and see connections that you wouldn't otherwise see. Through a lot of those kinds of conversations and periods of thought, I had a wonderful time denying God. I just couldn't allow myself to embrace very much of this God idea because that would've put me in bed with these people that I now had this big hard-on about, the Catholic faith. So I rather rigidly denied God at my own cost. First of all, one of my basic personal attributes is a tendency to deny my feelings. I have worked a lot to balance that so it's probably not true today that it costs me anything. I still, though, tend to be a thinker more than a feeler, and I think that's probably better than the other way around. I'd rather have that disability than to be constantly, *"Oh my God, look at the pigeons!!"* Because that's really terrible, and if you have no thinking side to take care of that, where are you going to go? But at least with the thinking side, you're free to go seek help and learn to feel more.

But for most of my life, I've thought and analyzed my way in and out of everything and denied my feelings because it saved my life. My injuries and hurts from childhood, real and perceived, arose from a father not ever being there and a mother being away at work. I just pushed those feelings down: "Well, that doesn't bother me, that's not even *here*. And if it does crop up, it's not something we have to deal with. I'll think my way through this, and I'll imagine my way through life." And that's where the creative side, I think, began to take hold. I needed an internal world to inhabit.

I think one way that I tried to achieve transcendence was through the world of thought, through examining and exploring my own brain, and by teaching myself the things I wanted and needed to further my art. Originally it was the art of the mimic, but then it became a pure vocal art — on the stoops, being funny in the neighborhood. I learned after a while that I had a brain to go with that, that it wasn't purely external, that I could invent and take ideas and change them and look for the distortions in life and find humor in the distortions in life, and by expressing that humor gain approval and acceptance. Whatever parts of me did not get the approval and acceptance and applause that I wanted as a child at home were able to get them by just expressing myself. So one of the ways I attempted to achieve transcendence was to be the center of attention, but at a quality level, not at all costs — not by jumping up on the table and putting a lampshade on my head — and then to make that into a career. I saw Danny Kaye when I was ten years old and I said, That's it! That's what ya gotta do! The movies were a dream factory for so many generations of young people, and I was no exception. From then on, that dream was real. My plan, even at fourteen, was to become an actor by being a disc jockey first and then a comedian, to go through certain stages so that they couldn't deny me what I wanted because I would have earned it. As it turned out, I've just done an acting part with Bette Midler and I'm getting ready to start a movie career. My early dream is gonna come true for me — it took a long time, but that's one area where I was willing to compromise because there was something in it for me.

But I transcended any kind of reality for myself by constant pursuit of that dream. The other way was through marijuana and beer. I didn't become a classic alcoholic because I never went for hard liquor, and it didn't seem like the beer got to a stage where it interrupted my pursuit of life and my relationships. But I certainly have an addictive component to my genetic structure, like so many people do. So I stayed high most of my adult life — a nice, even, pot-and-beer buzz. That was one other way of fulfilling that yearning. The later way would be when I finally came to terms with the notion of God — again, I'm going to have to use that very loaded word. Seven or eight years ago, I recognized that I was paying a penalty for my rigid denial of any sort of God thought. And I embraced it again. I said, Wait a minute now. I can invent this to my own satisfaction. I can create whatever He is for myself. And I really had been doing that all along.

If I were backstage — especially in Vegas in the years when I was not in command of the situation and I felt uncomfortable — I would be pacing while the overture was being played, and I would be going, "Hailmary-fullofgracethelordiswiththeeA*men!*" And this would help. Later I discovered that this was really a mantra and that it had a connection with relief of tension, so it worked for me. But I never for once believed that I was speaking to a woman who would intercede with God for me. The reason it worked was not only that it was a mantra but also because speaking that mantra put me in touch with that unity, with that yearning for the

Tao, for the One, to get back to the whole. It was only seven or eight years ago, as I said, that I realized that God and I had a relationship whether I wanted to or not and that I could find ways to use it to my advantage and, as a result, naturally, serve the cause of the universe.

I read so much about quantum physics now and cosmology, too. The inconsistencies that they're finding at the subatomic level are really exciting. The idea of the mystic in the subatomic — Fritjof Capra and the thing about Schradinger's cat, which is not dead or alive until we look in. Basically there are a number of critical values, such as the distance of the earth from the sun. These values include the strong force, which holds the nucleus of the atom together: if it were any stronger, then electrons couldn't spin around it; if it were any weaker, it would fly apart. It's within a narrow window of possibilities, and it's one of only a few of these kinds of values in the physical world that make life possible. It's possible to work backward from that and draw a conclusion that we were intended to be here or that man is, at least to some extent, the center of things.

And then there is the idea that nothing really happens unless it's observed, which is exciting in that it implies that existence requires an observer — and boy, can you have fun philosophically with that! These things, even though none of them is resolved, are wonderful food for this feeling that I now completely embrace that I am a part of something that I can "pray" to — and I use that word with heavy quotation marks — be in touch with, harmonize with, and count on to an extent. I do believe that there's some sort of "inevitability" that I don't understand at all — I don't even know if that's the right word, but I use it for want of a better word. And if Sister Richardine could hear *that* shit. . . .

Speaking of the nuns, I have a couple of stories that stem from the period after "The Seven Dirty Words" appeared on record. The first concerns my mother, who never liked the idea that I was using dirty words, attacking religion, or attacking big business — those were all sacred areas for her. She continued to live on our old block long after I had left, and two of the nuns from the school saw her on the street and mentioned how well I was doing — these were not nuns who taught me there but who had come later. They had seen me on Johnny Carson, and so on. And my mother said, "Oh, yes, Sister, but all the dirty language, the awful words. . . ." And they explained to her, "Mrs. Carlin, you must understand, he's using these words to show that the words in themselves have no meaning." Whatever it was, they explained it to her in such a way that forever after she was okay on that subject: she had gotten permission from the Church to like me again.

I got my own personal imprimatur when I was working in Chicago in the seventies, after about two years of really being hot with my albums. I had already done *Class Clown*, which had on it "I Used to Be Irish Catholic" and "The Seven Dirty Words." I got a note backstage at a concert in Chicago that Sister Marie Richard, my third grade teacher, was in the audience. She was now Sister Melitta Conlin, I found later, and she wore civilian clothes by this time, but she was still a Dominican nun. She came backstage afterward and said to me, among other things, "I am now involved in curriculum for the Dominican order, and I am involved in preparing our young sisters who are going to be teaching in the schools." She said, "I have used your routine 'I Used to Be Irish Catholic' in our discussion of comparative religion and the approach to the teaching of religion." She had also used "The Seven Dirty Words," and she told me that these things had been useful. This was a fabulous thing for me to hear because, in spite of what we say, we carry our guilts and our doubts around. For me to know, well, it was like being let off the hook. It was like the governor calling down and saying, "It's okay, George, we're gonna let you kill people." Then she told me that Sister Richardine was now at such and such house of prayer. I wrote to her and talked to her on the phone, and then I sent her a copy of the record after warning her about the language. She wrote back about a month later and said she had listened to the record but that some of the sisters had left the room during the routines. But in general she said that she saw what I was getting at, that it was okay, and that what I was doing had a purpose, and so on. That was the big one — those two.

It's also a further illustration of the permissive tone that I felt in that school.

It has occurred to me more than once that the Catholic experience — and this affects you even if you leave the Church and all its practices, though to a much lesser extent than if you remain and *buy it* — is an extremely limiting influence. I think the very nature of the belief system, with its narrow definitions and its narrow restrictions, its disavowal and discouragement of many human traits, longings, and needs, creates a person who not only in the spiritual realm but also in the intellectual and practical realms is somewhat limited. I mean this about people who really buy it — I don't mean the people who are still going to Mass in their forties because their family expects it and who sit there and daydream and don't really care about the miracles and the mysteries. But I think that those people who do buy it carefully are limited people in other aspects of their living. I think it makes a person less daring, less imaginative and inquisitive, less able to act on their own to create situations for themselves in life — not just situations of career or advancement but of living, of being able to maintain yourself healthily. I think there's a tendency to accept the restricted and limiting nature of things rather than to challenge that and to seek possibilities.

I'm probably referring here to people who were formed in the nineteen fifties and before. The argument I just made is less the case as we get closer to the present. Certainly you could find people in the arts and in business and many fields who would have seemingly contradicted what I just said. Then I would say, Look what they *might* have been. Or, At what cost did this happen? One of the other things about living as a Catholic among Catholics that I didn't like was the implicit and explicit judgmental attitude and tone present in the relationships. If you chose to be a little less careful about your practice of the religion, if you were a little less devout, you could detect in other people disapproval of you and, to the extent that that's true, some exclusion of you. I always felt that I was paying a price for my originality. It's in the body language. I always thought I could feel and detect things, and I don't mean anything paranoid, either. I just mean the way a shoulder is turned, the length of time a glance is laid on you. It always seemed to me that I was being asked not only to live up to God's expectations but to their interpretation of Him, which is even worse.

The question of a Catholic sense of humor also relates to my observation about the limiting quality placed on one by the Catholic experience. I can detect in Steve Allen and in Bob Newhart, for example, a certain constipation, a certain self-imposed — although they wouldn't know that — restrictive aspect to the very body language and choice of words, certainly the choice of subject areas. I sense a lack of freedom, a rigidity of posture.

One of the things that I'm thankful for about growing up in my neighborhood is the cross-cultural influences that we had. There is a freedom in the black body and in the black art, especially music, that is in complete contradiction to their economic and political loss of freedom. So I guess you find it where you can. The freedom of the black body language and street poetry — and by that I merely mean the speech itself — was very attractive to me as a kid and to some of the others in my group. A certain number of us very consciously tried to take the cool parts of being black and to adapt them to ourselves. I credit my exposure to that with at least part of the freedom that I feel to use my body in my work.

This is kind of perverse, but I would say that the Catholic experience gave me something to react against. It gave me something to respond to which caused me to find myself. Because I didn't have a standard home situation and because I had an interrupted formal education, I had to invent myself. I think the impetus came from my reaction to the confining nature of my religious training and indoctrination. I wonder how pronounced, how defined that self-exploration would have been if it had had to find its own way without that springboard. That's a true part of me, though, so that would be the extent to which I could say that it was positive. I really loved the songs, I gotta admit. And I love the Latin — I like the idea of learning a language no one speaks. They told us once, though, that the Pope *thinks* in Latin.

CHRISTOPHER BUCKLEY

God and Man at the Yale Club

I don't have conservative credentials. What I have are conservative genes.
—Christopher Buckley
  Interview, October 1982

"No writer leads a charmed life," Edmund Wilson once said. But at thirty-five, Christopher Buckley may have come as close as anyone. After graduating from Yale and joining the staff of *Esquire* in 1976, Buckley was on his way, he says, "to a hundred and twenty-five dollar a week job as a reporter for the Charleston, South Carolina, *Evening Post*" when he met *Esquire* editor Lee Eisenberg at a publishing party for his father, the author, television host, and conservative commentator William F. Buckley. Chris signed on as an editor at *Esquire* and within six months was promoted to managing editor and then to "something called 'roving editor,' which is the all-time wonderful job." In 1979, on the basis of a three-page proposal, publisher Congdon and Lattès gave him a thirty-five thousand dollar advance to write a book about his sea travels. "It came out to twelve thousand dollars a page," Buckley told one reporter. "That's the most I've ever earned."

In the summer of 1981, he received a phone call from a vice presidential assistant he had met earlier, offering him a full-time job as speechwriter for George Bush. Out of that experience Buckley later forged one of the day's most successful satirical novels, and certainly one of the wittiest. *The White House Mess*, his parody of the ubiquitous tell-all Washington memoirs — many of them spawned in the jail cells of convicted Watergate felons — not only sold well in Washington cir-

cles, as might have been expected, but also made the national best-
seller lists. Yet if the book was inspired by what Buckley called those
"wonderfully insufferable" memoirs, its real juice came from an in-
sider's knowledge of the pettifogging, Alice in Wonderland workings
of government functionaries whom he had witnessed firsthand while
working for the vice president.

Buckley's previous book, *Steaming to Bamboola*, was a nonfiction
account of life on board a tramp freighter. It may have been his first book,
but it wasn't his first tramp freighter. Ten years earlier, after the harrowing
experiences at Portsmouth Abbey which he details in this interview, Buckley decided to escape before college. With his father's help, he signed on
a Norwegian freighter called the *Fernbrook* for twenty dollars a week. It
proved to be an odd sort of escape, after all. "I grew up in Stamford,
Connecticut, and New York City," Buckley said later, "and the hardest
work I had ever done was conjugating French verbs into the future sub-
junctive." On the *Fernbrook*, work consisted of cleaning the ship's car-
buretor with kerosene for twelve hours a day and scrubbing a huge latex
hold with a compound made partly of urine. The book described in detail
the more than motley crew of his second sea voyage and was well met
by the critics, who praised its gritty, realistic tone along with the author's
"excellent eye, ear, and vivid precision of style."

Chris Buckley describes himself as "a right-wing nut," adding that
"all my friends are left-wing nuts." Not many of them were in evidence,
though, as we met in the lobby of the Yale Club, a place that's lousy
with history. Built near the spot where Nathan Hale was hanged, on
Manhattan's Vanderbilt Avenue, the club is one of those New York land-
marks that manages to carry an air of tradition while looking a bit frayed
around the edges. Across from James Harvey Young's portrait of Henry
Ward Camp—a Union officer with the Tenth Connecticut Infantry who
was killed in action in Virginia, and presumably a Yale alumnus—we
settled into rattan chairs fitted with blue cushions alongside bamboo window shades and vaguely Far Eastern lamps that lent a Conradian cast to
our conversation. Buckley was dressed in a dark, doubled-breasted suit
and pale pink knit tie—requisite attire in a conservative establishment
that only recently admitted women to its inner sanctum. He quickly made
it clear that despite an adolescent bout with religious angst and an occasional interest in psychedelic drugs, he considers his Catholic faith to be
the single most significant force in his life and the chief source of his
happiness. His play based on the life of Edmund Campion, the sixteenth-
century Jesuit martyr, opened this summer at the Williamstown Theater
Festival.

◄§ MY FIRST MEMORY, my first consciousness of God occurred in the semi-abandoned garage attached to my parents' house. It was the gardener's shed and it was full of must, dust, and broken-down things. I'm not sure if I was yet fully verbal, so I may have been younger than four years old. I looked up and saw tacked to the edge of a shelf a rendition of the Crucifixion which had been put there by our Cuban gardener. It was, I think, a pen and ink drawing, and it was one of those wonderfully gory Latino renditions. Nothing was spared: Christ's knees were bloody; blood was streaming down His face; the crown of thorns had been jammed tight into His skull; His fingers were clawed around the nub of the nail.

And it was arresting because I was still at the Mother Goose stage and not yet even into Grimm's fairy tales — in which you have the odd scary old woman and, perhaps, the slavering wolf, but *nothing* like this. It's a very clear, visual memory, as clear as yesterday, burned like a daguerreotype into my brain, and I have no way of accounting for it. I asked my father about it, but I didn't even have the vocabulary to describe what I'd seen. I don't recall his answer.

My next memory is of my father telling me about Jesus being put to death — and I was very concerned about that, as they say in Washington. You know, "What on earth had gotten into them?" And he explained in a very gentle, fabulistic, Aesopian way that it had to be. He sought to assure me that Jesus had not been surprised by this, that this wasn't a bad card they had suddenly dealt off the bottom of the deck, and that He had come to earth specifically to die. I was about five, and we were driving in a car.

Then, before I knew what was happening, I began to be instructed in catechism. This was done privately in a kind of carpool approach. They found a nice, unblemished, suburban Catholic girl who also had the advantage of being very pretty. There were about five or six of us and she sort of walked us through the Baltimore Catechism which, on the whole, seemed very much less interesting than that card which I had seen in the gardener's shed.

By this time I was going to Mass with my dad and, always, the servants. My mother is Episcopalian, so she did not participate — it was just my dad, me, and the maids, all of whom were Cuban. I had a healthy resentment about this intrusion on my Sunday mornings and took no interest in it. But I was curious about some of the vocabulary. I remember, for instance, poring through one of those old missals with the onionskin paper and red and black ink and all that — the Mass was still in Latin then, with the English translation. I noticed one particular passage which attributed the adjective "terrible" to God, as in "for He is terrible." This made absolutely no sense, so I leaned over to my dad — I had the sense that I was on to something, that I had just caught a *major* typo. And so I learned at a very early age that "terrible" has more than one meaning.

Just in passing I should add that I became immensely resentful of Pope John XXIII not long after this. I was enrolled in altar boy training, the major part of which in those days was having those 138 lines drummed into you. One week after I had it all down pat, Vatican II changed everything, and I felt as though the whole thing had been done to annoy me. So I continued for a while to mumble under my breath, "*Ad Deum qui laetificat juventutem meam.*"

What I remember mostly about first holy communion was the whiteness of the costumes and my special satisfaction in finally being allowed to wear long pants, for it would be many years before I was again allowed to wear long pants. There was a sense of something important going on. The movie cameras were out, the girls in their white dresses, the gold medallion with your name engraved on it. It was life's first ritual. There would be many rituals to follow, but that inflected all rituals with, I suppose, a subconscious religious content. However, *before* one got to first communion, there was The First Confession.

I think that the first confession is essential to the whole thing. You take an eight-year-old kid and you tell him to go into a dark booth with a man dressed in black and tell the priest — what was it? — "the things that you haven't even told your mother," I think was how they put it. I remember distinctly being handed a mimeographed sheet by a nun. My memory is muzzy, but I had gone from the pretty girl who taught me catechism past a brief gauntlet of nuns, who were not the sadistic concentration-camp matrons that they are popularly made out to be. Yet it was these nuns who caused a mimeographed sheet of sins to fall into my possession, given me for the examination of conscience prior to confession.

It's really rather an abstract concept, isn't it? Giving a child a mimeographed sheet — and it was crammed, it looked like a crib sheet. There was not much white space on it; there were something like forty or fifty choices, which was a lot for eight years old. So I took the sheet home. Now, there was a touch of Little Lord Fauntleroy about my childhood — I was the only child of devoted parents — and I found myself rather affronted by this sheet. "What do they want, anyway? What business is it of theirs that I've been stealing erasers from the local five and dime? Really, I'll keep this to myself, thank you very much."

I remember thinking quite a lot about this rather inconvenient step which had to be gone through in order to get that first wafer. I discussed it with my buddy from catechism class and we pored over it, and here life's first lesson in Catholic evasion was learned, which was Go the path of least resistance. So we settled on "disobeying our parents." We made that our buzz-sin. Still, stepping into that confessional for the first time is an experience that every Catholic writer has explored with an understandably surreal appreciation of the sudden darkness that has been imposed on an otherwise gay period of life. It prefigures—doesn't it?—the transition from innocence to experience. And you find yourself *speaking* to this darkened screen, trying to remember things. It's sobering. It's really the most sobering thing I can imagine happening to an eight-year-old, in a ritualistic sense—you know, short of losing your mother or father. It's pretty grim stuff.

And then iconographically there is a marked difference. You go from the first confession, which occurs in this darkened sound chamber, the next day into a church that is brilliant with light, and you're wearing white. Everything is lambent, coruscating. You know the minds that devised all this weren't dumb, they were good showmen.

At a deeper level, there is a certain rationale to all that—although I didn't come to realize it until years later, when I read G. K. Chesterton's *Orthodoxy*. And I still think, if you could read only one book on what it means to be a Christian, that's the book. Anyway, in a chapter which he calls "The Ethics of Elfland," where he describes being brought up in an utterly agnostic household in which God did not figure, he tells how he learned Christianity without even knowing it at his nurse's knee when she read him the fairy tales. And when he came to God many years later and he looked back on what he had learned in the nursery, he realized that it was all the same. He calls it the "doctrine of negative prohibition," which is to say that the happiness depends always on *not* doing something. The prince will return to his homeland if he doesn't kiss the warthog; the girl will not turn into a newt if she gets home by a certain time. He discerns in this, with typical Chestertonian majestic reasoning, a continuity of theme that he later found in Christianity.

Getting back to the confessional, I was already a confirmed criminal at that age—I stole regularly from the local five and dime. But that really was about it. Much too early for impure thoughts. The disobeying of parents, certainly, and not saying your prayers—I was very guilty on that count. But, you see, I was really raised by Protestant women who had no interest in any of this and thought of it as rather vulgar, certainly unseemly. God, after all, *was* an Englishman, and this was merely an unfortunate by-product of having married a Catholic. For my part, I remember being astounded when I found out, at about age ten, that Episcopalians had only three sacraments. I thought, Well, poor things, how do they manage?

Finally, by grade four, I was sent to a Catholic school — a Montessori school, no less. So I went from an idyllic white schoolhouse with a trampoline out front to the wonderful world of Roman Catholicism à la Maria Montessori — oh, yoiks! The teachers there at Whitby all wore, in the Oxford or Cambridge manner, black robes. I suppose the idea was to inculcate in you a degree of formalistic respect for the institution. They were not a grim bunch, but it was the first time I was introduced, outside of church, to organized prayer. We began the day with prayer in an assembly hall.

I remember very distinctly, one day in the middle of the afternoon, a teacher coming in and saying that they thought they had lost an astronaut, and we were all to come into the hallway immediately. They emptied all the classrooms into this long, shotgun hallway, maybe a hundred yards long and all cinderblock. So the effect was that of a sewer suddenly infested with penguins, by which I mean that we were all on our knees praying — for Gus Grissom, I think it was, the guy who blew it. It was not altogether lost on me that there was something very concrete to the power of prayer, that more was more.

By now we all knew that, as Jesus had said, "Where there are three or more of you in a room together praying, I am with you." Catholicism is remarkably precise in its pronouncements. I want at some point to get to what effect it has on the imagination. But it may have something to do with the fact that you're given a number of conflicting propositions. One is that God is always with you — Proposition A — and Proposition B: God is with you if there are three or more of you in a room together. I thought, Wait a minute, I thought he was with me anyway. You started to hear the voice of Bill Cosby there somewhere.

But otherwise, it was very freeform at Whitby. Grades three, four, and five were in the same homeroom, for instance, and you did clusters for instruction. It was very big on the "do whatever feels right" approach, which struck me as fine. I remember we had an English teacher who looked sort of like Luciano Pavarotti. He'd come in in this robe that looked impossibly small for him — I mean, it barely came down over his belt, so the overall effect was fairly ridiculous. And yet he was a dear, gentle character, kind of like a Friar Tuck. He taught creative writing, and he would come in and say, "Now, I want you all to put your heads down on your desks and relax . . . close your eyes, banish all your thoughts, and think of nothing. . . ." And somebody would go, "I can't think of nothing.'' But he'd go, ''Shhhhhhhhh,'' and after about a minute or so he'd actually succeed in lulling you in a semihypnotic fashion into a state resembling sleep. And then all of a sudden he'd go, ''Now, *create!*'' He was the Werner Erhard of Montessori education.

Then I went off to a school here in New York City called St. David's, which later became famous for having John-John Kennedy in kindergarten, whence Mrs. Kennedy removed him in a huff for some reason. Anyway, Catholic education then began in earnest. There was an honest-to-God chapel. There'd been no chapel at Whitby, it was all cinderblock — From His House to Bauhaus — and here there was a wood-paneled chapel with stained glass, pews, organ, the works, and I do mean the works. There were beatings — this was the beginning of corporal punishment — and very serious churching, right around the corner at St. Thomas More on East Eighty-ninth between Park and Madison. Now began the preparation for being a soldier of Christ: confirmation. Heavy stuff.

Once again, I was appalled when I learned that part of the ceremony would include being slapped in the face by Cardinal Spellman. The teachers went to great pains to say that this was a symbolic gesture, had nothing to do with how the cardinal felt about you personally, that it would in fact be a tap. But then the stories began to circulate that, you know, some kid's older brother, when he had been in Chicago, got a real *whack* across the face that left a five-fingered welt.

Then, at about grade six, it started to be important to get into the right prep school, so you'd get into the right college, so you'd get into the right life. My life was not very happy from about grade five to grade eight, because I would get back from a tough school, I would have an hour of piano practice, and then an hour of French from Genevieve, and then homework. Genevieve was my French governess, whose true calling obviously was to be a nun, and not of the nice variety. She was very Catholic and would give me punishments for rather minor infractions. Like once I walked back from receiving communion and I guess I forgot myself — instead of folding my hands in the attitude of prayer, I just let them hang down by my sides. Oh, boy, did she make me regret that. She somehow managed to combine French grammar with extra religious instruction in a way that made me view the whole schmeer with an increasing desire to have nothing more to do with it. It became a grim kind of world. All of a sudden there was very little light; it was all darkness. And at that point I sort of on the sly stopped going to confession.

Now that was at home. At school, we had one teacher who would beat you with a ruler with your pants down, and one who did sort of caning. We had a Latin teacher called Mr. Thompson, who was Scottish and

smoked a pipe. He would whack you over the head with this pipe, and
let me tell you, three ounces of briar, judiciously applied to the cranial
weak spot, produced stars. I got belted a couple of times in the face with
the back of the hand, but it was all pretty tame in comparison to what
most other Catholic friends of mine were going through. Those who went
off to the Christian Brothers were routinely beaten with leather straps.
And the ones who were with nuns. . . . One told me of a Sister
Immaculata—it's always Sister Immaculata—who kept a box of un-
cooked rice by her desk. This particular school had concrete floors. She
must have learned this at Buchenwald—she would sprinkle rice on the
floor, and you had to roll up your pants and kneel on it for two hours.
You ended up with bloody knees, and you ended up having to sort of
surgically extract the grains of rice with a tweezer.

Now, I suppose this was convenient for the parents. I guess any loving
parent would prefer not to beat their child and have someone else do it.
There's a Chinese proverb that says, "Beat your child at least once a
day—if you don't know why, the child does."

So that was St. David's. That was not a happy period. And then one
weekend my dad and I went to look at prep schools. We looked at three,
although there was a hidden agenda all along. We looked at Canterbury,
which I kind of liked; we looked at Taft, which I loved—it looked like
a miniature Yale or Harvard, out in the country with no evidence of
religion; and then we went to Portsmouth Priory, run by the Benedictine
monastery. I'd never seen a monk before, and it was a cold sort of cheerless
place looking out on a bay that froze over in the winter, and I thought,
My God, get me out of here. The monk who showed us around was a
wonderfully gentle man who did much to set me at ease. A little over a
year ago, that same monk married my wife and me. He's my closest
spiritual adviser, but that gets rather ahead of the story.

My father didn't want to force anything down my throat, yet it was
very clear that the deck was stacked. He said, "Well, what did you think?"
I said, "God, I hate it." He said, "Well, what didn't you like about it?"
I said, "Everything. Taft, great place." He said, "I tell you what makes
sense whenever you're trying to make a tough decision—you make a
list. On one side you put pros and on the other side you put cons. Shall
we do that?" I said, "Sure." He said, "Okay, let's take Portsmouth.
Now, on the pro side is the fact of Catholic education. . . ." I said,
"What's so *pro* about that?" At that point I think he gave up for the
moment.

I remember distinctly he and my mother having a real argument over
dinner—it was just the three of us and my dad had basically informed

her that I was going to Portsmouth. She was asserting her right to have a say in where I went, not as a religious matter but as a sort of turf battle. But she signed away those rights when she married my dad — all women who marry Catholics do. I mean, it's signed, sealed, and delivered; the Church gets it in writing. But I remember a nasty argument because she knew clearly that I wanted nothing to do with Portsmouth, and I just wished they would stop, it was traumatic. But . . . off I went.

I was thirteen years old, and it was the most miserable time of my life. I cried myself to sleep every night for three months. It was the closest thing to a British public school experience that I think you could get on this side of the Atlantic — minus the Catholicism, of course. But it was a gray, cheerless, miserable September 13, 1966. My dad wept as he hugged me goodbye — my mother wasn't speaking to him, because how could he do this to her? But he knew what he was doing.

I say that because Portsmouth is responsible for my having faith. Portsmouth itself I did not enjoy at the time I was there. It was very strict: thirty-six hours for Thanksgiving, no weekends, prayer every morning at seven, midday prayer, grace before meals — if you opened your mouth to put a Baby Ruth in, someone whapped a grace on you — vespers, evening prayer, Mass three times a week, and one of them was at six forty-five A.M. The bell would go at six fifteen, and in the winter it was dark and cold, and you would find yourself marching through snowdrifts up a hill with freezing toes to attend Mass. It was ridiculous. Did they really think that this was going to leave you with a love of God?

And then, of course, there were Christian doctrine courses — mandatory, nothing elective about them. One found oneself reading the Monarch Notes to the Old Testament: "All right now, which one was Amos?" But there were some characters among the monks. The headmaster was a man called Father Leo Van Winkle, who had worked with Edward Teller on the atom bomb as a young genius just out of Yale graduate school. The story went that some student from a previous generation had left photographs of Hiroshima taped to the front of his prayer carrel.

The one thing that is extraordinary about any *contained* Catholic institution, by which I suppose I simply mean boarding school, is the level of sadism. There was one Jewish kid at that school — what he was doing there I don't know — but he was the butt of every anti-Semitic joke, taunt, and raw cruelty, oven jokes, the works. Aloud. And I'm ashamed to say that I used to engage in that. We became friends, somehow — he somehow had the extraordinary grace to forgive. He was, incidentally, about the smartest kid there. And for some odd reason, part of the deal was that he had to attend Mass. He was not expected to take communion or anything, but maybe they saw no sense in exempting him from what everyone else had to go through. I don't know.

And then there was a kid who had a ghastly case of acne—how he was made to suffer for that. One night they got him out of bed, smeared chocolate all over his face, and paraded him about with a crown as King Hershey. When you look at the parallel, it's something like the Passion —he was taunted and mocked. And what do you know, he was killed in a car crash a year after graduation. So somewhere there are thirty kids who probably don't feel very good about one episode in their youth, and perhaps there's something there.

A couple of the monks were sort of queer. There was no overt homosexuality, but there were some who took a perhaps indecent interest in gym, and one who was sort of into spanking boys for not very serious provocations. And then there was a lay Latin professor, an old, florid-faced, white-haired English guy, rather decent really, called Cecil J. Acheson. But he had certain lapses. We were translating the *Aeneid*, and he had given us a word the class before. He said, "When you get to the fifth line of this translation, be alert to the word"—and I remember it very well—"*denique*. It's not a word you'll find in the dictionary. It means 'in a nutshell.' It's rather an interesting word." Well, this class he called on a kid to translate the first five lines and the kid, sure enough, forgot *denique*. Acheson went absolutely vermillion. And his glasses would fog up—this sounds like a movie but he had those owl, Coke-bottle glasses—and he turned to the kid in a voice seething with hatred and he said, "I don't understand why they don't send more of your kind to Vietnam. You're so expendable. Now let's go to Mass. God loves you; I don't."

So these were some of the things that happened at Portsmouth. I have obviously highlighted the grim. The caliber of the education was extraordinary. These monks may have been dotty, some of them, but they were all really authentic geniuses. In a class of sixty, in my senior year, ten of us were accepted at Harvard, and seven or eight at Yale, and then a hefty level of acceptances at Columbia, Dartmouth, Williams, Stanford. So they did their job.

That, of course, was the last time I saw the inside of a church for quite some time. I then shipped out on the merchant marine as a deck boy on a Norwegian freighter and worked my way around the world. And that was a very different experience. I mean, there were no Saturdays, there were no Sundays, and there were certainly no churches. There were Indian temples and Buddhist temples, but there were also the Mosquito Bar, the LeGaspi Rosegarden, rather more of that. I fell into probably what everyone does, which is the lapsed moment, and that endured through the summer of my sophomore year in 1972.

At that time an incident happened which I have to think maybe was put there. I was out drinking with some friends at a hotel in British Columbia where I was visiting my grandmother. I went into the men's room to wash my hands and have a pee. As I was washing my hands, I became aware of someone there who was neither having a pee nor washing his hands. I had taken self-defense, so I went into yellow alert. He said something innocuous, and I turned and saw that he was a pudding of a man with nothing harmful in his aspect. He was slightly flabby, very pale but kempt. But he looked very sad, so I asked him if there was something wrong. He said, "Well, up until yesterday I was a Benedictine monk, and I've left the Order. And I don't really know where to go." And I had no advice.

A few days later I found myself in the basement of a house where I had set up a temporary desk. At this point I had started dabbling in some creative writing and so I thought to write a short story about the incident. Halfway into the short story I found myself weeping — weeping with prodigality. I thought, I have betrayed these good men. The word is overused, but this was an *epiphany*, a sudden and unanticipated revelation of something — namely that these were truly godly men who, for all their dottiness, were holy. I ended the story, which was a rather crude attempt at fiction, with the monk walking out of the men's room — and he hears a cock crowing. Genius, huh?

So I was brought back to the Church by a chance encounter with a defrocked monk in a men's room in the Hotel Vancouver, and I've been back ever since. I remember explaining to my dad a year after returning from the merchant marine that I no longer went to church. He got very quiet, then he said, "You've got to, you've got to." And I said, "Well, look, I'll do it for you. I'll sit and listen to the music, but it ain't gonna reach me." But he was willing to settle for that. Of course, I didn't. Later on, I used to do all sorts of terrible things, like drop acid on Good Friday — not specifically because it was Good Friday, it just happened to be Good Friday. This was after I had gone back to the Church, but it was still a rather unstructured period. That sort of thing wasn't covered on the mimeographed sheets the nuns had given me when I was eight. But it was really a rather exuberant re-entry.

The Church and I never did differ on matters of doctrine. It had nothing at all to do with that. It was just unthinking revolution, although to call it revolution is to put too sophisticated a construction on it. If you've been under the supervision of a French governess and then thirty Benedictine

monks, and then you are let free, and suddenly no one's observing you
—I'm willing to bet that this happened to ninety-five percent of the people
I went to Portsmouth with—it's, you know, Thank God. It's *Ite, missa est:* thank God it's over.

At that point, you see, I hadn't come to Chesterton. Chesterton had a
lot to do with it. My dad and I once went down to Taxco, Mexico, for
the purpose of reading aloud to each other G. K. Chesterton's *Orthodoxy.*
And it was fabulous, in almost literally that way. It explains everything,
and it was so beautifully written that reading it aloud makes it almost your
own. It was kind of a crash course in the poetry of faith, which I had
never quite grasped through the formal education. Formal education was
linear, doctrinal, austere. They never sought to try to relate, say, Shake-
speare to it, or Rimbaud. I hadn't discovered the wonderful, poetical
qualities of Catholicism, so that when I chanced onto the line written by
H. L. Mencken in a superb essay called "Holy Writ," I felt as though
something very important had been illuminated. And I was very grateful to
such a sturdy and robust atheist as Mencken for having come up with the
sentence: "The Latin Church, which I find myself admiring more and
more despite its frequent, astounding imbecilities, has always kept clearly
before it the fact that religion is not a syllogism but a poem."

All of a sudden it all began to fall into place, that it wasn't just a
lawyer's brief on how to make it all the way, but an interpretation of how
it had all come about. I believe in Darwin *and* Genesis. I find nothing
contradictory in the theory of evolution and Christianity. Whittaker Cham-
bers writes in *Witness* that what brought *him* to belief in God was sitting
in the kitchen one night feeding his three-year-old daughter. He found
himself observing her ear, this perfect, delicate little ear, and he decided
this was not an accident, not a random accretion of molecules—it was
designed.

It's very hard to say what goes into writing, whether it be religion or
anything else, for that matter. You know, someone once complimented
Winston Churchill on a speech he had just made and said, "Winnie, how
long did it take you to write that?" Churchill said, "Six hours . . . plus
seventy years." A writer's capital is his life. But I'll tell you something
very concrete. I'm a big fan of St. Thomas More, and I keep next to the
screen of my word processor a postcard of the Holbein from the Frick
Museum, the famous portrait of Thomas More. And I keep it there for a
reason: He keeps me straight. It's actually happened that when, in the
course of doing a magazine piece or whatever, I'm tempted to fudge a
quote—if I think, Well, this quote doesn't do exactly what I want it to

do, so I'll just fix it up — then I look at More and I unfudge it. Now I really should have A. J. Liebling or E. B. White there, but I refer this to a higher authority perhaps than another journalistic buddy of mine might do.

Right now I'm embarked upon a very distinctly Catholic project. I'm writing a play on the life of Edmund Campion, the Jesuit martyr under Elizabeth I, whose life was illuminated to me by Evelyn Waugh's book on Campion. And I'm doing it with James MacGuire, a friend of mine from Portsmouth. After watching *Brideshead Revisited*, he had the idea to do a saga of the recusants, a term from the sixteenth century used to describe one who refused to attend the Anglican services.

I suppose I have a fairly Manichaeistic imagination, and I tend to divide things into good and evil. I believe in genuine evil. Watching *The Exorcist* was for me a truly horrifying experience. As someone else might put it, I *believe* in that shit. I don't believe in ghosts, but I do believe in miracles.

There's a line in *Orthodoxy*, which I shall now render clumsily, and it's Chesterton's answer to the scientific denunciation of the existence of God. He says he has absolutely nothing against skeptics except — and here's the very Chestertonian trademark — they're not skeptical enough. He says, "It seems to me fine to say that you cannot believe in God because you can't see Him with your senses; but how is it that you can believe in a dandelion? What is it that is so rational, obvious, logical about a dandelion or a butterfly?" He does that rather well.

Here's a true story told to me by a very good friend of Graham Greene, concerning Greene and Padre Pio. Padre Pio, who died not long ago, was an Italian priest who received the stigmata early on, and he became as such almost an embarrassment to the Church. You know, the Church is very wary of miracles. The Catholic Church has taken pains to keep the Shroud of Turin quiet. They take it out every twenty-five or thirty years, but that's about it.

But here they had a guy with the stigmata, and the crowds were starting to come. His hands would bleed at the moment of the elevation of the host; otherwise, he wore gloves. So they sent him to a very remote parish in Italy that was hard to get to — precisely because they didn't want headlines saying, you know, THE AMAZING BLEEDING PRIEST. They wanted to secrete him. And there are a number of miracles associated with his life, which are the subject of a fairly fascinating book, recently written.

Anyway, Graham Greene, who is a rather complicated Catholic — I have no window to look into another man's soul, but he's a pretty skeptical dude — heard about Padre Pio, and he went to visit. He located the village on a Sunday. Everyone was packed into Mass, and he got into the back of the church. At the moment of the elevation, sure enough, Padre Pio began bleeding. Greene was horrified by it and he fled, he had to get out of there. He went to the edge of town and had a drink. He was sitting there with a bottle, getting ready to leave, when he saw a young priest running in the street. The priest ran right up to him and said, "I have a message from Padre Pio. The message is this: Be at peace. God does not ask anything from us that we cannot give Him." And he left.

That's a true story. I'm not sure if Greene has ever told it—he may possibly still be freaked out. But it was told me by someone very close to him, who is also a Catholic. Interesting.

ELIZABETH MCALISTER

"Where's the Church?"

We were excommunicated because we dared exercise our conscience with regard to one another. But we are Roman Catholics . . . the Church has given us everything and we are deeply indebted to it. But we will continue to speak out against the excesses of myopia, cowardice and hypocrisy. It is probably the best service we can do the Church.
—Philip Berrigan
   New York Times, September 18, 1973

"Have you ever had *soy*sage?" The woman named Sunshine was making dinner in the kitchen of Jonah House, a religious commune set in a modest row house in the Reservoir Hill section of Baltimore. Once a classy neighborhood that over the years had become run-down and ghettoized, Reservoir Hill is making a comeback with the aid of what my cabbie called "a few courageous people." The folks in Jonah House are apparently among them.

Asked what soysage consists of, Sunshine explained that it's got some buckwheat, some spices, and, of course, some soymeal. Squeezing limes in a forty-year-old Juice-O-Mat, she went on to say that for twenty-five dollars a month, the commune buys the right to go through the local dumpster where they often find sacks of potatoes and onions and cases of pineapple juice that have fallen off trucks and been partially damaged. This procedure allows them to feed a lot of people for a little money. Jonah House is inhabited by Roman Catholics devoted to opposing their government's policies of nuclear proliferation and is presided over by what is perhaps America's foremost alternative Catholic couple (a designation they'd most likely reject): Philip Berrigan and Elizabeth McAlister.

When I told my cabbie on the way in from the train station about the book I was writing, the first thing he asked was whether I'd talked yet to Dan and Phil Berrigan. He had no idea that they lived at the address he was taking me to, but he knew they were in Baltimore somewhere. Nor had he heard of Elizabeth McAlister, Phil's wife, whom I *had* come to interview. If, during the sixties, Daniel and Philip Berrigan were in large measure the conscience of the radical Catholic Left, in the seventies that role expanded to include Elizabeth McAlister. The radical nun McAlister was arrested and convicted along with Phil Berrigan for smuggling contraband letters out of prison — the only charge the government was able to win in its case against an alleged conspiracy to kidnap Henry Kissinger. McAlister subsequently left the Sisters of the Sacred Heart to marry Berrigan, an ordained priest. Both were summarily excommunicated.

Since then, they have continued to put their bodies on the line to protest what they consider a string of related social injustices ranging from hunger and homelessness to the proliferation of nuclear weapons. Because they are also raising three children (Frida, age twelve, Jerome, eleven, and Kathleen, four and a half) they have to coordinate their acts of civil disobedience so that one of them is home to take care of the kids during the other's sojourn in jail. Besides participating in direct actions as part of Plowshares, a nationwide disarmament group, McAlister helps put out an antiwar newsletter called *Year One.*

When I spoke with McAlister in Jonah House, she had just returned from the Federal Correctional Institution in Alderson, West Virginia, where she had finished serving two years of a three-year sentence for beating up on a B-52 bomber in 1983. But apart from her yellow T-shirt — a prison souvenir which reads, "Sickle Cell Drive, Black History Month, F.C.I. Alderson, Feb. 1983" — she looked like any other mother of three. McAlister's gray eyes give one a feeling not so much of the militant or the fanatic as of someone in love with her work. On the Baldwin upright, as if placed there by a set designer, stood the sheet music for "Amazing Grace." A couple of handmade crucifixes adorned the walls, along with the more conventional trappings of an American home — children's artwork and the like. Her one concession to the unholistic way of life appears to be the Winstons she smokes with alarming frequency.

MY PARENTS WERE BOTH BORN and raised in the north of Ireland, and they were Roman Catholic. So there was something about being an oppressed minority there that gave them both a very deep sense of their own faith and its meaning. They met in this country, though. Mom had come with her family first, and when my father came over with one of his sisters, he was told to look up my mother, who was a friend of the family, and that was how they met.

There were seven children in my family. I came along as one of twins at places five and six. My parents were practicing Catholics, and to them Catholic education was central. All of us went to parochial schools until we moved to Montclair, New Jersey, when I was about ten, and there was no parochial school connected with our parish. They opted to send the remaining four of us to private schools to make sure we got a Catholic education. All of us except my youngest brother had Catholic education all through school, which means into college. It required a sacrifice on the part of my parents to make that possible, but it was something to which they were committed. That was their priority.

Dad was a contractor and was doing well for a good number of years, but then because he would not play the political games in New Jersey he went out of business. I'm not too clear on exactly what those games were, but there were constant under-the-table payments, underbidding and over-pricing, and all kinds of things that were expected. It was not a nice game, and he was an honest man. The value that he held up to us was the value of truthfulness. As children, I remember, it didn't matter what we did. If we didn't tell the truth about it, that was the worst thing we could do. And he carried that out in his own work life. As a result, he ended up working as clerk of the works on contracting jobs rather than being an independent contractor. He just would not deal with dishonesty. But both my parents also had an attitude that you didn't buy anything on time; if you couldn't pay for it, you didn't have it, period. So at least we were never in debt.

Religious life, to them, was part of family life. There would be a regular family rosary in the evening. My father would announce it, and we'd all endure it, pretty much. It was part of the ritual. I know they took that very seriously. I think that few if any of us ever had great devotion to the rosary. It seemed to us kids very repetitive prayer and not one that met our needs. We didn't enjoy it. We tried to bring the dog in or the cat, something to distract ourselves through it. Dad became a member of the Serra Club, a club of Catholic laymen which fostered vocations to the religious life among young people. It was a high hope of his that one or more of us would go in that direction, and I did. That was a deep joy of his.

Aside from schooling and prayer and fidelity to basic religious practices, he also led us in an interest in religious questions as they touched upon our individual and family lives. He would often initiate these and would be very interested in hearing from us about theology discussions that we were having in school. My father was the kind of person who was concerned about learning all his life, and he was not afraid to learn from us—which was quite a boost. He'd raise questions that he had thought about, and he was interested in knowing what we were being taught about them. If they were insights that he thought valuable, he'd respond very deeply to that. So there was a sense through that kind of exchange that religious questions weren't just part of Sunday Mass attendance but were part of life.

Initially, as a little one, I remember being very fond of the nun who taught us in kindergarten and first grade. After that I was pretty intimidated by them. In high school I began running into nuns for whom I didn't have a whole lot of respect as people exhibiting a life choice. That's a hard thing to say, but it's true. There were a couple that I could relate fairly deeply to, but they were the exception rather than the rule. When I went to college I ran into a good number of nuns whom I could deeply respect. Eventually I stopped regarding them as a group and began to see them as individuals.

My desire to become a nun stemmed from what I would have to call a very clear vocation, something that I met in my own very limited and yet even at that stage very real prayer life, and it was something that I resisted for a long time. It was only after I accepted it consciously and willingly that any attraction to that life grew. And it probably wouldn't have grown except in the context of the college where I was going and the life that was depicted by the nuns who taught there. I was at Marymount College in Tarrytown, New York, run by the religious of the Sacred Heart of Mary, which was the Community that I did enter and was part of for fourteen years. There was a spirit among them that was very fine and seemed to combine an ability to be friendly and human with a certain spirituality and an orientation toward growth. They were willing to change, to learn, and to grow as people. There was none of the artificiality of being shocked by certain forms of behavior that had become so apparent to me in the high school situation.

I knew that my father would be pleased by a vocation, but by that time I also had three married sisters and a married brother, and that life was also appreciated—as were the grandchildren. So I didn't feel any pressure from him at all. In fact, there's an interesting story that relates to this. My next oldest sister was in college at the time and was dating a guy there whom the brothers at the university had pinpointed as one with a priestly vocation. This emerged as their relationship developed, and so they talked about it with my father, who suggested that they go see the monsignor who headed up his group. They did, and after several discussions the monsignor advised that they not see each other again, that the boy go into the priesthood and my sister go into religious life. They were both brokenhearted by his advice and by his manner. My father told her: "Nonsense, do what you think best." And they got back together again, rapidly; they have eight children now. So when I told my parents where I was leaning, I was half expecting the appointment with the monsignor, which never came. But somewhere along the line, the monsignor heard that I would be entering the Community in a week. The monsignor came up to my father later and said, "Bill, you've been holding out on me." Dad just brushed it off. When I asked him why he hadn't told the monsignor, he said, "He spoiled one vocation on me. You think I'd give him a whack at another?"

I was in college for two years, and toward the end of my first year I went through a long period of wrestling with the vocation. There was a very clear sense that I would not be able to continue praying without saying yes to this. Then the question became What do I do with it? I saw a priest there who was a teacher but also the chaplain. He advised me just to accept the vocation and leave it alone for the time being, to let it grow. Which turned out to be wise — about the middle of the following year I began to feel that was indeed what I wanted to do. So I entered the Community after two years of college, in 1959. Those were the vocation boom years, so to speak, and I entered, as one of a group of sixty-one postulants, a large, very structured, pre–Vatican II novitiate. It was all very new to me. I'd say that on many levels they were good years, although I left the novitiate not knowing what it was all about. Maybe that was the best thing about it because I didn't have a whole lot to unlearn.

After I was professed, the first profession, I went to our House of Studies and completed my college. I truncated the last two years of college into one, taking twenty-two or twenty-three hours a week in courses. Then I was sent to graduate school and took a master's degree in history of art, came back to Marymount, and began teaching there in June of sixty-three. I got my master's at Hunter College in New York City, and there was a flavor in the air, but it didn't come into relief for me until I had come back and was teaching at Marymount. I was given the responsibility of caring for the bulletin boards, so I would put up articles from periodicals and journals on different political issues. I was doing a lot of reading along those lines, reading in a way that I had never read before, which is to say, not believing that our presence in Vietnam could be justified and feeling very deeply that it did not square with any kind of moral or biblical position. I felt that a patriotism that demanded such actions was somehow at odds with who God was. I also began to question the position of America in the world—"America first" didn't square with any religious belief that I was aware of.

The Second Vatican Council was beginning then, and that had a tremendous impact on me. Being at the college at Tarrytown with a religious community of eighty-six women, many of whom were pretty extraordinary human beings, both intellectually and spiritually, I was kept aware of what was going on in the council all the time. We had nuns at universities all over the country, and they'd come home for vacations and bring back a tremendous vitality. Many of the theologians who had been at the council came to the college and visited. They'd give a lecture and then we'd meet with them afterward and go far into the night questioning, searching. It was a very alive time, very challenging.

By that time, my political involvement was also overt. In 1965 and 1966 I was participating in marches and demonstrations and vigils and fasts and even doing some speaking on the war-peace question. I was associating with a loosely structured but growing community of people who came at their concern for the war-peace issue out of moral or religious grounds. There was a lot of nurturing and sustaining that went back and forth among us. It was during that time that I became involved with the Catholic Worker and Pax Christi. In sixty-five, Clergy and Laity Concerned About the War in Vietnam was founded, and one of the founding members was Rabbi [Abraham] Heschel, who had been a real source of inspiration for me through his writings. Dan Berrigan and Pastor [Richard] Neuhaus were the others responsible for the group, and that was when I first met Dan.

In 1970, I was involved in my first active participation in resisting the war, a draft board action in Delaware. Before that, I had been invited to be part of the Catonsville Nine, but I felt I wasn't ready for that. In Delaware, we were willing to face the consequences of our action, but the government couldn't get it together to move on us. So the first time I was subjected to arrest was in what came to be known as the Harrisburg Conspiracy. The indictment came down in January of 1971, and the trial started a year later. I had met Philip Berrigan in 1966, when he was celebrating the funeral Mass for one of the Catholic Workers who had been mugged and killed. Later on, he and three others did an action down here in Baltimore at the Customs House for which he was arrested, and a number of us came down on a regular basis for each of the phases of that trial. That was a radicalizing experience for me and for all of us who made the trip. It seemed like the way one should go; it seemed right.

In seventy-two we finished the Harrisburg trial, and Philip and I were convicted of writing letters and were sentenced for that.* He was paroled in December of seventy-two, and then we were legally married in 1973. But there was a definite sense of a commitment to each other that dated back to sixty-nine. He had been in prison pretty much the whole time between sixty-nine and seventy-three, off and on.

The case concerning our marriage was probably a little bit more black and white for me than for him. With him the issue was priestly celibacy. I held a hope and a vision that there could one day be a religious community that would involve both married and celibate people, and in fact there is a sense of that emerging right now with many religious communities, including my own. My Community even has a calendar of retreats and dialogues and family weekends. Up in Sag Harbor they have an annual gathering for folks who have been part of the Community and want to maintain that relationship to come with their families and share a combination of fun and reflection. They have retreats now with people who are still part of the Community and people who have been. My proposal for that kind of association was a little too soon.

I did request a dispensation from vows — though I requested it saying I would really rather not — and left the Order before the legalization of the marriage. We were actually excommunicated on the grounds that Phil is still a priest — he had never gone through the laicization process. I felt that, in essence, our marriage would enable the fulfillment of my vocation in a deeper sense, although it meant a very real change of lifestyle. I think that we live with a greater sense of poverty than I did in the Community and a greater sense of risk, in an effort to live in a spirit of obedience to the gospels. I was aware that the relationship with the Community was going to end as it had been, but I held the hope that it could continue in some new ways. That was wrenching, and yet I felt that it also was right. What was surprising about being excommunicated was that we found out about it through the newspapers. Nobody even gave us a written note about it. My reaction was "If this is how they do it, what does it mean? Thrown out of the community of believers — well, what community? And who says?"

I am part of the community of believers — the community of believers who have for many years raised the question "Where's the Church?" Years and years ago we stood outside St. Patrick's Cathedral to demon-

---

*They were actually charged with smuggling letters in and out of prison — Berrigan was in jail and McAlister was on the outside — an infraction that, according to most accounts at the time of the trial, is usually overlooked but that the government chose to prosecute in this instance.

strate our support for people of conscience who were in jeopardy with the law. We had seen the representatives of the cardinal when the Catonsville Nine were going for sentencing and asked that this be part of a prayer of the faithful. They said no. So we had a liturgy outside of the church that same Sunday, and it really raised the question "Where's the Church?" Is it inside there or is it among the people? We have picked up the definition of the Church that the Church is the people of God, that it's wherever people gather in God's name. By that time we'd been over a number of these hurdles with the Church, where you're celebrating the Eucharist behind closed doors like the early Christians—because you dare to celebrate marriage, because you dare to use regular bread, because you dare to share the cup.

The only times the excommunication has become an issue for us have been those times when we've been in prison and have dealt with a very conventional chaplain. I've only experienced that once; Phil has hit it a number of times where the chaplain has said, "I'm not going to give you the Eucharist." He's got to stick to his conscience, but then you create alternatives: have your own Eucharist with whoever chooses to have it with you. The priest we had at Alderson who came for Catholic Mass was rather traditional in many respects, and I wondered if he would bring it up. But he didn't, so I never did. But if he had brought it up, I wouldn't have made an issue of it because that would have seemed a lack of respect for his conscience. We met it with my younger brother, who asked us to be godparents for his youngest child. I said, "Father Brown will never agree." He asked Father Brown, and I was right. He came back and said, "I still want you to be the godparents." So she was baptized at home and we were the godparents. But it hasn't become an issue in most instances. And I think that the more the Church throws excommunication around without any kind of process, the less meaning it has. I mean, why don't they excommunicate people who are obvious war criminals?

On the other hand, the discipline of the Church on marriage and sexuality is something that, in time, I've come to appreciate, because there are deeper reasons for virginity and celibacy until there's a point of commitment. Growing up, that would have been a strict discipline. But I became in my adulthood deeply grateful for that discipline because it prevented me from experimenting and thus enabled me to avoid many of the deep emotional and physical wounds that come out of that. But it was taught so badly, it was taught as rigid right and wrong, and seldom were you told the wisdom of it. Either you learned its wisdom on your own, or you abandoned the discipline and then abandoned the Church.

.   .   .

We have three children and we didn't plan any of them. I'm really grateful for all three children. The littlest one came at a very inconvenient time. I became pregnant with Katy between the time Phil was released from prison after the Plowshares Eight action and his sentencing. Phil was given a three-to-ten-year sentence for that, so it took some real adjusting. She's a marvelous child, but if we believed in abortion, that would've been the time that I think my faithlessness would have led me to it. I would have a very rough time personally with abortion because I stand deeply for preserving life in all of its forms. It doesn't help me to say that life begins at such and such a time. I don't think we know that. My experience of pregnancy in the very early stages is that you know you're pregnant; you know that something very mysterious, something beyond you is going on.

To me that's valuing life, and where does that value come from in this country and in the Church when life is *not* valued? I find that starting with an emphasis on abortion is starting at the wrong end of the stick. I have had great difficulty in my encounters with the pro-life movement. With very few exceptions, the pro-lifers are saying, "I'm for the right of the unborn, but nuclear weapons are fine, and the death penalty's fine. . . ." I think it was Cardinal Bernardin who initiated the "seamless garment" ethic in terms of valuing life, and I feel deeply committed to that seamless garment, which encompasses war and nuclear weapons and abortion and capital punishment and the availability of guns and Saturday night specials, the emphasis on hunting and hunting licenses in any form—it's all of a piece. Until we begin seriously to address that, I don't think we can talk with any authenticity to a woman in deep trouble with an unwanted or unexpected pregnancy.

So that's my own kind of web, if you will. I was deeply offended by the ad that was placed in the *New York Times** a couple of years back— I wrote a whole letter of response to that which the *National Catholic Reporter* ended up publishing. What I think is much more to the point in all of this would be for women to share with one another the content of their own conscience on the issue of abortion, rather than to say simply that a variety of opinions exist among committed Catholics on the issue of abortion. That isn't helpful in promoting any kind of growth. It would have been more helpful for the people involved to explain what their

---

*"A Catholic Statement on Pluralism and Abortion" appeared as a full-page ad in the *Times* on October 7, 1984, asserting that "a diversity of opinion regarding abortion exists among committed Catholics" and calling for "candid and respectful discussion" of the issue. The signatories included two priests, two religious brothers, and twenty-six nuns. In November, the Vatican sent a letter to the superiors of those religious who had signed the ad requiring the signers to retract publicly or face dismissal from their communities.

personal attitude is, where it came from, what principles it was based on, and how they got to that point. Share that, so it can help somebody else in the formation of her own conscience.

On the other hand, the way the Church handled that situation is typical of their authoritarian response to any departure from their official dogma. I happen to disagree both with those who signed the ad and with the Church's response on this issue. I would rather see a dialogue opened up to discuss the possibilities for meaningful alternatives to both those courses of action.

I see everything that happens in our bodies as a consequence of what we do to them, or do with them, or put into them. If I put in a lot of junk food, I'm going to get sick or fat. If I put in a lot of alcohol, I'm going to get sick or drunk. If I have sex at certain periods of my cycle, I'm going to get pregnant. There's an organic principle here: I'm free to choose to eat or not to eat those foods that are going to make me ill or fat. And I'm free to opt for sex or not-sex at a particular time. But once I've had sex, the consequences are consequences of those actions, and that's where the argument breaks down for me that abortion is woman's ultimate right to control her own body. Where freedom comes is to say yes or no beforehand or to take certain precautions beforehand, either you or he. We have a right to control our own bodies, yes — to a degree. But our bodies are affected by what we do with and to them.

When I was pregnant with our youngest, I was forty-one years old, and I found that an incredible change in prenatal care had taken place. There were something like fourteen tests that were recommended that I take to ensure that the fetus was well and healthy. The supposition from these tests was that if it weren't, I would opt for an abortion. I chose not to take any of the tests. But because of the number of lawsuits that had come against doctors and other people, I had to give a written statement that I was advised of these dangers and I opted not to take these tests because of what they were leading to. *Fourteen* of them — and there had been none of that six years earlier. That was mind-boggling to me, and it sort of suggested that you were shopping for the perfect product, and if you couldn't get the perfect product, of course you wouldn't have any. It seems to neglect the value in our lives of people like Robert [the learning-impaired man who visits McAlister at the communal house]. We need them for our growth, we need them for our health, we need them to teach us who we should be and how we can care for our world.

But on birth control, I think people need a certain freedom because without that, married life can become very difficult.

. . .

When I was in prison down in Alderson, we had a very interesting process. Bishop Sullivan and Eileen Dooley, who heads the Office of Justice and Peace in the Richmond diocese, came every three months to see a number of us who were down there. At the time they started coming, the American bishops were talking about a pastoral on women in the Church. So a number of the women in Richmond got together and drew up a retreat process called "Women Listening to Women," which was then effected throughout the diocese. In this way, they were able to glean all the reflections from the many groups who met throughout the whole diocese and bring them to the bishops' conference. The net result of this was to say to the bishops, in effect, "Hey, don't even try it—you can't write a pastoral about women in the Church because you don't know anything about it."

But a group of us down there did go through the process together, in which people were asked to answer three or four questions during each of four sessions. I don't recall all of the questions, but the ones I do recall had to with who our role models were in growing up. There weren't any—there weren't *any*. I didn't know Dorothy Day and the Catholic Worker then. I wasn't into movie stars, so they weren't role models, although they substituted for that with many women. I couldn't get into the saints that much, and Mary—the role model that was pushed on us all the time—didn't cut the mustard. We weren't conceived without original sin, we weren't mothers of Jesus. That was one of the more astounding things to me—that there weren't any. When we got to the last session, we were asked about women we looked up to now, which for me would include some of the older women who were faithful in their lives—people like Mother Jones and the woman who heads up the Gray Panthers and the marvelous Meridel le Soeur, the writer and lifelong activist—because they bespeak a fidelity in their lives that is something one wants to aspire to.

Other questions included moments of great affirmation of yourself in the Church. *They* don't exist either. From the time we were little kids and the boys could be altar boys and we couldn't, it seemed very unfair. It seemed like you were a nobody. They could be priests and you couldn't—well, you could be a nun, but that wasn't the same. It just wasn't. I was interested in being a priest, I was not interested in being a nun. It's only in certain processes where women will talk to one another about spirituality and about our ability to create a Church, to be Church, that there's a sense of a whole now.

I think the Church as an institution behaves as all institutions, which is to say that it will continue to do what it has to do to survive. It seems to me that puts the onus of responsibility on us to remain in some marginal contact with it, to create forms that have a bit more vitality, that are attractive, and that the Church will have to incorporate if it's going to stay solvent. The Church will be catching up with its people, and it's up to the people to be the leaders and let the institutional Church follow for its own survival. And I think that's what's been happening all along with anything that makes any sense in the Church. The whole liturgical renewal thing came from the people, and the Church incorporated what it could of that. There's the phenomenon now of more and more house-church things going on, where people get together and pray—before long, the Church will be blessing that and saying that's a way to go.

That's the tradition out of which I come. I also think that we aren't going to gain a whole lot just by being critical, but we do have a responsibility to effect change. I don't think I'd want to be a cardinal in the Church today because I think they do carry the weight of responsibility for what continues to go on in the Church. We've been talking to bishops for years now about the fact that a large majority of the people who've been in prison for conscience and for resistance come from a Roman Catholic background and maintain some kind of healthy tension with that background. So that while I see a responsibility on the part of the Church, I also see a responsibility on the part of those of us who believe that we are the Church.

It's very interesting to go through the process of dealing with the Church on something like liturgical reform and then to begin dealing with the Church on the issue of your freedom to witness for peace—you learn what it is to go up against a bureaucracy, and you learn how slowly a bureaucracy moves at all. And then you go up against the state. The two involve the same kind of dynamics. So it's as if you cut your teeth on resistance within the Church to prepare you for what resistance in the state means. When you're talking about the Church and what it means to be part of a Church, are you talking about the institutional Church or are you talking about God's people who try to live in a spirit of obedience to that? That, after all, is a biblical mandate to all of us. If the Church has any hope as an institution, that's where it lies.

If we as people of God want to look at the Church and its relevance to many contemporary problems, we could do some good things. There must be millions of acres of Church land that would make marvelous communal homesteads for people who are misemployed and for whom life has no meaning. Philip and the kids and I were at Maryknoll the week after I came home from prison, and you look with hunger at the kind of land that they're sitting on. There aren't the monies anymore to keep it up the way it used to be kept up. And you could see what that could become very easily. Unfortunately, we aren't going in that direction, although at Gethsemane [the site of the Trappist monastery in eastern Kentucky] they had ten families living on their land outside the gates farming for about ten years—a fine concept that could be multiplied.

The Church itself is going to have to face up to some realities of its own very soon, with the decline in enrollments in religious orders. In West Virginia, where I was for two years, there aren't enough priests, so nuns are running those parishes. And that's good. But what needs to go on right now is some very creative, in-depth thinking about this, and where is that coming from? I think more and more that Christians have to get to their bishops and be a bug in their ear, not leave them alone. Any of the movement that I have seen on the part of bishops in the country who are outspoken on the issues of justice and peace and nuclear weapons I can trace to peace activists who have been privately nudging them for a long time. I can trace a direct line back to a community of people who have been consistently in dialogue with those bishops regarding their responsibility as bishops. And I hold that out as something that we're responsible to do, to keep pricking their consciences, because they are pretty isolated by the institutional nature of their lives. I know that the meetings we had on a regular basis with Bishop Sullivan were very powerful for all of us—for him, too, by his own admission, however begrudging. He's got a good sense of humor and we need that.

Our children Jerry and Frida are in public school; Katy begins this fall. For us, Catholic schools would be a privileged education. We don't have a local parish school, so it would mean paying a heavy-duty tuition. It's not generally something people can afford to do, and it's not something *we* can afford to do. Not that we couldn't raise the money for tuition—we could, because we do work. But it would be a way of opting for privileges for our children that are not common. So the responsibility for moral and religious education becomes our own, and that we do take very seriously. Phil sits down with the older children at least once a week and does their Scripture study. And he would tell you that he learns more from them in their studies than he does with adults because their questions are more incisive. We have at least a weekly liturgy here in the house-church that they participate in; we have an evening of community prayer and reflection on the Scripture at least one other time a week. That will often go on for an hour and a half, and then we have the Eucharist as a community with friends who come in specifically for that. It's very simple but real to our life together. It's a source of judgment and clarification and nurturing for that life too.

Jonah House is a community of people committed to nonviolent resistance. The focus is on the nuclear arms race; we can see other political and social problems in the light of that and in the web of violence that seems to find its culmination in the intention to destroy the earth with nuclear weapons. Other things that go on as social evils seem utterly consistent with that intent. The people who share our fear are people who are drawn to share in our commitment, which they have seen fleshed out. Some come for brief periods of time, at the end of which they decide either to go elsewhere and look further or to remain and commit their lives in this way. It's a fluid place in the sense that we move from large numbers of people being here to small numbers of people, depending on who's in prison and who's traveling. Right now it's a community of six plus the children. In addition to the folks who are here now, there are still three people from the community who are in prison. So when they come back it will be a substantially larger place — but probably not for long because someone else may be in prison. It has that kind of fluidity to it.

We founded the House in 1973 with a focus on the continuing war in Indochina. After Schlesinger's announcement of the change in U.S. targeting policy from "mutually assured destruction" to "flexible and strategic targeting options," we began to think that we should be focusing on the arms race and what had been going on with that while we'd had our eyes on Indochina. Since 1976, our resistance has been focused on the Pentagon. We go there regularly to witness for peace; we also frequent places like the White House, the State Department, periodically the Capitol — but more at the Pentagon because that's where this government is run from. We put out a newsletter four times a year. We do a tremendous amount of speaking and praying on these issues, retreats and simple lectures; we try to maintain a sense of network with people concerned about the issues of justice and peace and about what's happening with the arms race. That network includes folks who have been involved scientifically and technically in the production and development of these weapons and who have since abandoned those posts and have become marvelous resource people with their information.

We do contract painting, house painting, to support ourselves. We can get enough of that to enable us to remain solvent, and we can still pretty much regulate it so that we aren't working five days a week, or forty hours a week, and we have time for concerns that are much more important.

When you live in community, you can live much more cheaply than when you live separately.

Ultimately, when you talk about the issues within the Church that need to be addressed, you're talking about the emphasis on narrow moral issues and the abandonment of the wider issues of justice. When you read the prophets, when you read the gospels, where they focused on issues of justice, it becomes really astonishing to consider how we were taught. Eating meat on Friday was much more important than feeding the hungry — one was a sin, and the other was just a nice thing to do.

BRUCE WRIGHT

Catholic Justice

Aunt Catherine, in the large fullness of her flesh,
nightly blocked my bedroom door
with God's vigilance;
never agile in my kneeling, I nevertheless
made the posture she enjoined,
closed my eyes and sought in vain
to clasp a vision to my mind.
I was programmed in my bedtime repetitions,
compelled by loving oppression
to address her triple icons,
all certified by priest and pope.
Thus bent to reluctant duty,
I alerted God to bless my aunt
and ease her smiting
in the passion of belief
and see in me at least some virtues of The Good Thief.
— Bruce Wright
  "Catherine's Wheel"

Dressed in striped tie, pale yellow button-down Oxford shirt, khaki trousers, and brown loafers, Bruce McMarion Wright looks pretty much like
any other graying prep school grad capping a respectable legal and juridical
career with a tenure as state supreme court justice. So much so, in fact,
that it's hard to visualize the whitecaps of outrage that have swirled around
him for the past fifteen years as he sailed the high seas of the New York
courts. Could it have something to do with the fact that he's black — or
merely that he won't let anyone forget it?

For Justice Wright, notoriety began in 1970 with his appointment to the criminal court by New York Mayor John Lindsay, but the storms had arisen long before that. Wright was born sixty-eight years ago in Princeton, New Jersey, which he refers to with only a trace of sarcasm as "a Southern plantation town in those days." He was awarded a four-year scholarship to Princeton University but once he arrived was emphatically discouraged from attending by the dean, as he explains in the interview. Wright then suffered a similar contretemps at Notre Dame. He wound up attending Lincoln University, a predominantly black school in Pennsylvania and, after graduating in 1942, entered the army. A career with a law firm that wouldn't make him a partner "because clients weren't ready for it" and then in private practice led to work as legal counsel for the Human Resources Administration and to the criminal court appointment. During his career as a lawyer, Bruce Wright represented some of the greatest American musicians of the day, including John Coltrane, Miles Davis, Max Roach, and Charles Mingus, and the estate of Billie Holiday.

Following hard upon his appointment to the bench, Judge Wright attracted the attention of the press and the indignation of the Patrolmen's Benevolent Association through his policy of setting low bail where he felt it was justified. Wright's contention is that bail should be imposed only to ensure the defendant's presence at trial and ought to be based on the defendant's character, employment, finances, and roots in the community, as well as his previous record. Although the law appeared to back him in theory, bail was not customarily handled that way, according to Wright, because in New York City defendants tend to be black and most judges are white. "Bail is not a game of money," he said, "to be won only by the rich. It is to ensure the appearance in court of the accused. If he has roots in the community, there is no [high] bail." Wright once defined excessive bail this way: "If you come into my court and you have one penny, and my bail is two cents, that's excessive." The judge soon put his theory to the test, setting bail at five hundred dollars for a man accused of shooting a policeman. Even though Wright's percentage of no-shows wasn't any worse than that of other judges, the police quickly labeled him "Turn 'Em Loose Bruce," and the battle was joined.

In 1975, Wright was reassigned from criminal to civil court through political pressure brought by the PBA but was eventually reinstated after threatening to sue. The case that brought him national headlines occurred in 1979, when a thirty-year-old black man named Jerome Singleton was accused of slashing the neck of a decoy cop disguised as a Bowery bum. The defendant was married with two children, held a job, and had no criminal record, prompting Wright to release him without bail, on his own recognizance. Famed wordsmith Mayor Ed Koch immediately pronounced the decision ''bizarre,'' and the PBA resuscitated its ''Turn 'Em Loose'' sobriquet. This time civil rights organizations supported Judge Wright. Singleton showed up for trial and was aquitted by a jury of the attempted murder charge.

Wright's experience of social injustice was not limited to university entrance policies and the court system. He met it in the army (where he served in the infantry from 1942 to 1946, winning a Bronze Star and other decorations), and he encountered it in the Catholic Church. The witty and often whimsical manner of his comments and anecdotes — the judge is an inveterate punster, a composer of doggerel, and a published poet — tends to camouflage, but not conceal, some of his indignation. The child of an Irish Catholic mother and a West Indian agnostic father, Bruce Wright may, after all, have been raised a reluctant communicant. But to hear him tell it, the Church did little to quicken his belief.

◄ꜱ MY MOTHER WAS IRISH — in fact, five of her brothers became police officers, including her twin brother. No clergy in the family, we're all too sensible for that — too sensual, also. My mother was born here in New York, as her father was, on West Eighteenth Street. But their people came over from Ireland in the eighteen forties. My father came to this country in 1917 from Montserrat, which is located about forty miles off the coast of Antigua and still pays allegiance to the Queen. My father was a baker. He was a bitter man because, being black, he couldn't join the craft unions in those days. He was a baker, a short-order cook, and he learned how to look under the hoods of automobiles, though he was much better at putting gas in the tank — it was easier. He was a nice guy. He was not a Catholic, good Lord, no — that's how I got my name. He saw that my mother was looking through the dictionary of saints' names to get a proper name when I was born, and he didn't like that at all. So she named me Bruce, after him, with the middle name McMarion. It was a year when they were venerating the Virgin Mary, called the Marian Year, and so I became McMarion, the son of the Virgin — guess it fooled the old man a little bit.

My father was not violently opposed to the Church, but he was certainly not a member of any religious group. He was a semi–free thinker, I suppose. I say ''semi'' because he was illiterate — he certainly wasn't educated, and he wouldn't have known what a free thinker is. He was a phonetic writer, though he wouldn't have known what *that* is either. But he was a nice guy, a very gentle soul. That's why I am a pacifist, I assume.

I was in law school when my father died, after World War II. He was only fifty-nine, but he died of cancer, unfortunately. The last two years of his life were very painful. Although I never knew his parents, I was fortunate enough to know my father very well. However, I was pretty much reared by my Aunt Catherine, one of my mother's sisters, who thought I was cute. Her sole exercise, other than driving one of a series of Oldsmobiles, was crossing herself and praying to Saint Jude, the patron saint of hopeless cases, for Bruce Wright. It didn't do much good. She thought I was a hopeless case because I wasn't religious enough, because when serving as an altar boy I was a truant half the time, because I spent my Sunday school money on Tootsie Rolls, and because I was a *naughty* boy. She would make notes on those cold, winter days when I was naughty. Then, on the days when the sun was shining and I could hear the guys out in the street playing, she would say, "Bruce, do you remember this and that?" And she would literally tie me to the bed and make me read the Bible.

My sister said that my Aunt Catherine also beat me, but I don't remember that. I was just a kid, about ten or eleven. I suppose she was a good Irish Catholic, and there was an attempt at Catholic training at home. I did attend parochial school, the Church of the Resurrection on 152nd Street between Macombs Place and Eighth Avenue. They have a black priest there now, Father Lawrence Lucas. In fact, he wrote a book called *Black Priest in a White Church*. It's his protest against the Church rampant, which he allowed was not rampant enough, especially in catering to the special needs of its black members and those whom it recruited under the Society for the Propagation of the Faith. He's rather angry — on account of which he is no doubt guaranteed to remain nothing more than a parish priest for the rest of his life. In the nineteen thirties, when I attended the Church of the Resurrection, they did not have a black pastor; there wasn't one black priest to be found in Harlem at that time. We did have nuns who beat the hell out of you, though. They heard me say, "Hail Mary, full of grapes, Shirley goodness and Murphy," etc., etc. But everybody said that. It was just that my voice seemed to carry. I have the marks on me to this day.

I was a true believer for a while, I suppose, until I discovered the truth about mythology and pious fictions. That was when I was fifteen. I had received a four-year scholarship to Princeton and had the chutzpah to turn up to register, trunk and all, only to be taken out of the registration line and told by Dean Radcliffe Heermance, who had the girth of Sir John Falstaff: "Professor Weiss did not say you were colored when he arranged your scholarship." He looked down upon me as though I happened to be a disgusting specimen under a microscope. He said I wouldn't be happy at Princeton, that there were too many Southerners there. Then I was immediately referred to the dean of the chapel, Robert Russell Wickes, and after talking to him I never thereafter trusted people with three names. He told me that he had had close intercourse with God, and he pointed to his bookshelf where there were several books he had written on the subject—presumably they were diaries. He said the race problem was beyond solution and did I come to Princeton to make a problem? And did I want to be like a certain citizen of Princeton named McCormick, who was a Communist and who wanted to be places where he was not wanted? And, he added, I must stop my agitation because the race problem is beyond solution in this country.

He may be right, of course. Obviously, he thought I was a precursor of the civil rights movement and I was going to do a sit-in at Princeton. Radcliffe Heermance told me that he had no animosity toward my race and that his colored cook lived under the same roof with his family and that, indeed, in World War I he had had a colored orderly, I think he called it. His patriotism was beyond dispute. Well, at fifteen, to have that kind of dream shattered, and to be a long way from home, was shocking to me. I didn't cry until later. My mother, very sensibly calling upon her totems, said to my father, "Bruce, we should have sent him to Notre Dame." Of course, the priests were rallied around, and we tried to make arrangements for Notre Dame. But Notre Dame wrote a letter to me, which of course will be a footnote in my book. They were pretty much the same as Princeton, saying that the Church had done enough work in the South, that there were many Southerners at Notre Dame, and they had to accept the situation as it was. The only difference in their letter was that they added a line that read, "But you will be happy to know that our first President freed his slaves before taking up his duties at South Bend." So I thought I should attend a Mass of celebration for that little item.

Notre Dame really dismayed me. And then *after* the war to be so *pious* about having blacks there on the football team and saying that they were very happy. I've got *that* letter they wrote to me, too. They said, "We have three Negroes in attendance and they all seem very happy." I must tell you that the first black person to attend Notre Dame was a guy who weighed two ninety and was a football player, but he wasn't too keen *up here*. Do you know what his name was? It was Entes Shine—a very unfortunate name.

So that really did it for me with the Church. Before I even knew the term, there were "bare ruined choirs," before I had ever heard of Garry Wills—I assume I am much older than he is. In any case, that's what did it, changed my whole attitude. Indeed, it almost estranged me from my mother and my Aunt Catherine. But my Aunt Catherine had a new Oldsmobile each year so it didn't estrange me too far.

The Church is not liberal. They issue epistles promoting social justice every so often, but it's easy to say that. Who would be against that, Atilla the Hun? The thinking of the Church goes up to a certain point, but beyond that it is all faith and belief and trust and strict allegiance. I've been down to the chancery twice when Cardinal Spellman was the head of the archdiocese here. On the first occasion, a group of alleged intellectuals was summoned and the inquiry was "Why aren't more Roman Catholics winning the Nobel Prize in one category or another?" Some of us made bold to suggest that if you were going to be a good Catholic, your thought processes have to stop at a certain point. To win a Nobel Prize, generally, you have to give your thoughts free rein, be creative and original. Look what they did to John Rock [the Roman Catholic scientist and author of *The Time Has Come*], who was inventing a contraceptive pill. He's on the Index of Forbidden Books. Look what they do to women who marry divorced men. My second wife, whom I love dearly — a wonderful woman; indeed, she practiced law with me for several years — had to sneak around to various churches because I was a divorced man when she married me.

The other time, Cardinal Spellman called me down to the church because he had been told that I was a Catholic poet. Jimmy Dumpson, who used to be the commissioner of Human Resources in New York City, among other things, told him that. He was a convert, naturally more zealous than people who were reared in the faith. Cardinal Manning, Cardinal Newman, they all shot up to the red hat in a hurry over people who were born into the faith. On this occasion, Spellman decided that there were not enough black Catholics in New York. So he got twelve black intellectuals to come down, and he wanted us to go throughout Harlem and the South Bronx and Bedford-Stuyvesant to help convert *other* black intellectuals to the true faith. I thought that was rather funny. I had a good time there. I can drink tea and eat cookies with the best of them. Nothing came of that meeting, of course. He made a terrible mistake. Spellman was a lousy poet, by the way — like somebody in the fourth grade.

The Church's attitude toward black Catholics? Condescending, paternalistic, superior. We were treated as what the French call *évolués*, those who are evolving. That's the way they treated their African intellectuals. They did not realize that the rituals of the Church are as barbaric and filled with superstition and images as any African jungle voodoo belief. The pottery may be more refined; the chalice may be silver. You know the poem?

There was a young woman named Alice,
Who pissed in the archbishop's chalice,
   'Twas common belief
   She peed for relief
And not out of Protestant malice.

Well, you've got it now—feel free to copy Wright. But I thought the Church's attitude was entirely paternalistic. They looked down upon us as being of an inferior intellectual status and quality, and I found that to be true when I was at Fordham Law School. In those days the law school was in the Woolworth Building on the twenty-eighth floor, and there was a crucifix over the desk of each professor. They don't have that now because when the law school moved to public property near Lincoln Center, they had to agree that they would be open to everybody. That's why they keep Rose Hill in the Bronx, so they can indulge their Jesuit fantasies there.

When I got to high school there was one black woman teacher—*one* black on the faculty—who taught me more in one semester than I ever learned from the Church in all the years of my life. She was a woman who was a Catholic, but she taught me about Denmark Vesey [the black American insurrectionist]. I knew about Marcus Garvey from my father. I learned more black history from that woman—she opened up secrets and I *learned* how suppressed black history has been. If you want to deprive a people—make them nothing—you make them believe they have no history, and that's what has been done to blacks in this country. The Catholic Church has *not* done as much as it could. It is certainly the richest church in the world, as far as I'm concerned. At least my paltry little library on the wealth of the Church and the papacy and so forth leads me to believe that. After all, it is the *Vatican* that owns the water works and electricity works that supply Rome. No, I don't think I learned anything very exalting from the Church.

The Church is superstition to me. I'm a lawyer, and I look for evidence: haven't seen a Holy Ghost, haven't seen a God or anything of that sort. And I read the Bible and I instruct my children to know something about biblical history—either as literature or as fiction, as they wish. I think they *should* know something about it, especially when you have a season such as Christmas and they might be strangers or babes in the woods.

I have no religion. I am what probably would be called an atheist. Probably, by other people, yes, I often am. But that's their problem, that's not my problem. I have given my body to Columbia University's College of Physicians and Surgeons—to pick it apart, do whatever they wish with it. And if any friends of mine wish to have a memorial service to remember me, which is unlikely, I have insisted that they play a certain tape that I have prepared, which is my funeral oration. There is some music on it, and they are admonished to obey the lyrics of that tune, which start: "Do nothing till you hear from me." It's the old Duke Ellington tune, played by Randy Weston, one of my former clients.

One of my closest friends is Father Louis Gioia, a Jesuit. He teaches medieval history and classics at Baruch College. I think his salary is about thirty-seven thousand dollars a year, and Bishop Mugavero in Brooklyn wants that money. He says, "*I* will distribute it to the poor. You took a vow of poverty." And Lou says, "Screw you, I've a poor, black, and Hispanic parish, and I pay their rent, I buy their food." And he *does*. If Lou didn't have parents who live in Bay Ridge, he wouldn't make it. He gives his money away. He doesn't even give it to tax-deductible units. So we have to go to his mother's house sometimes to eat. I don't think they let him perform marriages anymore. He and I had projects where we tried to get prisoners out and rehabilitate them, all over the country, not just here in New York. He's wonderful at that.

Phil Berrigan, I think, clings to the vestige of the Catholic faith just to spite the Church. I don't think he is a devout Roman Catholic in the true sense of the word. He's too sensible, and yet his poetry is certainly Roman Catholic. It represents the theology of liberation. I spent till three A.M. with him one night when we were both on the same speaking program. So we meet now and then. He is very impressive as a human being. And I vote for him for Pope — except I guess I'd have to make him a cardinal first, wouldn't I? We can buy a red hat.

The Pope is not concerned about the theology of liberation any more than he is about the American theologians. He squelches those people. The Pope is a dictator, an *absolute* dictator. I don't think anybody can quarrel with that. Not even the Conference of Bishops, talking about the Holy Father — he is our universe and that sort of thing. Of *course* he's a dictator. He's also an actor, a consummate actor. He is to the Church what Ronald Reagan is to the Republican party. The Great Communicator . . . the Great Tourist, that's what he is. You have to give him credit, though — he's brave enough not to care about being shot. But I don't know what he wants to do or what he's worried about. He wouldn't have very much trouble, I shouldn't think, converting Africans, for example, or Haitians in the jungle, because there's very little difference between voodoo and the formal Catholic Church — little images of worship and so forth. The Jews have it right: no big altar, no images, certainly no idols. Have you been to the marvelous Greco-Roman imitation in Paris, the Madeleine? You must go in there sometime, it's full of images and statues.

The other thing that made me distrust the Church happened when I was in the army. I was in the infantry, and as we pushed our way around Munich, going through the woods, we would be frightened to death. Those goddamn Nazis had statues all over the place, all kinds of bloody saints in the woods, and so forth — scare the hell out of you, especially at night. Look at the Nazis — look at the Ku Klux Klan in *this* country — they're all deeply religious. Now they're welcoming *Catholics*. We're done for.

My parents were married at a time when Jack Johnson was catching hell for fooling around with white women. But you must understand one thing I learned from my mother's father. Keep in mind that he was born in 1857, the year of the Dred Scott decision. The Irish were known here in New York City as the white niggers. They shared, with blacks, the dirtiest, filthiest jobs they had — the "night soil" job, for example, before plumbing was universal. They called it "night soil" because they had outhouses, and you did your dookie into the soil and, because of the danger to the water supply, they had to be emptied. The Irish and the blacks did that.

If you were Irish, when my grandfather was a boy, you couldn't go to Macy's unless you went with the lady who employed you, who was generally a white Protestant. When the potato famine drove millions of the Irish here and to Boston, the first thing they saw were police officers dressed as London bobbies — as they were in those days — and this symbol of British authority offended them. The Irish bully boys used to travel in gangs and beat the hell out of the police. Finally, the man in charge of the police, who was not a commissioner, allowed them to dress in mufti and wear a shield. Not only did they beat them up, but they called them "coppers" because the shield was made of copper. Now that's been shortened to "cops" and they still call them cops, although the shield is no longer made of copper. The Irish couldn't go to certain bars; they couldn't go to Delmonico's, that's for sure. And they went into the police force finally because the mayor decided, "We can't have these fellows beating up our police — if we can't beat them, let them join us." And they folded them all in without the benefit of a civil service examination, and they brought their cousins, their uncles, and everybody else over to join the police force. And so we've had the Irish mafia for a number of years. That's disappearing; the Italians are coming into prominence on the force now.

The fire department is pretty much the same. Everything was volunteer in the old days, and the Irish formed volunteer fire brigades and relied upon the generosity of whoever owned the building they were trying to save. But unfortunately, many of them competed. They'd both get to the same fire at the same time and fight each other for the honor of putting out the fire—meanwhile, the fire wasn't waiting. You could tell those who had money because they had a horse pulling their wagon. Those who didn't have money had Negroes pulling their water wagons.

And it was very interesting to hear my grandfather tell about those early days, with a pipe in his mouth and a smile which was rather tolerant. But today there are no more shanty Irish, I think—they're all lace curtain. And now the Catholics in Belfast sing the same songs that we sang in the civil rights movement here; they have adopted "We Shall Overcome."

The animosity between blacks and the Irish police built up in those early days. Look at the so-called Second Rebellion during the Civil War, when if you had three hundred dollars, you could buy freedom from service. And the Irish said, "We don't have three hundred dollars, but we're not going to fight to free the niggers." And they burned down the Colored Orphan Home, which used to be right where Bryant Park is now, where the Public Library is at Forty-second Street and Fifth Avenue. And they killed the blacks. It was an Irish serving-girl who spread the story that black slaves were trying to take over the city in 1741 when they had the so-called Negro Plot, and they almost wiped out the entire black population of the city of New York.

Many people thought that judgeships were bought. In fact, we had a Seabury investigation in the thirties and a book written on that subject called *The Tin Cup*. When Lindsay called me over to city hall and asked me how I'd like to be a judge, I was shocked. I said I didn't have any money to buy a judgeship. And he blanched, properly and innocently, and said that I needed no money. I said, "I'll think about it," because I didn't think it was realistic. I didn't even belong to a party, and I certainly had never been in politics. But there are many people—as a matter of fact, a black guy who is now a judge stopped me and asked me how much I paid. He said, "I was supposed to be the next black judge. How did you do that?" Anyway, he's a schmuck, I never cared for him. I think it's reality but I have no proof. Sure, I don't know why people want to be a judge. If you see the work I have to do around here—it's well-paid slavery. Not well paid enough, however, for a man who has been married four times.

I've never been married in a church. I've never even had a ring for any of my wives. It's a symbol: "The endless circle of love, the oneness."

The Church loves that sort of thing. Now guys wear rings. Never had a ring on my finger—had one through my nose, I guess.

I majored in philosophy, so I suppose some humanitarian instinct was bound to rub off. When I was at Fordham, I liked the natural law. It almost got me in jail. The natural law says that if something is evil and wicked, you're supposed to resist it. So I prepared a little speech when I went to my draft board, and it went this way: "This country has examined me and found me fit to fight for it. I've examined the country and found it not fit to be fought for." And the guys says, "Whaddaya say, young fella?" And I said, "Aw, shit, what do I have to do?" And I went into the bloody army. That's not the only time I said "shit." I said "shit" in front of a priest once. It was the third time I got wounded. They left me lying in the snow for almost eighteen hours. I was a mess. Sometimes I was conscious and sometimes I wasn't, and once I came to and I saw a cross, and I said, "Oh, shit." Then I heard *Et spiritus sanctus. . . .*" The priest was giving me the last rites, and I said, "Father, I *will* be the last Wright, unless you get me out of here." But he had no sense of humor.

Yes, I spent some time as an altar boy—doesn't everybody? But there was a priest who kept chasing me, so I complained to my Aunt Catherine to get out of going to church anymore. He liked little boys. You know what happens when you renounce sex and take to whiskey and things like that: chasing lads. Well, it happens. All I can say is that it's something that happens. But I was not that fond of ritual at all, pomp and ceremony was a waste of my time when I could have been much more fruitful out in the streets. I was never fond of the Church.

Being an altar boy, of course, is something that's bestowed on males —women didn't have a chance. That didn't offend me till later. I thought it was normal, and it was, that's the way things were. It took me until fifteen to start protesting against "things as they were" and to realize that they didn't have to be that way. And perhaps should not be that way. It took some time to see the hypocrisy of the Church and the timidity of the Church. I thought the Church could get away with anything, that no one would call them Communists. People would respect them because they were clergy, because they did have a Roman collar on. And then I learned that if you're a black priest, you're going to be a parish priest the rest of your life, especially if you're militant. What's the black bishop's name in Harlem? Emerson Moore—he knows how to kiss the proper ass. Where did the Pope stop when he came to Harlem? Emerson Moore's church.

I was an absolutist. I would never vote for Roosevelt because he went to Hot Springs, Georgia. Blacks couldn't go to Georgia and be human beings. I didn't speak to my friends who went to Florida on vacation and who pretended they didn't see the signs: "Colored" this, "Colored" that. You had to sit in the back of the bus, that sort of thing. They pretended they didn't see those things. They were not my friends. Yes, I was an absolutist about it. I was furious. And I have been furious to this day that whites with Southern accents can come to New York and be big shots.

Eugene McCarthy

Religion in Politics, Midwest Variety

One could tell, after a certain amount of talk with Senator Eugene McCarthy, that he was a Catholic, though theology had not formally been brought up or discussed. He uses casually such giveaway phrases as "occasion of sin," and "having scruples," and "particular friendship," and "rash judgment," and "special dispensation"—not terribly exotic expressions, but each with a special meaning for Catholics.
—Garry Wills
  "Memories of a Catholic Boyhood"
  in *Bare Ruined Choirs*

You'd have to look long and hard to find another man who so haplessly deflated the idealistic hopes of a generation as did the former senator from Minnesota. There was something amorphous and decidedly uncathartic about the ultimate fizzling out of McCarthy's campaign for president in 1968, which left his most ardent followers feeling, eight years before Jimmy Carter would allude to it, a vague sense of malaise about the state of politics in America. It seemed like the Age of Aquarius came crashing to a halt seconds after it had got done dawning.

"A man may be good indeed, and thoroughly informed," McCarthy wrote in *Frontiers in American Democracy*, "but failure and inadequacy in the art of politics should disqualify him as a politician." One assumes he didn't intend that to be his epitaph. In fact, his numerous accomplishments in the House and Senate and even his quixotic early opposition to another senator named McCarthy—when Gene was young and Joe's star was situated just north of Bethlehem—are in danger of being overshadowed by his inability to acquire what is known in the trade as a "mandate."

Looking back over old footage of the Kennedy years, one soon finds that the famous Kennedy wit was really rather bogus and was mainly deployed when necessary to deflect media barbs and queries (a style Ronald Reagan imitated and, until recently at least, profited from). But McCarthy's wit was both more catholic and more Catholic. "When the showdown comes, the Irish reviewers kind of stand by you," he once said in response to John Cogley's favorable review of his latest book. "The Irish will fight you up to the last minute, but they'll stand by you then. That's why they're so good at wakes." And he showed a saltiness on the record that appears to belie his tag of mild-mannered intellectual. Asked during the '68 campaign how he felt about birth control in India, the Senator replied, "I would favor putting intrauterine devices into all sacred cows." Evaluating the record of the Johnson-Humphrey administration back in '67, McCarthy would only say, "Well, it's hard to write a good critical review of an accordion concert."

The question about birth control may be the closest religion came to obtruding on the '68 campaign, Kennedy having presumably settled that issue. But few politicians then or since have given as much thought to the role religion ought to play in government—particularly where morally inflected issues such as abortion are concerned. McCarthy's ruminations on that subject in the context of recent debates between Mario Cuomo and Geraldine Ferraro and the archbishop of New York are particularly relevant in light of an upcoming presidential campaign that is likely to pit Catholic candidates against non-Catholics and, conceivably, against the hierarchy of their own Church.

In Gene McCarthy's stories of growing up on a Minnesota farm, one can savor a less hurried and less harried way of living, one that is reflected in the way the religion was taught. His manner is itself casual and off-handed almost to distraction, and he tends to elide the beginnings and ends of thoughts—requiring one to fill in some of the blanks. But the wit is still there, still as slyly pungent. After our interview in the Washington offices of McCarthy's publisher, he encountered a couple of friends in the hallway. George Bush's name was mentioned and McCarthy had a quick characterization. "Bush is the kind of guy you want if you need someone for a carpool in a high-occupancy vehicle," the senator said. "He's clean and he smells good."

◄§ I WAS BORN in Watkins, Minnesota, which was, like so many other towns in the Midwest, a place of no visible distinction. The town had two doctors, one Catholic and one Protestant, and two hospitals with maybe four rooms apiece. My grandparents had married in Germany and had come here as part of the emigration that followed the Revolution of 1848. My father's father, who was Irish, died shortly before I was born. I'm told that he was something of a scholar and a historian. He was particularly learned about the British treatment of the Irish over the years. My maternal grandfather, Chris Baden, founded a mill and became a blacksmith because there wasn't one in town. His appeared to be the only German family in a sea of Irish.

My mother was a pillar of tolerance and strength, security and gentleness. Her life was not one of ''quiet desperation'' but rather of quiet hope. My father died in 1973 at the age of ninety-eight. His life span, one-twentieth of the time since Christ, covered the period of the greatest technological change the world has ever known. He was born in 1875 on a 160-acre farm in central Minnesota. He bought cattle in Minnesota, North and South Dakota, and Montana for shipment to the South St. Paul stockyards. He also worked as the postmaster in Watkins until he was ousted by the Democrats after Woodrow Wilson won the 1912 election. That turned him against the Democrats, but after he wasn't reappointed by the Republicans following their return to power in 1920, he had even less regard for the GOP.

The Irish in Minnesota were strongly influenced by Archbishop John Ireland, a Republican who banned the Jesuits from the state. My father was tolerant of priests, doubtful of all politicians, generally suspicious of doctors, and slow to take pride in sons or daughters. He was wary of seed dealers and farm organizers. ''Watch out for farmers,'' he would say, ''who put signs at their gates or let people paint ads on their barns that read, 'Member of Farmers' Organization,' or 'De Laval Cream Separator Used Here.' The next sign you'll see here will be 'Farm for Sale.' '' As we drove through the countryside, he observed, ''You can tell a German's farm from an Irishman's. The Germans start with a big barn and a small house. The big house comes later. The Irish start with a large house and a small barn. Neither is ever changed.''

The core of culture in Watkins and the adjacent country was the Church or, rather, religion. Our church was named St. Anthony's—not after St. Anthony of Padua, who was known for his traditional power to help people find lost objects, but for another St. Anthony. Our St. Anthony was one of the desert fathers best known for having resisted the temptations of the devil, who appeared at his desert hut in the form of a pig. Just what the temptation was, and how it was presented through the pig, was never made clear. In any case, the pig's appearance before St. Anthony and his rejection of same were represented in four stained glass windows set above the confessional on the south side of the church. I was especially attracted to these windows because, as was clearly indicated in the glass, they had been donated by my father, M. J. McCarthy, in memory of his father.

The pig in the window was small and rather attractive. In repelling it, St. Anthony had a staff in hand, and there it was, above the confessional most used by the parish priest, on the side of the church where the afternoon sun lit up the stained glass and made the confessions less threatening. The confessionals on the darker, north side of the church were used by visiting missionaries who probably attracted people who either had more serious sins to confess or who had not gone to confession for a long time. Fallen away from the Church, they were now returning in the shadows, as it were. The parish priests were, in order of succession, Fathers Willman, Roemer, and Bozja. They all spoke German and English, which was necessary in that parish, and they gave sermons in both languages at the same Mass. The rosary, which was said on Wednesday nights in May, was recited in German, but Stations of the Cross were in English. High Mass was sung in a mixture of Latin and German, but children's Masses were in English, as I recall. We used to say that sins were committed in English, confessed in German, and pardoned in Latin. Vespers were in English, but the hymns were in high Latin, particularly "Salve Regina" and "Tantum Ergo." But the hymn that we used to wrap up the more serious devotions, such as forty hours or high Mass, "Holy God We Praise Thy Name," was sung in German.

Religious instructions were the province of the Benedictine nuns, who ran the school. They placed an adequate emphasis on guilt, but not enough to develop in us the neurotic hang-ups that have been duly reported in those ubiquitous memoirs — or possibly imaginations — of Catholic childhood. That sort of thing was simply not as prominent in the Midwest as it may have been in other parts of the country. Sins were classified, of course, into mortal and venial and, above all, the sacrilege, which left an indelible mark on the soul. That was a particularly meaningful phrase at a time when we still used indelible pencils, the kind that when dipped in water or moistened with saliva would leave a mark on your tongue or hand like a tattoo, lasting for weeks. The only sacrilege we could remember ever having occurred took place after a couple of boys shooting marbles in the church basement (which was allowed in winter months) came to blows. Sister Lucretta, who had the reputation of being the toughest nun in the school, stepped in to break things up when one of the boys, apparently swinging away while still on his knees in shooting position, struck her accidentally below the belt — or in her case, below the rosary.

Sister Lucretta immediately announced that a sacrilege had been committed — the consecrated body of a bride of Christ had been struck.

As young amateur moralists, we held that since it had been an accident, no true sacrilege had been perpetrated. Nonetheless, we watched the kid closely for the next few months to see if any physical change might afflict him, maybe a withering of the hand. Other than that event, sins were basically broken down into the areas of obedience, fighting, stealing, and lying. And of course, there were the sins against the sixth commandment. Swimming naked in Clear Water Creek, for example, was considered a matter for confession, although that was really a seasonal sin. Skating with girls was suspect, depending on how you held them — crossed arms behind the back was banned.

But if there was guilt, there was also plenty of forgiveness available and easy atonement. In addition, we had more than our share of protective and supplemental prayer practices: plenary and partial indulgences, making the nine First Fridays — to which we added the nine First Saturdays — forty hour devotions, and missions. There were a few girls who fainted regularly during the First Friday ceremonies, including my sister. The fainting was considered a sign of piety, and the possible effect of fasting from midnight was discounted as an explanation.

We also had a lot of school and social groups associated with the Church, mainly for fund-raising — the Christian Mothers, the Young Ladies' Sodality, and the St. Anthony's Men's Society. The Knights of Columbus were recognized but weren't intimately involved in parish activities — they were thought of as being somehow outside the ramparts, on guard against the Masons. We also had a parish unit of the Catholic Order of Foresters, mostly German parishioners concerned more with secular insurance. The annual church bazaar, focused around bingo, was the big social event of the year, as I recall.

My parents' concerns, though, centered on their children's progression through various levels of serving Mass. The most important part of this was memorizing the Latin responses, something that began as early as second grade. They didn't try to teach you the meaning of the Latin words, only the phonetic syllables in the proper order. Of course, the priest had most of the best lines — except for the *Suscipiat*. It was tough to say and took off from the priest's introduction: *Suscipiat Dominus sacrificium de manibus tuis ad laudem et gloriam nominis sui, ad utilitatem quoque nostram, totiusque Ecclesiae suae sanctae.* The *ad utilitatem* was the break point because once you made it past that you usually made it to the end in a rush.

The server on the right side of the altar had the most important jobs, and the requirements were not just intellectual or spiritual. He needed a steady hand and nerve — for lighting the high Mass candles, say, or mastering the art of the clapper, the wooden substitute for bells during Lent.

Our first and second grade teacher was a delicate, sensitive nun named Sister Ancilla. Her interests were writing and art, and she introduced us to the Palmer method, which was supposed to make for proficiency in handwriting. You pursued this method all through grade school, winning along the way pins and certificates of progress comparable to those given by the Red Cross for swimming. Sister Ancilla's special side interest was ransoming pagan babies — mostly Chinese girl babies. To hear her tell it, they were lined up on the banks of the Yangtze and Yellow rivers after having been abandoned by their parents, and might be drowned if they weren't ransomed. Money, canceled postage stamps, and tinfoil — the kind they used to wrap Hershey bars and Eskimo Pies — were accepted in exchange for the babies, who were then promptly baptized.

Watkins was about twenty miles from Collegeville, home of St. John's Abbey. After I finished high school at St. John's Prep, I went on to college there. In my first year in college I decided that ideas were important and that I wanted to pursue an academic career. The only two professions recognized at the time were law and medicine, and neither one attracted me.

The school itself grew out of a Benedictine base that was established in 1856 when a Benedictine priest, two clerics, and two brothers arrived in Minnesota Territory under the auspices of Bishop Cretin of St. Paul. At the time, "Yankees" — German and Irish Protestants from New England — were moving to the area in expectation of statehood being granted. Between 1854 and 1857, the population of the territory grew from thirty-two thousand to one hundred fifty thousand. The prime mover behind all this was a Benedictine monk and future abbot named Boniface Wimmer, who obtained a grant from Ludwig, king of Bavaria, to provide clergy for Minnesota's twenty thousand German Catholics to prevent their seduction by the Methodists. Over a hundred years later, the Methodist threat may still be palpable, since all the best Catholic basketball players prefer to go to Hamline University, a Methodist institution, instead of the Benedictine St. John's.

By the 1930s, the college had begun to take on a distinctive character, largely through the direction of one of the monks, Dom Virgil Michel. Father Virgil was a man of broad, almost universal interests who, before his death in 1938, had set in motion or promoted three significant programs. One was the liturgical movement, a sophisticated and historically advanced application of the Benedictine commitment to work and prayer as the essence of the creative and re-creative role of man. The second area was social action — he moved the school and the monastery to a deep and continuing concern for social justice, which was the dominant concept

of Catholic and Christian emphasis in the thirties. The school supported
rural cooperatives, agricultural economies, and the Catholic Rural Life
Movement. Its leader, Monsignor Ligutti, worked to integrate the coal
mining industry, if it could be called that, of Granger, Iowa, with agri-
culture. He moved from that to leadership in international agricultural
policy and programs and, as adviser to Popes, finally to a house on the
Appian Way. The last time I saw him, at the Rome airport, I said,
"Monsignor, it's a long way from Granger, Iowa, to the Appian Way,
isn't it?" He answered, "No," and raised his eyebrows.

"Distributive justice" was the controlling and directing intellectual
concept of the day, as opposed to our current words like "equality"—
which was never mentioned in either the Declaration of Independence or
the Constitution—or "fairness," which has neither historical nor philosophical bearing. At St. John's Abbey I met Dorothy Day and Peter Maurin
of the Catholic Worker movement, the apostles of the poor, preaching in
a kind of second coming the "gospel to the rich," not distinguishing
between the deserving and the undeserving poor—a distinction which
can be made among the rich. I remember Dorothy for many things, but
most fondly for a remark attributed to her at the time when, during extremely cold weather in New York, the Mott Street quarters were heated
minimally by turning on the gas oven and opening the oven door. When
someone observed that this was a rather expensive and inefficient way to
heat an apartment, Dorothy supposedly said, "The poor are never eco-
nomical."

I also met the Baroness de Heuck, who later married a man named
Eddie Dougherty, who led another group concerned about the poor, especially the blacks, in an organization called Friendship House. The Baroness startled the monks in one of her lectures—it may have been the
last she ever gave on campus—when she said the coming revolution
would include monks hanging like dead crows from the telephone poles
along the twelve-mile highway from the monastery to the city of St. Cloud.

I finished my college course at St. John's in three years, mainly to
relieve my parents of the cost of another year's education, and tried to
make a living. But after applying for several teaching appointments and
receiving none, I decided to go on to graduate school in September 1935.
I tried to borrow enough money from my hometown bank to finance one
quarter at the University of Minnesota grad school—about two hundred
dollars, including room and board! But I was refused for lack of collateral,
and ever since I've favored government loans for college students—which
didn't exist at the time.

Eventually I got a teaching job and for the next four years taught high school English and coached basketball and baseball at various times. Those years were memorable mostly for testing my patience and endurance. The one clear breakout from boredom, near despair, was graduation exercises, because I could really sense the joy of the students. Most graduates weren't going on to college and had been educated beyond their parents' level. And for the parents, the graduation was the realization of their own lost hopes. That visible joy and satisfaction made the long, boring months of the term seem pretty much worthwhile.

Since I'd obtained a master's degree while teaching, I returned to St. John's as a faculty member. The years there and after World War II on the faculty of St. Thomas College in St. Paul were considerably more significant. During those years the Catholic intellectual movement sprang up here. The core of the movement was medieval studies, especially a revived study of Thomistic philosophy and natural law. Jacques Maritain was the acknowledged leader and spokesman, but there were also Étienne Gilson, Ives Simon, Christopher Dawson, and others. The writings of G. K. Chesterton and Hilaire Belloc were included for spice and accent. Teilhard de Chardin gave scope to the cosmology of the time. Dom Verner Moore and Abbot Butler, with later contributions from German theologians such as Karl Rahner and Hans Küng, helped set the stage for the Vatican Council meetings to come. For artistic support we read the novels of Evelyn Waugh, Graham Greene, Léon Bloy, George Bernanos, Dorothy Parker, and J. F. Powers, the poets Allen Tate and Robert Lowell, and Fulton Sheen converts like Heywood Broun and Clare Boothe Luce.

The years from 1946 to 1948, when I was elected to the House, were pretty good ones. In my courses on social problems, I used to emphasize the need for federal legislation in housing, medical care, education, economic security, and civil rights, and I argued for the need for political action to achieve that. But I still hadn't given any thought to direct participation. That came almost by accident or default. There was a lot of political activity in Minnesota in 1946, which involved a professor on the St. Thomas campus who was interested in the reform of the Democratic Farmer Labor party, an effort being led by the then mayor of Minneapolis, Hubert Humphrey. They nominated me as their chairman in the spring of 1948, and by early summer I'd decided to run for Congress against an incumbent Republican. It was a good year for Democrats and, running with Harry Truman, I got elected.

In the House my main concerns were civil rights legislation, which had become a central plank in the Democratic party platform, and the political economy. The critical committees were the House Ways and Means Committee, with jurisdiction over taxes, social welfare including social se-

curity, and trade, and in the Senate the comparable Finance Committee.
For sixteen of my twenty-two years in the Congress—four in the House
and twelve in the Senate—I served on those two committees. They were
good, productive years in which the general welfare was advanced further,
I believe, than in any other sixteen years in the history of the country.

As far as religion and politics go, you can't really separate the two.
Religion should have an influence, always has had, especially if it touches
on public life—you expect it to. If religion means anything, you expect
it to cross over by persons or religious institutions taking a stand if the
issue is compelling enough—like civil rights, for instance.

In government, you certainly get into moral issues. For instance, the
fundamentalists made an issue of alcohol. They thought it was important
enough to make it a political issue. When you get into behavior or morality,
you're in a much more relative world, and the Church ought to hesitate
about getting into something like that. On issues that require political
action, like birth control, which is fairly noncontroversial now, the Church
did stay out of that. They played around a little bit—in 1960 it was a
marginal issue—but the Church really didn't push it. I don't think they
ever went after a particular candidate and said, "Let's beat this guy because
he's for birth control." Abortion is a much more serious problem now
than birth control. But back in the forties even rhythm was questioned—
so-called natural birth control was considered wrong by the Church. They
said that everybody had to have as many children as they could.

At one point, *Time* magazine ran a story—and I don't know whether
it was true or not, or proven—alleging that a bishop in the Congo had
said that the nuns could take birth control pills if they thought they were
going to be raped. Well, there goes the natural law. If it was true, you
could say *that* was the point where the birth control case was lost. There
are some pro-life people who say no abortion after rape and incest, and
in a way that's logically consistent with the natural law. They say that
life begins at conception and anything after that is murder. It's a pure
position. They assume that they know where life begins.

If one thinks it's crucial to any kind of order or stability in society, or
that the next step is infanticide or euthanasia, then I suppose one has to
take one's stand. The subcommittee of the Senate determined that life
begins at the moment of conception, but it hasn't been accepted by the
full committee. You've got to be careful about what a subcommittee of
the Senate will do. They'll rush in where both fools and angels fear to
tread. If they establish *that* ruling, then maybe we can get a decision on
life after death—we might solve two of the major religious problems of

all time by following the determination of the Senate subcommittee. This is the new moral authority.

You can have one of two things when it comes to religious beliefs in the political arena: either a vague religion strongly held—which was what Eisenhower had—or a strong religion weakly held, which John Kennedy had. The trouble with Mario Cuomo is that he has a strong belief and he can't decide whether to hold it strongly or weakly. He's stuck in between. Kennedy said that if the great crisis of conscience came—a conflict between his religious beliefs and his duty to lead the people—he would quit. Whereas Cuomo seems to say, "Well, I'll find the consensus." Consensus is a pretty weak position, I'd say. How do you know it's a consensus, and how long does the consensus last? Until the next television show. Of course he's challenged the bishops to a showdown—at least Cardinal O'Connor. You never would have gotten Kennedy into a position like that. Whether he would have been able to use Cardinal Cushing as a defender under any circumstances, he would have had at least one bishop on his side. Cuomo has made it almost a challenge to the bishops. Ferraro never got it together at all, but if she had articulated it, her position would have been almost the same as Cuomo's.

Cuomo is also being belligerent about religion. Of course, my campaign was not typical. We had one issue, and that's all you really had to talk about—the war. Other issues came up occasionally, but they were sort of incidental. You'd get somebody asking you about Catholicism or birth control, and at one point I just said, "That's a question you leave for vice presidential candidates. Like birth control, or the authenticity of certain bones that were found under St. Peter's, the Holy Shroud of Turin, and the liquefaction of the blood of St. Januarius." That was my standard answer, implying that the issue of religion was out of the picture.

I don't think that this new wave of repression coming out of Rome will create a schism in the American Church. I think people will just leave—they'll drift off and come back and drift off again. We all know people who would've been excommunicated years ago yet who continued to go to communion and receive the sacraments. I presume that the parish priests knew what was happening but didn't do anything about it. There seem to be two Churches now, operating out of the same building, as it were, under the same hierarchy. In earlier times, they would have had a showdown, I suppose—nail some theses to the door—but they don't do that anymore. The nun who recently made a public show against the Pope would've been burned at the stake four hundred years ago.

The fundamentalist presence is always there, but I don't see it as having an impact that could be considered bad. Just in the nature of an open, democratic society, you have to fight these things off. I knew [TV evangelist] Pat Robertson's father, Willis Robertson, when I was in the Senate — I also read where Willis's father had been a preacher, so it skipped one generation. When I first came to Congress, I was invited to what they called prayer breakfasts — which was a strange kind of religion anyway — and being an active Catholic, I said I'd go. I lived in the suburbs and I had to get up at six thirty to get in for those breakfasts. About the second or third morning, Willis Robertson was giving the meditation. This was in forty-nine at the height of the civil rights fight, which we'd had as a campaign issue even though we didn't do anything about it until sixty-four, practically. Willis got up and said, "Ah'd lahk to be fer the Negroes, but the Bible won't let me." And he went on with quotations about Cham and Japhet and I don't know what. Hell, I never went back to the prayer breakfasts after that. I said, "My God, I'm not going to get up at six thirty in the morning to come in and hear some old nut like this." So here it is forty years later and the kid is running for office with the same ideas the old man had — and the same idea that the grandfather had. He's sort of combined the grandfather and the father — that's how it runs, I guess.

Sam Houston told de Tocqueville that there were two things that you didn't give Indians: one was brandy and the other was Christianity, because it was a highly destabilizing force. The Indian culture had a sense of tribal responsibility. Houston said that — especially in light of Protestant Christianity with its individualism — whereas an Indian might steal from another tribe, he would not steal *within* the tribe. But once the Indian got a private morality, he would steal from anybody. So the last state was worse than the first. That may be what the problem was with the Irish — they've had liquor and Christianity together. According to Houston it didn't work with Indians, so maybe it didn't work with Celts.

Indeed, the Church in America is kind of an Irish Jansenist Church. Actually, the whole Church is probably pretty Jansenist, even in Ireland. When they came over here they influenced — with Archbishop Ireland in Minnesota, who was a great leader in the Anti-Saloon League — the whole standard of behavior. The Germans were equally strict in many parts of the country. They were a strict construction bunch, almost as bad as the Irish in the Midwest, although they were a little easier. The influence on *our* church, as I've said, was pretty much German. Did you ever run into the group known as the Detachers — Father Hugo? There was an ascetic movement in the Church in the forties that held ideas such as "Don't have an automobile," "Don't have a radio," "Sleep on the floor." There was a celibate ideal, too—a husband and wife living together but leading a celibate life. Hugo was a Canadian and he got a lot of attention. He had a particularly ascetic retreat for priests, and they were coming back from it, so the story goes, when they picked up four or five priests and rode together. And the last one they picked up was named Father Bozja —he was Bohemian and was the pastor in my hometown. They'd really been affected by the retreat and were keeping the silence on the way back. Just as they got to the parish church, Father Bozja said, "Would anybody come in and have a beer?" They all came in and had a beer, I guess. So the discipline with those German priests lasted for twenty miles after the retreat was over.

But with the Irish Church in Ireland still, it's the same—they denounce drink. It's primarily just drink and sex that they're most concerned about in Irish discipline. The Irish in the eighteenth century were altogether different before the famine, the potato failure—they married young then, not like afterward when they would wait as long as they could. Of course, they could maintain millions of them with potatoes before the blight. So the morality may have come as a way of just disciplining people—saying that you've got to behave this way because you can't get married anyway and so you'd better make a virtue out of it. The alcohol was sort of an escape, so then they tried to keep them from the escape. I suppose it could all be explained. I know they make a strong case for the good life before the famines came—even Yeats writes about the eighteenth century, the lords and ladies and the good life and the peasants and the rest of it. That may or may not be true.

When you ask me if the current government under Reagan would qualify as a "Christian" government the way I outlined it in my book [*Frontiers in American Democracy*], then I have to say that, while it's relative, I don't think it's as Christian as one could have said the government was in the thirties or in the early postwar period. I say that on two counts. One is its belligerency or militarism, which gets into a religious area: the question of a theology of hope which you apply to something as massive as nuclear war. The other is the question of social justice. Even though in terms of poverty and so on things are better than they were in the thirties, the human involvement and the playback from the economy to the person is less Christian and less humane than it was then. I fault the bishops for that. They're still talking as though if you just had more distribution, somehow it would be more Christian. But some of what's in the old encyclicals—and you get snatches of it now—has to do with the human satisfaction of having a job and knowing that you have it, not just of being given a dole. As they push it, it gets almost to the point of saying that if you do enough for the poor and equalize taxes, then the Christian objective will be achieved. They really ought to be beyond that now in terms of practical programs. I've been advocating for ten years the redistribution of work: instead of saying we have to create more jobs, let's just take what we've got.

In Reagan's case, you don't really quite hold him responsible for what appears to be his failure to live up to Christian principles. It's as though he lives in a clearing. He just doesn't have any sense of history, or even of what he's said himself. It's just "Put me down here and I'll talk," and "Put me down *here* and I'll talk. I may contradict myself over here." He was talking to Tip O'Neill and said, "Now don't put the pressure on me about the space thing [the Strategic Defense Initiative] so I can go over and negotiate [at the pre-summit meetings in Iceland]." So Tip doesn't do it and Reagan goes over and he doesn't negotiate a thing. O'Neill and those guys should have said, "Look, we're going to send you over in a position where you may have to give on space."

What it comes down to with Reagan is that he just doesn't know what's in between, he doesn't know what's in the jungle. There are clearings—country clubs and party rallies and football games—but there's no sense of historical continuity. What's Nancy's interest? It's drugs. Well there again, it's quite isolated from general social problems. At least Eleanor Roosevelt went into the coal fields. They all get into drugs or mental retardation—some kind of specialized individual defect rather than a social one.

I don't blame that on Ronald, but I do think the clearing image is a valid one. I debated him once, shortly before he announced for the 1980 campaign, someplace in New Jersey. That's when I first heard about the welfare queen—the woman in Chicago who was getting twenty checks or something. Someone said they never could find her. He was told that, and he just kept giving the speech anyway. It didn't make any difference. Reporters would say, "Where is this woman? We're looking for her and we can't find her." Reagan would only say, "She's there, you just haven't found her."

He went with this same statistical stuff, about the abuses of welfare. So I just gave up. What do you say—"She only got six checks, not twenty?" And the stuff about how he read the paper and there were all those ads, and there couldn't be real unemployment because the L.A. *Times* had six pages, small print, of help-wanted ads. I said, "What do they want them for—security jobs and bill collectors?'' But he said, ''There's no problem with unemployment for those who can work.'' And the stuff about how nobody has to be hungry in America. You have to say, ''But people *are* hungry.'' And he'll just say, ''Well, they don't have to be. If they just go get the food, we're ready to give them food. They can work in the fields.'' It was a strange experience. It wasn't like a direct confrontation—he didn't respond to anything I said. He said stuff that was just nonsense, stuff that wasn't true. But he was happy about it, just going on. So nothing he does now surprises me.

As I've remarked already, I think the Congress from 1945 to the passage of the civil rights legislation was a good time whether one was a personal success or not—just being a part of that Congress was an honor. As to particulars, I could list half a dozen things that wouldn't or shouldn't have happened or would've happened sooner if what I had recommended had been done. I consistently challenged that anti-Communist stuff in the fifties. I offered amendments to protect people; I debated Joe McCarthy in fifty-two when nobody would debate him. I escorted John Connally up the aisle when he was being questioned by the House Un-American Activities Committee in May. I made a speech against Joe McCarthy three months after his famous West Virginia speech to the Holy Name Society of Montgomery County. I was only in Congress about two years. I said that Holy Name Societies really ought to take up more than God's name. I said, ''God can pretty well take care of His name—what you ought to be concerned about is the abuse of the good name of persons who are being attacked by McCarthy.'' That was a quintessentially Catholic issue. In any case my speech was less than a full success then. As I said, I was just a new member of Congress, but that was one of the things I was committed to, and I think it was out of a Catholic personalist manifesto approach that I brought with me.

I had a feeling that if others had stood up against him and that whole thing at that period, it could've been blunted. A lot of the things that happened in the fifties that destroyed people's lives and had a terrible impact on society could've been stopped if people of greater stature in Congress had stood up. They could not get anyone to debate Joe McCarthy, nobody in the Senate would take him on on public television. I knew he was Irish. He was just kind of bullying people. He said to me before he died, ''Gene, we don't want to have this be an Irish brawl, do we?''

In Vietnam, the Catholic population was concentrated in the south, so the Church position was closely identified with them, even though eventually there were bishops who said, "Let's stop it, it's gone far enough." But in the beginning, to a large extent, Catholics supported the war because of the Catholic missionaries—and Protestant missionaries, too. I do think the Church could play an important role in American political life now, the way it did in the thirties. It came slowly on civil rights, but it was ultimately all right. It didn't come on the war at all. But it could have a powerful effect on the issue of nuclear arms because that's an issue that has almost moved into the area of prophecy and theology and hope and all the virtues—the area where religion is finally supposed to live or die. There are hints that the Church will come, it just doesn't quite go all the way. And it could have more of an impact in the nonmilitary area if it took some of the principles it's laid out and insisted on following them: personalism, for example, and the right to a job and to the security of a job, the use of our agricultural potential. I don't know if it will, for example, challenge corporate power, which depersonalizes everyone in the corporation. The Church is pretty dependent on corporate contributions, and the Catholic schools certainly are. The whole area of individual liberty is more and more restrictive, and the Church ought not just to speak in general principle but lay out four or five actual programs as we had in the New Deal and press for economic security or justice of some kind. Still in all, it does seem like the Church is running a little bit ahead of the Democratic party.

Unfortunately, the Church has run into a kind of trap on the issues of abortion and nuclear war. Maybe it's not a trap, but the Church's response is that their abortion stand is justified because they're against nuclear war. The liberals, being pro-choice and antiwar, don't want anybody to be born but they want everybody who's already alive to live forever. Whereas the conservatives want everyone to be born that can be but they don't care how long they live or under what conditions—you can blow them up or starve them, just get them born. Those are the irreconcilable positions now.

CHRISTOPHER DURANG

Unanswered Prayers

SISTER: Are all our prayers answered? Yes, they are; what people who ask
that question often don't realize is that sometimes the answer to our prayer
is no.
—*Sister Mary Ignatius Explains It All for You*

I write occasionally maniacal and angry plays that are sometimes funny.
I'm a very *unfunny* person until you get to know me; I'm sort of quiet. Not
only do I not look like what I write but I tend—and this is my Catholic
training—to be very polite, and my plays aren't polite. I work out a lot
of aggression in them.
—Christopher Durang
  Interview, October 1982

Like Bob Dylan, Bob Marley, Bruce Springsteen, Sylvester Stallone, and
a number of other prominent figures who have riled people for various
reasons over the last twenty years, Christopher Durang is not big in stature.
And although he's not nearly as famous as any of those pop icons, Durang
has a similar ability to get under folks' skin, causing his audiences either
to admire him or to want to run him out of town on a rail. But unlike the
typical self-serious hierophant, Durang has a redeeming gift for comedy
(he may be the only professional playwright who has been a guest host
on *Saturday Night Live*). That humor can sometimes be obscured by the
sheer vitriol that seems to spring unbidden from his plays and splash in
your face, thereby grabbing your attention—like the gun that Sister Mary
Ignatius suddenly fires in his most famous work—but comedy is still the
strongest single element in his writing. Theatrical comedy, as a rule,
doesn't read especially well, and yet it's hard to get through even a few
pages of Durang's *Beyond Therapy*, say, without laughing out loud.

It would be folly to argue that the dark side of Durang is somehow less significant than his wit—for one thing, the two are as tangled as any crown of thorns. In fact, one could probably make the case that, at least in certain sensibilities, an unhappy Catholic upbringing can spawn both the bleak vision and the surrealist comic leaven that then makes life possible. Yet Durang is so often accused of gratuitous bile that it's necessary to place his anger in context.

Christopher Durang has had a couple of brief runs on Broadway, but his best-known and most commercially successful work is a one-act play called *Sister Mary Ignatius Explains It All for You*, which originated off-Broadway and has played in regional theaters around the country (usually in tandem with his curtain raiser, *An Actor's Nightmare*). Though the impact of Catholic education on the playwright pops up in several of his works, in *Sister Mary Ignatius* he deals with it through a furious exorcism of ineffectual religious ideals. Directed as much against the pain that comes when those ideals let one down as against the Catholic Church per se, the play was viewed by many within the Church as nothing less than a frontal assault. In St. Louis, a city with more than half a million Catholics, *Sister Mary Ignatius* touched off unusually intense opposition, including a call for a boycott by Archbishop John May (a moderate in Church politics, May is the current president of the National Conference of Catholic Bishops). May attacked the play in the archdiocesan weekly as a "vile diatribe against all things Catholic." Even B'nai B'rith got into the act, labeling the work "offensive, unfair and demeaning." Durang himself was quoted in the *New York Times* as having previously stated, "I didn't write this play to throw water in the face of those who believe. My purpose wasn't to make people angry but to get off my chest how I look at things."

The Catholic League for Religious and Civil Rights, according to the *Times* report, performed "a brief skit attacking the play" in the form of "an irreverent satire by a board member," which must have been quite a performance in its own right. The show, in the best tradition of the theater, went on. As often happens in such situations, the publicity caused by the Church's criticism resulted in sold-out performances.

In this interview, Durang explains the play's provenance and Sister Mary's actual prototype in detail. Some of the complaints voiced in the play will be seen to grow directly from the playwright's own experiences. Non-Catholic readers, or Catholics who had a milder time of it in grammar school, may tend to look on such anecdotes as wildly melodramatic exaggerations. Yet how can one explain that the reality was sometimes far more surreal?

I think that the crux of *Sister Mary Ignatius* can be found in a few lines spoken by Diane, one of four former pupils who come more or less to confront Sister Mary with the aftermath of her, and the Church's, dogmatism. Asked why she would want to embarrass Sister, Diane tells her simply, "Because I believed you. I believed how you said the world worked, and that God loved us, and the story of the Good Shepherd and the lost sheep; and I don't think you should lie to people." Diane then launches a long monologue about her mother's painfully protracted death from cancer that is clearly based on Durang's own past.

Diane appears to be getting at much of what Martin Scorsese intended in *Mean Streets* when his alter ego, played by Harvey Keitel, complains that he took the priests at their word. It seems to me that Scorsese ultimately forgave the Church, while somewhat generously laying blame for the misunderstanding on his own innocence. I think it's fair to say that Christopher Durang is somewhat less forgiving, but his sense of humor finally carries more weight than his burden of anger.

I HAD DOMINICAN NUNS from first grade through sixth grade at Our Lady of Peace in New Providence, New Jersey. Seventh and eighth grades I went to a school called Delbarton in Morristown, New Jersey, which was taught by Benedictine priests and goes from seventh grade to twelfth. I pretty much liked that school. The curriculum was somewhat accelerated, and the priests tended, in that kind of prep school way, to call you "Mister." So then when I went in ninth grade to a place in New Brunswick called Union Catholic Boys High School — because my parents had separated and financially we couldn't afford Delbarton anymore — I went from being assigned *Gulliver's Travels* and *Candide* to being assigned *Cheaper by the Dozen* and *God Is My Co-Pilot*. That was what we read in English class, which is *horrible* — so forget that it was Catholic, it was just stupid. Also, the boys' school and girls' school were separated but on the same grounds; and you shared the same lunchroom, but with a plastic curtain separating the two sides. You were not at all allowed to deal with the girls, except on the buses, which made everybody hysterical.

When I was at Delbarton, I had written a play in the eighth grade that the seniors put on, and they got girls from an accompanying school to be in it. I thought, trying to be constructive, that since Union Catholic didn't have a drama school I should start a drama club as a freshman. Because we had girls on the premises, I thought we should be allowed to change the rules a little and have it be coed. The Marist brother in charge said no, this could not be. So I guess that meant we could only do *Twelve*

Angry Men over and over. I said the hell with it, I guess I won't start a drama club. I had an awful time at the school. I was just about to demand to be sent to a public high school when, out of the blue, Delbarton decided to give me a scholarship back there. A priest and a lay teacher there had kept in touch with me and saw that I was really sinking at the other school and spoke up for me. That was a very significant thing.

I was being a very bad student at Union Catholic because I was so angry at being made to read *God Is My Co-Pilot* — still one of the least worthwhile books imaginable. I liked English and I liked reading, so it was like being put back five years or something. I mean, I had actually read *Cheaper by the Dozen* — it's amusing, but I didn't expect to be taught it in school. Union was so oddly disciplined in a stupid way. It was the kind of school where, when you left a classroom, you had to turn right whether your next class was to the left or not, just to keep this antlike flow going, which was such a terrible waste of time.

With the nuns, I think I saw some quirkiness, but I didn't have a bad experience per se. Often people ask me if Sister Mary Ignatius is based on a specific nun, and she really is not. She is (a) fictional and (b) a reaction to a dogmatism I got from being a literal-minded and rather obedient child. I really took what they said on their word. This dogmatism was also echoed in some of my relatives. The only thing that I should mention about my education is that I think that the religion I was taught by the nuns and the Marist Brothers and some of the Benedictine priests was very much that pre–Vatican II rigid dogmatism, which is also what my parents' generation had. The play *Sister Mary Ignatius* pokes a great deal of fun and criticism at that kind of teaching.

However, at the Benedictine school I was rather drawn to the liberal side of the Church. I got involved with the priests and lay Catholics who were marching against the war in Vietnam — instead of my senior prom, I went to a meeting at the Catholic Worker. And I feel good about that aspect of Catholicism.

I grew up in New Jersey, mostly in a small town called Berkeley Heights. I was in the generation that was taught with the Baltimore Catechism, question-and-answer style. In retrospect I think it was kind of a hangover from the immigration experience — as Catholics we were told that it was dangerous to be around non-Catholics because we'd lose our faith. We were told, for instance, that if we went to a fair or bazaar at a Lutheran church, we were supporting another church. My grandparents' generation felt that made sense — it was a ghetto mentality which dictates that when a group feels threatened it sticks together — whereas my parents' generation became very assimilated. I remember feeling somewhat guilty because after a while my mother *would* go to the Lutheran fair. I remember thinking, I've been told this is wrong, but my mother seems a fairly sensible person so I guess it mustn't be *that* wrong.

We would also be made to stand up and take that damned pledge about the Legion of Decency every year. Because I loved movies and would follow things, I actually knew which movies got rated what, while my parents would take the oath but not really know what anything was rated. I remember in 1959 when I was ten years old, *Some Like It Hot* came out and I could tell that it must be a very funny movie. It was rated B — Morally Objectionable in Part for All — presumably because of Marilyn Monroe's dresses, which she was kind of hanging out of. My parents took me to it, and I decided not to tell them that it was morally objectionable. First of all, they wouldn't have cared. I had a wonderful time but I was aware that they were breaking their oath.

The kind of Catholicism around me was sort of more Irish than anything else. The pastors of the various parishes all tended to be Irish — my father was an architect who designed church buildings and church schools, and his father did the same, so that meant we had direct dealings with pastors. The specific parish that I grew up in had a lot of Italian parishioners but they always had Irishmen as pastors, and there was quite a bit of tension about this. My last name is French, but there's an awful lot of Irish blood in my family on both sides; I've always felt that I was more Irish.

At Yale drama school, I became friends with Albert Innaurato, and when he and I would exchange nun stories, he turned out to have been taught by what I would describe as violent Italian nuns who were always banging people against the wall or holding them between their legs (if he's not making it up) — violent things which informed a lot of his plays. By contrast, I would say that my experience involved more *repressive* Irish nuns. It's funny: one understood so clearly from them how wrong sex was on every level without really much discussion of it. It was just implied.

One of my mother's sisters, who was kind of my favorite aunt — she was my godmother — was very religious and, indeed, was in the convent for a while. She left for health reasons but always felt conflicted about having left and kept a lot of religious artifacts around. Both of my parents were churchgoers who took it seriously, and they were initially disturbed when I stopped going, although after a while they accepted it. They weren't particularly zealous — in fact, they were somewhat lackadaisical.

The first nun I had was very sweet and gentle. And our principal was actually rather fun — she had a bit of a temper but she also had this show business streak in her. She reminded me of Ethel Merman. I say that because she would have the school put on shows every year in which each class would get up and perform, and she would choreograph and direct them all. So she would be in her nun's outfit doing Charlestons and so forth, and she was actually terribly engaging. Then I remember the third grade nun was very gaunt and grouchy, and she would lose her temper a lot. The fourth grade nun also would lose her temper a lot — she was jolly, but then she would get in a foul humor. She had a very red face and was slightly overweight, and the white piece of her veil seemed to be *digging* into her forehead, it seemed to be very starched. I do remember once that she was trying to explain long division to someone who was not getting it, and she just turned purple with rage and started to *scream* about long division.

Of course, Catholic schools then were so overcrowded. In fourth, fifth, and sixth grades we did have fifty children in the class. I have the character in *Sister Mary* who never can get to the bathroom because the nun won't recognize him. Well, I remember in the fifth grade — it was not all that traumatic, but it happened — after lunch, always around two thirty, I would need to urinate. I was in the last row of, I guess it was *sixty* children by then, and it would take an hour and fifteen minutes before the various other children could all go. Why they wouldn't just have a bathroom break is beyond me, but you know how they are about not wanting children to go to the bathroom at the same time lest they have ten-year-old orgies in there or something. Needless to say, I couldn't listen to a single word the nun said for that hour and fifteen minutes; it was extremely annoying.

The religious teaching was monolithic. Everyone said the same thing, and there was really an answer for just about everything. I got this from my favorite aunt before I even went to school. Before kindergarten I was made aware of the so-called fact of mortal and venial sin: mortal sin sent you to hell forever and ever; for venial sins most of us had to expect to be in purgatory. They never said how *long* you were going to be in purgatory that I remember.

I wasn't particularly angry at the Church when I wrote *Sister Mary*, but I've become genuinely angry since all the various groups have protested it. The thrust of the protest is often that they disagree with what I say and so they feel that somehow I should be shut up. That makes me very angry. For instance, my mother's family was also politically conservative. I was too small to know about Joe McCarthy, but they all liked Joe McCarthy and thought he was just fine. And when people began to be against the war in Vietnam, including a lot of the priests in the school I was at, my religious aunt, who was rather tender-hearted, started to feel that maybe the war was wrong too — even though she came to that much later than a lot of other people did. But my grandmother and uncle, who were very conservative, told my aunt that she was wrong and, furthermore, she must shut up about it. It was not to be discussed.

It also makes you think of some of the discussions in *Portrait of the Artist as a Young Man.* There's something both very Irish and very Catholic about "We're right, and shut up." There was that feeling that ideas were dangerous. I know that some of my relatives have said about my play that it will lead the faithful astray. That fits right in with the Index of Forbidden Books and the Legion of Decency.

My anger or disappointment with Catholic teaching occurred more in retrospect than when I was going through it. The anger comes from my belief that a lot of what was taught caused a lot of people whom I know — and sometimes myself — unnecessary psychological difficulties. Certainly just about everything about sex has been very traumatized for me — although I do think of that Feiffer cartoon where a man is impotent with a woman. He keeps talking about how sex is this wonderful expression of love between two people, and finally she says, "No, it isn't, it's dirty, it's dirty." And then he gets excited again and he can function. I sometimes wonder if sex could be so exciting were it not for how forbidden they've made it.

Somewhere along the way — I don't know where — I picked up the understanding that mortal sins not only send you to hell, they also pound the nails into Christ's body — sort of working in retrospect. And you know you're causing our all-loving Lord this infinite agony by something you've done. In studying the Ten Commandments, I picked up pretty fast that, first of all, there weren't too many sexual *venial* sins — they tended to go to mortal very quickly. And they seemed to be the most likely mortal sin you would commit unless you were the sort who liked to rob things. (I loved the distinction there that if you stole a dime from your mother, that was really a venial sin, but if you stole a dime from somebody who only had a quarter to his name, that would be a mortal sin.)

It made me angry after a while, those intricate and exhausting laws concerning sex. I guess not everybody takes it as seriously, but it strikes me as a great waste of time. I remember being told by my grandmother about my uncle, who married a non-Catholic and moved away from home to Chicago — which was two strikes against him. Anyway, at college he was going to get honors but he didn't because he disagreed with his religion teacher on birth control. And my grandmother, in telling the story, then said to me, "And, of course, he shouldn't have done that." I understood that she meant that he should have been practical enough to get the honors; but she also meant, as a supporter of Joe McCarthy, that she and the Church knew what was right, and it was better just to follow.

Now that my grandmother is dead, I hope my living relatives won't be too offended if I acknowledge that, unconsciously, a lot of *Sister Mary* comes from my grandmother. My grandmother was a very charming woman, but *extremely* dominant and opinionated. For example, I remember the times I would spend there after school at Delbarton—the bus would leave me near her house and I would wait there for forty-five minutes for my mother to pick me up. I always had a very nice visit with her because often the grandchildren get the best of the grandparents. Well, I had been studying a poem called "The Listeners." In it, some traveler had been knocking on the door of a castle and got no answer, and he couldn't tell if there were people inside listening or whether it was empty. My grandmother asked what I thought it meant. I said that it either means there is no God or that there is a God but that he is, for whatever reason, silent. And my grandmother said that she didn't think anyone should be allowed to say that.

Twenty years later, I realized that this was the same thing that people were saying to me about *Sister Mary Ignatius*. And I hate that kind of thinking, it makes me livid. But getting back to my uncle, some years after that story, when I was becoming involved in post–Vatican II liberal Catholicism, I came to believe that as soon as one decides that sex doesn't have to be just for procreation, then birth control suddenly doesn't seem an issue. It seems sort of like tooth decay prevention. To be against it is like saying, "No, you can't go to the dentist, you can't learn to floss your teeth. God meant you to get cavities—get them!" And then your teeth will fall out at age fifty as they're meant to. I don't know, that's a crazy metaphor—and aren't teeth falling out a weird sexual thing in dreams anyway?

But there's a very specific way in which the Church's teachings on birth control harm people, aside from all the psychological ramifications of it. There was a woman my mother knew whose husband was an alcoholic and who had to get married when she was seventeen; she was now twenty-five and she had five children. She had an awful life because of this awful brute, but it was very hard to leave him because of the five children. Her husband would come back in these frightening drunken rages and, since his father was a judge, it didn't do much good when she called the police. After a while she went to the local parish priest and asked him if she might use birth control in case her husband raped her in a drunken rage. The priest thought about it over dinner, and his answer was no. So she didn't, and she did have a sixth child.

One of the things that makes me angriest about people who believe in God—and it isn't just Catholics at this point—is the idea that God is watching over everything. I mean, I wish that it were true and that everything awful that happened and everything good that happened had something to do with God. I think it's hilarious when people thank God at the Tony Awards, as if God has any *care* who wins the Tony Awards. I suppose, though, that the priest I just mentioned felt one couldn't block the possibility that God might work through mysterious ways and the husband raping his wife would produce a child for which He had special plans.

It just strikes me as a very strange and illogical thing. When you look at the Third World nations and all the praise of Mother Teresa, I think I would think better of her if she were more of a visionary and suddenly woke up and said, Hmm, I think we should work for population control as *well* as feeding these hundreds of thousands of starving people.

I was talking to a girl I know who was raised Catholic and who made me realize that there was a lot that was taught to the girls that wasn't taught to the boys. The girls were often taught, for instance, that the boys were *so* out of control with sex that it really fell *especially* to them (the girls) to stop things. The girl also told me a story that I can see haunts her to this day. It's about the kind of crazy, nonhumane thinking that comes out of this dogmatism. It also results from the kind of thing I did as well, which was to take people at their word, to believe what they said and digest it.

We were all taught back then that when you received communion, you weren't allowed to chew the host. That has since been changed, but the nuns really did a big number on this notion that the host would bleed and it was a great sacrilege, and blah, blah, blah. But something that never came up in my classes did come up in this girl's class: Somebody asked what happens if, as soon as you take communion, you throw up? What do you then have to do with the vomit? This question was treated seriously, and the nun said, Well, it still has the sacred host in it and it's consecrated. You can't clean it up yourself—you have to get a priest to do it. I guess this little girl of six or seven so identified with this dilemma that on the day of her first communion, needless to say, in the parking lot outside the church she vomited, undoubtedly out of fear that she would.

There she was, totally humiliated and also feeling that it somehow meant that God hated her or that she was doomed. She was with her mother, who was apparently a fairly normal person who said, "Don't worry, dear, I'll clean it up." And the little girl said, "No, no, you can't, you must get a priest to clean it up." The mother thought about it a second and said, "No, it's really all right, I'll do it." The little girl let her mother do it, knowing that her mother's conscience was okay but that she herself had created an incredible sacrilege because *she* knew that the priest had to get it and that she didn't fight hard enough. And so this woman, who is now in her late thirties, is still haunted by this. She just feels that she's cursed by Catholicism and that in some of her romantic attachments there are things very unhappy and wrong that are traceable to the things she was taught.

This is what happens if you're seven and you buy into that kind of overresponsibility. They just make so many crazy rules—I mean, who would think to worry about the vomit? So I was not taught about the consecrated vomit. Gee, that's the title of my next play, *The Consecrated Vomit*.

In terms of guilt, I went through a somewhat similar dilemma which I bet must be fairly common. Masturbation is a mortal sin, so that did become an enormous problem for me, because I would genuinely try to stop it. But then when I was thirteen I confessed it to some priest who rather traumatized me with his response. He said that it was *so* terrible that I couldn't bring myself to go back to confession. And so for two years I lived in mortal sin because I was too afraid to go back to confession. And yet, since my mother would comment if I didn't go to communion —you know, "What's the matter with you?"—I created all these sacrileges by going to communion with this mortal sin on my soul. And, of course, it's all about sex again.

A few years ago, I saw a liberal priest I knew from high school whom I liked, and just out of curiosity I asked him whether they still taught that masturbation was a mortal sin. To my surprise, he wasn't willing to say it was a mortal sin, but he wasn't willing to say it wasn't, either. It's such a strange thing, if you look at the evils in the world, to think that people are all worried about masturbation; it really, really seems wildly out of proportion. That was a needless psychological thing to go through for a couple of years.

But I didn't leave the Church over that. It's funny, they have that phrase "the loss of faith" that we used to discuss—almost as if you'd misplace it or it would mysteriously disappear one day. And mine really mysteriously disappeared one day. There were two causes for this. One was the prevalence of a kind of hopelessness that came from growing up in an alcoholic family—which I wrote about somewhat in my play *The Marriage of Bette and Boo*—this feeling that very few things could be solved. Then, as a liberal Catholic, I had become very strongly opposed to the war in Vietnam by my junior year in high school. But by the end of freshman year in college, I'm afraid I stopped believing that anything could be done about it.

I was at Harvard, and the other Catholics at the so-called Catholic Club there were very preppy and didn't seem concerned about the war. I then found some graduate students at the divinity school and I went for most of the year to this experimental Mass at a Jesuit house. At one service one of the nuns was speaking about the war, saying that despite the escalation and all, she still felt hope. And I just thought to myself, I don't. And I never went back. I suddenly did not feel any hope at all. I was unable to reconcile the all-powerful God who is also all-good coming up with this world — it just didn't make sense to me. I spent a little time thinking that maybe God is evolving like the rest of us, but I was so used to His being all-powerful from the teaching that I couldn't make sense out of an evolving God. I couldn't pray; I had no idea what prayer was for. None of it made sense to me. And that's what stopped me going to church.

I then went into a deep depression for two years. Pauline Kael, in putting down some movie that she didn't like in a review, said it reminded her of a Catholic college friend of hers who'd bored everyone on the dorm floor by saying, "Well, if you don't believe in God, what do you base your life on?" Reading that, on the one hand I felt great sympathy with this "boring" girl who didn't know enough to be sophisticated and didn't realize that we're all cosmopolitan and get around without God. And on the other hand, I realized that I was just like that — I didn't go around asking people the question, but I still thoroughly believed in this all-powerful God and that somehow things made sense. When I see people going to est or all these self-improvement things, I realize that they're looking for something to make these things make sense, so I have sympathy for it all.

When I got out of my depression, it was like getting used to not having God as the starting point. In my sophomore year at Harvard, I had a roommate who was Jewish — I refer to him, I hope not offensively, as my first New York Jew, since I had not known any before then. I had befriended him in my freshman year because, of all the people in the dorm, we were most interested in spiritual matters and were both against the war. We made some odd connection between my being a so-called serious Catholic and his being serious about his Judaism.

Two things were very odd. He, like many Jews, doesn't believe in God; but he would still follow the dietary laws. It was actually fairly inconvenient at school to follow them — they'd make special meals for you but you had to wait in a longer line. I always found that rather mysterious. Then, as soon as I lost my faith at the end of that year, suddenly he and I had very little in common. I know many Jews who don't believe in God, and still Passover is important to them. But if you're

Catholic and stop believing in God, you don't keep going to communion just out of social tradition. It really all starts with the basic premise that there is a God. I think that maybe the teaching is quite successful in communicating this primary cause theory to children because other people seem to cope somewhat better without believing in it than we seem to do.

And that's why it was very important to me when I was writing my play that the title was *Explains It ALL for You*. I had stopped going to church and really had stopped thinking about Catholic things for ten years and was just living my life. But because my mother was dying of cancer, there was a lot of pressure from my religious aunt to pray for my mother. I didn't believe in God, but I got to thinking that, if I did, what was the prayer supposed to mean? That if she did suffer — because she had a rather lengthy death — did He then have some purpose to it? I realized that I didn't understand what they meant.

It was also very painful because in the context of the Church you can go to the person who's dying and say, "Don't worry, you're going on to the next life." And if you *don't* believe, it's sort of like, "Well, so long! I hope it's not bad, but we'll see!" Needless to say, I didn't say that to my mother, but I really did become so . . . nostalgic is not quite the right word, but I was aware that, given somebody dying, there were comforting things to be said from religion and I had nothing comforting to say, which was awkward.

I just got thinking about religion. I sometimes just start writing on a blank page, and the blank page was a nun giving a lecture in which she explained *everything*, the answer to everything. So that was the impulse of the play. And then as I was writing it, I realized that since, for instance, non-Catholics wouldn't understand the meaning of mortal and venial sin, I'd better have her talking to non-Catholics as well. So she started explaining things, and as she started explaining things, I started to remember these things that I had just forgotten or not thought of for a long time. For example, the notion that they had to say that unbaptized babies went to limbo is to me, in retrospect, *hilarious* — and yet we were taught it.

I even came across a book after I wrote the play — which is kind of scary because if anybody saw the book they'd think I took the play from it. It was in the form of questions and answers written by a priest; maybe they were taken from a newspaper column or something. Some woman writes in to him saying that she has so much difficulty reconciling her sadness that her baby may be in limbo because it wasn't baptized and died right at birth, and so on. And the priest's answer was that basically God knows best and he means you to concern yourself more with your children who *are* living. And don't worry, limbo is fine and I'm sure your baby is very happy, because he doesn't realize he's missing God. That seems to me insane.

I know that some of the people who protested my play picked up a line in my introduction to my six plays [*Christopher Durang Explains It All for You*]: "Because ten years had passed since I'd thought about all this, I felt like a tourist in my own past, and what I'd accepted as a child and forgotten about as a young adult now seemed on a new viewing as the sincere ravings of a semilunatic." And I can see that if you believe everything that Sister Mary says, that must sound like an offensive thing to say. But just focusing on limbo for a moment, it seems so crazy. You know, if you have crazy parents who say, "We eat with our feet," and you eat with your feet for ten years and then you go out in the world and see that people eat with their hands, you're so struck with the total sincerity with which you were told to eat with your feet that it just knocks you out. By the same token, according to what we were taught, Eichmann would go to hell and a child who masturbates would go to hell. Maybe hell's a little worse for Eichmann, but even so. . . .

MAURA MOYNIHAN

Christ and Krishna

I think that my going away from the Church for those years and immersing
myself in an entirely different tradition has made me come back to it with
fresh eyes. I'm not just going through the rote motions because I learned
them as a child. I came to it of my own volition and my own longing,
without any kind of judgment — considering myself a Hindu, not thinking
of myself as a Catholic — and have rediscovered how wonderful the Catholic
service is.

—Maura Moynihan

There is only one religion, though there are a hundred versions of it.
—George Bernard Shaw
Preface to *Plays Pleasant and
Unpleasant* (1898)

"I've just returned from a year in India where I was working for the
Smithsonian. Prior to that I worked as a journalist at the *New York Post*
and *Interview*, and I'm freelancing now for *Vogue, American Heritage,*
and the *New Republic.* I'm also an actress and singer and I have a band.
I've been in five movies and several plays and television series like *The
New Show*; I gave that up temporarily because it just wasn't satisfying
enough, but now I'm back at it. I'm planning to do a children's book on
Hindu and Buddhist myths. I'm also very active in politics and am toying
with the idea of pursuing politics as a career. I guess you could say I'm
at a crossroads in my life."

So Maura Moynihan described her career to date, interrupting the narrative long enough to brew a cup of lemon zinger and light a stick of
incense. Now, incense is as much a part of the Catholic experience as
mortal sin and Mass wine — in fact, you could almost say that, properly

spooned over a glowing square of charcoal in the base of a thurible during Benediction, it is the official smell of the Roman Catholic Church. But that odor is distinct from the joss stick that was burning between us. Moynihan's apartment off Madison Avenue in midtown Manhattan is sparsely decorated, apart from a few photographs of her father, the well-known senior senator from New York, and a collection of religious icons and images that would baffle the most ecumenical spirit. Amid pictures of Christ, the Blessed Mother, and St. Clare are representations of Chaitanya (the great Bhakti saint), Ganesh (the Hindu elephant god), Durga and Kali (manifestations of the mother/female principle), Venus and Cupid, a phial of water from the Ganges, and Hanuman, the monkey god.

Moynihan finds no contradiction in being both a practicing Catholic and a devout Hindu. In fact, as she went on to describe her bifurcated belief system, it became clear that her embracing of Hinduism in India (when her father had been stationed there as American ambassador) may have helped more than anything else to resurrect her moribund Catholicism. She chooses to stress the similarities in the two religions, the correspondences in, say, the lives of Christ and of Krishna, and by doing that to show how the faiths can enhance each other. At least one thing is clear: Catholicism and Hinduism exercise a synergistic effect on Moynihan's religious consciousness. For another thing, Maura Moynihan has a lot of fun with her religions; as seriously as she takes them, she does have a sense of humor about the situation. She was quick to point out, for instance, the number of days one could take off from work by combining two sets of religious holidays. "If I could somehow stick Judaism in, too," she added, "I might never have to go to work again."

Wearing a black-and-white-striped tunic, turtleneck, and large hoop earrings, the twenty-eight-year-old Moynihan at times closed her eyes fiercely and clenched both hands while making a point. Then again, she would occasionally lapse into a kind of Punjabi accent which she used not sarcastically but simply as a way of expressing a foreign mode of thought — one that she may have felt she couldn't do justice to in flat-out American English. Indirectly that raises a point that has not been addressed by any official voice within the Roman Church. Large numbers of Catholics have been feeling a more intense need for some direct emotional involvement in their religion, an emotionalism that may have inadvertently been sifted from the Church during Vatican II. The rise of the Catholic Charismatic Renewal and the appeal to certain lapsed Catholics of the Evangelical or Pentecostalist sects indicate that the yearning is clearly there. Maura Moynihan describes another path — unusual and inventive, to be sure, but one that works for her.

⌐§ FAITH IS WITHOUT ANY QUESTION the most important thing in my life—having a personal relationship with God. In this society, people laugh at you for saying that. You're considered a nut if you say you believe in God, a little off. I find that very frightening. When I had a rock 'n' roll band, I used to try to talk about mysticism and religion. I wrote songs about it and people laughed, so I stopped and went back to teenage angst.

My earliest years were spent in upstate New York, but I don't remember them at all. Then my family moved to Washington, D.C., when I was in kindergarten and my father was working for John F. Kennedy as assistant secretary of labor. I had an extremely happy childhood, and I feel very blessed. During those years in Washington, my family and I were more involved in the Church as a family than we were ever to be again—which makes me very sad. We had our communions, my brother was confirmed. My father used to take me to the National Cathedral in Washington, and I was awed by the size and scale of it. I suppose religious buildings are supposed to inspire awe and reverence, and they do—it works.

I was very attracted to all the stories about Mary, the Virgin Mother. I'm named for Mary: my name Maura is the Gaelic for Mary. You're named for saints—or, in India, for gods—because that particular saint—or god—will protect you. So I feel that I have the protection of the Virgin Mother, and I feel grateful for that.

There is a certain distinct personality type that is definitely Catholic and that is defined by a certain energy. They like to flaunt their neuroses. That doesn't mean we hang out together. In fact, my closest friends when I was growing up were all Jewish. I was always a little bit envious of them because they had better festivals and holidays. Then I went to India and became exceedingly jealous of my Hindu friends. Their rituals seemed more participatory than the Christian ones, but I've since come around and changed my mind. I go to synagogues, too, and I think you can't really understand Christianity unless you know something about Judaism.

Catholics are also perennially childlike in some ways. I don't know why that is, but all the Catholics I know have that sense of wonder and awe in them. There is something very mystical and strange in the Catholic ritual, in the liturgy, that's missing in the Protestant and that I think always fills you with awe of the unknown. Catholics also tend to be more superstitious, and they're always trying to blame something on someone else or on some external force. I assume that derives from confession, from trying to exonerate yourself with the words and the incantation.

My first spiritual experience took place at the National Cathedral in Washington with my dad. I was listening to the music, the censer was swinging, and suddenly the whole altar seemed to glow, to acquire an aura that had not been there previously. I was in first grade, but I remember this moment quite vividly. I used to be afraid of church a little because it was so large and almost forbidding. No one really explains the rituals to you very well. I find the image of Jesus on the cross absolutely terrifying, and I think it's quite wrong that there's been such an emphasis on that in the two thousand years of Christianity—or since whenever it was that the emphasis shifted from the Resurrection to the Crucifixion. That's all wrong. It terrified me as a child, and it still frightens me when I go into a church and I see Christ's agony.

The real miracle of Christ is the Resurrection. But I remember as a child being frightened of the crucifix and not understanding the Crucifixion at all. I feel the same way about the language in a lot of the hymns: He who suffered for us, the Lamb who left His blood. And what about taking communion, the Body of Christ and the Blood of Christ? It seemed to me that the Crucifixion was like a human sacrifice—and of the most hideous kind if He was the Son of God and a Man of peace. But now I try to think more of the Resurrection because I don't like that emphasis on our sin, I don't like that emphasis on evil, I don't like that emphasis on torture and murder.

There's so much superstition in Catholicism. I'd ask in Sunday school, "But *why* was He crucified?" "*Because* of your sins! Shut up!" You're a child, you don't know. But to compensate for that socially, the largest Christian festival in the United States is Christmas—not Easter, not Good Friday, not Pentecost. It's Christmas, the *birth* of Christ. When I was a child I loved Christmas so much. It was the most important part of the year, a unifying experience for my family, for the community, for society, for the world. In India there are large festivals on the scale of Christmas five or six times a year. But you don't have that in Christianity anymore; it's lost. The only real festival we still practice is Christmas, and it has all the elements of a festival: the spiritual message, the merchandising aspect of it, everything.

People say that without the Crucifixion you couldn't have had the Resurrection, but I don't know about that. The Buddha wasn't crucified. The Buddha died in his sleep and *then* the Nirvana came. Mary wasn't crucified; she ascended body and soul to heaven. I don't accept that about the Crucifixion. I think it probably was a terrible tragedy and that He was terrified. Besides, there's more truth in what the artist portrays than in what the theologian will tell you. Look at the face of Christ on the cross:

the horror. That's not a very comforting notion, nor is it what He meant
when He was teaching and spreading His message of love.

My parents were divorced, and the nuns used to tell stories about
children of divorced parents and how their feet and hands would turn into
animals' hooves. Isn't that horribly irresponsible? It's terribly frightening
for a child when she's eight years old. In Catholic education, you are
instilled from the very beginning with all kinds of phantasms of fear. It's
like Zoroastrianism and the duality in those early years, in the sense that
they're trying to instill in you a reverence for God and a terror of the
devil. But it wasn't the devil who was a prominent player in my early
childhood fantasies and myths so much as *myself* and the evil in me —
being tainted and being sinful and going to hell.

Something about Catholicism and its emphasis on ritual, which inspired
the Reformation and God knows what else, does sort of lead one to think
it's a system and you can buck it — that if you just go in and say so many
Hail Marys you'll be cleansed. So it was as a child in Sunday school that
I first began to question Catholicism. My Sunday school teacher was a
very sweet and lovely lady who told us some lovely biblical stories,
although not enough. In fact, I wish we'd had more stories and less practice
of genuflection. Instead she would tell us, "Now go into the confessional
and say, 'I lied ten times, I stole five times, and I was mean to my brother
six times.' So every single one of us went in and repeated exactly what
she said. There wasn't enough emphasis on really examining your conscience and really taking responsibility for confessing and then perse-
vering and resolving not to sin again. Something seemed false about that,
and it made me doubt the efficacy of prayer and ritual when I was very
young.

I think that what's lacking in Christian education today is an emphasis
on myth and mysticism and understanding Christianity through the arts,
because that's how religion comes alive. Then it's not something threatening, then it's not just a moral dictum. That's why I was very strongly
attracted to Hinduism when I first got to India. In India, religion is an
integral part of your life — to the extent that there's no secular art to speak
of. Well, now there is with films, which are a Western technology imported
to the Third World. But all the plays and songs and art and music of India
are extolling the great achievements and powers of the many, many, many,
many gods. That's how I've come to reach Christianity again, through
music and visual arts.

Yet in my early Sunday school education and my education in general,
there wasn't enough emphasis on trying to conform as closely as possible
to Christ's teachings and His message of love and forgiveness. There was

more justifying and explaining the Crucifixion. I think that's misplacing much of our faith and our focus. That's my problem with Catholicism and Christianity, so I've tried to come back to it in my own way. And I have, through Indian religion, come to a new acceptance and understanding of Christianity. I was born a Christian and that's very important. I wasn't born a Hindu in this life, although I do believe in reincarnation. I know, for instance, that the doctrine of reincarnation was described in the early Christian Scriptures and that it was removed at the Council of Nicea.

I went to public school from the first to the fourth grade, then I went to private school from the fourth grade to the beginning of tenth, following which I attended the American International School in New Delhi for high school. I moved to India when I was fifteen, when my dad was appointed ambassador there. My father goes to church all the time. I remember going to church with him as a child and feeling very proud and excited. But we were the only two members of the family who ended up going. My mother had a terrible reaction against religion and Catholicism. She went to parochial schools her whole life, and she has terrible stories about it.

This is a funny story—I don't know what she'll think but I'll tell it anyway because it's very revealing about Catholic childhood. I was playing with my little brother in the bathtub one day. I was in kindergarten or first grade, and we had just been preparing for first holy communion. So I said, "John, don't you know that gasoline is a car's host?" I thought cars ate gasoline, just like we ate the host at communion. Mom heard that and, perhaps reflexively after years of getting her knuckles whacked in parochial school, she came in like a torrent, pulled me out of the tub, and shoved a bar of soap in my mouth. It was like a Dickens novel or something. I was kind of confused and didn't know what I'd done wrong, because to me it seemed perfectly sensible.

They never considered sending us to parochial school, I think because of my mother's bad experience with the nuns. A lot of my friends went to parochial school, though, and there were always nuns coming to visit the family because we were actively involved with the Church. I was very sorry that I wasn't confirmed—we were moving a lot at that time and my parents never got around to it. And I think that sense of community and cultural identity that comes with belonging to the Church started slipping away as my parents no longer enforced any kind of religious discipline on the family. That started to slip away, and with it went my whole sense of who I was. I think religion is important not just for spiritual or ethical structure, but also for a sense of your cultural identity. I always envy my Indian friends so much because they know exactly who they are and where they come from and how they fit in to the larger historical tradition. We don't in America—we've lost so much of that. All the distinctions are blurred and our individuality and our sense of belonging to a tradition are gone.

I regret that. And if I ever have children I don't know how I'll bring them up, because I really am a pantheist/universalist. I go to church, but I also go to the Hindu temple—to me there's no conflict at all. I'll go to a synagogue and a mosque, and I'll have the same intensity of spiritual communion in any holy place. I felt that way at Stonehenge. I also felt that way when I was in Greece and I went to Delphi. In fact, at Delphi I had one of the most powerful mystical experiences of my life.

As I said, I moved to India when I was fifteen, and I fell in love with India the moment I stepped off the plane. It just felt to me like home. People are seldom indifferent to India—either they love it or they can't stand it. I loved it instantly. The first thing one learns about Indian philosophy, which one hears from speaking to the pundits, is that all things are divine, all things have jiva, which means soul. You do really feel that you're in an integral universe there, that everything has its purpose and its place and is working as part of a larger scheme. The whole notion of time and space is so vast and so grand in India. I majored in Hindu studies at college because I love reading the texts and the mythology.

In the Judeo-Christian tradition in the West, what are erroneously called the pagan myths or fairy tales have been disavowed as being part of a religious tradition by the Church, and a schism has grown up between the two. That shouldn't be at all, and in Hinduism they're not at variance with one another. They're integral parts of the same cultural religious tradition, and they can coexist and cross-pollinate. "Truth is many, God is one," is one Hindu axiom I love. No, "Paths are many, truth is one." I'm sorry.

Hinduism is very tolerant. It acknowledges the legitimacy of every religious experience and every religious leader. Through my Hindu studies, I started understanding Jesus again. If you ask the holy men about Jesus they'll say, "Yes, He is also an avatar." So I began to think of Jesus as an avatar. But I have a lot of trouble with Catholics who told me that He's the one God, the only God, the only Way. I don't believe that still, though I do consider myself a good Christian. I believe very much in Jesus' message, and I don't think Jesus would like their attitude. I think He'd be very upset that His message has been distorted and that crimes have been committed in His name.

I became strongly attracted to Shiva. He's the God of destruction and he's very strange, the God of the Saddhus—he's blue and has a snake around his neck. And then I had an extraordinary mystical experience in Vrindavan, where Krishna was born. I have always thought that Krishna and Christ shared many attributes and qualities. The Krishna myth has elements of Moses and of the Christ myth and of certain Greek and Roman myths, too. Krishna was born in a palace, smuggled out at night on a bed of reeds, and floated down the river, like Moses. He was a carpenter, a cowherd, and led a simple life among simple people, like Christ. And, like Christ, his message is very much for the poor: Blessed are the meek, for they shall inherit the earth. You find that over and over again in the doctrine of bhakti, which is the notion of reaching God through love only, not through exact performance of ritual or understanding of doctrine— because that keeps religion in the hands of the educated classes and away from the poor man. That's a problem particularly in India, with its caste system.

So Krishna came along, and he was a radical and a revolutionary very much like Jesus. He performed miracles, but much more than Jesus did —Jesus was very modest about it, Krishna wasn't. But I don't know if Krishna was a god or a man. I think he was probably a myth. I don't know if Krishna lived, but I think there's evidence that Christ really took human incarnation. It doesn't matter in India, no one cares. There's no real Indian history. There are hundreds and hundreds of years, after the Greeks left and before the Moghuls and the British came, when no one kept any records. The reason it doesn't matter in India is that the divine and the actual get mixed up.

But in India my faith and my involvement in religion were reawakened, and I guess that says something for what's lacking in our Christian education or upbringing here in the West. I studied Hinduism in school and I loved it because it's so colorful and exciting. I was attracted by the sensual, physical qualities of the worship—the brilliantly colored temples, the vast mythology with many, many gods, and the sound and smells and richness of it. It's what I would call the spiritualization of the physical. Contrast that with the irony and, some would say, even the hypocrisy of the Catholic upbringing which on the one hand is so sensual and on the other teaches you to deny and fear and reject the flesh and the physical world. That always made me very uncomfortable, and that's something which Catholics always struggle with. Catholics have a very difficult time with sex, although it's something of a paradox. They're afraid of it, and yet they're passionate.

What's wonderful about Hinduism is that there are so many different belief systems that contradict one another—there are many different sects you can follow — yet all are part of the Hindu religion, and they're all perfectly acceptable. You can choose the path that's suitable for *you*. There aren't the terrible conflicts between different sects and schools of thought that exist elsewhere. But I was first attracted to the sight, the sound, the smell of it, which is a very important part of religion. Like the incense and the lilies in church, all that's very important — the outward forms of ritual and symbol and practice.

My parents' generation was different. For them, the answers were much clearer. World War II had a tremendous impact on their values and beliefs and their faith in the age-old struggle of good and evil. That was a war in which it was very clear that there was Good and there was Evil. It wasn't that way for us, as you know. We don't know what we are. In the sixties the social revolutionaries were defying everything that was established, and that meant the Church, too. But that was a great loss. My father taught at Harvard, so I was hanging around the Harvard campus all through the sixties rebellions. David Stockman was my live-in baby-sitter, so it's all my fault in a way: I tortured him so much that he turned into that weirdo who destroyed the economy!

All my father's closest friends were Jewish — Norman Podhoretz, Nathan Glazer, Irving Kristol — so I was surrounded by all those rabbis, those brilliant Jewish intellectuals. I was always going to Hillel House with my friends — they'd have Hanukkah parties and Passover dinners and I'd always tag along. That was a lot of fun. We Catholics on the block never had anything like Hillel House. I do think that the Church didn't reach out and grab us enough. *I* made an effort to come back to it; it hasn't come after *me*. Most people desperately need some kind of spiritual guidance — not just spiritual, but also a sense of cultural identity, which a lot of American Catholics are losing. That's one reason I became a passionate Hindu for many years.

Then in the temple in Vrindavan, where Krishna was born, I had the experience similar to the one I had had in Washington, only more intense. I went in really just as a student with my notebook and my sunglasses and left my sandals outside. And suddenly I just began to tremble all over, and I felt this . . . I can't describe what it was but it's sometimes known as the kundalini awakening. It was an experience of kundalini rising, and I felt an extraordinary communion with all the animating and divine power of the universe. And I fainted. I stayed in Vrindavan for two weeks, just walking around in a daze. It was a moment of absolute communion with God. Then I came down very fast, which can happen with kundalini. But I became a fervent devotee of Krishna — though I'm not a Hare Krishna at all, which is a different sect. Then I began to meditate and visualize Krishna and use the Krishna mantra.

When I went to temples, I felt a tremendous sense of security in that I belonged to something and a feeling that God was very close and accessible — something that I had not felt in the Church in a very long time. I can't explain why. You can never explain faith. And then I had another mystical experience in Delphi, in which I saw . . . well, you can't describe these experiences, so I'll just leave it at that. I had another in Jerusalem at the Dome of the Rock and the Wailing Wall and then at the Church of the Holy Sepulcher. I felt frightened and confused, though, to think that these three great monotheistic traditions had warred with each other so much over the centuries. No one in the Church has ever explained that to me. In Jerusalem I met, at the age of nineteen, a man from the Greek Orthodox Church who took me around the Old City. For the first time in my life, I saw someone with a halo, which is the aura — I saw it around him.

I took a year off from college and went back to India, and I lived the life of a true pilgrim. I had very few possessions, and I walked many places visiting holy sites. I lived in an ashram for a very long time. I always wore a sari over my head, and beads. That was a strange and beautiful time, now that I think of it. I spent many hours a day meditating and praying. I was also unhappy at that time, longing for some answer to all my deepest prayers. I hope this doesn't sound silly — I think when you describe your own spiritual journey it sounds silly to people.

I had come to accept, from meeting those holy men and reading the vast literature of Hindu and Buddhist canons, a belief in reincarnation and the idea of karma. What we have in America is a lot of karma, but not dharma. Dharma is the corollary principle: it is the law that you must obey. If you are a Hindu, you are born with your dharma, which is very clear. In America, we don't have dharma — we can be anything. We can be a street sweeper or the president, it doesn't matter. So I was searching for my dharma.

At that time in my life I was very unhappy and I sought refuge and solace in temples and churches, really out of desperation — in much the same way that you'll see a bagman passed out in front of St. Patrick's. I felt almost like that. Still, if you go to the Church out of desperation, it does not desert you then. I was very poor at this time, I had no money and was all on my own. I was sort of working my way around Paris at odd jobs. I sang at sidewalk cafés, making forty-five dollars a night passing the hat, doing street theater, and living hand to mouth.

One day I went to Notre Dame and had another overwhelming feeling of faith. I burst into tears and felt a reawakening of faith that had not happened to me for a very long time. I used to go to church to feel close to God but didn't feel that *personal* ecstasy that I felt at Hindu temples.

But this day I decided that it was my dharma to be a Catholic — after all, why was I *born* a Catholic? But I decided that I was not going to reject Hinduism, I was just going to incorporate what I'd learned. To me, Hinduism still had a lot of answers that I wasn't getting from Christianity, from a priest, from Catholic friends, or from going to Mass on Sunday.

I went back to the United States and started going to church again — but combining it with my visits to the Hindu temple, which I still do. I don't have any problem reconciling that and believing in both. They both satisfy different needs for me. I still find Christianity stranger and more elusive than I find Hinduism. I find the Catholic ritual and liturgy more peculiar and almost more *supernatural* than the Hindu, which seems much more down to earth. It's back to the Crucifixion, and the sacrifice of God's only Son, and the drinking of His blood — that just seems strange and supernatural. Hinduism is also much more physical: the priest will *fling* holy water at the faithful, and they'll *scream*. It's more like a Baptist church — more hysterical, in a way, more ecstatic.

I think that my going away from the Church for those years and immersing myself in an entirely different tradition has made me come back to it with entirely fresh eyes. I'm not just going through the rote motions because I learned them as a child. I came to it entirely of my own volition and my own longing, without any kind of judgment — considering myself a Hindu, not thinking of myself as a Catholic — and have rediscovered how wonderful the Catholic service is and how much it is trying to instill love, forgiveness, and brotherhood. I know it sounds corny and prosaic to say things like that, but good God, that's what the human race needs, isn't it? Still, I think that the Church isn't doing enough to bring back young people who have lapsed.

I would like to reinvolve people in faith because it means so much to me, especially in the nuclear era. If I didn't have faith, I don't think I would be able to get up in the morning, I don't think I'd be able to live. I went through a period a few years ago when my faith was very badly shaken, right after Ronald Reagan was re-elected and we embarked on a massive rearmament program while funds for everything else were being cut. It was terrible to read the paper in the morning, and I couldn't even get out of bed sometimes, I was so scared. It is only through almost militantly reasserting my faith that I feel I can keep on living and that nuclear war can be stopped — if enough people turn to God and discipline themselves ethically and spiritually. Nuclear war is just a symptom, isn't it? But in the history of the human race as we know it, we've never faced anything like it before now.

The Church, through the bishops' conference, has been very responsible about that, and I'm glad. I don't think anyone can challenge the moral authority of the Church on that issue. It's not just like a citizens' action group—politicians can't turn away from it. I've worked with the nuclear freeze, but I plan to get more deeply involved with the disarmament movements that are tied to the Church because they have the most persuasive arguments. I'm also interested in the sanctuary movement and the Church's role in Central America. I think the Church could be even more active on issues of disarmament and of military intervention and war— then again, look at the Crusades! But I think you can forgive mistakes that have been made along the way.

It seems to me that during the Inquisition, for instance, the Church must have been invaded by some demonic force. I believe in the duality of good and evil—that's what I liked about my early Catholic instruction, the idea of two combating principles. Zoroastrianism describes them very well: Asha and Druj represent two angels inside the soul who compete for the individual throughout his life. I think there's much duality in Christianity. The iconography of the devil has not been very well developed; otherwise we wouldn't have the same kind of fear and anxiety about sin that we do. In Hinduism, the notion of evil and the devil is much more sophisticated and more visible, in the form of the goddess Kali. You worship her and pay homage to that principle of destruction and violence. They don't call it evil—it doesn't have that moral connotation to it. But you recognize it and ask it to protect you. That doesn't exist in Christianity, and it's another thing that attracted me to Hinduism. It was dealt with in a healthier way. The devil has more power over you if you are afraid of him—you attract him through fear. There's less fear in the Hindu psyche. Kali is depicted as being black, like the devil; she wears a necklace of human skulls; she wears a skirt of human arms; she spouts blood. So you can see why the Victorian ladies were a little confused when they first arrived on the subcontinent.

How do my parents feel about my Hinduism? I haven't talked to them about it too much. I think they were a bit bemused by my attraction to Hinduism, frankly, in the early years. They were very confused by it. They didn't take to it immediately and instinctively, like I did. I don't think they know the extent to which I'm involved in my meditation and my personal practice, because I keep it fairly private. I've been a vegetarian since I was a child, they know that. But many of my odysseys in India were solitary, not with them. I think they're glad that I'm involved with the Church again, but I don't think they care one way or the other.

It's not a big deal in India. You can talk about your guru and your meditation and your mysticism at any cocktail party and it's not considered to be offbeat or nutty. Whereas here, as I said before, if you say that you believe in God, people think you're a little off, and they're suspicious of you. But certainly my parents have seen the change in me since I made a greater commitment to faith—how much happier I am and how much more responsible I am. I do believe that you get divine guidance. I believe in the old axiom that if you take one step toward God, He takes ten steps toward you. Christ is a very good exemplar and model for that. But I don't know what Christ would feel about the divisions in His Church. I wonder what He thinks. I feel very strongly, for example, that there should be more unity between Christians and Jews. I go to synagogues, which my parents always encouraged a lot. My father goes to synagogues, too, and he's been a great champion of Israel. And yet he's a good Catholic. So there's always been a great involvement with Jewish culture in my family, and I feel very privileged to have had that when I was growing up. It shaped my values a great deal. I think there should be more of an effort on the part of Catholic and Jewish leaders to emphasize what is common to both traditions and to create a greater unity. Judaism is fascinating—the language and music—and to think that Christianity is part of that makes Christianity seem a richer and more varied tradition than it sometimes appears. God knows, it can often seem stodgy and boring. Go to a Hassidic synagogue in Brooklyn and, my God! There should be more joy in the Catholic service.

Going to Italy also had a hand in making me rediscover Christianity and enjoy it more and find more pleasure in it. Ritual should be pleasurable, it should be esthetic. The Catholic Church in Italy, God knows, is spectacular—the color and the light. Again, as in a Hindu temple, it's the spiritualization of the physical, which you see in the Buddhist and Hindu traditions and which often seems to be lacking in contemporary Catholicism and Christianity. Also, I never learned much about the saints and always wanted to. They're like all the Greco-Roman gods. One thing the Church should do is to revive the folklore and mythology. Italy is like India with its spiritual topography, because you have the place where a miracle occurred and then the home of a saint. In every temple in India the priest will come up and tell you that it's the holiest place in all of India.

What is it we're missing in America? Maybe it's because we're a nation of immigrants and we don't have roots that go down too far—we're transplanted. In India and in Jerusalem and in Italy you feel a deep connection to the source. It was in France and Jerusalem that I had my reawakening, and when I went to Assisi it just all came to life.

ROBERT HOYT

A Catholic Reporter

The Catholic press represents the Catholic mind at work; if it shows no
interest in the "secular" environment; if it is never "present" in the slums,
at school board and city council meetings, in the union halls and the Chamber
of Commerce luncheons; if it reviews only works of hagiography and meditation, but not books of social criticism unless they are written by Catholics;
if it is unconcerned about the impact of a new farm law; if it has nothing
to say about music and art and discusses novels and films only when they
are denounceable—to the extent that we are absent from these spheres, we
*mis*represent the Catholic mind; we teach that grace builds on a vacuum.
—Robert Hoyt
  America, January 30, 1960

Sitting at his office desk in the basement level of a West Eighty-seventh
Street townhouse, Robert Hoyt is excited over the cover of the current
issue of the *National Catholic Reporter*, a paper which he helped to found
but with which he has not been associated for many years. Because of a
generally tepid response among American clergy to the public humbling
of Seattle's Archbishop Raymond Hunthausen, the *NCR* had decided to
run its letters to the editor on the cover, something Hoyt finds to be a
sensational move, "a stroke of genius" in fact. "It's not exactly detached
newspapering," he says, "but I think it accurately reflects the amount of
concern among the laity." One senses that he is not simply going out of
his way to praise the publication that fired him after he had built it during
the 1960s into the single most influential Catholic newspaper in America.
No, Hoyt genuinely enjoys seeing the paper make a daring editorial move.

    A more objective observer, John Deedy, wrote in a recent issue of the
Critic that the *NCR* "is hardly the Peck's Bad Boy it once was. . . . *NCR*,
in fact, rather than being counter-institutional or hostile is just plain

churchy.'' Deedy adds that in it, ''one's interests are not cultivated or consciously engaged, as one remembers them being during Bob Hoyt's time.'' And yet the paper that broke the tradition of a protective and apologetic Catholic press in this country — for example, by running an article by a priest who questioned the value of clerical celibacy, or by publishing the secret recommendations submitted to Pope Paul VI by the Papal Commission on Birth Control (the majority report, which the Pope rejected, favored the use of contraception), or by printing a piece about papal infallibility headlined ''How to Get the Papal Monkey Off the Catholic Back'' — will always have a place in American Church history. As will its soft-spoken but effectual founder and first editor.

But to appreciate the role Hoyt and the *Reporter* played in the American Catholic press, one has to recall that as late as 1965, during *NCR*'s first year of publication, *Time* magazine was able to report, ''All but a handful of Roman Catholic magazines and newspapers in the U.S. are published by dioceses or religious orders — and usually display a nervous, reverential caution in telling what goes on inside the church.'' *Time* was intrigued by what it called ''a cheeky one-year-old exception . . . owned and edited by laymen who take orders from no one'' and went on to quote a Boston monsignor who referred to it as ''the freshest thing that has appeared in Catholic journalism.''

The *NCR*'s stated purpose was ''to report the life of the church in the world'' and, according to Hoyt, to serve as ''primarily a newspaper, meaning that its function will be to report what is going on in the church, not to explain or defend it.'' Although some lay-operated Catholic journals of opinion such as *Commonweal* were already having an impact, there was no major independent Catholic newspaper. The distinction is what set the *NCR* apart from all the rest. Opinion, theory, and advocacy, no matter how radical or persuasive, lack the unambiguous authority of simply reporting the facts as they are, an activity which, in the long run, makes it more difficult for any hierarchy to function arbitrarily.

One example of that principle in action was reported in no less secular a publication than the *Wall Street Journal* in 1968. When Cardinal James F. McIntyre of Los Angeles moved to halt a liberalization program adopted by the Immaculate Heart of Mary sisters — a teaching order known for its innovative methods — the *NCR* stepped in, allotting ''considerable news space'' to the dispute. According to the *Journal*, ''The upshot . . . was that the nuns were allowed to vote their preferences, and the liberalization moves were overwhelmingly approved. The publicity that *NCR* gave the matter 'probably saved the Immaculate Heart sisters,' says one priest who was close to the situation.'' The same article quoted the managing editor of the archdiocesan newspaper of Newark, New Jersey, as saying that "the presence of *NCR* has helped us all gain greater editorial freedom — it has broadened the limits of what we can publish."

Though the *Reporter* championed liturgical and other forms of Church renewal in its unabashedly liberal editorials, it was scrupulous about giving space to conservative commentators. The *NCR* ran lengthy defenses of the natural-law argument against contraception, balanced the column of liberal John Leo with one by then-conservative Garry Wills, and added the perspectives of Rabbi Arthur Herzberg and influential Lutheran theologian Martin Marty. But all that ecumenical fervor apparently didn't sit well with the paper's original sponsor, Bishop Charles Helmsing of Kansas City–St. Joseph. In October 1968, Bishop Helmsing issued an official condemnation of the paper that had been nourished in his diocese, charging it with "imbalance" and a "poisonous character." He accused the paper of "exploiting . . . situations of apparent or real conflict between various classes of the church — between the bishops and their priests, or between the clergy and the laity." Threatening some members of the staff with excommunication (the threat was never carried out), Helmsing demanded that the word *Catholic* be removed from the paper's masthead.

With an equanimity that perhaps came of having locked horns with the institutional authorities of the Church so many times along the way, Hoyt brushed off the attacks, and the paper continued to thrive. Several years later, declining circulation and intrastaff disputes, not the opposition of the hierarchy, drove him from the publication he had nurtured into prominence. Now, at the age of sixty-five, Robert Hoyt is working on a book about the nature of institutions, based on his experiences at the *NCR* and his dealings with the institutional Church. In this interview he gives an account of those early dealings and of a life in heartland American Catholicism.

◈ MY FATHER WAS NOT CATHOLIC. I don't know the story very well, but my parents were married outside the Church. I think my father had been divorced, which may have caused some ill feeling among my mother's Catholic friends. But evidently there was no conflict between them as to our religious upbringing. My older brother, Jim, and I were raised Catholic even though my mother wasn't in good standing, and I'm sure she repaired that after my father's death.

My father died when I was five, and my mother sent us to boarding school very early on. I started in kindergarten or first grade, and that lasted until she got training as a beautician and set up her own shop. I went to a variety of schools, actually — all Catholic schools — in Iowa and Michigan and Windsor, Ontario, until I was in the fifth grade and we went to Detroit, where my mother had started her beauty shop. We lived in an apartment behind the shop. I went to grade school in the local parish, which was run by Jesuits, and then spent a year and a half at the University of Detroit High School — also Jesuit — until my mother died, partly of pneumonia but partly from hopelessness — it was 1936, the depths of the Depression, and her business was failing. The extent of religious influence on my life can be shown by the fact that the pastor of the parish presided over what was going to happen to my brother and me after her death. There were a number of people in the parish who were my mother's customers and who offered to take care of us; he chose the richest. We were sent to a foster home for the rest of that year and the first half of my sophomore year, and then they shipped us off to a boarding school, St. Norbert High School in De Pere, Wisconsin, near Green Bay.

After high school my brother, James, who was two years older than I was to the day, continued in college for two years. At the end of my freshman year of college, I entered the Order — the Norbertines, or Canons Regular of Prémontré, an ancient order not well known in this country. Their focus in this country has been mostly on education. They modeled themselves on the Jesuits, I think, in their educational practices and were essentially second team Jesuits. But my entire education was religious — I didn't enter a secular institution until I was a teacher in Kansas City and I had to get some education credits to qualify. I can't recall the names of all the orders that taught me, and that's too bad, because at least some of the teachers were pretty good, particularly at Gesu parish school in Detroit.

One result was that I never felt the sense of astonishment that the Second Vatican Council brought to so many people. Both the nuns and the Jesuits, who taught the formal religion classes at Gesu, and, later, the Norbertines, or some of them, portrayed a Church in which the Pope was very much a man and very much capable of sin and of mistakes. It was very much a human Church and I always thought of it that way. That's my orthodoxy. People who saw the Church changing its mind or being open and semidemocratic during the council were often quite astonished. I simply welcomed it as the implementation of what I'd always thought. So I think that schooling had a very profound influence on me.

The early experience of religion in the boarding schools we attended was pretty intense. When I first went to Gesu, I remember leaving after Mass, filing out with my classmates, and I've got my hands clasped in that prayerful pose. And I suddenly realized that nobody else was doing it.

We had some nuns who were strict, but I don't remember any real severity or any trauma coming out of that experience. I didn't have a "Sister Mary Ignatius," for instance. A few years ago a group of us went to see that play [Christopher Durang's *Sister Mary Ignatius Explains It All for You*], and we found it funny but nevertheless offensive. It seemed to us an example of a guy getting his revenge. Most of the people I saw it with were ex-Catholics, but they were mostly from the Midwest, where things weren't so rigid. That business of growing up Catholic as nothing but "don'ts" and whacks doesn't correspond to my experience, which I remember as being rather benevolent.

I think it was probably more friendship, and maybe looking for a home, that impelled me to get pious enough to want to join the priesthood. The only relative I was in touch with at the time was my brother. The people who took care of us didn't take us into their homes — we weren't adopted, they simply made us wards. What made me believe I had a vocation was that my closest friends were going in. That was after my freshman year in college. After a year in the novitiate and after completing college, I was sent to teach at the Order's high school in Philadelphia. While teaching, we were also taking theology courses, taught in Latin, so it was a pretty heavy load. Two things intervened, though, before I was scheduled to take solemn vows. One, the war was on, and I was patriotic; the other was that I decided I wasn't cut out to be a celibate. Yet it was very hard to leave the seminary because we had a close-knit group in my year — five of us were very close. The other four went on to be ordained.

I would've been drafted anyway, but I enlisted so I could be an aviation cadet. I turned out not to have certain skills necessary to fly airplanes — I tended to bounce them off the ground when trying to land — but because of a government experiment I spent the war going through one training school after another. I don't know why, but every time we completed the training, a certain group of us would be sent to another school while everybody else would be put into a unit and shipped overseas. So I never did get sent overseas. My last station was Lowry Field in Denver.

After being discharged, I stayed in Denver because I liked it and had no place else to go. I discovered that there was a provision of the GI Bill that gave you a hundred bucks a month for being self-employed. So I declared myself a freelance writer, and for six months or so I read books and the standard writers' magazines about how to aim for the *Saturday Evening Post* and *Collier's* and so forth, how to write for the "slick" magazines and the "pulps." But my manuscripts bounced just about the way my airplanes did — they came back very fast. I began feeling guilty about taking the government's money, so when I learned of a job opening with a Catholic paper I applied and got it. That was in forty-six.

Actually, it was not one paper but a flock of them. The Register System of Newspapers, as it was officially known, was headquartered then in Denver, and it was a huge operation that put out upwards of thirty-five editions at its peak. It processed diocesan newspapers. Monsignor Matthew "Matt" Smith, LL.D. — a self-awarded degree — was editor-in-chief of the overall operation, which included a plant at which the papers were all assembled and which Smith used to brag was the second largest printing plant west of the Mississippi. The copy came from Wheeling, West Virginia, Helena, Montana, Cincinnati and Fresno, Santa Fe, Peoria and Green Bay, and all over, from the editors of the local diocesan newspapers who chose — basically for economic reasons — to have their papers edited, composed, typeset, laid out, printed, and, in most cases, mailed from the central Register plant in Denver.

What it was, was economy of scale. A lot of these dioceses could never have had papers except for the enormous saving involved in centralizing it in one plant. There was a copy chief who would choose the front-page stories for most of the editions and plan the layout of those, select the size of the headlines and type size for all the stories. The rest of us would do the detailed copyediting, but most of us also would do the layout for one or two editions — say, the *Eastern Kansas Register* or the *Kansas City–St. Joseph Register* or the *Cincinnati Telegraph-Register*. And besides all those, there was the parent paper, called simply the *Register*, national edition, which was sold in pamphlet racks in dioceses that didn't belong to the Register System. It had a circulation of maybe eight hundred thousand. It survives, after a fashion, to this day.

The local editions all had a version of the national incorporated into them, so that unless they wanted to, they didn't have to pay any attention to national or international news — some did, some didn't. They all looked pretty much alike and had the same type with some variations. I was in charge of the Grand Island, Nebraska, edition, for instance — and making a good-looking front page for the diocesan newspaper of Grand Island, Nebraska, was some feat because there wasn't a hell of a lot going on there.

When I applied for the Register job, I was in many ways your ideal candidate — graduated from a Catholic college, a philosophy major, an ex-seminarian with some exposure to theology, and so forth. I started there as a proofreader, where, like everyone else, I was available to the city editor of the local edition, the *Denver Catholic Register*, for doing local feature stories. Then the next step was to move into the editorial room as associate editor, mark up copy, write headlines, page proof, and still do some local stories as well.

And then, of course, there was the Register College of Journalism—quite an astonishing institution. No matter how long you worked for the Register—and one guy had been there seventeen years—you still had to take theology classes. You had to take two years of English—classic composition, which was very well taught, the rules of rhetoric and grammar. You could get out of that after the two years were up, but then you took theology forever. You had to show up every Saturday morning, and it was biblical theology, moral theology, dogmatic, and every variety. Most of it was quite arid and very conservative. You didn't actually have to take tests or hand in papers—mostly you just sat. But you did get degrees eventually, which were in fact recognized by the state. So everybody who wrote columns on the paper had at least a Litt.M. or an M.A.

I ended up getting married to another young proofreader, Bernadette Lyon. The proof room was not just a workplace but a matching game because you had young, fairly intense Catholic boys just out of the service or out of college and girls, as we called them then, with the same history and the same interests and ideals. So there were several marriages that developed while I was there.

Soon after our marriage, Bernadette and I got active in interracial matters. There was an old, hardbitten Jesuit, Father William Markoe, there who had bounced around from place to place because he was always in trouble with his superiors over race. If he saw any white people with similar inclinations, he'd bring them together with blacks, or "Negroes." Finally we founded a De Porres Interracial Council—named for Blessed [now Saint] Martin de Porres, who was living proof of the benefits of miscegenation. Father Markoe made sure that we got in trouble, too. He had spies in the chancery and found out that they were going to start a parish gerrymandered to be all black. He got us to take a door-to-door survey, asking black Catholics in particular what they thought of this idea. A lot of them didn't like it—and just asking the question killed the plan by making it public before it could become a *fait accompli*. Of course, it was the archbishop's plan, and if you worked for the Register, you were working for the archbishop. I didn't get fired over that, but I was chastised. A black lawyer named Wendell Sayers and I were called to the chancery to get roasted by His Excellency in person.

Maybe the reason I wasn't fired was that I was doing pretty well. The local edition started a sports section and I was made sports editor—meaning that I covered the sports of all the Catholic high schools and the one Catholic men's college. A little later, the woman who had been writing the advice to the lovelorn column for the national edition quit to get married and I was asked whether I would take over for her under a pseudonym. I chose "Roberta Guidon." It was a terrible column. It generated very little mail from readers, so I was inventing the questions as well as the answers. But then I got a real letter with a real problem. It came from a woman at a secular college. Some of her classmates were sleeping with men and she wanted to know whether she had to quit school to get away from the occasion of sin. I was then under the influence of a magazine called *Integrity*, sort of an offshoot of the *Catholic Worker*, run by Ed Willock and Carol Jackson. It dealt with the lay apostolate, or Catholic Action, terms you hear much less often now. Borrowing from the *Integrity* ideology in answering, I said that of course you have to be aware of peer pressure, *but* you can't run away from all temptations—and if you stay you can set an example of how to be happy though pure. Some printer set it in type. He'd probably been there for years and was fully imbued with the Register's attitude toward sexual matters, so he brought a galley proof to the managing director, Monsignor John Cavanaugh, who brought it to Monsignor Smith. I was called into the monsignor's office, and he raged and raged, convinced that I had invented the question—when for once I hadn't. Everybody thought I'd be fired then. I wasn't, but Roberta Guidon died a quick death.

What eventually happened was this. There was a Maryknoll priest named Don Hessler who had been converted to Catholic Action in a Japanese concentration camp in China. After the war he had been sent to New Mexico to recover his health. I guess he recovered, but not by resting. He went around the state converting priests to the lay apostolate and to self-sacrifice; he was both holy and charismatic. I met him when he came through Denver. He was close to the archbishop of Santa Fe, Archbishop Byrne, and suggested to him that he should make his paper, which was part of the Register System, a little more *au courant*. The archbishop agreed, and Hessler said he had just the man for the job. So Bernadette and I went down and met the archbishop and I was hired. We started to sell our home, and quarters were obtained for us in Santa Fe. I submitted my resignation to John Cavanaugh, and Bernadette and I and our first child, Michael, were about to leave when a telegram came from the chancellor in Santa Fe: "Owing to circumstances beyond our control, the job offer is withdrawn." The circumstance beyond their control, Hessler found out, was that Monsignor Smith, my boss, had told Byrne that he could hire whomever he wanted as editor of his paper, but it couldn't be part of the Register chain if he hired Robert Hoyt. At the time, papers like the one in Santa Fe were heavily dependent on Denver—they couldn't afford to have enough staff or do their own printing. I then tried to withdraw my resignation, but Cavanaugh said that "other arrangements" had been made.

A little earlier, Carol Jackson, the coeditor of *Integrity*, had made a speaking tour around the nation, and when she came to Denver, she stayed in our home. When she got back to New York, she sent letters around to some of the people she'd met asking if they'd like to work for a Catholic daily. Some of us wrote back and said, "Sure, where do we apply?" And her answer was, "Well, there isn't one. Why don't you start one?" Well, by courtesy of Monsignors Smith and Cavanaugh, I was now loose, and others who had joined in with similar responses were available.

So when I lost my job in Denver, we all got together in Chicago to start a Catholic daily, and we did eventually, though not in Chicago. It was originally to be called the *Morning Star*, because that was one of the many titles of the Blessed Virgin, but it also sounded like a newspaper. We were well on the way to launching the paper when I had a phone call from an assistant chancellor who read me a statement from the Chicago archdiocese — obviously from the cardinal — saying that if we persisted we would be denounced from every pulpit and possibly excommunicated.

So we went bishop-shopping. We would've been accepted in St. Paul — we might have been accepted in a number of other places — but we settled on Kansas City, Missouri, partly because Geraldine Carrigan, a member of our group, had her home there, had a wide circle of friends, and was very close to the bishop of Kansas City, Edwin V. O'Hara. She was sort of his favorite lay apostle. We did get under way eventually, and we published from October 1950 until April 1951 under the name the *Sun Herald* — a translation of "Morning Star," which is the herald of the sun. After the paper folded, I drove a cab for a while, and then I was managing editor of a little daily in Independence, Missouri, which was published by the guy who had printed the *Sun Herald*. I was fired when I asked for a raise and ended up teaching in the local Jesuit high school for four years.

At one point, I asked the bishop who had accepted the *Sun Herald*, Bishop O'Hara, whether he'd like me to spruce up his diocesan paper. He said he would not put a lay person in charge of it. When he died, his successor was John Cody, who *did* want a better paper. It was clear that he wanted to be known, and sprucing up his paper was one way of becoming known. He was not in all respects an admirable guy, but he did pick very able young priests for his chancery staff. Two of them happened to be friends of mine, and when he asked his own staff if there was anyone around who could make his paper better, they both independently suggested me.

He offered me the job and made one of the priests, Vince Lovett, a very able and gutsy guy, business manager. I insisted on the title of editor—one of the first times I knew what I was about in dealing with the hierarchy. It was at that point that one of the Register people, the same Monsignor Cavanaugh who had maneuvered me off the staff in Denver, came to see Cody and warned him not to hire me. Cody's paper, you see, was part of the Register chain. By this time, though, the balance of power between the Register System and the individual papers had changed. Cheaper printing methods had developed, some dioceses had become more prosperous, and the Register could no longer just say, "Get out." So I became editor. Cody went back over the records of the existing paper to see how much money it had earned over the years. He then credited the paper with all that money—and it was a lot of money, which we proceeded to spend very fast. Because of that, we were able to attract a very gifted journalist, Jack Heher, to leave the Register headquarters in Denver and become our managing editor.

Cavanaugh and Smith must have guessed that it was our plan to get out of the Register System when we could. In two years we did—instead of the *Kansas City–St. Joseph Register*, we became the *Catholic Reporter*. We had a meeting with Cody about what the name of the paper would be. He had a great inspiration and he just beamed when he said it: "*Veritas!*" Our staff had already settled on *Catholic Reporter* because that was what was missing in the diocesan press—the reporting function. So it was wonderful. I just said to him, "Only one problem with *Veritas*—it means the same as *Pravda*." His face just fell apart—but he got the point right away.

It was a muddy first edition, but it contained a declaration written by me and signed by Cody that nothing in the paper was to be considered the official teaching or directive of the diocese unless it appeared over the bishop's signature, with the word "Official" printed above it. Later, because the paper began to get kudos—and it also began to get circulation outside of the diocese, which was very unusual aside from the *Davenport Catholic Messenger*—Cody was invited to be the keynote speaker at the annual meeting of the Catholic Press Association in Omaha. The CPA was then a large and thriving group, if somewhat obscure to outsiders. Cody asked me to write his speech, and I handed it to him as he was on his way to the plane—it wasn't by design, it's just that I never meet deadlines ahead of time. And so he gave the speech, word for word. I quoted it for years—a whole philosophy of freedom of the Catholic press, about which I became a great bore.

When Cody was transferred to New Orleans, his successor was Charles Helmsing. We were enjoying extradiocesan circulation, the paper was becoming well known and widely quoted, and what were we going to do about it? Vince Lovett, Mike Greene (who had succeeded Jack Heher), and I thought about doing a Sunday supplement like *Parade*, but that seemed impractical. Instead, the idea of creating a spinoff of the diocesan paper came to mind. Some local lay people were interested, and so was Dan Herr of the Thomas More Association in Chicago, who agreed to join the board. Eventually Martin Marty joined the board, and Robert E. Burns, the executive editor of *U.S. Catholic*, a magazine published by the Claretians in Chicago. We got a fifteen thousand dollar loan from St. John's Abbey in Collegeville, Minnesota, and we raised fifteen thousand dollars in Kansas City. But the biggest boost came from Bishop Helmsing, who agreed to let us keep on putting out the local paper while also launching the national, using the same office space and equipment and, at first, hiring only one new staffer, Bob Olmstead of the Associated Press. Helmsing was then in the first flush of his enthusiasm for Vatican II, and so he agreed to more than he thought he was agreeing to. He said that he agreed to our being independent, but he added, "Of course, you will accept my guidance." What he meant by that was that if he didn't like it, we wouldn't print it, and what we meant was that we'd listen and then decide, because we were independent and we were set up corporately that way.

The *National Catholic Reporter* started off with a circulation of eleven thousand and at its peak got up to a few hundred short of a hundred thousand. What accounted for that was, first, its near uniqueness — you had independent lay-controlled journals like *Commonweal*, but they weren't news gatherers, primarily — and then the spirit of the time. I remember, during the height of the Vatican Council, everybody was following every nuance of every story every day. You could print three stories about the same event at the council, and people would gobble up every word.

On the front page of the first edition, we had a story out of Los Angeles, part of which I did myself by phone. I was astonished to find that they would answer when I said, "This is the *National Catholic Reporter* calling." It was just a totally different sensation from calling up and saying that you were from the *Catholic Reporter*, because then they would say, "That's a diocesan paper, what the hell business is it of yours? That's what the [National Catholic] News Service in Washington is for." I was further astonished, then and many times later, that they answered at all. There was a lack of sophistication — it was as though "No comment" had never been invented. They could have killed off a lot of stories by stonewalling. Anyway, that story had something to do with the racial policies in the diocese, and it wouldn't have been covered, indeed, was *not* covered by the rest of the Catholic press.

Of course, once such a medium exists, you don't always have to find the news—a lot of it walks in or comes through the mail. I think our front-page humor column—"Cry Pax!"—also had something to do with the paper's popularity. It got tired, because it was a very formulaic thing, and I finally pushed it to the back page and then killed it. But I think that in the first several years it was terribly refreshing to a lot of people to have this kind of mostly gentle but still pointed *kidding* on the front page of a Catholic paper, talking about the charming and not so charming quirks of the Church institutional. We also had great columnists like [*Commonweal* editor] John Leo—I think we did something for him, but he certainly did something for *NCR*. He was gutsy and he writes clearly. And Garry Wills, who *became* a columnist really while writing for us. Wills was at *National Review* at the time and was, in fact, nominated by Bill Buckley for the job of being our loyal opposition. He wrote occasional articles for *National Review*, but not as a columnist. His first efforts for *NCR* were extremely scholarly and academic—high flown, highfalutin, and too long. He would tend to write a series of three columns on the same topic, which you just don't do in a weekly—I mean, who remembers?

Leo and Wills enjoyed a particular kind of repartee and became very close friends. Oddly now, Leo has become more conservative over the years, and although Wills is hard to characterize, he's moved away from Buckleyism. I also asked Wilfrid Sheed to be the movie reviewer for *NCR*—although it might have been the local edition at the time—and he said, "I don't go to the movies—you can't smoke in the movies." A month or so later he turned up as the movie critic for *Esquire*, but, of course, he was seeing his movies in screening rooms then where the rules are different.

If a bias toward openness is a liberal bias, then we had a liberal bias. I just think it was a bias toward a proper use of the press. Martin Marty, in one chapter of a book called *The Religious Press*, said that from Gutenberg's time, religion put the press in the service of the program. That's his terminology—I would say "in the service of the institution"—but all he meant was that the religious press was essentially a public relations instrument, not a journalistic one. The notion of journalism as free and independent but responsible and governed by criteria of fairness is a secular gift. It ought to have come out of the Church, in my view, but it didn't. Actually, most of the earliest local Catholic papers were independent and sometimes enterprising, even those that were owned and edited by individual priests. Gradually, that tradition died—they were bought out or

forced out because the bishops were nervous about their very independence. They didn't want newspapers, they wanted house organs.

One thing I haven't mentioned yet is the time we broke the story about
the secret papal Birth Control Commission reports. A lay Catholic journalist then in Rome named Gary MacEoin, who had covered a number
of stories for us, suggested to the people who had gotten hold of these
documents that they should go to *NCR* as well as to *Le Monde*. When the
word came to release the texts, I was at my desk for thirty-six hours
straight, helping to finish translating them from the Latin and French and
writing the story and editorial to go with the reports. Then *Le Monde* for
some reason didn't publish on the day it should have to be simultaneous
with us. So we were out there all alone, and we had telephone calls from
Australia and West Germany and all over. All three television networks
were in our offices, and the story got major play all over the world. The
point of recalling all this is Gary's reason for choosing *NCR* over, say,
the *New York Times*. He knew we would handle it better and that the
Times and the other media would still see it as an important story. And
I think he thought it was right for the story to be broken by an independent
Catholic paper.

The impact of the celibacy issue was interesting because we hadn't thought
about it much — it hadn't come up in the Vatican Council. We got a piece
from an assistant priest in some parish in Montana who wrote a reflection
on celibacy — its negatives, the variations in the tradition, and so forth
— that seemed to cover everything. I think it was a slow news week, and
we dubbed it "News Analysis" or something like that and put it on the
front page. An uproar! I mean not just of denunciation, but indicative of
an enormous latent interest.

Celibacy was one of the three or four issues that eventually soured
Bishop Helmsing on *NCR*. Helmsing had given us the go-ahead out of
the same instinct that governed his life: This is what the Church is doing,
this is what the Holy Father wants, whether the Holy Father is John XXIII
or Paul VI. Helmsing was neither liberal nor conservative. He was the
very model of the "good boy." So that when Helmsing first began to
hear from other bishops in this country, including those that outranked
him, he stood up to them for quite a while. He got a lot of crap thrown
at him by the bishops over *NCR* and he stood up to it for a long time —
as Cody had before, by the way, in connection with the *Catholic Reporter*.

But eventually Helmsing began to make his displeasure known. One
of our first offenses against Helmsing came when we ran a piece on how
Cody was being received in Chicago in his first six months there. It was

an evenhanded appraisal of what the priests and lay organizations there thought of him, and it revealed that they didn't like him very much. Cody was offended by this piece and withdrew his acceptance of an invitation to come to speak in Kansas City at the dedication of a high school that was to be named for him. Helmsing was grieved on that account. I said it was a fair story, that that was what people said to our reporter and what we should print. But increasingly it became doctrinal matters and sexual issues that we differed on.

At one point, Pope Paul VI talked with several bishops about certain Catholic publications in America. And Bishop Helmsing called me down to receive the news that the Pope was concerned about our brashness and rashness. Helmsing could be very grave about such matters. But he didn't have any control. He didn't assert it soon enough—had he done so, he probably could have cowed us or scared away readers. By the time he got serious, it was too late. I don't know if an excommunication—as he once threatened in the press—would have taken.

Ultimately, it was not a papal warning or a threat of excommunication that drove me out, but a good old-fashioned power struggle. Circulation was falling, and our publisher, Donald Thorman, blamed it on me. Some of his criticisms may have had some merit—I was tired and I was distracted by personal issues. But everyone else's circulation was falling, too: *Commonweal* was going down, *America* was going down, so were the liberal Protestant journals. After the publication of *Humanae Vitae*, the papal encyclical condemning "artificial" contraception, in 1968, a great many of the people who had been excited by Vatican II lost interest. A lot of them quit the Church and a lot of priests left the priesthood.

My hindsight feeling is that the *NCR* changed things instantly, or damn near. Other papers were not seeking out the news and printing it without fear or favor. The National Catholic News Service had to change. It was becoming more professional before *NCR*, but it was still very much a controlled instrument—it still is, to an extent. But now they can't *not* cover a story because the story is already out. I think that to most readers *NCR* was clearly out to live up to its name—which, as you know, was very carefully chosen. It wasn't out to get anybody. We weren't the only competent paper around, but we *were* competent and set some standards there, too. I think the paper's intellectual level was such that the increasingly educated Catholic lay and religious readers respected it and were able to make judgments about our fairness.

Now it's clear that we touched on areas that previously had been regarded as private matters to be dealt with by the corporate structure. But we were going under the postconciliar assumptions that it was everybody's Church and, so, everybody's business. Editorially, it's true, we would normally come down on the liberal side of issues, whether in the Church or in the world. But just by *reporting* stuff that wasn't supposed to be reported, we were perceived as being terrifically biased. Well, it was a journalistic rather than a theological or political stance. It may have had theological grounding that was liberal, and Charles Curran [the Catholic University priest recently censured by the Vatican over issues of sexual morality] today would uphold it. Of course, guys like him benefited from it.

On the other hand, we did lean over backward many times to be fair. There were plenty of people—hundreds of people, it now seems to me—who suggested that we take the word *Catholic* out of our title before Helmsing actually issued his statement demanding that we do precisely that. I always make the comparison to being Jewish—how do you stop being Jewish? I can't stop being Catholic in some way. I'm totally formed in that tradition—and I like it. I like the help that it has given to me in thinking, even in thinking my way out of some of what it's taught me. I just don't give anybody a license to determine that. If you were doing an essay, you'd have to write your way around the contradictions in this because authority is certainly part of the tradition. But I think it has always been the case that everybody defined Catholicism for himself or herself, and there are millions and billions of Catholicisms running around embodied that don't fit the standard operating definition.

About the effect of *NCR*, one thing I recall is a couple of letters that came in response to the editorial on *Humanae Vitae*. One of them was from a woman who said she was grateful for the editorial because it enabled her to leave the Church comfortably and in good conscience. The other was from a priest who said that because of the editorial, for the first time he understood what the doctrine was and why it was defendable. I wasn't after either of those objectives, but I felt good about that pair of responses. They suggest that people find it easier to think for themselves when they see others doing it.

Journalistically, one example of the change I'm talking about is that the documentation service now provided by the National Catholic News Service, called *Origins*, is something new under the Catholic sun. Lately they've been on a bit of a kick about authority and relations between bishops and theologians, and a recent issue carried a full statement by Father Curran. Twenty-five years ago that would have been inconceivable. This is the bishops' instrument, how can it print things that challenge the system?

How significant is that, you might ask? Curran is still fired. What difference does it make that Archbishop Hunthausen's troubles have brewed what looks like a real storm? You can say he's still shorn of his balls. My instinctive comment to Tom Fox, now editor of *NCR*, was Let's think about it as a phase. Nobody gives away power. You cannot strive for the kind of change that people are fumbling toward and trying to define for themselves without encountering resistance. It happens that the resistance is very ably led and that John Paul II is no pushover. I don't think Cardinal Ratzinger in the Vatican is very formidable intellectually, but just in terms of determination and consistency and brainpower, John Paul is a pretty unfortunate enemy.

I don't feel like emigrating because Ronald Reagan is president, although he's not *my* president and it's not *my* country that's bombing villages in Nicaragua, and so forth. There's no way to quit the Church that's appealing to me. And such phases have come and gone in the past. After John XXIII it did not appear possible ever to revert even this far. I think we're somewhat ahead of where we were with Pius XII. Most people don't have a memory of that time and of how even *liberal* Catholics were Pope worshipers, or damn near. I remember when Garry Wills was working for *National Review* and they ran an editorial on John XXIII's 1961 encyclical *Mater et Magistra*, and Garry wrote the headline "*Mater Si, Magistra No.*" It was openly and sharply critical of the economics in that encyclical and said that the Pope has no special faculties to write off the mysteries of free enterprise. That editorial — probably the headline more than the column, which I believe William F. Buckley wrote — caused a real furor. The liberal Catholic press attacked Buckley viciously as disloyal if not heretical. The *Catholic Reporter* and maybe one other paper defended his right to publish that kind of critique.

What I'm trying to get at is that what has happened since, and what's happening now because of this current wave of suppression, is that those Catholics who still care are better able to free themselves from distorted mystifications of traditional authority, the mumbo jumbo and the pseudosacralization of anything the people in charge want to defend, particularly if it is something that keeps them in charge, such as papal infallibility and the denial of power to women. That's Dan Callahan talking, but that perception is profound, the use of doctrine for power purposes. I find it unfortunate — and I'm sure Sidney [Callahan, Dan's wife] does as well — that Dan felt that he would be a hypocrite to keep on calling himself a Catholic when he can't accept the definition of Catholicism that is being exemplified in these kinds of repressive actions. But that's giving away the store, that's giving away the ball game.

All institutions—which is what my book would like to be about, if I can get at it—are potentially repressive and regressive and power hungry. And yet you have to have institutions. I think religion must be institutionalized in order to survive and serve, to be effective. So if it starts to go bad, some people will fight back. If I had been brought up a Mormon, I might have felt free to quit. But I admire that Mormon woman I've read about who puts out an unofficial Mormon magazine and hangs right in there. She's been excommunicated or whatever their term is, but she just goes on and is starting a liberation movement within the Mormon church. On the other hand, I still think there is something other than institutionalism in *this* institution, the Catholic Church.

FRANK ZAPPA

Wrinkled Shoes

Dominus Vo-bisque 'em
Et come spear a tu-tu, oh!
Won't you eat my sleazy pancakes
Just for Saintly Alfonzo
They're so light 'n fluffy-white
We'll make a fortune by tonite.
—Frank Zappa
  "St. Alfonzo's Pancake Breakfast" on *Apostrophe (')*

That's right, remember there is a big
difference between kneeling down
and bending over . . .
—Frank Zappa
  "Heavenly Bank Account" on *You Are What You Is*

The titles of the songs Frank Zappa has written over the past twenty years convey the information that their author is someone who does just about what he wants to do. And if compositions such as "Chrome Plated Megaphone of Destiny," "Call Any Vegetable," or "The Voice of Cheese" sound like the work of a drug-frayed sensibility, Zappa will tell you quite convincingly that he can't even smoke a joint without falling asleep. ("The '60s were just one big chemical experiment put on by the CIA," he once told the *Washington Post*. "Taking drugs and dropping out. *Rolling Stone* magazine, you know, is a CIA plot—has been since 1968.") Nevertheless, Zappa has been credited with originating the "free-form mixture of what would become, for many, psychedelic or acid-rock." Like a kind of pop music Peter Schickele, Zappa created some of the earliest rock parodies ("Duke of Prunes") and had the temerity, at a time when the

Beatles were not merely gods but the future of the music industry, to produce an album-length parody of *Sgt. Pepper* called *We're Only in It for the Money*. His first LP, the 1966 *Freak Out!*, has been described as "a precursor of today's punk," whereas it was really rock's first "concept" album.

Influenced by black rhythm and blues of the late fifties and the work of Edgard Varèse, Zappa's music managed to offend as many people as possible and to find only a modest audience in this country. Like jazz and other recent classical music forms, his work continues to be more popular in Europe and Japan than in the States. Although the song titles may read like a raunchier P.D.Q. Bach ("The Dog Breath Variations" or "Prelude to the Afternoon of a Sexually Aroused Gas Mask"), the music that has fun with myriad musical idioms from Nashville to *Sprechstimme*. In 1970, he joined forces with Zubin Mehta and the Los Angeles Philharmonic to stage the première of Zappa's *200 Motels*, a concatenation of "serious" and "nonserious" music that stretched both about as far as they should ever go. When the sheet music called for the violin section to belch, literally, the musicians drew the line and said "Blurp" instead. Zappa's only major hit single was a 1974 song called "Don't Eat the Yellow Snow." His 1982 collaboration with his daughter Moon Unit, "Valley Girl," not only brought Zappa back into the spotlight but put phrases like "grody to the max" and "gag me with a spoon" into the national vocabulary — much to Zappa's dismay. More recently, Zappa has become an outspoken opponent of government attempts to censor song lyrics.

Even a casual familiarity with Zappa's work will alert one to the fact that he enjoys being thought a blasphemer. He recently created a radio satire on show business with monologist Eric Bogosian. *Blood on the Canvas* purports to be a musical comedy about onstage castration and death and, says Zappa, "it's probably the most blasphemous thing anyone has ever heard." Or maybe he just likes to go against the grain: asked what he was planning to name his fourth child, Zappa said, "If it's a boy, we'll name it Burt Reynolds, and if it's a girl, Clint Eastwood." He has written songs called "Catholic Girls" and "Jewish Princess," but most of his religious fervor has been reserved for the fundamentalist right, in songs such as "Heavenly Bank Account" and "The Meek Shall Inherit Nothing." Like those compositions, his remarks in this interview were on the record well before recent scandals focused national attention on the foibles of television evangelists. In fact, the reader will be quick to realize that Frank Zappa has no use for organized religion of any sort — which may come as a major relief to clerics the world over.

I'M CERTAINLY NOT a devouter, but I did used to be. I was pretty devout up until the time I was eighteen, and then I said, What the fuck is going on here? But it wasn't really connected with the rigamarole of the Church. If I'd been raised in any other kind of religion, I think I would've been just as devout because it felt correct at that time in my life to be devout. But the more you get into the rigamarole and look at what the dogma is and see how the machinery of the Church shuts people's minds off, and the more you learn about the business end of the Church and the history of the Church, from an objective point of view, then the more chance there is that you will decide that it is possible for a human being still to be quite fond of Jesus and wind up hating *any* church. That's a theoretical possibility.

By the time I was eighteen, I'd read enough about other different types of religion, seen enough examples of hypocrisy just at a local church level, that I had to say to myself, This is not for me. It's not something that I wish to continue to participate in, so that's it: thanks a lot, goodbye. Now, nobody was banging me over the head. I didn't come from a family where everybody was kneeling and squirming all over the place in holy water fonts. I just liked it. It felt right for me — I was that kind of a kid. Some kids have that mystical bent, they can envision the whole aura of religion and it gets to them. That was my style at that time. It does blow over — you *can* escape.

Sure, I had religious feelings, but that's not something that you quantize by whether or not Jesus, or a replica or representative thereof, is whispering in your ear. I don't think that necessarily has anything to do with spiritual feelings. It's like when you listen to music: you either get it or you don't. A real religious feeling transcends the brand of the religion. It doesn't make any difference if it's Hebrew or Moslem or any of the little splinter Christian things. You got it or you don't have it, and no amount of banging you over the head is going to instill it in you. You can't inflict that on somebody. That's the thing you can really learn to hate about the dogma, because it *is* like, "Repeat after me." And then you have to ask yourself, Why am I repeating after *you?* Who in the fuck are *you?* Why are you so terrific? You dress like Halloween, but other than that, what are you telling me? Why are you improving my spiritual health here? Because I've already got it, I don't need you.

You can practice spirituality and lead a good life without going through the dogmatic machinery of any kind of religion. I think that many people have found that for themselves — one of the statistics is that there are forty million unchurched in the United States today. That does not mean that they're atheists or that they're hateful people; it just means simply that they do not subscribe to any particular brand of rigamarole. Nor do they invest in it. I would consider myself to be religious but unchurched. I intend to remain that way, and I'm going to continue to raise my children that way. And I would advise anybody who has the chance to escape from an organized religion right now to get his ass out as fast as possible. The reason I say that is that basically every religion has revealed itself to be a real estate scam, especially in the United States. The whole thing is tied to real estate. A wise man once said that the only difference between a cult and a religion is the amount of real estate they own. Guys who start off in a storefront wind up conning the people who want some sort of spirituality into donating money. In the United States this is all tax exempt. They can't be audited by the IRS, they're protected by a lot of different laws. They take this money and instead of sending it to that little black child with flies on its nose that you saw on television, they put it into some real estate investment someplace. And that investment is spun off into something else, and the next thing you know you've got a guy in a silk suit with a Southern accent, a lot of political power, and a lot of money in the bank, telling a lot of lies and leading people down the primrose path, and that's got nothing to do with spirituality.

I hate that kind of religion, and I think that that gives a bad name to religious feeling. It should be done away with because it's like bunco. There should be a religious Bunco Squad to go out there and clean this stuff up. And if Jesus came back today, He would be the Sergeant on the religious Bunco Squad. Look at what's happening with the rise of the fundamentalist right. How can they presume to be any more moral or religious than anyone else? That is not a conclusion that one could draw from their behavior or the way in which they advise various governmental leaders on foreign policy. You've got Pat Robertson advocating assassination—nice religious man he is, and he wants to run for president. Apparently he doesn't know about some of the laws that are already on the books. I find this reprehensible.

There are too many inconsistencies, too much ego involved in the people who are earning their living beating on a Bible or beating on anything else. The same sort of religious ignorance extends to every one of the religions that you can look at in the world today. When one guy says, "God's talkin' to me, and we're right, we're the chosen ones, only you an' me are goin' to heaven and everybody else is an infidel and they oughta die"—that's what gives you wars and shit. I think it would be a good idea to get away from religion as fast as possible, especially that kind.

. . .

My father's dead; my mother still goes to church, but she's not fanatical. When I was a kid, they took me to Mass. I didn't make it every week nonstop, but it was the usual stuff: you didn't eat meat on Friday, you went to church, you went to confession. I did all that stuff—I had communion, I had confirmation, and I bailed out. I went to parochial school for two weeks. They hit me on the hand with a ruler, and I said this is not for me, and I refused to go back. My folks wanted me to be an altar boy—all Catholic parents want their son to be an altar boy. This was in Maryland, by the way, a very Catholic state. They have some funny rules there. For example, the existing law defines pornography as showing depictions of illicit sex—and the first item in the definition of illicit sex is "sexual intercourse."

I went to catechism classes, though—the Baltimore Catechism, remember that one? I remember them showing me something like a map chart with big pictures: "Here is limbo . . . here's hell, wooooooo." And they flip the page: "You don't want to go there, do you?" They had little competitions where the prize was that you got a relic if you recited certain things. I remember receiving a relic, a little cardboard card and a little package with something sewn up in it—under pain of death you may not open this thing to find out what the fuck is lurking in there.

Then there was the scapular business—you're never supposed to take it off. How can you do this? These strings are gonna rot from sweat, y'know? You go through life with brown felt stinky things with a picture sewn on one side and some strings that are full of sweat going over your shoulder. You're supposed to wear this under your clothes for the rest of your life? I didn't like that. Then there were the brown corduroy pants they wanted you to wear. And the other thing was a lot of kneeling down—and the way that it crinkles your shoes. That really used to bother me. How would you like to go around with the toes of your shoes pointing up with wrinkles across them? You could spot Catholics a mile away.

I don't think that I ever really had the desire to be a priest because I found out early on that they didn't get to have sex. But I do have the kind of mentality for monklike detail work, which is a requisite for doing musical composition when you get into writing dots. It could take you sixteen hours to draw one page, one orchestral page, which occupies two to three seconds of music in real time. You've gotta have a bit of a monklike attitude to want to write something like that, especially knowing that in America the chances of its ever getting played are minimal. I'd say there is a certain correlation to something like that. I did have a monastic mentality for doing that kind of stuff, but celibacy—not a terrific plan.

There's a lot to be said for having a vocation, if you think that you're going to do good for your fellow man.

Anyway, around the time I was sixteen I started reading books on comparative religion. In fact, there was one book called *Comparative Religions* that had everything from Zoroastrianism to Buddhism. I didn't just read that book and go, Aw, now this is all horseshit and I'm quitting. It wasn't like that. But I read a bunch of stuff, and by the time I was eighteen I bailed out. I just refused to go anymore to Mass, I would no longer go to confession or do any of that kind of stuff. I said, That's it, cancel — which horrified my parents. They thought, Oh my God, oh no. My boy is goin' to hell. He's goin' to page three of that big chart in the catechism class.

I started reading about Zen, which I found the most attractive of all the philosophical points of view at the time that I was studying that stuff. I thought, Now look, *this* makes sense. This is real. Why didn't somebody tell me about this before? Because given the choice between Zen Buddhism and being a Catholic, I would say Zen is probably a better investment.

You hear people talking about how you're supposed to be a good this and a good that. You hear 'em talking about it, but you want to see 'em do it. You want to see an example. And when the examples don't match the rhetoric, you have to question whether or not there's any value to the rhetoric. And I haven't seen any examples of people living up to their faith. I wanna see a saint. Show me a saint. I don't want just a little card with a bone chip in a packet. I don't believe in saints; show me a real saint guy.

I wasn't very political at the point where I left the Church. My main interests in life were sex and rock 'n' roll — or rather, sex and rhythm and blues. I just couldn't see how it was humanly correct the way the Church was approaching sex. A devout Catholic would probably say, "Well, how arrogant of *you* to set yourself up against the Church and decide for your own self that the Church is wrong and you're right." And to that I would say, "If you feel that I'll be going to hell, then I have the right to disagree with you." To me it was stupid and wrong. If you're gonna play the game, you're gonna play it all the way. If you're gonna be that devout, you gotta do all the rigamarole. I'm not a halfway guy. If I couldn't do the whole thing, I wasn't going to do any of it. It just didn't add up.

I would never deny anybody else the right to go for it all the way. The manager of that TV station who wouldn't put a condom ad on the air and believes that if he did he would go to hell, he is *welcome* to that guilt, to whatever he imagines his heaven is going to be. Anybody who wants it can have it, just don't inflict it on me. I think free will is more important.

I've always liked the sound of Gregorian chants, that sort of monastic monody. I like that medieval aroma. In fact, I can still remember the tune of the "Kyrie" that they were singing at my confirmation. That lick pops into my head sometimes, and I've wound up playing it on the guitar in the middle of solos—I swear to God. It's a great tune, and I just hear it and I'll say, Yeah, that would fit right in there. There's all different kinds of "Kyries," but that particular one stuck with me.

I like the medieval-sounding stuff because the minute I first heard it, it just had a familiar ring to me: I've been there before, I remember that one, that's real to me. And the other music that I really like is black church music, gospel. I used to have those albums along with the rhythm and blues albums—the Mighty Clouds of Joy, the original Staples Singers stuff, the Five Blind Boys, great stuff. I can't stand those bland-o Christian hymns that they have on Falwell's show.

I was never that crazy about the incense. Burning balsam is not my idea of a good time; it used to gag me. But there's something I'll always remember from my grandmother's funeral. The choir was singing and I could see from the way that the candle flames were wavering that they were responding to the sound waves coming from the choir. That was when I realized that sound, music, had a physical presence and that it could move the air around.

This was long before I even thought of writing music. My parents did not have a record player—the only music I would hear would be by accident, if I heard it on somebody's radio or if I heard the singing in church. I do not come from what you would describe as a musical family. The earliest music that I remember hearing was those Gregorian chants in the church and, one time, I don't remember where, Arab music. I immediately liked it. But up until the time I was fourteen or fifteen, there was absolutely no way to play music in the house. If I would be riding in the car and turn the station to any kind of rock 'n' roll or rhythm and blues, they would turn it off. I couldn't even hear it. No classical music, nothing.

In a way that was really great because I didn't grow up with my parents' musical taste—they didn't have any. So I didn't have any preconceived notions dumped on me by what my parents listened to. I'll give you an idea of my parents' taste in music. When I finally got a record player, it was a Decca, the kind with legs and the speaker on the bottom—this cheesoid little thing. With the record player you got two free records from the store. One of them was "The Little Shoemaker" by some singing group on Mercury. It was from the same mentality as "How Much Is That Doggie in the Window?" "He would tap, tap, tap, tap. . . ." You know? That kind of stuff. My mother liked that record and would play it while she was ironing, and it was the only one she had. Within a week or so of getting that record player, I had bought the Edgard Varèse album, volume one. And since the record player was located next to the ironing board, you can imagine the turmoil that was caused when I put on *Ionisation*. So it wasn't too long afterward that the record player was permanently moved from next to the ironing board to my bedroom, where I could listen to that "crap" all by myself.

What music is literally is a recipe for sculpted air, because that's the way you hear it. Now, your sensation of the piece is going to be determined by where you hear it: in your living room, in a corner of the cathedral, front row center in front of the orchestra. It could be the same piece, but depending on where you hear it, you're hearing a different version of the sculpture. You have a volume of air in an enclosed space, the loudspeakers or the instruments perturb the air, the air is sculpted into a shape, the ear detects the shape and converts that into a sensation, and you compute it: good, bad, or indifferent. So if you don't think about what you're doing to air molecules when you write music, you're missing part of the message. And if you don't realize how people perceive it or what the mechanism of perception is, then you're overlooking one of the more important facets of the craft—that you're an air sculptor.

That day at the catechism class when they were flipping the page over and saying, "Here's hell," it didn't even scare me at the time, I thought it was *laughable*. Even as a kid, and wanting to be religious and wanting to believe in stuff, I felt that that was a rather useless thing to do in a catechism class, to show a kid an illustration of bogus demons and stuff. That was a really dumb medieval scare tactic.

I think that there are different psychological and physiological types, and some types of people have an affinity for mystical or spiritual or religious or ethereal stuff—it's in 'em from birth. Other people have total interests in sports and nothing else; other people, math. Whatever it is, if you come to terms with it yourself and realize what kind of type you are and feel comfortable inside your own skin, with your own aptitudes and liability, then you can get on with your own life. Not all children are like that. You can't just say that children are naturally drawn to religion. Some go for it in a big way—it feels good to them because it seems right, it's in phase with who and what they are. And I was one of those kids, that's it.

But a kid like that has got really high expectations of performance from the people who represent that phenomenon that is natural to them. Let's say you're a very religious kid or one of those mystical kids, and that's natural to you. And then you're put in the context of an organized religion, and the religion is playing upon and reinforcing that natural instinct. If the practitioners of that religion do not live up to your expectations of how holy they should be, you have a "phase aberration." It's as if the lip-synch is bad, it's not quite registering right.

The other tendency that I would presume for kids with that type of mentality is that they themselves are perfectionists and demand certain levels of perfection—usually unattainable—from the people around them. And they try to ask the same kind of shit from themselves up until the point when they find out what they can and cannot accomplish. Some people will always try to attain more than they can realistically do and wind up being totally miserable and eventually find out, You can do this but you can't do that. That doesn't mean that you settle for *shit*, but you start looking for achievable goals, and that becomes your idea of your perfection.

The sooner you let any child discover what that level of expectable attainment is, then the better you're going to be able to let the child get on with his or her life rather than always holding out, "There's heaven out there and you have to be *this good* to get there." Because that way you're going to thwart that kid, you're going to make him weird, you're gonna twist him.

In my case, there's no specific incident that I could point to and say, "And then so and so let me down." It wasn't like that. I have a kind of analytical mind. I take a situation and I look at it and try to figure out what's really going on. I hear this, I hear that; I see this, I see that. Add it up, what do you get? If what you get is out of phase, then you have two choices: you either phase up to the artificiality of what you've been presented with, and thereby thwart yourself; or you say, Fuck this, and go for what you know and let *them* be out of phase. And you let *them* get the ulcers.

There are reasonable things that could be stated in the philosophy of *any* religion. You can always find something in there of which you could say, Yeah, that's true and it works! But it's all the fine print and the dogma that the priests or practitioners in each of these religions have embroidered on to the basic goodness of their philosophy that make the money—it's all the boilerplate that they add in there. It's like when you sign a contract with a record company: the deal points are okay, but the boilerplate takes them all back, you know? The zinger is on page twenty-seven and you need a microscope to find it. And that's the same way it is in most of the religions.

I don't sit my kids down and say, Now I'm gonna tell you about the Ten Commandments. But what I do say is this: The minute people start talking to you about Jesus, get away from 'em. And any time you see a television show with a phone number at the bottom of the screen, turn it.

Daniel Callahan and Sidney Callahan

Spiritual Tennis

I became a Catholic at twenty. Now, I've been a Catholic forever, but you know they always think you're a convert no matter how long it's been. But everyone's always been kind and wonderful to me, I've never had any bad experiences at all in the Church, so I think that's quite a different feeling from many people I've known who've been born Catholic.
— Sidney Callahan

I might as well have been born in 1968.
— Daniel Callahan
  Quoted in the *Critic*, Fall 1977

I was a sophomore at St. John's University in New York in the fall of 1965 when twenty-one faculty members were summarily fired by the Vincentian-run institution. One of the hit songs blasting out of the radio of my '57 Ford Fairlane that summer was Barry McGuire's ode to pop apocalypse, "Eve of Destruction," and it must have seemed to me at the time that at least a little chunk of the prophecy was coming true. One minute my friends and I were sitting around the Honors Program lounge reading *Christ and Apollo*, *The Heart of Man*, and Maritain and Bonhoeffer and thrilling to the changes of Vatican II; the next we were out on the street, picketing and trying to keep out of the draft. We felt doubly deserted by the Catholic educational system, betrayed, in fact, with few lights to steer by.

One of the Catholic writers taking this kind of ferment seriously was Daniel Callahan, the young *Commonweal* editor who had just written a book called *Honesty in the Church*. (No doctrinaire liberal, Callahan questioned the honesty not merely of the Catholic bureaucracy but also of the liberal reformers.) Fellow Harvard alumnus and Church reformer Michael Novak wrote at the time, "No one has better articulated the experience, aspirations, and dilemmas of liberal Catholics in America than Daniel Callahan." And so we felt. Callahan went on to publish a book of essays (*The New Church*) in which he made clear his priorities as a Catholic. "I, for one," he wrote, "would be perfectly willing to see the ruination of the Church if that was the price necessary for personal freedom." It was an exhilarating statement for an exhilarating time in the life of Catholic intellectuals, but in retrospect it appears to have been an adumbration of Callahan's disaffection for the faith itself. By 1970, he had produced the classic *Abortion: Law, Choice and Morality*, in which he tried to discover a sane middle ground between the Church's bias toward fetal life alone and abortion on request, which he felt was based solely on women's rights. At that point Callahan was gone from *Commonweal* and on his way out of the Church, too, although that didn't discourage the Thomas More Association from naming *Abortion* the best Catholic book of the year.

But his fascination with ethical dilemmas was already manifest. Around that time, Callahan cofounded the Hastings Center in Hastings-on-Hudson, New York — a think-tank approach to ethical issues in biomedicine. Today he serves as the center's director, with a staff of twenty-five who consult and question each other about the ethics of involuntary sterilization, organ transplants, drug-induced behavior control, genetic engineering, euthanasia, and other moral issues that may have replaced the debates over papal infallibility and the perpetual virginity of Mary which once preoccupied him. "There are things I miss that I enjoyed at *Commonweal*," Callahan told John Deedy in the *Critic* some years later. "Like the personal feuds that are a part of the Catholic experience — the running fights, for instance, with Andrew Greeley. Like having sport with the bishops. There's not room for funny doings in this work."

Sidney Cornelia de Shazo converted to Catholicism shortly before marrying Daniel Callahan. By her own admission a refugee from a formalized Southern Methodist agnosticism, she was at one time mistakenly called the Catholic Betty Friedan — mistakenly because Friedan herself accused Sidney of being a sellout for saying she enjoyed housework. Yet in the course of bearing and raising six children, Callahan wrote as many books and became an award-winning syndicated columnist for the *National Catholic Reporter*. (Talk about having it all.) Her 1965 book *The Illusion of Eve: Modern Woman's Search for Identity* was a ground-breaking Catholic feminist work which *Time* called "both a defense of traditional femininity and a plea for the right of women to find creative expression outside the home." An outspoken feminist and pro-life advocate, Callahan has consistently refused to adopt a party line if it goes against her personal religious beliefs and is often called out to debate other feminists for breaking ranks. With her husband she edited *Abortion: Understanding Differences*, a series of interviews with women on the subject.

In talking about a topic such as abortion, Daniel and Sidney Callahan can be seen to contend like familiar adversaries on the tennis court— trading volleys, charging the net, looking for an opening, and loving every minute of it. Daniel, the ex-Catholic who has evolved a rather idiosyncratic pro-choice position, at one point found his lectures being leafleted by protesters with copies of his staunchly Catholic wife's pro-life articles. (Apparently the protesters were unaware of the conjugal link between the speaker and the unwitting broadsider, the kind of plot element that in a made-for-TV movie would elicit groans and a sudden craving for Cheez Doodles.) Sidney and Dan still haven't resolved their differences, as is evident from much of this interview, but after thirty-three years of marriage they wouldn't have it any other way.

DANIEL: I grew up in Washington, D.C., which was an unusual city to grow up in as a Catholic because it didn't have many Catholics. I moved to Boston later in life and I discovered there were twenty-five Daniel J. Callahans in the phone book. But in Washington, D.C., there was only one, the man I was named after. So there really wasn't any Irish ghetto. My father was in radio. He started out as a newspaper reporter, then he managed a number of radio stations in Washington, New Orleans, Boston, and then ended up back in D.C. publishing newspapers. We were sort of upper middle class.

I went to Catholic school in Washington — St. John's College, which was actually a high school — starting in the eighth grade. When I hear about other people's Catholic education, I realize ours was comparatively relaxed. We had Christian Brothers who were fairly genial and not academically high-powered by any means, so the atmosphere was certainly Catholic but it was never oppressive — although I did have some nuns in grammar school who were mean, at St. Thomas the Apostle by Twenty-seventh Street.

My father was a kind of lapsed Catholic. Like a lot of Catholic males, he seemed to *believe* but he didn't go to church very much. He made sure that I went to church, but he didn't go. Toward the end of his life he went, but for a long period, about twenty to twenty-five years, he didn't go. My mother was more pious, but she was a more sophisticated Catholic woman than many others of her generation. She was born in Washington in 1895.

But the environment was Catholic enough that when I wanted to go to Yale everybody thought that was a rather daring thing to do. It was not only different socially, but also it was thought that you ended up atheist if you went to a non-Catholic or Ivy League college. William Buckley was the Big Man on Campus at the time—in fact, he was brought in to assure us that one could be Catholic at Yale. But it helped to be preppy, which he was. Coming from a Catholic high school in Washington, D.C., was not prep school background.

I was comfortable with my religious training to that point, because it was the only thing I knew. It was so much a part of the culture that I grew up in that I just took it for granted. I guess most of our friends were Catholic, too, so it wasn't as if I had much to compare it with. Our neighborhood wasn't so much Catholic, but I guess by virtue of going to Catholic schools, most of my friends were Catholic. It all seemed perfectly natural.

I was never an altar boy. My parents were never too eager to have me be one. I was never asked and had no interest in doing it, which made me one of the few people who didn't, particularly if you were at all pious, as I was during high school—mildly so, that is. But I never got anywhere near that. I got pretty religious in high school and stayed that way until my mid-thirties—from about sixteen through thirty-five I was pretty pious, I would say. In fact, that's when I began to be interested professionally and wrote about it also. Even though Sidney remembers my once talking about becoming a priest, I never really pursued it. A surprising number of Catholics who were active intellectual Catholics and writers were in the seminary for a short time, but I never was.

In grammar school we had Holy Cross nuns; they used to go back and forth to the Holy Cross Academy. They weren't an impressive group, as I recall.

SIDNEY: They impressed *me*.

DANIEL: I had always had philosophical inclinations—even in high school I was asking a lot of questions. I thought I discovered those things later in life, until I ran across somebody I used to sit next to in high school, and he said, "Oh no, you were always interested in those things." I hadn't realized that. But I guess it was as I went along in college that

I became more intellectually interested in Catholicism, philosophy, and theology. By the time I was near the end of college I decided I wanted to go into philosophy professionally. That's also when I started to write about things Catholic. It was a big thing in those days to become a "Catholic intellectual." I had met some interesting Catholics at Yale, but back then it was still fairly anti-Catholic. I mean, a Buckley did okay, but the rest of us didn't, unless you were from old or very wealthy Catholic stock. But not a lot of Catholics went to those places who came from Catholic schools. So there was always a very strong clash of cultures and values. We all had certain professors who took glee in assaulting Catholics. There used to be almost a type in college, the aggressive atheist, and every college seemed to have an aggressive atheist who really evangelized atheism. At Yale there were two or three such people who were famous for assaulting everybody's religion, but I don't hear about those people on campuses anymore.

SIDNEY: They've lost the faith, too.

DANIEL: Religion is not such an interesting target to attack anymore, for whatever reason. They were sort of aggressive secular humanists—often ex–religious believers themselves, who wanted to spend the rest of their career attacking the whole thing. By my senior year in college I was very religious and interested in things Catholic intellectual and wanted to make my career in that field. I turned all of my personal interests into a career—whereupon I met Sidney.

SIDNEY: My parents had left any religious identity behind them when they came north from Alabama. My father was decidedly antireligious. He believed in science and the Enlightenment and hated the old superstitious Baptist-Presbyterian-Methodist background he had come from, but it's hard to get Calvinism out of the system. All his family was very religious, so when people ask me, "What were you raised?" I always say, "Lapsed Calvinist." It's a kind of secular but still Protestant view, although they really weren't interested in religion at all. Both of my parents were born in Alabama. I was always interested in religion, but I can't decide whether it was because of my aunts or because of the black servants who told us about those things that I always had a sense of God's presence and a keen interest in religious things.

I didn't ever go to any church until one day when somebody came to our school. In those days there wasn't division of church and state; we were taught religion in the schools. A woman came to school and she was just this marvelous person. She talked about death and dying, about how caterpillars become butterflies, and about how God loves us. Then she said, "Now you have to go to Sunday school, and you have a little chart here and you put a gold star in every time you go to Sunday school." Well, I was a good little girl and anything to get gold stars, my heavens, or maybe it was butterflies, I don't remember, but anyway I started going to the Methodist Sunday school with my friend. We would get up in the morning, and my parents would be hung over. The house would be a mess from their party—they were big drinking, socialite types. I'd pick my way through and go to Sunday school feeling soooo, so smug—better than all of them, right?

But I really believed, too, and I was trying to get it all together. I was a little person who read all the time; I just read the local library. It all went together with the little girls' books, with the idealism of Louisa May Alcott. It was a special kind of almost nineteenth-century childhood in some funny ways—I've thought about that a lot. I think I'm really much more akin to the nineteenth century than the twentieth because I was formed in this Victorian idealism. The books that I read and the schools that I went to and my parents' ideals—they weren't religious ideals, just a simple message: "Be perfect." At least girls were supposed to be perfect—I just had one sister. My father was allowed to be totally the way he wanted to be, but women were supposed to be perfect. And I *was* just perfect—never told a lie, never did anything wrong, got all A's.

My aunts were a big influence on me in the sense that my parents had been divorced and I was raised by my father. Then he remarried and I had a stepmother, so all these feminine influences were very important. I've thought a lot about how strong the women were in my family. Although it was a very machismo, male-dominated setup, the really great people were the women, black and white. I always had an uneasy feeling that my parents *should* be religious—I know that it's right to be religious because that's the way it should be, and why weren't they? And then I went to Sunday school, where that was reinforced. My father's reaction to my going to Sunday school was interesting. He said, "I don't believe in that, but if you want to that's fine. But if you *start*, you *have to finish*." This was the message of perseverance and finishing things. I've thought about that many times: finishing is the important thing. So I wound up becoming a Methodist, because that was the Sunday school I went to. They came to visit my parents, and my parents said, "Okay, you can do it."

Then, during the war, we moved around to various places and finally to Washington. My father got out of the navy and started a practice in Washington, D.C. I went to the Baptist church. It wasn't very exciting. When my father went back to sea—he went back into the navy—my stepmother, who was residually religious — she didn't do it while he was around — went around the corner from our house to this interesting new little church that had just been started which turned out to be famous later, the Church of the Savior in Washington. It started the Potter's House and all these wonderful things, but it was started by a young Baptist minister who had come back from the war, and he called it an ecumenical church. It involved study and discipline and tithing. They read all the Christian classics in education and I just think what my life would have been if I hadn't met that church because it had just the most wonderful people. They were about twenty-eight or thirty, and I wondered would I ever be that old, will I ever be able to be as grown up as they are? They were wonderful models for a young person of thirteen or fourteen. I became interested in the church and joined. My sister and I were the youngest members. My father was unhappy about this because it was really a much more religious commitment, but it was just a wonderful experience.

By this time I was going to a fancy girls' school, since my father had taken us out of public school. I was going back to Holton Arms where I had gone in first grade. My parents weren't too much on women being intellectuals but felt they should be ladies. That created a great conflict with my religious thought because it was very worldly there. The thing was to "come out," to have a debut, or to be very preppy, so I had a sense of conflict. At Holton Arms my headmistress said, "Sidney, I've thought about you, and you should go to Bryn Mawr." I said, "What, where, what's that?" I only knew about Sweet Briar and Southern schools, and my stepmother had been to Duke, so I thought I would go to Duke or Sweet Briar or something like that. But I won a scholarship and went off to Bryn Mawr. I loved it there. Everything my parents feared would happen, happened. It was okay to be an intellectual there, so it was a very broadening kind of experience.

You see, my parents knew about horrible girls who went to Radcliffe and became very left wing and liberal. I was constantly in conflict with my family because I had these advanced views. I didn't believe in segregation, didn't believe in this and that, was a feminist of sorts — but we got along pretty well. They were very proud of me at the same time that we'd fight and struggle.

I was a member of the Church of the Savior in Washington, D.C., but when I went to college, I started seeking someplace to worship. I went to a Methodist church, which was terrible; the Presbyterian church was worse; finally I went to the Quakers and that was wonderful. I had a whole year when I was very interested in the Quakers, and then that really wasn't quite right for me, and I went to the Episcopal church.

First the Low Episcopal church, then the High Episcopal church, and then finally I burst out of my cocoon into the Roman Catholic Church. And it was such a wonderful thing to do, I cannot tell you how *unhappy* it made my parents. It was so terrific, adolescent rebellion: screw your parents! Phooey on you, Miss Lerton and Holton Arms! And all right, you Bryn Mawr snobs, I'm going to become a Catholic — which was like getting leprosy.

DANIEL: You see, both of us had this experience. So many Catholics grew up with all Catholics and they had to fight against it, whereas both of us grew up with a lot of prejudice against Catholics. So you had a sense of being persecuted by the people outside, not the people inside, and that made a real difference. Bryn Mawr was even worse than Yale. At least Yale was large and sophisticated, but Bryn Mawr had *no* Catholics at all.

SIDNEY: Bryn Mawr was very antireligious, period. I had been very religious when I came and they wouldn't allow anything on campus because it would be divisive. All my professors were atheists — the aggressive atheist type. It was a real culture shock in that way, but it did make me even more interested in religion. You know, there's nothing like persecution to make you more ardent. To become a Catholic was such a wonderful thing, but you get caught in these adolescent rebellions forever, right? These wonderful gestures that change your life.

Anna Freud said somewhere that the adolescent defense against the upsurge of sexuality and instinctual drives is to take up asceticism and intellectuality. In a certain sense, those are wonderful defenses and I took them up with great fervor. It keeps you out of trouble like nothing else, to be a very religious person and a very intellectual person. In my case it also started me on a life of achievement, so it was a wonderful adolescent period compared to what some other children had. Plus, in those days, before the sexual revolution, it was possible to do all those things that I did and still go out every single night with *thousands* of men. It was great! I'd never kiss *anybody*. You just went to parties and dances, and it was always romantic. That's why I say it was a nineteenth-century girlhood in a sense. I just had a ball. A Southern belle I was on the outside; I was an intellectual, but it didn't show. My parents told me, "Don't be too smart; nobody will marry you." But going to a girls' school, it was fine: you just were very smart in school and very fun outside.

I was about twenty when I converted to Catholicism. My father kept me up the whole night before I went, arguing about how horrible it was. He didn't think he'd ever live to see the day when this would happen. It made me all the more determined. It was both déclassé and superstitious. Of all the religions, it was the worst, and it was not acceptable as far as society was concerned. Alabama was very anti-Catholic, although it could have been worse. I could have become Jewish or married a Jew. One of my cousins was going to marry a Jew and I thought the whole family was going to faint. Catholics were the next worst, and blacks would have been unthinkable, absolutely unthinkable.

Now that I think back, the ceremonies surrounding my conversion were terrible. That's not the way they do it today. They made me be rebaptized. I think I've been baptized three times. It turned out that I had been baptized Episcopalian — I didn't know that my mother had had me baptized in the Episcopalian Cathedral — and then I had been baptized as a Methodist. But you only have to be baptized once. I waltzed into St. Matthew's Cathedral with *Commonweal* in my hand, and the priest said, "Why have you come here?" And I said, "Because I hate the architecture and I know Joe McCarthy comes here, and I decided that I should enter the Church at the pits so that it could never get any worse."

This guy turned out to be McCarthy's friend who had married him, an old, fat, slobby, horrible man. He said, "I don't think you and I are going to get along." So he turned me over to another priest. This was a lovely French priest about whom he said, "He's a French Huguenot heretic, too." He already knew I was going to be a heretic. The French priest had come back from India. He was a mystical person and we just believed in the Holy Spirit together. I said, "Well what about the Index?" And he said, "Oh, don't worry about that." And I said, "Oh, I didn't think I would!" We sailed through instruction. I had already bred myself in the Church anyway. Then he baptized me and I went to confession and first communion and that was it. It was very nice. This was in 1953, after I had met Dan. I wouldn't have done it, I don't think, without—

DANIEL: I was interested and then Sidney got interested. You always denied that it was because of me. You said that I was the occasion, not the cause.

SIDNEY: I wouldn't sell my soul. People always used to say, "Oh wasn't that nice of you to do it for Dan," and I thought, What do they think I am that I would change my religion because of somebody? I had a friend at Bryn Mawr who also became a Catholic at that time. I wouldn't have known about *Commonweal* except for my friend Elizabeth — she and I were sort of seeking together.

DANIEL: We met when Sidney was a freshman at Bryn Mawr and I was a senior at Yale. We met at a party in Washington and we started going out.

SIDNEY: No, we met in your junior year, because it was the junior prom. I couldn't remember what he looked like but I had never been to Yale so I said I'd go.

DANIEL: Another thing that got her in trouble. In fact, my being a Catholic was a big obstacle for a while. Because in those days you didn't marry a non-Catholic, if you were pious as I was. So it was a big crisis, but it was going to be resolved by my going into the army. I would presumably get shipped off to Germany and we would have all this time apart. So I got sent to Washington, D.C., instead.

SIDNEY: First he got sent to Indiantown Gap, which is an hour from Bryn Mawr. So we ended up getting married at the end of my junior year, in 1954. But I had worked it out so that I would finish Bryn Mawr no matter what. I had already worked out my courses so I could come back and graduate.

DANIEL: I lived at home with my parents during my military career. I was in the Counter-Intelligence Corps. We really did counterintelligence, security checks. One of the advantages to being in the CIC was that you didn't live on army bases and you wore civilian clothes. Saved a lot of money and took the bus to the Pentagon. Basically what we did was walk around the Pentagon at night and check to see whether people had locked their safes and locked their drawers. You can imagine spending two years, midnight to eight A.M., walking around the Pentagon—not high-level stuff. But I tell my children about my war career, and it sounds really dramatic.

When I was still in the army, I went to graduate school in philosophy at Georgetown. I knew by the time I had graduated from college that I wanted to go into philosophy, so I was able to start at Georgetown. Interestingly, I had been born in the old Georgetown University Hospital, and when I went back they had built a new one, but the old one had been turned into offices and the department of philosophy was there, so it was . . .

SIDNEY: Back to the womb.

DANIEL: It really was—back in the building I was born in. I went to get my master's about 1955, then went to Harvard in the fall of 1956, by which time I did have an M.A. from Georgetown. I suppose the first article I ever did was one Sidney and I did together in 1958, on Catholic colleges.

SIDNEY: Neither of us had ever seen a Catholic school.

DANIEL: Telling everybody what was wrong with Catholic education.

SIDNEY: Typical.

DANIEL: Anyway, I went into straight philosophy, which I came to despise thoroughly. It was very boring and technical and tiresome and not what I had hoped philosophy to be. It wasn't directly antithetical to Catholicism, but it was just indifferent to the whole thing. They weren't even interested in religious issues, so there was nobody who even cared.

SIDNEY: There was a lot of persecution. They thought that Catholics were stupid.

DANIEL: They really did think that Catholics were stupid, so you had to answer a certain number of ridiculous questions about all kinds of stuff. I went into philosophy at Harvard. I was still very interested in religious issues, but the Harvard philosophy department was just hostile to those interests. It was very strong in analytic philosophy. I had to satisfy my religious interests by spending time at the Harvard Divinity School. Those were the first days of ecumenism and we had a little circle of interested Catholics and Protestant students. And then there was a famous Catholic historian, Christopher Dawson, who got the first Catholic chair at Harvard [the Chauncey Stillman Chair of Roman Catholic Studies]. By that time I had started writing a little bit in *Commonweal*, and I had been active in the Catholic Club—

SIDNEY: We sort of started the Catholic Club there.

DANIEL: So they got to know me and eventually I was asked to work with Dawson, as his assistant. That was pretty interesting because he was a cultural historian involved in religious culture. That kept alive a lot of my interest, which was utterly unsatisfied in the philosophy department. I went there from fifty-six to sixty-one, and we were very active in Catholic affairs there. I was already writing for *Commonweal*, mainly book reviews. The first book I wrote was on the ecumenical movement, a collection of essays by Catholics and Protestants which was published in 1961, called *Christianity Divided*. That was one of the first books published on ecumenism in those days. I had a kind of split career at Harvard. I was doing straight philosophy, but I was also hanging out at the divinity school and doing all these other things on the side. I guess around 1960 or 1961 I started to get known a little bit, because I met an editor at Scribner's who was looking for some books by Catholics. I had an idea to do a book about the Catholic laity, which turned out to be *The Mind of the Catholic Layman*, which I started when I was a graduate student. That came out in 1963.

So I had this funny career; the two parts of my psyche were operating in different parts of Harvard University, and there wasn't much overlap. In 1961, I guess when I finished all my work and actually had to go out and get a job, I originally intended to teach but decided it might be fun to be a *Commonweal* editor. So I applied for a job there. I intended to work for *Commonweal* for a couple of years and then go back to academic philosophy, but I never did get back to it. I found that I enjoyed New York. And I guess it's still true that New York is one of the few cities where you can have an intellectual life apart from the university. They didn't let us know about that at Harvard, where the assumption was that intelligent people are only at universities. And I just liked the style and pace. *Commonweal*'s offices were at Thirty-ninth Street and Madison and I started there as associate editor.

It was also an interesting, dynamic time in Catholicism, the time of the Ecumenical Council. It was ideal for somebody like me who grew up in a Catholic environment, got to Yale where there were all kinds of countercurrents against that, and turned my personal problems into my profession.

SIDNEY: We were very excited about the council because we were the *Commonweal* Catholics and very interested in Dorothy Day and the Catholic Worker movement. That had been a great influence on us, so we were trying to live the life that Dorothy Day would want us to live, which was dedicated to poverty and Providence. I had often thought that I had never gotten my life so together as at that period because your intellectual life, your family life, your liturgical life was all unified in this very exciting way. It all worked together—a very intense time for us, also a very brilliant time. And because we were very poor and being persecuted, we were in an even more manic state to survive—and one of the things at that time was trusting in Providence. You wouldn't use contraception, nor would you use rhythm if you were really a "truster." So we didn't and what happened was that we had seven children in ten years, and that's what I was doing. I was living the intellectual life, but at the same time I was leading a life of intense physical activity. You can imagine, doing all the work and all the physical care, while Daniel was often at the library. At Christmas he would study, at Easter he would study—and I was coping, the "earth mother." We had babies in the charity clinic, and along the way I had decided that I should have all these children by natural childbirth. They had never heard about that. So here I was, fighting them—fighting Harvard, fighting my family, fighting the obstetricians.

DANIEL: There is something about all this that is very difficult especially for my non-Catholic friends to understand, and that is the combination of being a left-wing liberal and a pious Catholic. They don't understand that you could be liberals while you were having all of these children. That was a strange mix.

SIDNEY: We were taking the Franciscan and the Jesuit ideals and trying to live them as lay persons—highly intellectual and believing in Providence. And merging the two. On the one hand, we had the Benedictine ideal of manual labor, which said that you were sanctified in the world by your work. I didn't feel as if I was being oppressed. I felt that this was the way to be a saint! To be doing your manual labor at the same time as you were doing your intellectual work. We had interesting friends.

DANIEL: Many people were at Harvard at the same time: John Noonan, Michael Novak, Harvey Cox, a lot of people who later became prominent writers. But in the late fifties and early sixties they were all graduate students.

SIDNEY: Here I was, having these babies and reading, with all these interesting people to talk to. Basically, I don't think I had any difficulties. I crashed when we moved to Hastings. For one, we had had a tragedy—one of our boys died suddenly, our fourth boy, and that was just *horrible*. As I look back, I think I must have been depressed anyway, really. I was never very open to anything psychological in those days because I'd relinquished all that, and so I just wasn't attuned to the fact that this might be a psychological problem. I had difficulty overcoming that. Dan went off to work, and there I was, stuck in that house, with those three little children. I didn't know anybody, there were no intellectuals around—those were tough times for me at that period.

Then I decided I couldn't wait to go back to graduate school. I was going to have six children by the time I was thirty and a Ph.D. by the time I was thirty-five. Then I was going to work by forty. I had this all planned out when we got married. Dan wanted twelve children, and I said, "I can't have twelve children; I'm going to have six children because I want a career." The idea was that this was going to be a little magical family because at that time, of course, neither one of us had seen a baby. We were spoiled. We'd had servants, we didn't know anything. Dan had one brother, I had one sister; we didn't know what kind of work it would be. We had ideals and set ideas about things. Our parents used to say, "Isn't it nice that Dan and Sidney found each other?"

DANIEL: Sidney's father was particularly distressed because I was going into philosophy. Which meant I was going to be a student forever— no money, a Catholic who wouldn't use contraception. As a son-in-law, I was a bad scene in every possible respect.

SIDNEY: I was so sad that my father never lived to see Dan's triumph. Although the *rest* of my relatives did! I did *better* than them all! My husband is more successful than any of *their* husbands. So it was great, it was delightful.

But getting back to the story, I was really depressed and lonesome in Hastings. Dan was down in the city and I was stuck with the kiddies, whom I adored—but it was always much more fun when there were loads of other young mothers and children around whom I could talk to, like at Harvard with the graduate students. It must have been around that time I decided that I had to do something. Philip Sharper, a Catholic editor, said, "Why don't you write a book about women?" I agreed. I said, "Sure, if Dan can write a book, I can write a book." Very competitive. "All the other people we know can write books, I'll write a book." I had written one book review up until this time, mind you. So I started to write a book, and I don't know how I did it. People said, "How did you do all that?" and I would say, "It must have been somebody else." I was desperate, I guess. I needed to have some intellectual stimulation. I would get a baby-sitter for two hours a day. That was my writing time. Later, I did have a column in the *NCR*. But I just wrote this book, *The Illusion of Eve*, and delivered it—boom, here it is. By the way, I had two more children by the time I was I finished with the book—and the day I delivered the manuscript I must have been pregnant because then I had another child by the time the book came out. The book was a big success and it was published in different languages. It was one of the first Christian feminist books. I was trying to bring it all together, which led to this career going around the country and talking—which led to another book, then eventually to the column, which led to another book. But still, I wanted to go to graduate school. Finally, I went to Sarah Lawrence and got a master's degree and practiced psychotherapy for a while. Then I went to CUNY and got a Ph.D. in 1980 and I taught for a while. My education took twenty-five years. I always tell my students I studied on the twenty-five-year plan. It was *terribly* difficult at that time to keep the family going, keep Dan going, keep graduate school going, keep work going—I was also working three days a week. It was a very hard period.

DANIEL: I went to work for *Commonweal* in 1961. I was an editor there from 1961 to 1968 and I guess it was somewhere around 1967 or 1968 that I started fading from Catholicism. In fact, I wrote some articles which, if anyone had read carefully at the time, might have shown what was going on. I wrote one article saying that people left the Church in two ways. Most people left the Church because they got angry at the Church, and there were a lot of people in the sixties who did that. Some became Protestants, but not too many — John Cogley became Episcopalian, as a matter of fact, but that was rare. Most of them didn't become anything, yet they remained religious. Then there were the others who weren't angry at the Church but ceased really being theist and religious believers. I was among the latter group, which I think was a smaller group. I was never particularly angry at the Church one way or the other. Even when I was writing on things Catholic I was considered a reformer and radical type. We knew many angry people, and I was very mild in comparison with the genuinely unhappy people.

In my own case, I think that the first symptom of falling away was that I couldn't stand any worship service or any literature. I would get just absolutely, exquisitely bored going to church under any circumstances. It wasn't the fact that they were suddenly having folk Masses that turned me off. Although I had written an article at one point saying that I had known a fair number of Catholics who were unhappy as Catholics in a lot of vague ways who had placed a lot of hope in the Catholic reforms and still they were unhappy. They realized that whatever their problems had been, they weren't going to be solved by having the reforms. I faded out from the whole thing and ceased being a believer, ceased going to church, never particularly becoming angry, and I suppose respecting the whole thing all the while and remaining interested in it, which I am to this day. To many of my nonreligious colleagues, I am just another Catholic. An ex-Catholic is a Catholic — it's a kind of Catholic. It's just a matter of whether you believe or not, which is a trivial matter. As far as they can see, I'm Catholic because I'm always saying, "No, the Pope didn't boil the baby. No, the Pope doesn't have mistresses." And, they say, "Oh, you Catholics." I could write a funny piece to correct other people's mistaken notions of Catholicism. People just say such absolutely stupid things. I am always defending Catholicism. I remain friendly with all my Catholic circle.

SIDNEY: I felt totally betrayed by Dan's loss of faith. It was horrible, but that's the way it was. I thought he would believe if he could, so I just accepted it. I had to accept it: what else was there to do? I think we argued and it was very painful for a long period, but then we just stopped talking about it. I think there is pain on both sides if you change your beliefs or your thoughts about something. That's just part of living with somebody and being married. You do change and you have to accept that if you're going to stay married. Besides, Christians believe love overcomes everything. So you're committed to that.

There was a fear that it would carry over into our personal life, a great fear. I didn't think it would affect my belief. The real crux of the whole matter for a while was that Dan thought, "I'm leaving, now aren't you going to leave, too?" I said, "What's that got to do with me?" But everybody I knew was leaving. It was a great trial in the sixties, one of the two great trials. The other trial was that those who were staying Catholic were going off into crazy, violent things while I was a pacifist. The people who gave me great sustenance during that period were people like Dan Berrigan and Dorothy Day because they never wavered in their belief. So with all the people who left around me, which was almost everyone, there was still enough support from those people whom I admired. I was able to survive. Sometimes, in my worst moments, I thought that I had driven everybody away so I could be the only one going to church again, like in my childhood. Here I am all by myself, going to church! I could feel persecuted again.

The worst thing was trying to keep the children within the Church, because I was then left all by myself to do that. I taught Sunday school for seven years. My major response to any struggle or any sort of problem is to try harder: I will overcome this, I will try harder. So I tried harder. The children weren't in parochial school. Our school was terrible. I wouldn't have sent a dog there. When we first moved there, one nun was dying of cancer and she would put the children in waste-paper baskets, beat them up, that kind of thing. I would never have sent anyone there. It's always been a poor parish, but there is more hope now. Things are better now. But it became clear to me that you couldn't raise children to be Catholics without a Catholic community. Especially if one parent is not a Catholic, you need to have the community.

It was a horrible time to be raising children, period. The Vietnam War — it was just like being in a war at home, I really think it was. I think we should all get medals for having survived. You talk to any parents who had children at the time, and they'll tell you what a terrible period that was. There are people who are still walking wounded from that period. Drugs came to the middle classes for the first time and nobody knew what to do. All authorities were crumbling and the Church was a mess — not a mess, but at least there was confusion. All in all, it was a very difficult period to be raising children. Most of my children, who are now between the ages of twenty-two and thirty-two, are no longer in the Church. But Mark, my oldest one, says he's a Catholic. But I say, "If you're a Catholic, how would anybody know? What are you going to do about it?"

DANIEL: I think they know, in a certain sense, that they are culturally Catholic. But they don't go to church.

SIDNEY: I don't think the little ones know if they're Catholic. The three
little ones. At least I got the first three through confirmation. But since
they made confirmation an individual, free choice, I couldn't force the
others to do it anymore.

DANIEL: Our kids were all highly rebellious types, too.

SIDNEY: Where did they get that from? I think we deserved it. When I
think of all the trouble I gave my parents. If my parents could have
lived to see how I got back everything I gave them, in spades. . . .
But now we're all great, jolly friends, the kids and us, so it's wonderful.

DANIEL: They were never super down on us. They rebelled at school,
but we never had terrible struggles with them.

SIDNEY: Sweetie, you just weren't around.

DANIEL: I don't interpret that as being against us, so much as against a
lot of other things.

SIDNEY: Oh, that's nice. They don't remember any of it. Mark was just
the most awful, horrible child. Now he thinks that he was just the
perfect child. He doesn't understand young people today. They brought
it up, too. They can't remember a thing. Memory is wonderful. Time
is wonderful. Time heals so many things.

DANIEL: My interest in ethics was always there. When I was religious I
had an interest in ethics, maybe not as pronounced as it is now, but
even as a graduate student of philosophy, ethics was one of my stronger
points. After I'd worked at *Commonweal* for about seven years, I was
fading from the Church, but, frankly, I was just tired of being a magazine
editor. Particularly a weekly, which is a very repetitious routine, and
so I really wanted to leave. I got a grant to write *Abortion: Law, Choice
and Morality*, and I left *Commonweal* and stayed home to work on my
book. I did the book on abortion not so much because I was trying to
promote a particular viewpoint but mainly because I wanted to show
how a philosopher might handle a problem like that. In those days
philosophers really didn't deal with factual questions of that sort. It
was during that period that I discovered medical ethics. I was forced
to try to figure out what I was doing with my own career since I had
decided I didn't like teaching, and I didn't think I wanted to go back
to working for a magazine. I started the Hastings Center in part because
the issues seemed important but also because it solved my own career
problem.

I got interested in the issues in about 1968, when I was doing my
work on abortion, and then spent about a year and a half with this vague
idea of getting a center together to work on these issues. Then I met

Willard Gaylin, a psychiatrist whom I had come to know socially in Hastings, and presented him with this idea I had to start a center and asked if he would be interested. And he was. We really took off after that. We recruited other people. The center was in my house until the fall of 1970. As it stands now, the center is a nonprofit organization supported by grants, individual contributions, some corporate contributions, and our membership program. We have a budget of one and a half million dollars.

In terms of religion and Catholicism, in one sense, certainly, there was discontinuity when I left religion, both personally and professionally. I went into a different field, and now I spend my time around doctors and lawyers. I've worked with a lot of people, many of whom have never *heard* of *Commonweal*, much less about me and my earlier career. Once in a while I'll meet someone who remembers me at *Commonweal*, but for the most part I work with people who are secular, not religious. However, by virtue of my background I have brought different things to the center from other people. Ethics is a very heavily secular field. Although there are some theologians of some importance in the field, most of the people are rather secular types. In the beginning, in the sixties and early seventies, there were more theologians who were influential in the field, but it began to change as it became larger and more popular. I would say the theological influences declined and the secular ones became stronger. What made me different from my colleagues at the center was that I remained, at least intellectually, religious. I was able to bring Catholics in, even after I had left the Church. I wasn't alienated and I felt the Catholic sensibility was important and should be represented, though it was often a struggle because some people were very down on religion or just thought it was irrelevant.

When I am questioned as to what I might base my ethical principles on, if not on the notion of a Supreme Being and religious beliefs, I remind people that ethics has had a whole secular history going back to Socrates and Aristotle's *Ethics*. It *has* had a religious history — obviously, Judaism and Christianity have been very powerful — but there is a secular tradition of ethics as well. The main argument that has always gone on in ethics is What are the necessary foundations of morality? There would be some who would say that you eventually have to move ethics into a religious belief system and others who would argue that that is not true at all. Philosophically, ethics has always had a basic problem with its own foundations: how can you develop ethics on the basis of reason alone? Many people over the years have said you can, and others have said you can't. But even if they said, "No, you can't,'' for many it doesn't drive them back to religion — it makes them more relativist, or skeptics. It's a two-thousand-year-old argument that continues.

As regards secular humanism, I always felt I didn't want to leave one religion to join another. There is a kind of secular humanism that is just as dopey and dogmatic in its way as Catholicism ever was. There is a sort of liberal fundamentalism and some very authoritarian dogmatic types, each of whom claims that he or she is an authority on the subject. But they have as many dogmatic clichés about their own values as any Catholic ever had. I never found it that appealing, and I never came out feeling that any other community was any better. In fact, in working with things ethical, I find a certain rigorously secular temperament rather narrow. It's not a very rich tradition. Catholics always seemed to me to have far more varied intellectual perspectives and traditions than your typical nonreligious atheist, who often has an intellectually narrow point of view. But when I work in ethics, I find that you have to bring in different perspectives and keep stirring up the pot. My joke is that you can't raise children under the credo of the ACLU.

Looking at the resurgence of Christian fundamentalism, I think we see a need for something that secular humanism cannot fill. The question is Why did people go to that rather than liberal Protestantism or mainline Protestantism? It might be because it is far more emotional, maybe embodying a sense of community. An awful lot of mainline ethics in this country is dominated by individualism. The principal moral value is autonomy — our primary values would lie somewhere between autonomy and equality. That has always seemed inadequate to me. It says to me that the purpose of ethics is to give people free choice, and they can use their free choice however they wish as long as they don't harm others. Taking an ethic straight out of John Stuart Mill — liberty — I find that too thin. I don't think it is adequate, and certainly I don't think it works with a lot of serious issues in medical ethics. However, there are people who think that it's fine, and in a pluralistic society that's the way we can have it, because it maximizes individuality. I have been trying to develop a notion of medical ethics which would have a more communal basis, which would find some way to look at morality other than to begin and end with autonomy and equality. There are a lot of critiques around of liberal individualism, not all of them right wing. In fact, there are eternal debates within liberalism itself, and I find those interesting.

The book I wrote after *Abortion: Law, Choice and Morality*, around 1980, was actually based on an idea of Sidney's. We had been arguing about abortion all that time, and I guess it would be fair to say that although each of us was on a different side in the abortion debate, we are both in the general spectrum of views probably considered to be maverick. Even though I am clearly pro-choice, I am something of a troublemaker within the pro-choice camp because I press certain questions that I don't think they care to see pressed. For instance, I ended the book on abortion by asking how women should use their freedom morally. I think that, for a lot of feminists, it is a tough question. Women are supposed to be free and we're not supposed to ask what they're to do with their freedom. But I think it *is* important, as a matter of ethics. Not that it would differ from what men should do with their freedom—the point is, I would like to see public *discussion* of the *use* of freedoms. Most of the debate turned on ''Let's have women free and have the law leave them alone,'' and we got that with *Roe v. Wade*. Now, I am interested in what I have always been interested in, which is What do women morally think about when they use their freedom? How should they morally decide whether to have an abortion or not to have an abortion? It seems to me that subject should be one for open moral debate, but generally speaking, most feminists don't think so. They think that is a way of chipping away at women's freedom. I feel that the pro-choice movement is going to be in serious trouble in the long run unless those women who are in it are prepared to have some moral debate and not simply emphasize freedom under the law, as if that is the end of the discussion—which is what they tend to do.

What I mean by trouble is that, first of all, there are many pressures from the pro-life side that have chipped away at them. This is not so much true of the older generation—the first reformers, women in their forties, fifties, and sixties now—but there is a younger generation of women coming along who have slightly different attitudes, and they are comparatively more open to the arguments of the pro-lifers than some of the initial reformers are. Much of the abortion reform movement is so resistant to talking about any of these things, so dismissive about any concern for the fetus, about any concern about women's use of their freedom, that I think they're just hiding from some important realities that are a part of the abortion debate. They have to take them much more seriously, and, I find, as in so many debates, people say one thing in public and another in private. There are many troubled pro-choice people who know they have problems, but they feel that for political reasons they can't talk about these things publicly, even with each other, and I think that is a foolish course to follow. I was told when I wrote my abortion book—at that time I was no longer a

Catholic — that only a Catholic would have spent so much time on the fetus, that the number of pages itself betrayed me. It is interesting to see, just by looking at the index of any book on abortion, how much space is given to the subject: maybe one page in a book by a feminist, whereas the pro-life people are the other way around, pages and pages on the fetus, but nothing on women. You can watch people's biases just by the quantity of space they accord a given issue.

In the book, I oversimplified my views. I thought the fetus's status was uncertain, at least early in pregnancy, and for purposes of the law, given that uncertainty, we should favor women, let them make the choice; but later, in the second trimester, it's a different matter.

Meanwhile, I think women should be very sparing with their use of abortion. Given the large number of abortions in this country, it is hard to believe there is enough moral seriousness about the issue. Whether or not you consider the fetus to be a human being, you should worry about whether it is — one should really wrestle with oneself. And beyond that, the law leaves room because it's morally uncertain, but in your individual conscience you might have a higher system and you have to ask what you do in the face of the uncertainty. I think a woman has to have a very serious reason to have an abortion. I have been persuaded by Sidney over the years that if you ask this question of most feminists — "Do you think women are tough, strong; can they work ten, twelve, fourteen hours a day, can they compete with men in the marketplace?" — the answer is "*Right on!*" But if you ask if they think they can raise a baby, then it's "Oh, gee, I don't know." Pregnancy has been managed for centuries, and the question a woman has to ask is What do you do about any crisis in your life that poses a threat? What difference is it going to make in the long run? People can rise above their immediate crises. I suppose our own experience has something to do with that, having had children under all sorts of unfavorable circumstances, and things worked out. I don't want to condemn such women, but I want them to take this whole thing seriously and not immediately assume they can't do it. Social reforms would make things much easier for women, undoubtedly. There are some who don't want the emotional burdens, and then there are the borderline cases — women who could manage if someone could help them to do so. But they often think they can't. It seems that women find it a much bigger deal than it was twenty-five years ago. I don't know if it actually is, but it certainly is perceived that way.

SIDNEY: I often receive opposition from feminists on my pro-life stand. I feel that a pro-life position is a truer feminist position in the sense that it's more in tune with women's bodies and women's real well-being. Letting women have abortions doesn't solve the problems women are having. We need to have a lot more support and be able to be who we are. We don't have to turn our bodies into male bodies in order to get into the world. We should be able to work and have education *and* have reproduction if that's what we're doing. I want the world to change, not for us to mutilate ourselves to join the team.

DANIEL: If I'm a kind of conservative pro-choice, Sidney's a liberal pro-life. Most of the pro-life people have a reputation of being conservative and right wing.

SIDNEY: No, I think that, interestingly enough, the Catholic bishops, like Cardinal Bernardin in Chicago, have advanced the consistent life ethic — they're against abortion but also against capital punishment and nuclear weapons and so on. Because I'm a pacifist, I'm against any violent solution and am pro-life. For the first time in my life, the bishops are where I think they ought to be, leading in the direction of peace and against capital punishment, against war, and against abortion, so I'm very happy.

DANIEL: I'm not a pacifist, so I believe there can be just wars and, in hard situations, just abortions. I don't have a consistent pro-life ethic in the same sense, but I'm being consistent too.

SIDNEY: I always felt that you thought that abortion ought to be available to women but that there weren't any immoral abortions that would ever be conducted under your system.

DANIEL: No, I wouldn't say not *any*. Not a lot, maybe.

SIDNEY: Whereas I'm always very soft, and anybody who actually has an abortion I understand totally.

DANIEL: Well, we used to laugh and say that my position is that abortion ought to be legal but no woman ought ever to choose one, and Sidney's was that it ought to be illegal, but no woman should ever be prosecuted. So that's the absolutely perfect solution.

SIDNEY: I feel that for women to have abortions is like men having to go to Vietnam. You can understand that the whole society set you up to do it — there's absolutely total pressure. To resist pressure to have an abortion today is almost like being a conscientious objector when you're eighteen years old. And I feel the same way about people who came back from Vietnam as I do about women who've had abortions — I would never judge anyone on their choice of what they did. I can work to make a different kind of society where nobody goes to war and where abortions won't be necessary, but I wouldn't judge women who have them.

. . .

DANIEL: A lot of my moral positions are ones that I feel I've arrived at by purely rational means. But if you asked my non-Catholic colleagues, they would say, "Yeah, but he always seems to come out with positions that are more like Catholic positions than our atheist positions." For instance, I'm against euthanasia, and I think there are perfectly solid philosophical reasons to be against euthanasia. But the point is that most people who are against euthanasia are Catholic. Anybody would then have to say that obviously my background makes the difference. Of course, I point out to my secular friends that they have backgrounds too, and if they think they just got there by reason alone, I'll ask them why it is that everybody from their background also believes the same. There's no more reason to believe that they've achieved their position by pure reason than that I have.

   But if you want to address my lack of religious belief today, I would say that I certainly don't feel I've replaced it in any way, and I don't care. I don't feel any need for it at all. I suppose there are certain times when intellectually it would be nice to have a coherent understanding of the world, of a sort which religious belief gives one, but then I don't find any of the available religious beliefs plausible. Having had it, I know how nice it is to have that kind of view — were it only true. In my case, I fell away because I got sort of tone deaf toward the worship and the liturgy, whereas for many people that would be the last thing to go. It was like getting symptoms of cancer. I was absolutely bored at Mass, I just could not keep my mind on the whole thing. I would say, "Something's wrong here. I'm just not with this anymore." I wrote an article, in fact, called "Religious Slum Dwellers," where I admitted that I was in an unusual position because most of my fellow believers talked about experiences of transcendence and I didn't have any at all. That made it very difficult for me to appreciate a lot of things, which is why I referred to people like me as religious slum dwellers, who had to try to make do without these experiences. And I found that I couldn't make do for very long.

SIDNEY: Did you have them when you were in high school and college, and then they stopped?

DANIEL: Yeah, I guess so. I did, but then they all seemed to fade out eventually. So I guess to me — which is probably the hardest thing for Sidney — it's just an absolute big blank. It's as if people say, "What do you think of Mount Shasta?" And I say, "Nothing. I don't have any feeling for Mount Shasta." Literally, this doesn't exist in my psyche — there's a hole there. I don't think ethics explains all the problems of life and the problems of meaning; there are a variety of other things that ethics does not adequately deal with. In fact, there are ethical problems it *can't* deal with. That's the problem when you do ethics without a religious perspective. There are certain kinds of issues you come up against where it's very hard to do that: explaining the meaning of suffering or the kind of sacrifice that some kinds of moral situations can require of somebody. If you don't have a religious perspective, it's extraordinarily hard to know how in the world you would ever justify sacrifice. I'm writing now on the elderly, where some family member, who usually turns out to be a daughter, is forced to give up her life and happiness and take care of an elderly sick parent. It's pretty hard to find any basis in the secular ethic to do that kind of thing.

By and large, that would be the difference between religious and nonreligious people, I think. I would say that if you took a poll, the nonreligious people would say that she doesn't have an obligation to her parents, you can't ask that of someone — if she does that it's nice, but she doesn't have a duty. Whereas I think most religious people would say, Well, it's a lousy deal but ya gotta do it anyway. I think the religious attitude is clearly preferable, but it's also harder to justify intellectually. It may be that you can only *do* it if you have a religious view of life and you have a way of making sense of this.

As a believer, I guess I was always more rationalistic than most. To me, the important thing about religion was not the spirit or feeling, but a certain coherent view of the world. So by extension, the person who takes care of the elderly parent does so because he believes that the world is a certain way. They may have some religious feelings that keep this alive within them. But I still think that they would feel, This is not a crazy, absurd, unjust world. If you do the morally right thing, which may require great demands of you, you will not in the end be confounded. You will be satisfied in some ultimate reckoning.

SIDNEY: I was just going to say to Dan that he said it was a lack of transcendent experience that made it impossible for him to go on. I think of religion as something that you *do*, more than a concept. It's very important that it's rationally all there — I'm a rationalist too, and I do believe that you can reason through to *almost* faith. Faith is just one little leap beyond reason — not even a huge gap — and I think reason can take you a long way. But ultimately it's the experiential quality of religion that really makes it live. And that's the thing that makes you able to keep doing the things that reason tells you you *should* do but you can't do unless you have an experience of feeling, and it's all about love and forgiveness and compassion. You can't do that without the prayer and the sense of somehow being in contact with God. It's almost like . . . electricity, juice. The images in the gospel are very interesting: you'll wither without the vine; salt loses its savor. If I don't continue going to Mass, I just don't care about anybody, I get very selfish. I can just see myself withering immediately. So that's why I always say to the kids when they ask me why I have to go to Mass, "Because I'm so much worse a person than all of you. You're all naturally good. If I don't go to Mass, I get mean as anything." I do have a sense of needing it.

SIDNEY: I'm very alarmed by the retrenchment in the Church from the Vatican II reforms. I've been spending a lot of time and energy lately not only trying to hang on to the reforms that we've had, but pushing onward to get even more structural changes that I think we need. I'm worried about the American Church on a superficial political level.

DANIEL: But you can't imagine leaving the Church. The Pope could go around shooting people and you'd say, "Well, he's a jerk and he shouldn't do it"—but you're not going to leave the Church. Yet you know a lot of others who really do think of leaving the Church if they get unhappy enough. Sidney is certainly strongly in favor of ordination of women and so forth, but then there's another group of feminists who might well leave the Church over it.

SIDNEY: That would be just a peripheral issue to me. I can't imagine going off for that reason. I think all this silencing of Curran and Hunt-hausen is horrible, and I work like a dog to protest and write against it, but that's still way up there in the political sphere to a certain extent. I think it's symptomatic of original sin and a corruption of our community, but what else is new? If you want to be a religious person, a Christian, where else would you go? Once you get out of the Church, then they win. They win immediately if you leave.

DANIEL: They've been at it a longer time than you have—say, two thousand years. They're well used to dealing with heretics and schismatics.

SIDNEY: But there isn't any "they," really. It's "we." The hierarchy is just one little surface phenomenon, to a certain extent. But they can cause a lot of trouble.

DANIEL: I really think there are two kinds of Catholics. This is oversimplifying, but there are a lot of angry ones who were raised in very rigid backgrounds, and in a funny way they totally buy the version of Catholicism they were given. They were told that if you don't accept the Pope, you have to leave the Church—and they accept that. Whereas there's another group like Sidney who say, "Don't buy that vision!" So they're not going to leave the Church. The Pope could say, "Sidney

Callahan's excommunicated," and she'd say, "Screw you, you can't get rid of me." Wouldn't you?

SIDNEY: I wouldn't say, "Screw you!" I'd keep going to Mass. I would not leave. I'd wait for Jesus to tell me at the moment of death — then I'd know it was real, that I'd really got the word! The people who were raised most rigidly, when they'd rebel they'd go crazy in the other direction. And I would think, Oh, if they'd only been raised a little more laxly! But other than that, I think that religion has something to do with everyday life. I've gone up and down, been lax and had more difficulties. But whenever I have any crisis or suffering come into my life, then it works in the sense that it becomes the thing that keeps me alive. So all the Psalms are right: You rescue me out of the depths, and so forth. I hope it will continue, because I think life must get harder as you go into your old age. I just got a letter from my stepmother that said, "Old age is hell!"

I do have one pet peeve about people who leave the Church, and that is that people who leave criticize the reforms and changes that have taken place in the Church. They left, but they want the Church to remain the same old awful thing that they had to leave. They resent the fact that it's trying to get its act together and change, that it's a living community that's going on. Somebody like Anthony Burgess is like that a little bit. He writes about how decadent and terrible the Church is now, and why couldn't it have stayed its good old Roman self? The Church we loved to hate!

DANIEL: I think that there's a subtle explanation for this. I think that a fair number of people who've stopped believing believe that believers engage in an enormous amount of self-deceit. In a sense, they feel that the very nature of being a religious believer is that you fool yourself, talk yourself into what is not intrinsically plausible. Therefore they feel that believers are constantly adjusting the world to what they want it to be and that believers feel whatever state the Church is in is the real Church, but that's only because they've talked themselves into it.

SIDNEY: No, the problem is that they thought the Church they grew up in was better, so they are nostalgic for that. That's what I don't like. If you said the whole thing is horrible — "It was horrible then and it's horrible now, I'm glad I'm out" — that's one thing. But they say, "I left and it was horrible, but why are they changing it?" I think the self-deception argument is one nobody should ever engage in because you can say that everybody who *leaves* is self-deceived.

DANIEL: It's not a matter of self-deception. Nonbelievers feel that believers are excessively credulous people who believe more than one ought to believe. The nonbeliever is saying, "What I reject is a way

of looking at the world which is willing to swallow as much as you're
prepared to swallow'' — it's a particular type of self-deception.

SIDNEY: I think that people who believe and people who have left shouldn't
try to explain the others.

DANIEL: But you really have to do that because you have to make some
sense of why people who are otherwise as intelligent as you are behave
the way they do.

SIDNEY: I thought you just gave an explanation, which is that there *is* no
explanation.

DANIEL: I don't find any that's satisfying, but I think it's worth pursuing.

SIDNEY: Haha ha ha ha! Well! You should see Dan and me play tennis.
We played every day for three months this summer, and we came out
exactly even.

DANIEL: It's too bad we don't come out even intellectually, but. . . .

SIDNEY: Too bad about you. We know what happens to old philosophers.
But at least we never thought that either one was the smarter. I think
that in your dominance struggle in a marriage it's very important that
you should come out as a draw, and it's hard for it to come out as a
draw in this culture because women start out behind and they get further
behind as the world goes on.

DANIEL: On the other hand, women live longer, so they win in the end.

SIDNEY: I don't know — then they're lonesome.

DANIEL: As for Sidney's continuing belief in Catholicism, I guess I see
it as highly idiosyncratic. It just doesn't impress me one way or the
other. There's this thing she likes that I don't, and that's why people
are different. But it doesn't awe me.

SIDNEY: But you know other people who believe, so why is it idiosyncratic?

DANIEL: I do find it idiosyncratic. I don't know why some people believe
and others don't. To me there's no rational explanation. I long ago gave
up the notion that some were just smarter than others — things don't
break down that way. Literally, it's in the same category as some people
like classical music and others don't. I'm interested in ultimate questions
and deep philosophical issues, but belief is a direction that doesn't mean
anything to me. I was once that kind of person myself, but I faded
away. I guess it's like my high school girlfriend — I know she's there,
but I don't feel anything for her anymore. It's not only that I don't miss
the faith, I'm ever thankful that I don't have to go to church anymore.
It's a living relief. I just came to dislike it so much.

SIDNEY: And I can't live without it, so there we are.

Selected Bibliography

Breslin, Jimmy. *The World of Jimmy Breslin*. Annotated by James C. Bellows and Richard C. Wald. New York: Viking Press, 1967.
———. *The World According to Breslin*. Annotated by Michael J. O'Neill and William Brink. New York: Ticknor & Fields, 1984.
———. *Table Money*. New York: Ticknor & Fields, 1986.
Buckley, Christopher T. *Steaming to Bamboola: The World of a Tramp Freighter*. New York: Congdon & Lattès, 1982.
———. *The White House Mess*. New York: Alfred A. Knopf, 1986.
Callahan, Daniel. *The New Church: Essays in Catholic Reform*. New York: Scribner's, 1966.
———. *Abortion: Law, Choice and Morality*. New York: Macmillan, 1970.
Callahan, Sidney. *The Illusion of Eve: Modern Woman's Quest for Identity*. New York: Sheed & Ward, 1965.
———. *Beyond Birth Control: The Christian Experience*. New York: Sheed & Ward, 1968.
———. *The Working Mother*. New York: Macmillan, 1971.
Callahan, Sidney, and Daniel Callahan, eds. *Abortion: Understanding Differences*. New York: Plenum Press, 1984.
Carlin, George. *Class Clown*. Little David Records LD 1004, 1972.
Chittister, Joan D., O.S.B. *Women, Church and Ministry*. Ramsey: Paulist Press, 1979.
———. *Psalm Journal*. Kansas City: Sheed & Ward, 1985.
———. *Winds of Change*. Kansas City: Sheed & Ward, 1986.
Chittister, Joan D., O.S.B., and Stephanie Campbell, O.S.B., Mary Collins, O.S.B., Ernestine Johann, O.S.B., and Johnette Putnam, O.S.B. *Climb Along the Cutting Edge*. Ramsey: Paulist Press, 1977.
Durang, Christopher. *Christopher Durang Explains It All for You*. New York: Avon Books, 1983.
Editors of the *National Catholic Reporter. Special to the N.C.R.* Kansas City: National Catholic Reporter Publishing Co., 1969.

Gordon, Mary. *Final Payments*. New York: Random House, 1978.

———. *The Company of Women*. New York: Random House, 1981.

———. *Men and Angels*. New York: Random House, 1985.

Huxley, Aldous. *The Devils of Loudun*. New York: Harper & Row, 1952.

Kelly, Mary Pat. *Martin Scorsese: The First Decade*. Pleasantville, N.Y.: Redgrave, 1980.

Kennedy, Eugene. *Re-Imagining American Catholicism*. New York: Vintage, 1985.

McCarthy, Eugene J. *Frontiers in American Democracy*. Cleveland: World, 1960.

———. *Complexities and Contraries: Essays of Mild Discontent*. New York: Harcourt Brace Jovanovich, 1982.

McCarthy, Mary. *Memories of a Catholic Girlhood*. 1957. Reprint. New York: Harcourt Brace Jovanovich, 1981.

New Saint Joseph Baltimore Catechism No. 2. Official revised ed. New York: Catholic Book Publishing Co., 1969.

Novak, Michael. *The Open Church: Vatican II, Act II*. New York: Macmillan, 1964.

———. *Belief and Unbelief: A Philosophy of Self-Knowledge*. New York: Macmillan, 1965.

———. *The Spirit of Democratic Capitalism*. New York: Simon & Schuster, 1982.

Pick, John, ed. *A Hopkins Reader*. Garden City, N.Y.: Image, 1966.

Rinzler, Carol E., ed. *Frankly McCarthy*. Washington, D.C.: Public Affairs Press, 1969.

Scorsese, Martin. "Tapping the Intensity of the City." *New York Times Magazine*, Part 2, Nov. 9, 1986.

Sheed, Wilfrid. *The Good Word and Other Words*. New York: E. P. Dutton, 1978.

———. *Transatlantic Blues*. New York: E. P. Dutton, 1978.

———. *Frank and Maisie: A Memoir with Parents*. New York: Simon & Schuster, 1985.

Stone, Robert. *A Hall of Mirrors*. New York: Houghton Mifflin, 1964.

———. *A Flag for Sunrise*. New York: Alfred A. Knopf, 1977.

———. *Children of Light*. New York: Alfred A. Knopf, 1986.

Sweeney, Terrance A. *Streets of Anger, Streets of Hope: Youth Gangs in East Los Angeles*. Glendale: Great Western Publishing Co., 1980.

———. *God &: Thirty Interviews*. Minneapolis: Winston-Seabury Press, 1985.

Torres, José. *Sting Like a Bee: The Muhammad Ali Story*. New York: Abelard-Schuman, 1971.

Unamuno, Miguel de. *Tragic Sense of Life*. Translated by J.E.C. Flitch. New York: Dover, 1954.

Wills, Garry. *Bare Ruined Choirs*. New York: Dell, 1972.

Woods, William Crawford. "The Art of Fiction XC: Robert Stone." *Paris Review* 98 (Winter 1985): 24–81.

Wright, Bruce McMarion. *From the Shaken Tower*. Cardiff, Wales: William Lewis Ltd., 1944.

————. *Repetitions*. New York: Third Press International, 1980.

Wright, Bruce McMarion, Langston Hughes, and Waring Cuney, eds. *Lincoln University Poets*. New York: Fine Editions Press, 1954.

Zappa, Frank. *Apostrophe (')*. Ryco RCD 40025, 1974. Compact disc.

————. *You Are What You Is*. EMI Records EN 5000, 1981. Import only. For information call 1-818-PUMPKIN.